The
French Overseas Empire

The
French Overseas Empire

Frederick Quinn

 PRAEGER

Westport, Connecticut
London

Library of Congress Cataloging-in-Publication Data

Quinn, Frederick.
    The French overseas empire / Frederick Quinn.
        p.   cm.
    Includes bibliographical references and index.
    ISBN 0–275–96799–9 (alk. paper)
    1. France—Colonies—History.   I. Title.
    JV1811.Q56 2000
    909'.0971244—dc21   99–046409

British Library Cataloguing in Publication Data is available.

Library of Congress Catalog Card Number: 99–046409
ISBN: 0–275–96799–9

First published in 2000

Praeger Publishers, 88 Post Road West, Westport, CT 06881
An imprint of Greenwood Publishing Group, Inc.
www.praeger.com

Printed in the United States of America

The paper used in this book complies with the
Permanent Paper Standard issued by the National
Information Standards Organization (Z39.48–1984).

10 9 8 7 6 5 4 3 2 1

Pour Eugen et Jacqueline Weber et Charlotte
encore et toujours

Contents

A photo essay follows page 105

Preface

I remember exactly when I decided to write this book. After two years of living in Yaounde, Cameroon, working as a diplomat in the American embassy and spending evenings and weekends among the Beti people of central Cameroon, I decided to expand my horizons and study the French Overseas Empire. French intrusions were everywhere in the rain forest and in Yaounde, where the French diplomatic, military, economic, and educational presence was strong in the new African capital. How did it all begin, I wanted to know, how extensive was it globally, and what was its history? The National Archives contained piles of quarterly reports from district administrators, plus end of service accounts, and correspondence. That gave me the story of the Beti-French encounter. A few intelligence reports discussed the political activity of post–World War II football clubs and similar associations. French district administrators complained that Nigerians, Indians, and American missionaries were agitating Cameroonians to push for independence. (One suggested that a mission hospital's newly arrived X-ray machine was a Geiger counter in disguise.) In the absence of understanding political change, suspicions mounted among the bush administrators, who knew only the *cercle* to which they were assigned. The winds of change were blowing everywhere, but the cautious local reports could only describe them without understanding the seismic shift in attitudes toward colonies that followed World War II. A wider picture began to emerge as I compared the French experience in Cameroon with other parts of Africa and Asia.

The Archives was a confused and confusing place to work. Consisting mostly of carefully penned entries in a large leather-bound book, the classification system had been abandoned by some transitory French administrator years ago. I quickly became friends with Daniel, the Cameroonian clerk and himself a Beti, who had once been a secretary to an important chief. Meanwhile, the Archives' director, from another ethnic group, and the Archives' French advisor, were suspicious of my interests. Why would an American diplomat rummage through the pre-independence archives? By the time my two-year assignment ended, both had become friendly. The director had a medical problem, and when I returned from home leave I brought him a needed medicament; the advisor was from La Rochelle, and he and I shared an interest in French Protestantism. None of this was evident, however, in the early months of my work. Archive regulations allowed researchers access to only one file at a time, and this usually took at least a half-hour to find and the results were never certain, owing to the archaic classification system. Daniel supported my work and gave me unrestricted access to the stacks, allowing me to scan quickly folders from various subdivisions. (Sometimes he served as my interpreter when I visited lineage heads in the rain forest.) The easier access to documents nearly ended when the French advisor ran into me while I was carrying an armful of folders to an empty table. I understood his protectiveness, but I had little time and wanted to complete the archival work quickly so I could begin conducting oral interviews with Beti elders. I remember once leaving a pile of important political dossiers on a table under one of several holes in the building's slate roof (the building had been a slaughterhouse), only to return several weeks later during the short rainy season and see water dripping a few inches from the frail, fading documents.

During that era no one would begin field research without a copy of a standard work, *Notes and Queries on Social Anthropology*. Its admonitions were to use a good quality paper that would not fade, carefully date and label your research notes, keep interviews to an hour, and so on. I quickly abandoned it as one Beti headman or informant led to another. I had assembled a folder of pictures of former Beti chiefs and German and French colonial administrators and often began an interview by asking, "What do you remember or know about this person?" Some interviews went for hours at a time and, when they knew *le chercheur* was coming, headmen would assemble lineage members, some of whom would weigh in with their own recollections while we sat on wide cement verandahs used for drying cocoa in the rain forest. At times, if they came to Yaounde, some of the Beti informants showed up at our house to add more information or continue the conversation. "You must keep this material for the young people," some would say, adding that such-and-such a headman had died last year and, had I interviewed him, he could have told the history of his people far better than anyone else in that region.

Cameroon was a French mandate territory from 1919 to 1946 before achieving independence in 1960. Max Abe Foudda, the last living *chef supérieur* of French colonial days, recalled in great detail his experiences with the French adminis-tration; the Abbé Theodore Tsala, Beti linguist and scholar, had virtually every book that had been written in German and French about the Beti or the Yaounde region, and he gave me much additional information. Another lineage head, during our last interview, stood up and with two hands presented me his raffia fly whisk, symbol of chiefly authority. Abbé Tsala said, "Oh, you young people. Don't you understand what has happened?" He was naming me as his successor.

I wish I could say that my French colleagues at the local university were helpful, but few were. Most were writing their dissertations and regarded Cameroon as a French research preserve. However, Henri Brunchweg, one of the leading French colonial historians of the postwar period, was unfailingly courteous and interested in my and my wife's work. (Charlotte was writing a book on the French, the British, and Islam in the Senegambia.) Claude Tardits, dean of Cameroonian anthropologists, stopped by the house often in the evening for a few drinks and stayed for one of our home-cooked meals, while we peeled through the layers of who was writing on which aspect of Cameroonian studies and what was happening in local politics. The French ambassador, a graduate of the École Normale Supérieur, shared reminiscences of leading French political personalities encountered in several overseas postings. Robert Cornevin and Robert Delavignette came as lecturers to the local university, attracting crowds of Cameroonian students and Africans who had once served with them. African intellectuals like Bernard Fonlon and Englebert Mveng shared many hours with us discussing African history, politics, and culture.

Thus the threads of interest in French interaction with overseas societies began to coalesce. My first overseas posting was to Morocco in 1958, just after its independence. Much of that assignment was spent learning French. I had a daily tutorial from a retired French oil company executive and, to practice on my own, bought a copy of André Malraux's *Voices of Silence*, one of the most difficult French texts I ever encountered, and tried to translate it page by page. The small but influential Reformed Church of France congregation welcomed me generously albeit formally and allowed me to practice my French, this time through songs from the starkly beautiful but archaic Geneva psalter. Of course other things were happening politically, but I was only marginally aware of them; independence had just come to Morocco. Rabat was filled with young Algerian leaders in exile, and they borrowed books and films from our embassy's cultural program, of which I was a part. Sometimes I had coffee with the young Algerians and other Moroccans who were followers of Ben Barka, a Moroccan opposition leader, but my French at that point was not adequate for me to interact fully with them. (The State Department did not believe it would be a prudent investment to first put me in an intensive French course.)

One Sunday morning I was walking from my apartment toward the embassy when an explosion shook the neighborhood. I watched a French woman wailing from her apartment's cement balcony, two small children huddled close to her. Below was the smoldering wreckage of a black Citroën car; in its shattered back window was wedged the body of a Frenchman with a billowing white shirt with large purple stripes. Local French terrorists had attached a bomb to the car's clutch. Later I learned he was a local attorney who supported the Moroccan independence movement, which infuriated the reactionary French planters, as rigid and violent as their Algerian counterparts, the *colons*.

In Haiti, from 1959 to 1961, I saw a different aspect of French colonial history. I made several trips to the north, to Cap Haitien and Henri Christophe's Citadel, the brooding fortress set high above the bay, which was never attacked, but which stood as a crumbling monument to Haitian counterviolence, and saw the ruined plantation gates and the outlines of what had once been vast estates. The archivist, whom we had just sent to the United States on a leader grant, showed me signatures of Toussaint Louverture and other documents of Haitian independence. By now my French was greatly improved, and I learned Haitian Creole and attended Sunday morning poetry readings at the French Cultural Center. François Duvalier was president then, and several of his close followers were cabinet ministers. To learn more about them, I read works of the *les Griots* school of negritude writers and met Dr. Jean Price-Mars, the ethnographer who wrote *Ainsi Parla l'Oncle* (Thus Spake the Uncle), which was credited with making Haitian studies a legitimate intellectual exercise. I also read the novels of several Haitian writers, including Jacques Roumain, who wrote *Gouverneurs de la Rosée* (Masters of the Dew), named for the servants who walked before any official delegation in the countryside in the early morning, shaking the dew from the tall grasses so that the important people would not get soaked. Often I accompanied visitors to meet Duvalier in his office. A snubbed-nosed silver pistol lay on a table next to his desk, pointed at the visitor's chair, and a guard with rifle, helmet, and bayonet watched intently as the president-for-life told *New York Times* and other journalists what he was doing for the people. I was deeply shaken when some of the intellectuals with whom I worked simply disappeared, killed in Tonton Macoute vendettas; others fled the country or sought jobs as United Nations or World Bank experts.

From Haiti I moved to Ouagadougou, Upper Volta, 1961–1963, as head of the embassy's cultural and educational programs. Independence had just come to this landlocked sub-Saharan country. Ironically, President Maurice Yameogo's private counselor, Nader Attie, was a longtime Haitian resident trader. I arrived with four cases of Haitian rum. Mr. Attie's cook knew how to prepare Haitian food, and we spent many Sunday evenings on his spacious verandah. President Yameogo often attended and told us stories of his meetings with General de Gaulle and various African leaders. It was a heady time, and sometimes, if the president didn't show up, we simply went *en bloc* to the palace to continue the conversation. The French ambassador, a former *préfet* of the Paris region, took an interest in me; my counterpart, the cultural attaché who had taught French at Vassar College, and several members of the embassy with long experience in Africa all shared their experiences with me. From an African perspective, Joseph Ki-Zerbo, at that time a young historian, and Frederic Guierma, Upper Volta's ambassador to the United Nations, shared their unique viewpoints on African-French relations. During the dry season I also went to the town's open-air motion picture theater which showed historic French films on Monday nights, including 1930s Foreign Legion films where impeccably dressed French soldiers pursued cunning Arab-looking aggressors to the cheers of African audiences seated on wooden benches close to the white-washed screen.

Politics and French culture were inseparable even at the farthest reaches of empire. I think of the African *commandant du cercle*, whom I visited on the edge of the Sahara, whose small bookshelf contained standard French classics and a *Manuel Pratique de Protocole* that was a constant companion to new African leaders. It contained information on how to greet people, send them letters, seat them at dinners, place them at receptions—to conduct the human intercourse required in a situation drastically different than in the past. The same official had a local artist's painting on his wall, more a political statement than a work of art. It showed two African porters depositing a sedan chair with a French official on the ground and walking away. Nearby the French flag was being lowered and the African state's flag was being raised on the *cercle* compound. It was Independence Day. Administrative hierarchies, uniforms, decorations, and ceremonies replicated those in France. A *café au lait* and *croissant* became a universal breakfast, *sapins de Noël* appeared in the tropics and sub-Sahara for Christmas Day, lilies of the valley and labor demonstrations were part of May 1, and the year climaxed with the annual Bastille Day celebration, carried out as lavishly as local French resources would allow. Ads ran in newspapers and were broadcast on national radio inviting all French citizens living in the country to visit the French embassy residence on Bastille Day for the celebration and the ambassador's speech.

In visiting such isolated former French outposts from Bobo-Dioulasso to Dalat, I experienced firsthand the way France tried to create a total presence in its overseas empire. Stationery, type fonts, and sizes of letters were the same everywhere, and buildings looked as if they had come from a central design office in Paris, albeit with Arabic or Oriental twists. What struck me most was how the geographic layout of French colonial cities and even the smallest, most isolated outposts reflected imperial ideas. The *cercle* was always on the choicest ground, with trees planted around it, and wide roads leading off in every direction, pointing to the colonial capital and to France itself. Avenue Binger, Rue de Strasbourg, Place Foch, Avenue de Dakar—somehow the empire was tied together in one master architectural plan of global dimensions, even if the reality did not extend much farther than the town's limits or the roads' ends. Decades after independence, when I visited some former colonial outposts, like rural administrative centers in Guinea or Chad, they resembled abandoned stage settings built for a pageant performed years ago, left to the elements after the actors had moved on.

My next overseas port of call was Saigon, Vietnam, where I was assigned as a province advisor during the height of the Vietnamese conflict, from 1964 to 1966. My office in Saigon was within walking distance of the National Archives, and I began to read books there by 19th century French explorers of Asia. All books were covered with brown butcher paper and shelved in order of the date of receipt, so there was no history section to look through. Chain-smoking and sipping endless glasses of lukewarm tea, and sitting at a small desk between rows of wrapped books, the *bibliothécaire* had a polished wooden card catalogue with book titles in it that told me what was available. A few French settlers remained. In Nha Trang a French widow, once married to a local Vietnamese official, now ran a small restaurant near Cam Ranh Bay, one of Asia's largest deepwater harbors. She told me how, when she and her husband were first assigned there in the 1930s, peasants paid for goods with Russian double eagle gold coins. Such coins remained in circulation in the mountainous region from the time when the Czar's fleet stopped there in 1905 to wait for its coaling ships while on its way to the Russo-Japanese war and its defeat.

On another occasion, I became acquainted with a Vietnamese pharmacist whose shop looked like the local equivalent of a French Third Republic establishment. Around glass-enclosed cabinets on three of its sides were exquisite period 19th century French apothecary jars, listing the names of chemicals and herbal compounds, surrounded by hand-painted flowers and trimmed with gold paint. Crowded with new merchandise, the shop contained paper displays of Japanese pharmaceutical products and a life-sized model of a French female model holding a box of pills. Her round eyes had been gently retouched by a local artist to make them look more elliptical and Oriental. It was clear from the crowded shop that its French presence was receding, and the owner was along in years. I said, "I know how much they mean to you, but if you ever decide to redesign your shop and want to sell those pharmaceutical jars, I'll give them a good home." "I could never part with them," he said, "but you can order your own." He disappeared into his small office and reappeared with a camphor-scented tissue paper–covered document. He unwrapped it as gently as if it were a wedding present and displayed an immaculately preserved catalogue printed on thick, high-quality paper. A delicately engraved set of designs and notices described the various pharmacist's jars and gave their prices. "You can order some for yourself," the owner said, pointing to the address in Paris. The date was 1914.

The incongruity of French and Vietnamese cultures was displayed for me one sweltering summer day. Dripping with sweat, my boots filled with water from walking through a stream after a bamboo bridge collapsed, I came to a small provincial Roman Catholic church whose principal possession was a meticulously preserved 19th century statue of a radiant Jeanne d'Arc in full battle dress, with sword, shield, and heavy metal head cover. I wondered how she could wear all that without rusting. In Mytho, the Vietnamese army commander, a former Montpellier law student, invited me to live in the province chief's residence during my six-month stay in that part of the Mekong Delta. It was a magnificent two-story high-ceilinged colonial-era villa with spacious gardens and a carefully maintained gravel walk that led to a dock on the Mekong River. The province *maître d'hôtel*, previously the librarian of the now-defunct *cercle colonial*, placed a complete set of the works of Victor Hugo in my smallish room. The books had been hidden since the French had left a decade ago. "Some day some one will use them again," he told me, while filling every shelf. A few volumes contained long-dead worms that had expired half way through eating their way into the glue-laced binding.

During three stays at the University of California at Los Angeles in 1964, 1966, and 1970, I completed separate masters' degrees in African studies and history and a doctorate in history. Above all, it was an opportunity to spend long days and some evenings in the graduate school library, which is superbly equipped with French history books and journals. Eugen Weber and his wife, Jacqueline, were gracious in the hospitality of their Sunset Boulevard home.

The present work, which draws on the resources of the Library of Congress, initially took shape in the 1970s. Foreign Service assignments in the next decade, plus raising two children and being married to a talented wife who had her own professional career as a historian and diplomat, meant that I could study individual volumes but had little time for writing. The book was put aside. Finally, with my foreign service retirement in the early 1990s, I was able to devote full time to the work. I revised the original text several times and added new material. I returned to the manuscript in the mid-1990s after spending a decade assisting several countries of the former Soviet Union, and some African countries, with the writing of constitutions and the modernization of their judicial systems. This allowed me to take a basic look at the French post–World War II constitutions and their antecedent laws, ranging from the 1685 Code Noir to the decrees giving bush administrators sweeping powers to employ the *indigénat* and *corvée*, systems of summary justice without legal proceedings and forced recruitment for work gangs. Although I had studied French colonial history, literature, and social anthropology, law had rarely been discussed in these disciplines as an aspect of colonial policy. Seeing how the authoritarian systems of Eastern Europe used law as a way to control society gave me a new awareness of how the French employed legal codes and ordinances as ways of regulating their overseas possessions. Not that communism and colonialism were similar, they weren't; the common point was how little access there was to full legal and political participation by subject peoples in either system.

I returned to French West Africa twice in the 1990s, once in 1992 with a Canadian colleague to assist Guinea with the writing of an electoral code under the auspices of the International Foundation for Electoral Systems, and again in 1993, with French and Haitian professionals on a United Nations mission, to advise the government of Chad on possible structures of government after a military government relinquished power. Guinea was experiencing a bumpy transition from authoritarian rule to pluralistic democracy after 26 years of Sekou Touré's dictatorship and a decade of military rule. My ride across Conakry, the capital, with a young lawyer was a drive across recent Guinean history. We passed a museum and statue honoring French explorers and a generic Soviet-era war memorial of Sekou Touré marking the defeat of an invasion by Portuguese and Guinean mercenaries in the 1970s. The latter reads, "The revolution is exigent. Imperialism found its tomb in Guinea."

The lawyer, one of 35 in a city of one million people, drove under the Castro bridge, a main crossroads with a crumbling cement overpass. Cars burning low-octane gas pinged through an intersection that resembled a giant pinball machine, dodging trucks loaded with people and firewood. Sekou Touré hanged political opponents beneath this crowded overpass without trial. "Even now it makes my stomach tighten," the driver reflected. "They were hung between two and four in the morning and left under guard until 6 P.M., when families could claim the bodies." Like many of his generation, the lawyer spent time at Camp Boiro, an infamous prison camp on the town's outskirts. Family and friends held a vigil at army headquarters until he was released.

"How do you find our constitution?" the lawyer asked. The image of Guinea that emerged to me after several days' discussion was of a car being driven on a narrow road, one foot on the gas, the other alternating on the brake, the driver fearful of swamps marked "anarchy" and "tyranny" on each side of the road. "I see it differently," the French-trained attorney continued. "We are in a car, half-filled with gas. We know where we must go, but we are not sure we will make it."[1]

* * *

The People's Palace rises mirage-like out of the flat landscape in N'Djamena, capital of Chad. Built by the People's Republic of China, its distinctly Oriental design and celestial blue colors contrast with the miles of desert flatland covered with single-story mud and cement buildings. Inside, more than a thousand Chadian leaders gathered in March 1993 for a Sovereign National Council. Such conferences have been held in several French-speaking African countries moving from dictatorships to democratic governments. Keen local interest was displayed in the conference. Human rights abuses and military raids on civilian communities were described in speeches carried on state radio and television in Arabic, French, and Sahra, the main language of southerners. Motor-scooter drivers steered with one hand and held a portable radio close to an ear with the other, following the debates.[2]

To the podium came speaker after speaker, politicians back from exile in France, farmers who had never used a microphone before, and members of the Chadian Human Rights League. Intense politicking took place in surrounding corridors and at coffee bars; turbaned Muslim northerners gestured at Christian southerners in colorful flowing garb. Delegates asked us, "Do you favor a strong presidency or a parliamentary state for Chad?" Chadians wanted information about direct versus proportional representation, the relationship between the state and religious groups, and the role of an independent judiciary. "You can explain these things to us," they often said, with expectant voices, suggesting that we somehow could help them find a way out of their present problems.

Only eight lawyers were in private practice in Chad. In N'Djamena 12 government attorneys were assigned to the Appeals Court, the nation's highest court. They shared one small room and four desks and five chairs. Those who arrived early got seats. The absence of law books and published court opinions hindered Chadians in determining what the law said. Many French legal codes were used, without a Chadian law saying they were applicable to Chad. Thus, if a local magistrate had been to France and could afford a copy of the French Commercial Code, he would apply it; another judge might be working from a 20-year-old text on the same subject. After our visit to the main courthouse, its shutters torn apart with bullet holes from the last coup attempt, my French colleague, André Baccard, who spent almost 40 years dealing with African legal issues, and who had been Chad's prosecutor general for nine years after independence, remarked, "*C'est la fin de l'état!*" It was not quite the end of the state in Chad, but it was close to it.

Toward the end of our visit, we drove to a local cemetery. Baccard stopped by the grave of an old friend, the first president of the Chadian Supreme Court (a judicial body that existed on paper only). The grave was marked with a simple sign—white letters on black paint on a rectangular piece of tin—"Here lies Pierre Djime, Lawyer, 7/3/1933–7/4/1979." Next to it was another tin sign whose epitaph had been scratched away by the strong desert wind and dust, but it still bore its original message: "Esso for sale here." It will take much more than expected oil revenues to create a viable modern state in Chad.

Thus, while living for almost a decade in francophone countries of Africa, the Caribbean, and Asia, I tried to put together the larger picture of how this empire originated, grew, and declined, the subject matter of this volume. My intention is not to pass judgment on several centuries of France's overseas activity, but rather to describe what happened. No thin red line exists of possessions held, lost, or added to. The map of France's overseas possessions changed each century. What is a constant throughout is France's amazing resiliency, the endurance of empire despite the obstacles. France kept sending explorers, soldiers, settlers, and traders abroad, and they remained a lasting overseas presence until the late 20th century.

Each chapter closes with a survey of the "empire of the mind," the overseas world envisioned by writers and artists, and later by politicians and journalists. In many ways, this imaginary empire was as important as the real one. After all, it was a colonial vision that drove French kings to send explorers and to charter trading companies; the vision reflected in French eyes what an expanding European power should be. The empire of the mind in each century cannot be separated from domestic political realities. Two different examples illustrate the point: the Royal Palace at Versailles included a Stairway of the Ambassadors leading to the royal apartments. Figures from the overseas world, including an American Indian, bowed before the Sun King, displaying their produce and adding glory and luster to the monarch, one of whose warships carried the caption "I am unique on the ocean wave as my king is in the world." Much later, at the beginning of World War II, both Vichy and Free French governments claimed overseas France as an integral part of their political vision. It was from Africa that de Gaulle began his long march to power; it was to an overseas department that France sent its gold reserves for safekeeping. The examples of this imaginary empire change in each century, but they always serve a single purpose: difficult as times might be at home, there was always an empire beyond the horizon.

ACKNOWLEDGMENTS

Gary Maurice Dwor-Frécaut, librarian of the French embassy, Washington, D.C., and the reference librarians at American University Library rendered invaluable assistance in locating books and photographs of the colonial era. The Ides Group, scientists and jurists with long-standing professional ties to France, have shared insights with me during monthly meetings organized by Judge Pauline Newman of the U.S. Court of Appeals for the Federal Circuit and Dr. Wilton S. Dillon, Senior Scholar and former Director of International Programs, the Smithsonian Institution. Members and officers of the Mississippi Historical Society, the French Colonial Historical Society, and the Society for French Historical Studies have provided stimulating venues for discussion of many of the ideas examined in this book. Professors William B. Cohen of Indiana University, Indianapolis, Indiana, and James Pritchard, Queen's University, Kingston, Ontario, Canada; Arthur J. Dommen, a historical researcher on Indochina; and Charlotte S. Quinn, who is completing a book on Islam in Contemporary Africa, read all or sections of the original manuscript and provided me with valuable insights, as well as much stimulating discussion, for which I am grateful. Larry A. Bowring of Bowring Cartographic, Arlington, Virginia, made the maps. I wish to thank also the Library of Congress for the illustrations they supplied.

NOTES

1. Frederick Quinn, "Down an Open Road on a Half-Tank of Gas, Guinea Goes Democratic," *Legal Times*, June 29, 1992, pp. 24–25.

2. Frederick Quinn, "Chad's Painful Journey to Democracy," Opinion and Commentary, *Legal Times*, April 26, 1993, pp. 26–27.

Introduction

From the early 16th century, when French fishermen sailed westward in the uncharted North Atlantic, to the closing years of the 19th century, when explorer-soldiers tracked inland to the Sudan and fought rebellious populations in Indochina, a basic continuity marked the history of the French Overseas Empire. Backed by the government and the heroic effort of its proconsuls, the Empire grew, tentatively at first in North America and the Caribbean, then, after setbacks, more rapidly in Africa and the Far East. Finally, it encompassed several million people around the globe, who increasingly identified themselves with France, whose economic and civilizing mission progressively transformed indigenous societies and profited the French economy.

This, in outline, is a popular theory of empire, but it is an inaccurate one. It reflects the empire of the popular press and the colonial handbooks of the early 20th century, a fabrication explicable in the context of the times. Theories of evolution, presented with the authority of scientific discoveries, provided a framework to describe the harmonious progress of the white race. Romanticism reinforced a cult of the exotic, of the less civilized cultures of Africa, America, and the Orient; and the militant nationalism of period historians depicted overseas societies responding to French initiatives in much the same way Europeans, in a pre-Copernican world, believed the spheres revolved around the Planet Earth.

Seen from a later period, and a more inclusive perspective, the story of the French Overseas Empire is often one of disjunctures and contradictions more so than of continuities. It was as much the product of chance exploration as of systematic design, of the effects of individual traders or small business groups who believed they knew of a profitable route to the East and set out to explore it, or stubborn individuals who established obscure outposts to further commercial, military, or religious ends. Generally, the French government was a sometimes player whose interests blew hot and cold. Troops and funds needed to secure potentially advantageous overseas colonies were rarely forthcoming, or when they were it was often a case of too few soldiers or colonists arriving too late to seize the opportunity fully. At home, overseas interests competed with the requirements of France's numerous continental wars, and with domestic political demands. France's frontiers, especially on the northeast, were difficult to defend and its sea-lanes were vulnerable. French colonization thus came in fits and starts. Despite the spread of commerce and the conquest of lands, at times French overseas expansion seemed, as one colonial administrator put it, "a vaudeville subject," reflecting, in a paraphrase of the playwright Molière, "the conqueror in spite of himself." Notwithstanding, one should look with amazement at France's colonial achievement. Resiliency was an aspect of France's imperial success. Time and again the French pushed forward in difficult terrains, braving tepid support at home and hostility abroad, to establish an imposing overseas presence.

This volume will survey the French Overseas Empire from the early 16th century, when it comprised little more than a few barren North Atlantic islands and fishing stations; through its apogee in 1931, when it encompassed almost 12 million square kilometers and 65 million people overseas on several continents; through to the late 20th century, when the once-global empire was in an advanced state of decline.

In addition to chronicling the spread of exploration and colonization, this study discusses why France's overseas interests and possessions changed markedly during succeeding centuries, how domestic and continental interests influenced French colonial policies, and how the French perceived their Empire in different historical periods. This is not a history of individual colonies, but of France's relations with and attitudes toward its colonies, extended to include what were technically protectorates and mandates, and to Algeria, which France treated like a colony but called a part of metropolitan France. Laos, Cambodia, French Guiana, and the islands of the South Pacific and the Caribbean, on the edge of the Empire, appear only when their activities measurably influence France or vice versa. Attention is devoted to expositions, films, books, and popular attitudes because the study of what French historians have called *les mentalités* is necessary to understand why France behaved as it did.

The literature on France overseas is vast, and I have cited it in chapter endnotes when works have been used in this narrative or to call attention to particularly interesting books or concepts. Citing each number and quotation would make for a much longer volume. French words not in common usage have been translated into English.

A work covering five centuries is also an exercise in what to include and what to omit. It has been said that historians are divided into two schools, lumpers and splitters; this volume is in the former category. It is carefully constructed in its outline, but not like a traditional political-military history. To such material I have appended information important to the larger picture of the Empire. Thus, a Vietnamese protest poem might appear not far from an account of diplomatic struggle, or the songs of African railway workers describing the harshness of their working conditions might be placed near a section on the rise of indigenous political parties.

It is important to state what this book is and is not. It is not a detailed history of France or its individual overseas possessions. This is not a work in the *les Annales* tradition, nor does it belong to the *Képi et tricolore* school of colonial historiography, the detailed accounts of French overseas military-colonial advancement. The domestic history of France is discussed only insofar as it affects overseas life, and particular colonies and possessions are chronicled as they are part of the larger picture of France in a particular century. This volume is not "history from below" but "history from within." A social history of an empire across five centuries would require an approach for which consistent evidence is not yet fully obtainable. Where possible, I describe the detailed interaction of societies at several key points within the larger political context. In recent years, there has been a flowering of works on colonial history, which take advantage of new approaches and methodologies and allow a greater exploration of the interaction between colonized and colonizer, expanding the historian's orbit to include classes and groups as diverse as trade unionists and household servants, petitioners in bush courts and railroad workers and allowing a depth to the writing of empire history not available earlier. Also, a revisiting of an earlier generation of colonial historians reveals insights and acuity of judgment that stand despite the obvious addition of new materials and the change of time. The Empire is long gone but, among historians, any announcement of its demise is premature.

The history of French imperial contact was much more than Julius Caesar's "Veni, vidi, vinci" (I came, I saw, I conquered). What actually happened was a series of complex interactions between colonized and colonizer that over time modified both societies in discrete ways. Initially, historians of the post–World War II period described this process as one of *résistance* or *accommodation*. Resistance included a military confrontation with the intruders, as in Algeria, Syria, or Vietnam. Accommodation was a melding with the colonial culture, retaining key aspects of indigenous structures and belief, as was the case of some smaller, less homogenous ethnic groups, such as the Baule of the Côte d'Ivoire or the Beti of Cameroon. The forms of interaction were more complex than might at first appear. They ranged from consistent militant opposition to the French military, political, economic, religious, and social-cultural presence to passive resistance, partial accommodation, or the capitulation of some overseas intellectuals who became "more French than the French."

To complete the picture, additional studies are needed of *le menu peuple* (small or marginal people), at the edge of the Empire, such as rural populations and villagers, liminal figures including religious figures or griots who assumed roles as prophets or arbitrators, women, and classes of *évolués* (educated persons or persons in positions of authority) including teachers, government workers, commercial entrepreneurs, trade unionists, and urban migrants, sometimes called *parachutistes*. History from the bottom, however, has its limits. Social groups like household servants and rickshaw drivers operate within a larger political framework; some political scaffolding is necessary if the groups' growth and interaction are to be more fully explained. Most likely, their accounts, available in fragments and through oral histories, will not redirect the flow of history but will enhance it, adding dimensionality to what the English historian Peter Laslett once called "The World We Have Lost."

If microcosmic studies demonstrate the complex interactions of colonized with colonizer and of the colonized with other colonized, the macrocosmic story is of larger scale interaction of overseas peoples with France demonstrably affecting both societies. The most obvious early example is the formation of a distinctive Canadian culture out of the long, complex French and Indian interaction and of the later limited but real transformation of French politics through its post–World War II interaction with figures as diverse as Léopold Sédar Senghor, Aimé Césaire, Ferhat Abbas, and Ho Chi Minh and the political interests they represented. After all, it was the Algerian crisis that precipitated the Fourth Republic's demise in 1958 and General Charles de Gaulle's subsequent return to power.

Each generation of historians of empires rediscovers the contributions of literary and visual artists and anthropologists to the wider study of overseas societies. Anthropological studies, however, are sometimes cast in a timeless "anthropological present," unaffected by political change, or if change is admitted, sometimes it is measured by a grid attuned to developmental studies, some of which are more theoretically consistent than they are historical in their explanations. The contributions of cultural history, broadened to include film, posters, postcards, and popular and travel literature, illustrate French perceptions of the world beyond the Hexagon, as France itself is referred to, from the *bibliothèques bleues* sold in marketplaces during the first days of printing, with their depictions of Turks and fantasy creatures, to the first generation of photographers who set up shop in Dakar and Saigon and created portraits and postcards that said as much about France as they did about indigenous societies.

The interaction always was more complex than a polar colonizer-colonized one, although that is what was initially most evident. But even in the earliest days of indigenous-French contact, there were multilayered exchanges, as with Jacques Cartier in New France and the French in Florida and the numerous local peoples with whom they came in contact. We ask what happened to the handfuls of indigenous peoples who made it to France—native inhabitants of Brazil and New France, a Vietnamese prince, Creoles from the Caribbean—and to the small numbers of French who went and stayed abroad—fur traders in New France in the 17th century, planters in Saint-Domingue in the 18th century, and the administrators and traders who remained in Africa and Asia. Such interactions were minimal during the first four centuries of colonial contact, but they exploded in the early 20th century when indigenous soldiers, workers, and students poured into France and administrators, missionaries, and traders headed toward overseas possessions in larger numbers than ever before. What emerged was a multilayered network of exchanges. These participants include those involved in (1) person-to-person contacts (administrator and concubine, administrator and protégé, etc.), (2) institution-to-person contacts (school and student, church and convert, police officer and citizen, etc.), (3) institution-to-institution relations (French army and indigenous *chefferie* or mandarinate), (4) government-to-government relations (the Vietnamese or Algerian governments and the French government), and, most recently, (5) the interactions of an emerging global community with augmented travel, easy access to media, heightened possibilities of communication, with, at the same time, a diminished role of the influences of the traditional nation-state. As globalism increased and became a category superseding earlier structures of cultural contact, the influence of *la francophonie* sharply diminished, both because of increased competition and because France no longer had the power and resources to play its earlier dominant military, economic, and cultural role.

EMPIRE AND ITS *MISSION CIVILISATRICE*

I have euphemistically called France's overseas presence the French Overseas Empire. In a strict sense, it was an empire only during the Napoleonic conquests. With the emperor's demise the word fell into disuse, to be revived by Napoléon III and in the draft Vichy constitution, which was never adopted. Morocco, Tunisia, Syria, Lebanon, Togo, and Cameroon were "protectorates" and the most complicated of all French North African holdings; Algeria was technically part of France for much of its recent history. Thus, what began as a monarchy ended as a republic, and it was not an empire, except briefly in the 19th century. French theorists fondly pointed to the Roman Empire as a model for their own efforts, with the idea of conquest, establishing order, and civilizing barbarian peoples as precedents for a *mission civilisatrice*. From at least the times of Charles VIII to Louis XIV, a religious, civilizing dimension was tagged on to the emperor's role. "God on Earth" is how the Hapsburgs phrased it, but the French kings used somewhat less elevated language. For example, the charter of the Acadian colony (1603) was an "attempt, with divine assistance, to bring the peoples . . . to the knowledge of the true God, to civilize them, and to instruct them in the faith." This gave Catholic missionaries and settlers their marching orders.

The idea of the *mission civilisatrice* was probably formed in French thought, although not as a clearly defined concept, when explorers and traders gave way to settlers and missionaries who needed an elevated purpose to put the best face on their activities. Indigenous peoples lost their land, were subjugated, and were made to work for the French. Education, *la francophonie*, the benefits of public health, and eventually, administrative roles and limited political participation were given to them; what more noble way to express such control of others than to label it a civilizing mission? Although Napoléon in Egypt was a self-declared architect of civilizing initiatives as a recipe for political control, the idea gained its widest currency during the Third Republic (1870–1940), and it endured until after World War II. Unlike another colonial term, *mise en valeur*, Albert Sarraut's 1923 concept of economic development, which translated into blueprints for ports and plans for roads, the *mission civilisatrice* always remained chimerical, useful when Bastille Day speakers in My Tho and Bobo Dioulasso needed a justification for their policies. The dark side of the *mission civilisatrice* was what Aimé Césaire, writer, Communist, and politician from Martinique, would call *"l'ensauvagement du continent,"* speaking of the significant loss of colonial peoples who served in Europe's 20th century wars. A Vietnamese writer and former judge of a French colonial court said, "Western civilization is only a thin coat of whitewash over a decaying wall."[1]

Another perspective on France's civilizing mission, different from that of the builders of Empire, was delivered by a schoolchild from Martinique in Patrick Chamoiseau's autobiographical *School Days* (1997). With Rabelaisian irony the writer from the Antilles viewed the civilizing mission through the filter of a recipient:

In those days, the blue-eyed Gaul with hair as yellow as wheat was everybody's ancestor. In those days, Europeans were the founders of history.... "Do you know, you Ostrogoths, that they brought to the New World iron, the wheel, the ox, the hog, the horse, wheat, rye, indigo, sugar cane?" ... "The superior races—this must be said openly, following the example of Jules Ferry—have, with regard to the primitive races, the right and duty of ci-vi-li-za-tion."[2]

The child not only absorbs the lesson but transfers its perspective to his moviegoing hours where the "American Indians of Buffalo Bill, the Zulus of Tarzan, the Chinese of Marco Polo, the Moors ambushing noble knights.... These savages demonstrated bloodthirsty brutality. They represented darkness confronted by the light. Howling madness struggling against the progress of civilization."[3]

DISEASE AND EMPIRE

The constant specter of disease was important to the French perceptions of empire, and it affected possibilities for conquest and settlement, especially in later centuries. European diseases also took their toll of indigenous peoples and reshaped their societies accordingly. The French, unknowingly, took smallpox to North America, yellow fever (*mal de Siam*) from the Far East to the West Indies, and fulciparum malaria from Africa to the American tropics, all with horrific consequences. The examples can be selected from almost any century and continent, a subject historians are only beginning to address. A yellow fever epidemic wiped out Napoléon's troops, who had just arrived in Saint-Domingue, contributing to the emperor's decision to leave the island, and a few years later the French suffered severe losses from the plague in Egypt, which reduced the number of effective troops from 30 thousand to 12 thousand in the ill-fated Syrian campaign. In August 1858 the French expeditionary forces landed in Vietnam in the middle of the monsoon season. Dysentery, malaria, cholera, and other tropical illnesses decimated the French ranks. Nearly 100 French soldiers died monthly from disease; often such deaths outnumbered the casualties of warfare. It was no better in Saigon, where disease reduced full companies to skeletal forces of from 20 to 30 troops.

In the next century, deaths from malaria were estimated to cause perhaps one-fourth of the French deaths in Indochina. In Algeria, the high cost of troops and colonists killed by disease and hostile action caused the French to remark that "the cemeteries are the only colonies that continually prosper in Algeria" and a 19th century Vietnamese commander spoke of malaria as an "ally" in the fight against the French.

A medical history of the French Overseas Empire remains to be written, but there is every indication that disease was as much a factor in limiting French expansion as hostile tribes and hesitant politicians in Paris.[4] Faced with debilitating climates and the prospect of illness, the French were reluctant to go abroad, and we can speculate on the effects of isolation, life in a hostile climate, and the additional stresses illness or the prospect of illness worked on the colonial psyche. Overseas French spoke knowingly of several colonies as "the white man's grave." The 1875 admonition of a professor of tropical medicine in Brest would have resonated in other centuries as well: "On the pestilential banks of the Atlantic, you will encounter the redoubtable sphinx of malaria, pernicious Protée, the delirious phantom of typhus, the livid, frozen specter of cholera, the yellow mask of black vomit. Be careful of the land and the water that exhale a poisonous breath."[5]

RACISM AND EMPIRE

As devastating as disease to the shaping of attitudes toward empire were the views most French held toward overseas peoples. Accurate accounts of traditional societies or respect for the dignity of local peoples were the exceptions in French colonial history. In the Middle Ages, it was believed that Cyclops, unipeds, and winged or beastlike creatures lived in distant countries. Later, actual inhabitants were described as "heathen infidels" or "happy savages." Is it any surprise that, given such warped appraisals of human life, slavery would become widespread and opposition to it would be minimal? Numerous late 20th century studies have documented the stereotypical roles given to Africans, Arabs, and Asians in French films, school books, comics, and literature. The list extends from Pierre Loti and Jules Verne to André Malraux and Albert Camus, whose enthusiasm for French leftist politics far outstripped their interests in accurately portraying the Asian and North African societies. Even when racism was not overt, it was clothed in the garb of stifling paternalism or amused curiosity about "lesser peoples," as in French colonial posters of the early 20th century which depict happy crouching Africans being led into battle by tall, stiff-spined French officers (Africans could rarely become officers and could not command French troops). Some solitary voices spoke against this tide: Robert Delavignette in colonial administration, André Gide in literature, Maurice Delafosse in anthropology, and several Roman Catholic missionaries who worked in obscurity collecting information on and writing about the value of indigenous religions, especially in Africa. Such figures, however, were rare in a country that laid just claim to being among the world's most civilized lands, a promoter of culture, reason, and the rule of law.

From the 18th century on, racism was thought to be based in science, as chronicled by William Cohen in *The French Encounter with Africans, White Response to Blacks, 1530–1880*.[6] Studies of physical anthropology drew on phrenology and physiogomics, the measurement of brain size and shape and physical characteristics. This produced rankings of inferior and superior races, temperaments, intelligence levels, and attitudes toward governance. For example, Gustave d'Eichtal, secretary of the Société ethnologique, argued that blacks represented a "female race" and "like the woman, the black is deprived of political and scientific intelligence; he has never created a great state . . . he has never accomplished anything in industrial mechanics. But on the other hand he has great virtues of sentiment. Like women he also likes jewelry, dancing, and singing."[7] Such supposedly scientific thought gave credibility to political decisions, justified armed conquest, and often harsh treatment of overseas peoples. Rich cultures were relegated to obscure museums and special study institutes, like the contents of *cabinets des curiosities*, the curio collections of bones, baskets, and artifacts wealthy collectors assembled from the 16th century onward.[8]

Racism's price in part was that effective political structures were not built because no basic trust existed between colonizer and colonized, reflecting the conditions Frantz Fanon and Albert Memmi railed against in the immediate decades before the French Overseas Empire's final collapse in 1962. In law, institutionalized racism pervaded the Code Noir (1685), the legal code through which slavery functioned despite showcase language protecting slaves' rights. Similar were post–French Revolutionary efforts to exclude non-*métropole* French, former slaves, or native inhabitants from full rights and freedoms, and later the *indigénat*, the amalgam of laws and decrees that, from 1834 to 1946, sharply limited human rights in colonies by prohibiting gatherings, allowing arbitrary arrest, and requiring people to join work gangs with penal sanctions for those who refused.[9] To these must be added the various postwar attempts made at union, federation, or community—legal Catherine wheels that spun in dazzling circles, but always with someone in Paris doing the spinning. In short, racism, like disease, crippled the prospects of a healthy relationship between France and its overseas possessions.

NOTES

1. Hoang Dao, quoted in Ngo Vinh Long, *Before the Revolution, The Vietnamese Peasants Under the French* (New York: Columbia University Press, 1991 reprint), p. 76.

2. Patrick Chamoiseau, *School Days*, trans. Linda Coverdale (Lincoln: University of Nebraska Press, 1997), pp. 121–122.

3. Ibid., p. 122.

4. Philip D. Curtin, *Death by Migration, Europe's Encounter with the Tropical World in the Nineteenth Century* (Cambridge: Cambridge University Press, 1998); Philip D. Curtin, *Disease and Empire, Military Medicine in the Conquest of Africa* (Cambridge: Cambridge University Press, 1998); Sheldon Watts, *Epidemics and History: Disease, Power, and Imperialism* (New Haven, Conn.: Yale University Press, 1997); William B. Cohen, "Malaria and French Imperialism," *Journal of African History* 24, no. 1 (1983), pp. 23–36.

5. Pierre Guillaume, *Le Monde Colonial, XIXe-XXe siècle* (Paris: Armand Colin, 1994, 2d ed.), p. 92.

6. William B. Cohen, *The French Encounter with Africans, White Response to Blacks, 1530–1880* (Bloomington: Indiana University Press, 1980); Tzvetan Todorov, *On Human Destiny, Nationalism, Racism and Exoticism in French Thought* (Cambridge: Harvard University Press, 1993).

7. Quoted in Cohen, *The French Encounter*, p. 236, from Gustave d'Eichtal and Ismail Urbain, *Lettres sur la race noire et la race blanche* (Paris, 1839), pp. 15–16, 22.

8. Michael Adas, *Machines as the Measure of Men, Science, Technology, and Ideologies of Western Dominance* (Ithaca, N.Y.: Cornell University Press, 1989), pp. 319–325.

9. Kristin Mann and Richard Roberts, eds. *Law in Colonial Africa* (Portsmouth, N.H.: Heinemann, 1991), p. 17.

1

The 16th Century: The Fishermen's and Sailors' Empire

Un beau navire dans le port de Brest
Je ne regrette que ma jeunesse,
Et lon lon li lon lon la,
Je ne regrette que ma jeunesse,
Car elle s'en va!

[A pretty ship from the port of Brest
I do not regret that my youth
is gone, gone, gone,
I do not regret that my youth
She is gone!]

—16th century French cod fishermen's song

FRANCE, THE FRAGMENTED KINGDOM

When its southern European neighbors surged out to claim world empires, France was primarily a European presence. Nevertheless, France had considerable success beyond its shores which eventually positioned it to become a global maritime power. Early in the sixteenth century, French ships from Atlantic and Mediterranean coastal ports made their way along the coasts of Africa and the Mediterranean and gradually to Brazil, where some settled to cut logwood for export, which incurred the wrath of the Portuguese in the 1530s and led to the permanent Portuguese conquest of Brazil. A growing market for French textiles in Spanish America also encouraged trade, and French slavers were active in the early Spanish Empire slave trade as well.[1]

In the North Atlantic, increasing numbers of French ships engaged in the growing cod fishing trade, contributing directly to the French navy's growth, the Canadian fur trade, and the expansion of such maritime industries as ship provisioning and marine insurance. Basque whale fisheries employed hundreds of men in the Gulf of Saint Lawrence. (Jacques Cartier encountered them during his Canadian explorations.) The Spanish Main was, during much of this century, an open road for individual or small bands of traders and privateers from Dieppe, Honfleur, La Rochelle, and other coastal ports. Such French armed ships, usually operating privately but with government encouragement, took on the Spanish, Portuguese, and English in global waters. Between 1522 and 1523 French plunderers captured nearly all the booty Hernán Cortés sent home from Mexico to Spain, and in 1529 the king of Portugal complained he had lost 300 ships to such corsairs. Jean Ango, a Dieppe mariner, tried to reach the Far East at this time while raiding Portuguese commerce freely, but he was only one of many such freebooting adventurers. Moreover, as Portuguese and Spanish ships approached the waters off Gibraltar between Madeira and the Azores, quickly mobile French privateers became a constant irritant, lying in wait for the slowly moving Spanish treasure and Brazilian sugar fleets. Although France established no land-based overseas empire to rival Spain and Portugal at this time, a French "fishermen's and sailors' empire" existed, a prosperous and expanding enterprise spread over the North Atlantic, pointing the way to France as a rising maritime power.

The reasons why France did not promote settler colonies at this time are understandable. A large and agriculturally rich country, France did not have the food and population problems that triggered the Portuguese expansion. François I (1515–1547), France's king of the Valois line, had hoped to become Holy Roman Emperor in 1519 when the title became vacant but, despite his bribes, the Electors awarded it to Charles of Austria, already a rival to France through the Spanish house of Aragon. The Hapsburg-French rivalry henceforth would be an enduring theme in European history, and the rivalry often spilled over into foreign waters and distant continents.

As the French monarchy gradually consolidated its power, François was determined to be a player in the international arena. He objected to growing Portuguese claims for territory and argued the only just claim to title of overseas lands came from occupancy. François once called his Portuguese counterpart "the grocer king" and reportedly said he "should be very happy to see the clause in Father Adam's will which excludes me from my share when the world was being divided." He persuaded the pope to agree that the bull *Inter caetera* (1456), which gave Spain all lands beyond an imaginary north-south line a hundred leagues west of the Azores and Cape Verde Islands, did not apply to lands subsequently discovered by other powers.[2] France was thus free to compete with its rivals without papal interference. As an added bonus, French kings were aided in their consolidation of power by general acceptance of patrilineal inheritance of property and title. This meant foreign marriage alliances would not result in French lands passing to other crowns and if the male line became extinct, land and title reverted to the crown. In this way, Anjou, Burgundy, Orleans, and Brittany, once bitter rivals of the king, all came under crown control by 1660.

Peace had been made with England after the Hundred Years' War, nobles were steadily losing out, and words like "majesty" and "state" entered the political vocabulary of the times, but unification came slowly to France. A traveler in 16th century France might change legal systems more frequently than horses, so the saying went. Along the Loire River there were nearly 120 toll stations in a 600 kilometer stretch. It was not until 1567 that civil jurisdiction in legal matters came under crown control. Besides provincial law courts, provincial currencies, tax systems, weights and measures, governing councils, and regional markets existed, some depending as much on commerce with Spain, Germany, or the Lowlands as with other parts of France.[3] Nevertheless, it is too easy to cite the fissiparous forces in French society to explain why France did not launch settler colonies abroad with the same frequency as its Iberian rivals. James Pritchard, a historian of the ancien régime, has noted,

State involvement in overseas expansion whether in the form of support for explorers or sponsorship of anti-Spanish settlements in Florida or Brazil it seems to me came a distinct fourth behind three non-state activities: fishing, trade and piracy, none of which involved settlement. Moreover, there could be no colonization until the notion itself became commercialized. Settlement does not logically follow exploration though exploitation may.[4]

Before France could fully consolidate its power it had to overcome two barriers, long wars with Italy and civil war at home, which, between them, spanned much of the 16th century. Italy, the lodestone for France that the New World was for Portugal and Spain, represented the gateway to Europe through which spices and silks poured from the Orient. If it conquered Italy, with its thriving ports like Venice, France believed it could attain easy access to the markets of Egypt, India, and China. The French believed that long-standing dynastic alliances gave them legitimate claims to parts of Italy, and during 40 years three different French kings used such claims as a pretext for invasions, but Italy sapped French arms, money, and lives until the Treaty of Câteau-Cambrésis (1559) was signed. Despite the lure of victory, France never conquered Italy, whose inhabitants remarked, "The French are chiefly remembered in Italy for the graves they left." No sooner had the French withdrawn from the costly Italian wars than France was engaged in a series of civil wars covering most of the next half-century. Called the Wars of Religion, these conflicts combined both Catholic-Protestant doctrinal disputes and personal feuds and rivalries. Energies spent on them drained resources France might otherwise have devoted to expanding its presence overseas.[5]

THE FISHERMEN'S EMPIRE: "BEEF FROM THE SEA"

It was in the North Atlantic, not in the sought-after Orient, that France found its most lucrative overseas holdings in this century. The term "fishermen's empire" is used illustratively, since the Breton, Norman, and other French mariners frequenting the banks claimed no territory as their own and founded no colonies. They rarely experienced the central government's power, except when the latter tried to collect taxes or ordered them to stop fishing and protect the channel harbors or attack the shipping of France's rivals. Yet, no French overseas activity was more significant in this century, and this fishermen's empire, a month's journey from Europe, was France's most profitable overseas venture in this hundred-year period. French ships were frequenting the North Atlantic in some numbers by the first decade of the 16th century. The sale of cod was encouraged by more than 150 annual Catholic fast days and the absence of meat in most peasants' diets. Also, dried or salted fish kept well, which was important in an age when food storage was a problem. The growing cod fishing industry became a thriving though risky international business, one with increasingly complex specialization, including sailors, fishers, splitters, headers, and salters. Several related occupations benefited from the expanding fishing industry, such as shipbuilding and provisioning, banking, and insurance. The fishing industry also provided sailors and ships in wartime, and the maritime provinces became prime sources of recruits for overseas settlers, missionaries, soldiers, and civilian administrators. Maritime and fishing questions, until now the concern of individual ports and owners, soon became important to France as a matter of national interest.

The vast codfish banks off the Canadian coast, encompassing nearly 40 thousand square miles, represented the kingdom French explorers otherwise never found, if the inexhaustible loads of fish from the North Atlantic are counted as overseas' riches. For most of the century, the industry employed hundreds of ships and thousands of sailors. This "beef from the sea" was as plentiful as precious metals were not, and an early voyager to the banks wrote of a sea covered with fish that could be taken both by line and by plunging baskets into the water and retrieving them full of fish. Located above the submerged continental shelf off North America, the fishing grounds were situated at the confluence of the warm gulf stream and the cold northern currents, giving the voracious cod a constant supply of plankton, smaller fish, and crustacea to feed on. Weighing six pounds and sometimes more than twenty pounds, the cod reproduced prolifically; a 40-inch female could spawn more than 3 million eggs, some reproducing in less than 20 days. Cod flesh was rich without being fatty, making the cod easy to dry and preserve for future trade.[6]

FISHERMEN AND MERCHANTS

As early as January or February, the small fishing boats left French port towns for the Newfoundland banks. Braving strong winter westerlies, with luck they returned with their first full loads of fish, called "prime," in time for the Lenten market, when the price was double what a full cargo would bring later in the year. They returned to the Grand Banks for a second expedition, called "tard," trying to reach port before the October gales. Fishing boats made the month-long trips through difficult waters with few navigational instruments. Violent storms wracked the North Atlantic in early spring and late autumn, and dense fog banks frequently rolled over the small fishing fleets, leaving them stranded for several days at a time. The usual plan followed by small ships departing France for Newfoundland was to set latitudinal bearings, calculated by eye, relating the ships' position to the sun and the North Star and about a month later begin to take soundings. When markings registered the presence of banks, they knew they had reached their destination. Mariners also used the drift of the sea, its color, the position of aquatic plants, and the presence of birds to locate their position. While the sea was seemingly without discernible land-marks, its features were widely known to sailors, and a skilled trader could often tell from which grounds a given barrel of cod might come.

The French cod fishing fleet grew substantially. By the middle of the 16th century it is likely that 500 or more ships from French ports were at the banks at any one time, with a possible catch of more than 15 thousand tons of cod yearly. Two types of fishing developed: green fishery, *la pêche errante*, at sea, and dry fishing, *la pêche sedentaire*, in which wooden flakes were set up on shores to dry fish by exposing them to sun and wind. At sea, the salted cod were cleaned on the fishing ships, stored in wooden barrels, and quickly returned to Europe for sale. Dried cod were spread on simple wooden shore racks and turned periodically. Fish were sold all over Europe and in markets as distant as the Baltics. Rouen sent more than 60 ships to the Newfoundland fisheries in January and February 1541, and between 1543 and 1545 approximately two ships a day left its harbor. Originally, fishing vessels came from more than 50 French ports, located mostly between the English Channel and the Atlantic. By the century's end, trade was concentrated in a handful of key ports: Saint-Malo, Rouen, Dieppe, and Honfleur. Ships used in the Atlantic fishing trade were variations of the long Portuguese or Biscayan caravel or the stockier Nordic cargo carriers, made for bulk, not for speed or for carrying armaments. Larger ships were soon built to accommodate the flourishing cod trade. The first *terre-neuvier* weighed between 30 and 40 tons and carried a crew of from 10 to 12. By century's end, ships of from 200 to 300 tons were bound for the North Atlantic carrying crews of from 50 to 70 sailors plus several novices and ship boys.

Shipboard life was vividly described in Pierre Loti's *Pêcheur d'Islande* (1886). Although written in the 19th century, its accounts of the difficulties of life at sea, the hard work, numerous deaths, and few satisfactions, reflected conditions that changed little through the centuries. A mariner's life was divided into three parts—the outward voyage, the time of fishing, and the homeward journey. On the voyage to the fishing grounds, which took about a month, times

of boredom for those aboard the ships alternated with keeping the ship moving
and readying gear. Once the ships reached the Newfoundland banks, activity
was intense for more than a month. Aboard larger ships, fishers sat inside large
half-barrels with a canopy over the back that somewhat protected them from
the elements. They fished, usually with single lines, using small fish as bait, or
the entrails of cod, or the content of the fishes' stomachs. Lines were lowered
to considerable depths as the cod were often found below twenty fathoms. Hauling them in was a laborious task, especially since the average crew member
caught more than 100 a day. At the day's end, the person with the largest catch
was called the "admiral" and was given a cup of eau-de-vie by the captain. After
the day's fishing was done, the sailors worked in teams chipping at the salt
blocks while singing a variety of songs. Each line was punctuated by removing
a shovelful of salt, after which "une" was cried:

> Un beau navire dans le port de Brest
> Je ne regrette que ma jeunesse,
> Et lon lon li lon lon la,
> Je ne regrette que ma jeunesse,
> Car elle s'en va![7]

at which point "deux" was shouted. After twenty verses, a new group of workers
took over.

Shore life followed a somewhat different pattern for the sailors drying cod.
The ship's party divided into groups of five persons to each longboat and, once
land was reached, they fished in a single location most of the season. Crews
were expected to fill the boat twice a day, dumping the catch on shore, where
the fish were cleaned and placed on drying racks. The smaller wind-dried fish
required only half as much salt as salted cod, but labor costs were greater because twice as many crew members were needed. When they were not thus
employed, the land-based crews hunted, grew vegetables, made pine branch beer
to drink, or traded with the Indians, which led to the important fur trade.

THE PORT TOWNS

Life was lively in the coastal port towns, especially when the fleets arrived
or departed. In addition to the crews, owners, and outfitters, there were lawyers
and notaries. In many towns, most citizens were involved in marine operations
for much of the year. At the heart of each port town was the quay with its long
stone docks where tub-like Dutch boats, hardly more than floating cargo rafts,
moored beside flute-like caravels of Portuguese traders and ships from Norse or
Germanic ports. Until the eclipse of the Italian ports, long galleys from the
Mediterranean regularly visited the Atlantic ports as well. Most towns had a
mariner's church and a lighthouse, fired by coal, at the harbor entry. Common

to all were waterfront taverns, which served as international centers for the exchange of information and gossip among sailors.

Separated from the quay by cobblestone walkways were various merchants' *hôtels*, impressive as their wealth would allow. Often these were four-story stone structures; business offices and storage space were on the ground floor, and the family lived above. Nearby was the customhouse where municipal and royal fees were collected on incoming and outgoing cargoes. Conspicuously near the ports were the stalls of the money changers, through whose hands passed a variety of national and regional coins of fluctuating value. Shops selling charts, instruments, and other supplies proliferated. On the town's edge, the warehouses of merchants and the government were built as were shipyards for storing timber, masts, and pitch. In towns like Saint-Malo, fish that did not have sufficient time to dry on the return from the Newfoundland banks were laid out on any available surface, giving the town an unmistakable odor.

One of the most important provisions used was salt, without which the fish would not keep. The marshes of Brittany, Poitou, and Brouage produced much of the salt used by the French fishing boats, but a government salt tax, the *gabelle*, doubled its cost and eventually accounted for as much as a quarter of the government's revenues. Leftover salt was stored in the Newfoundland caves or from one season to another in turf-covered earth cavities. Previously used salt could be reused, but it was supposedly stored in government warehouses in port towns to avoid the possibility of its being resold as fresh salt. Sometimes zealous port inspectors beat the salt from recently arrived barrels of fish to prevent sailors from selling it as new salt.

INTERNATIONAL RIVALRY ON THE FISHING BANKS

Throughout the century, French fishermen and mariners of other countries established a modus vivendi for operating in the cod banks, and, while an occasional cargo was seized, or a rival's boat sunk, no single country dominated the area. France had no monopoly on the cod trade. Craft from several nations were quickly drawn to the North Atlantic banks, including Spanish, Portuguese, English, Dutch, and, at times, Italian ships. The seas were also infested with individual pirate vessels, but pirates preferred gold and silver to salted cod and did not bother much with the fishing fleets.

The English presence in the banks increased sharply during the second half of the century, although there are examples of French-English encounters before that. Originally, the English interest in the fisheries was incidental to the search for a Northwest Passage, but eventually the vast underwater wealth commanded attention of its own. Raids by both sides increased, and in 1583 England took the decisive step of claiming parts of Newfoundland as English territory. The proclamation was a strange, dramatic event. Fishermen from various nations were assembled from their scattered ships, conveyed by the English to the wind-swept island, and were there read a proclamation, translated by those among them who knew another language, that Newfoundland was now an English island. Although control passed to the English, the French would return. Meanwhile, the cod fishers, who more frequently setting up their drying racks along the coastal shores, traded fish for furs on the side. Within a few decades, fish gave way to furs as the engine of French expansion into North America.

MID-CENTURY EXPLORATIONS AND SETTLEMENTS, 1524–1542, 1555–1563

Although France's North Atlantic fisheries flourished during the 16th century, providing wealth, jobs, and fish—a staple to the European diet—France was less interested in establishing a land presence. In an age when Portuguese and Spanish sailors visited the world's extremities and established settler colonies, the French established a shore presence in North America, Brazil, and Florida but only in Canada did France create a beachhead from which a successful colony flourished a century later. Giovanni da Verrazzano (14??–1528?) and Jacques Cartier (1491–1557) are known to history as the first French explorers of North America; both sought a Northwest Passage to China and the Spice Islands that would reward their backers and allow France to break the Spanish and Portuguese international trade monopoly. It is only with substantial qualification that Verrazzano's voyage can be called a French expedition, for it was the work of an Italian mariner, backed by Italians, living in France, and given only minimal support by the French king.

VERRAZZANO'S VOYAGE

Support for Verrazzano's voyage came, not from François I, but from the Florentine banking community resident in Lyon, which was interested in Verrazzano, a merchant-mariner of Florentine gentry origins, for purely commercial reasons.[8] Lyon, an important commercial city, risked becoming a backwater in the early 1500s when the center of overseas trade shifted from the Mediterranean to the Atlantic. The cheaper and quicker Portuguese-discovered ocean route around the Cape of Good Hope (1498) was supplanting the once-prosperous Mediterranean ports from Egypt to Italy. Knowing the winds of change were blowing about them, the Lyon merchants sought their own direct sea route to the source of Eastern wealth. Cartographers, sailors, and merchants had assured them that such a route existed; it would soon be discovered and the Florentine traders wanted Verrazzano to find it. Several sponsors raised money for the voyage; the king, whom they had tried with marginal success to interest in the project, contributed the *Dauphine*, one of the expedition's four hoped-for ships, and the shipmaster's salary. Verrazzano, 39 when he crossed the Atlantic in 1524, was educated in Italy. He had spent most of his adult life in the seaport

towns of northern France and may have sailed on earlier fishing voyages to
Newfoundland.

On January 17, 1524, the *Dauphine*, with 50 sailors and food for eight
months, passed the Madeira Islands and headed into the Atlantic. After more
than 50 days of sailing, Verrazzano encountered the shore of what he described
as "a new land which had never been seen before by any man, either ancient
or modern," although he acknowledged that it was inhabited. It was late March
and the land, the Carolina coast of North America, was covered with trees of
many colors "so beautiful and delightful they defy description . . . and these trees
emit a sweet fragrance a hundred leagues away, and even farther when they
were burning the cedars and the winds were blowing from the land." There was
"an abundance of animals, stag, deer, hare plus lakes and pools of running water
with various types of birds, perfect for all the delights and pleasures of the
hunt."[9]

His narrative contained only occasional passages about encounters with local
populations. Like many explorers, Verrazzano appeared to have been singularly
incurious about the indigenous people he met. In one passage he describes kid-
napping a child whose subsequent fate is unmentioned:

We met with a very old woman and a young girl of 18 to 20 years, who had hidden in
the grass in fear. The old woman had two little girls whom she carried on her shoulders,
and clinging to her neck was a boy—they were all about eight years old. . . . When we
met them, they began to shout. The old woman made signs to us that the men had fled
to the woods. We gave her some of our food to eat, which she accepted with great
pleasure: the young woman refused everything and threw it angrily to the ground. We
took the boy from the old woman to carry back to France, and we wanted to take the
young woman, who was very beautiful and tall, but it was impossible to take her to sea
because of the loud cries she uttered and, as we were a long way from the ship and had
to pass through several woods, we decided to leave her behind, and took only the boy.[10]

For the next three months Verrazzano sailed northward along the American
coastline from the Carolinas to what may have been Massachusetts. In the end,
he knew he had not found a direct route to Asia. He wrote, "I did not expect
to find such an obstacle of new land as I have found." The importance of
Verrazzano's first voyage lies in enlarging the world map then being pieced
together. The thousand miles of coastline Verrazzano explored, added to the
earlier Portuguese and Spanish discoveries, helped define the North American
continent as a separate landmass.

Verrazzano's achievements were twofold. First, he proved that a direct northern crossing could be accomplished without difficulty to a large mass of habitable land, although this was not the sought-for Cathay or Spice Islands. Second,
he established that territory between Florida and Newfoundland was part of the
same landmass and henceforth voyagers seeking a direct route to the East must
sail farther north or south. Verrazzano was an explorer, not a colonizer, and

since he anchored at sea, he failed to explore and claim for France several bays which the Dutch and English later found strategically and commercially impor- tant—the Chesapeake, the Delaware, and the entrance of the Hudson River. If François had ever been inclined to follow Verrazzano's explorations with other voyages and settlements, he could have claimed much of the eastern shore of North America. However François was concentrating on Italy at the time and was captured in 1525 at Pavia in Italy and imprisoned in Spain. France did not attempt another overseas exploration until a decade later.

CARTIER: *"VOILÀ UN DIAMANT DU CANADA"* (THERE IS A CANADIAN DIAMOND)

First Voyage: April 20–September 5, 1534—"The Land God Gave to Cain"

In 1532 François I met Jacques Cartier during a pilgrimage to the great abbey of Mont-Saint-Michel and authorized Cartier to seek the elusive route to Cathay and to search for gold and silver as well. François, his Spanish captivity behind him, was looking for ways to sting his rival, Charles V. Finding a quick, cheap sea route to the Orient would have been such a coup. Above all, he needed money to reduce the French war debt and to provide for his court's expenses. François also hoped to locate rich northern sources of silver and gold that, like the Spanish treasures of Mexico and Peru, must surely be there.

No copy of the royal commission survives, but there is a naval treasurer's notation that on March 18, 1534, Cartier received 6 thousand *livres tournois* (metallic money originally made at Tours which became the royal coinage) to equip his ships, pay his sailors, and "discover certain isles and countries where there is said to be found a vast quantity of gold and other rich things." Cartier had two ships, each under 60 tons, each with a crew of 60 sailors. Recruiting crews was not easy work. A royal decree banned recruitment for fishing vessels until Cartier had assembled his full crew, but Saint-Malo entrepreneurs with well-established fishing interests resented giving up some of the port's most able sailors for the long and uncertain voyage.[11]

Cartier began his five-month voyage on April 20, 1534, following a route leading almost directly across the Atlantic from Saint-Malo. His own explora- tions began slightly north of where Verrazzano's had ended, indicating famil- iarity with his predecessor's work. Although it was late May when Cartier arrived in the Gulf of Saint Lawrence, his ships met frequent ice floes. As they sailed from one bleak, rocky island to another, Cartier called it "the land God gave to Cain." "Were the soil as good as the harbors," he wrote, "it would be fine but this [coast] should not be called New Land, being composed of stones and frightful rocks and uneven places; for on this entire northern coast I saw not one cartload of earth, though I landed many places."[12] John James Audubon, the naturalist, later called it "poor, rugged, miserable country."[13] From there,

Cartier sailed along the wooded coast of Prince Edward Island in early summer. He found it a "marvelously beautiful and sweet smelling place" with open country nearby filled with numerous berries and "wild wheat like rye." His first encounter with Micmac Indians came in early July along the northern shore of Chaleur Bay. Approaching in two fleets, they held up several fur pelts on sticks, indicating they had met Europeans before.

Cartier described the Native Americans "dancing and making divers signs of joy and wanting our friendship." His men later "made them signs that we wished them no harm" and sent two men ashore "to deal with them, bringing knives and other cutlery, and a red cap to give their chief." Later, at Gaspé Bay, Cartier encountered perhaps 200 Huron Indians on a mackerel fishing trip in late July. He viewed them as "the poorest people there can be in the world, all their possessions, apart from the canoes and fishing nets, are not worth five *sous*." Before he left, Cartier raised a large cross with the inscription "Vive le Roy de France" with the royal arms on it. The local chief, Donnaconna, sensing the symbol was more than a decoration, objected to the ceremony, but he was placated and allowed two sons to accompany the Europeans. By August, Cartier had cruised about the bay for over two months, with no hint of the sought-for water route to the Orient. He assembled his "captains, pilots, masters and gentlemen volunteers" on August 1, 1534, to decide whether they should spend the winter in Canada or return to France. By now tidal currents were strong; heavy downstream winds and seasonal tempests had set in. Cartier wrote that "it was high time either to turn back or stay right there, and . . . if a succession of east winds caught us, we might be forced to stay." They decided to return to France, and the two ships lifted anchor on August 2, pausing only to encounter a party of Montagnais cod fishing for a French captain, indicating the region was already well known to French fishermen. Within three weeks they had crossed the Atlantic and arrived in Saint-Malo in early September 1534.

Cartier's disappointment with the voyage is reflected in the laconic tone of his published account, the *Bref réceit*. Neither the passage to China nor the gold and silver to rival the riches Spain was uncovering farther south had come his way. Other forms of wealth, unrecognized as such by Cartier, surrounded him. Ample supplies of fish, animal pelts, and timber were there for the taking, but he had no interest in fish or beaver and, although France's own timber supplies were fast depleting, the seemingly limitless strands of timber awaited France's interest in the next century.

The Long Second Voyage: May 19, 1536–July 16, 1537

Shortly after his return to France, Cartier received a commission for a second voyage "to explore beyond the new found lands" and "to discover certain far away countries." He was given three ships and, as in the previous voyage, the king provided a subsidy for half the expenses. The second voyage began on May 19, 1536, but it was not until August 17 that all three ships had entered the mouth of the Saint Lawrence. They arrived dangerously late in the year to begin explorations before the onset of the long Canadian winter. Two Hurons, who had accompanied Cartier to France, assured him that they were near "the great river of Hochelaga and the *Chemyn du Canada*." A rare note of excitement creeps into Cartier's otherwise matter-of-fact journal at this point. Was he on the verge of discovering the direct sea route to China, as he hoped, or at least a northern Peru, rich in gold and silver, as the accounts of the two Huron youths would indicate?

By early September, the French were at the site of the modern city of Québec. On September 8 the Huron chief, Donnaconna, and several warriors boarded Cartier's ships, where he talked at length with the two youths who had returned from France. Cartier unwittingly was in the middle of a struggle between Donnaconna and an upriver rival near what is now Montréal. Donnaconna objected to Cartier's continuing inland. At first, the two guides declined to continue with Cartier, then Donnaconna gave Cartier three of his children, hoping to dissuade him from continuing westward. When these ploys failed, Donnaconna said he would accompany Cartier to Hochelaga. However, on the next day, the French were surprised by a canoe full of local people "in black and white dog skins, with faces black as ink, and horns as long as a man's arm." One of them, "with fixed eyes, as of one piercing the secrets of futurity," began a long harangue, trying to keep the French from going upriver because supposedly "snows, tempests, and drifting ice would requite their rashness with inevitable ruin."[14]

Cartier and the smallest of his ships continued upstream, towing longboats. Finally, on October 2, Cartier and 30 followers reached the heights of Hochelaga, now Montréal, where a thousand people greeted them with gifts, including cornbread which "seemed to fall from the air."

Finally, Cartier and his crew saw the whole expanse of the Saint Lawrence Valley before them, and in the distance the Green Mountains, the Adirondacks, and the Laurentians. The otherwise spectacular natural panorama, however, contained a river that was blocked by numerous rapids. The wide river supposedly leading to the Orient suddenly funneled into a narrow, rapid-filled stream which the French sardonically named *Lachine* (China). The tone of Cartier's narrative shifted after he encountered the rapids. There was no more talk of reaching China. Cartier had to change his plans because the cold Canadian winter was fast approaching.

It was late now and instead of moving ahead, Cartier returned to a wooden fort his crew had constructed near Québec, where they prepared to spend the winter after making great stacks of firewood and salting enough fish and game to last until spring. A disastrous winter followed; ships were frozen solid, covered with thick ice and snow up to four feet deep. Scurvy struck both the Huron and the French, resulting in pain, rotting gums, loss of teeth, and swollen limbs.

From the Huron, the French learned about a bark drink that cured scurvy. The concoction, brewed from bark of the arborvitae tree, rich in vitamin C, was drunk by the sick every other day, and the residue was spread on swollen arms and legs. All who took it recovered, but by then 35 members of the expedition had died. Only three or four of Cartier's sailors remained healthy by mid-February. Fearing a Huron raid, the small French band feigned revelry and merriment and made loud noises.

Cartier and the remaining survivors planned to return to France in May 1537. The resourceful Donnaconna made one more attempt to lure the French into an expedition against a rival chief, suggesting Cartier take his opponent to France. Instead, Cartier planned to take Donnaconna back to France, presumably to tell the king about the riches of Saguenay. Cartier invited the Huron to the raising of a cross on Holyrood Day, May 3, after which some local inhabitants were seized and taken quickly to a waiting ship. Gunshots scattered the others who "scampered off like sheep before a wolf, some across the river and some to the forest, each for himself." The Huron regrouped and "cried and howled like wolves" all night at the river. None of the 10 Huron Cartier took with him ever returned; by Cartier's third voyage, all but one had died in France.

On June 19 the remaining two ships left Newfoundland for Saint-Malo and, three weeks later, ended the 14-month-long voyage. In addition to the Native Americans, Cartier brought back several barrels of glittering minerals. Portuguese fishermen who saw them reported the French had found gold and diamonds but, as in the past, the cargo was crystal quartz, iron pyrite, and mica-bearing rocks. Cartier had failed to find the direct route to China, but he was in a better position than before to approach the king and ask for a new expedition.

Donnaconna, a skilled storyteller, was able to present the golden kingdom of Saguenay dramatically to François and the court. He spoke of lands in the wilds of Canada with gold, silver, rubies, and other precious stones where nutmeg, peppers, oranges, and pomegranates grew. Unipeds peopled the land, as did men with wings like bats who flew from tree to tree. His story never varied in the telling. To skeptics he pointed out he had sworn to its veracity before a French notary. Donnaconna lived in France for four years, was baptized and given a pension, but he died while Cartier was planning his third voyage.

Cartier's Third Expedition: 1541–1542

Although he had supported three economically unremunerative explorations in the last decade, François agreed to back a fourth North American voyage, this one to find the passage to China and "the great country of Canada and Ochelaga," where a settler colony would be installed.

Cartier had headed the first two expeditions to Canada by himself, but in January 1541, three months before his scheduled departure, François awarded command of the voyage to Jean-François de la Roque, sieur de Roberval, a Huguenot nobleman and courtier. The expedition was ill-starred from the beginning. This was Cartier's roughest crossing, taking a month to make a familiar voyage requiring two-thirds that time in good weather. Ships were separated in storms, water ran short, and cider was given to goats and swine so they might survive. By August 23—late in the year for such an expedition—Cartier arrived near Québec, where the Huron chief, Agona, who had replaced his rival, Donnaconna, expressed no grief at news of Donnaconna's death in France.

Several miles upstream, at what is now Cap Rouge, Cartier established a settlement, which presumably would lead to the inland kingdom. Colonists, convicts, and cattle were landed, a garden was begun, and a fort was erected, called Charlesburg-Royal after the duc d'Orleans.

Again quantities of glittering quartz crystals, which Cartier mistook for diamonds, and iron pyrites, which he thought were gold, were quickly dispatched to the king by two ships with word that more such riches awaited the expedition. On September 7, with autumn approaching, Cartier set out for Saguenay. Cartier next reached the barrier that had barred his progress six years earlier. Laboriously he threaded past rapids which fell 42 feet in two miles, only to discover— not the wide, smooth river to Cathay—but a narrow, rapid-filled stream.

It was all over. Cartier turned back and ended his quest for the Northwest Passage. Equally grim realities awaited the leader on his return to the fort. The Canadian winter was fast approaching and Huron-French relations had worsened. Friendly visits to peddle fish and game ceased; the Huron attacked the fort and, surprising a party of wood cutters, killed 35 persons. The only surviving narrative breaks off at this point.

In June 1542, Cartier and the remnants of his settlement headed home, carrying with them more barrels of worthless stones. Approaching the harbor of what is now Saint John's, Newfoundland, they chanced upon Roberval's three ships, which had not left La Rochelle until April 16, 11 months after Cartier had sailed on the expedition Roberval supposedly commanded. Roberval ordered Cartier to accompany him back to Canada, which Cartier refused to do, and on the second night Cartier ordered his ships to steal silently away.

Seen against the wider picture of 16th century discovery, the results of Cartier's explorations were principally of interest to geographers and mariners. They proved that the North American continent stood in the way of any westward travel to China, and Cartier provided the first accurate information about the Saint Lawrence Gulf and River. Possibilities of a Northwest Passage or a fabulously wealthy northern kingdom were never again seriously considered by French explorers. Cartier found no gold or silver and showed no interest in timber, fur, and fish. Notwithstanding, a French connection to Canada was established that would bear fruit in subsequent centuries.

BRAZIL (1555–1560) AND FLORIDA (1562–1565)

During the century's middle years France again thought about overseas possessions, this time in Brazil and Florida. During the decades-long Wars of Religion, Gaspard de Coligny (1519–1572), an admiral of France and a Protestant leader, hoped to create French settler colonies overseas as a refuge for his persecuted coreligionists. Coligny wanted such settlements to be primarily French, not Huguenot, settlements believing that, unless they had broad national appeal, he could never obtain necessary support for them. Also, the admiral, as a soldier and patriot, constantly looked for ways to counter France's enemies, Portugal and Spain, and he thought territorial bases in Brazil and Florida would threaten both rival country's trading interests.[15] Coligny's overseas plans were ill-fated from the start. Brazil and Florida became case studies of all that could go wrong in overseas colonial settlement: inept leadership, planning errors, inadequate support, and bad luck.

THE FRENCH MOVE ON BRAZIL

Brazil was probably the overseas land best known to the French at this time; for many years, sailors had traded with the inhabitants for tropical woods and spices. Ties with coastal tribes were cordial, and many Frenchmen established trading stations along the coast and stayed for long periods where they lived with the local people. Such coastal settlements were numerous near Rio de Janeiro Bay, where the resident French established roles as intermediaries between local tribes and visiting ships.[16]

Support for taking Brazil from the Portuguese came from the large Rouen Protestant merchant community which staged an elaborate Brazilian festival when Henri II and his bride, Catherine de Medici, visited Rouen in 1550.[17] A large native village was built on the banks of the Seine, with wooden houses, parrots, and birds and animals brought from a local collector's menagerie. Brazilians swung in a hammock and shot at birds with bows and arrows. The cast included over 200 French sailors painted red and black and dressed as Brazilians and some South Americans who had been brought to France as well. Natives and traders bartered for wood with animated gestures when discussing prices. A mock combat between two tribes was staged, complete with showers of flaming arrows, and one tribe's storming another's fortress. A poetic narrative stressed Brazil's enmity toward Portugal and love of France, a thinly veiled plea for royal backing for a French colony in Brazil:

> Sire, il n'est pas jusques aux cannibales,
> Ils à tous fors à nos des loyalles,
> Ou ne soyons en bonne sûereté,
> Pour la faveur de vostre autorité.

> [Sir, there are not only cannibals,
> there are always us, the loyal ones
> who want to live in security
> under the favor of your authority.]

The Rouen merchants' proposal was accepted by the king. Shortly after his visit he ordered an accomplished mapmaker, Guillaume le Testu, to prepare a map of Brazil for use in future explorations. Coligny then took the necessary steps to create a settler colony, naming as its leader an ambitious adventurer, Nicholas Durand de Villegagnon, a mercurial personality who had established Protestant ties during his student days at the University of Paris, but who later became a knight of the Order of Saint John of Jerusalem, a militant pro-Catholic band of soldier-adventurers.

Six hundred colonists embarked for Brazil in late July 1555, and on November 3 the expedition arrived in the Bay of Rio de Janeiro. Here Villegagnon made the first of several decisions contributing to the colony's downfall. Instead of settling on shore, where French traders were already established, local inhabitants friendly, and conditions right for growing food crops, Villegagnon took the colonists to a small island in the middle of the bay and built a fortress, a "French Malta" which he called Fort Coligny. The island lacked fresh water or space for crops, and Villegagnon assumed French and Brazilian mainland inhabitants would supply him with food. However, over time, Villegagnon's rigidity permanently alienated both communities. The Brazilians were soon bitter about inadequate payment for foodstuffs and poor treatment from the fortress. Friction with the trading community developed when Villegagnon ordered a Norman merchant, who had been living with a local woman for seven years, to marry her or leave her. Dissention soon broke out in the colony, over the most minute issues, such as whether Indian corn bread could be used for the communion rite or whether water could be added to communion wine without diluting the wine's spiritual efficacy. Charges of heresy were exchanged, and about half the recent arrivals left the fort for the mainland. Some built a fragile craft to return to France. Their 20-week crossing was rough, supplies ran out quickly, and to survive they ate leather, rats, and finally the parrot they brought as a gift for Admiral Coligny.

In late 1559, Villegagnon ended his four years in Brazil and took 50 Brazilians with him back to France. He was well received by the king and the Catholic court; the adverse reports spread by the returned Calvinists were to no avail. The Brazil colony languished. Before France could decide what to do with it, the Portuguese struck on February 26, 1560, when Men de Sa, the Portuguese governor, began a sustained bombardment of the island fort. On March 15 Portuguese and Brazilians made a daring night raid on the fort, now defended by only a small band of French and Brazilians, and seized the remnants of the French presence in Brazil.

FLORIDA, 1562–1565

Coligny's intentions for Florida were the same as those for Brazil—to build an overseas haven for persecuted Protestants and to challenge France's neighbor and enemy, Spain. Catholics dominated the French government, so Coligny presented the colony as a national, not a sectarian, project. French strategy was simple: a successful Florida colony would threaten the Spanish lifeline, the route of the annual treasure fleets, eventually cutting Spain off from its sources of gold and silver. In Spain's view, the French intrusion clearly violated the long-established papal decree dividing the world between the two Iberian powers. A French military base in striking distance of the Spanish Main and the important port of Havana was a direct threat. In response, Philip II unleashed an attack on the "Lutheran" outpost comparable to what Spain had earlier loosed on the Moors.

The French party's leader, Jean Ribaul, a skilled Dieppe mariner, reached what is now South Carolina in mid-April 1562 with two antiquated boats full of soldiers and sailors after a two-month journey. Sailing along the coast until May 1, at what was later called Saint John's River, local peoples strewed laurel boughs in front of them as the party landed, chanting Huguenot psalms. The 19th century American historian Francis Parkman reconstructed the landing:

Never had they known a fairer May-day. The quaint old narrative is exuberant with delight. The tranquil air, the warm sun, grazing deer, herons, curlews, and the unknown fowl that waded in the ripple of the beach; cedars bearded from crown to root with long, gray moss; huge oaks smothering the folds of enormous grapevines; such were the objects that greeted them in their roamings, their newly-discovered land seemed the fairest, fruitfullest, and pleasantest of all the world.[18]

The land was called New Canaan, recalling the promised land of the wandering Hebrew tribes, and 30 members of the group remained to found a fort, which they called Charlesfort, after Charles IX, the weak, young king. Ribault and the ships then returned to France to report their success and to return with the permanent colonists.

For the small party that remained at the fort, the following months were as disastrous as anything faced by the French in Canada or Brazil. To begin with, settlers were drawn from one of two ranks, gentlemen adventurers and nobles, or unemployed soldiers of fortune who made their living by hiring out to various warring factions. Some knew how to fight, others were sharp in theological polemics, but no one knew anything about growing crops. Second, relations with local peoples soured quickly. Tensions flared when the French behaved with levity at a religious ceremony to which they had been invited, and the local chief temporarily confined his guests to his dwelling. Later, during the summer, food supplies dwindled and the Native Americans, who originally gave freely of their crops to the fort's inhabitants, withdrew, as their own supplies were low and the harvest was not yet due. Supplies soon gave out, and the daily ration of food was reduced to 12 kernels of maize, after which they ate shoes and other leather. By the end of 1562, the colony's first year was a disaster.[19]

THE SECOND ATTEMPT

In 1564 the time seemed right for Coligny to move ahead with plans to establish the main Florida colony. France's political climate was more favorable than in recent years. The Edict of Ambroise (1563) had temporarily ended hostilities, and Catherine de Medici, anxious to reach a rapprochement with Coligny, supported the colony. Coligny named René Goulaine de Laudonnière, an austere, indecisive Huguenot nobleman, to lead a new expedition. Three ships set sail with 150 soldiers, artisans, and traders. Drawn largely from the Protestant region of Dieppe, their numbers included unemployed soldiers and adventurers drawn from the quays. Once again, there were no farmers.

The French arrived in June 1564 and built a fort on a site on the bluff above Saint John's River near what is now Jacksonville, Florida. Their first serious mistake was intervening in a dispute on behalf of a chief who had befriended them, and who promised them great stores of nonexistent gold and silver in return for military aid against his enemies.

The colony's fortunes seemed to improve when Ribault arrived from France with seven ships and 600 colonists on August 28. Women and children joined the expedition, as did artisans and small landowners who had lost their possessions in the civil war. Farm animals came with this group, something not true of earlier expeditions.

The ever-cautious Philip II received reports that 4 thousand French were settled in Florida. He responded by sending a force of 2,640 troops—four times the size of the French expedition—and ten ships to Florida under an able soldier, Pedro Menéndez de Avilés, whom he named Spanish governor general of Florida. At the same time Ribault arrived in Saint John's River, Menéndez and part of his forces landed 40 miles to the south at what is now Saint Augustine.

For the French, the long months of indecision were over. They had to act quickly, little realizing that the colony's fate, two years in unfolding, would be settled within three weeks. The French had three possibilities. They could stay where they were, which meant losing their ships to the Spanish, but hopefully withstanding a direct attack. A second possibility, with the advantage of surprise, was to push quickly overland and attack the Spanish before they were fully positioned. However, this would leave the French ships unguarded and the fort poorly protected. The third course was to sweep down on the Spanish by sea. The distance was short, the route was well known, and the plan had the advantage of surprise, although it left the French fort unprotected. On the surface, the third choice, which the French adopted, looked the most attractive but, like everything else associated with the colony, it ended disastrously.

Ribault's 600 French soldiers and sailors headed southward by sea, while a Spanish force of 500 soldiers, guided by a French deserter, moved overland through a tropical storm and surprised the French fort, whose numbers were reduced to a few laborers, the ill, and women and children. Menéndez sent 50 women and children and six musicians to another Spanish colony and massacred the remaining captives. Menéndez then headed south with 150 soldiers, where he encountered an even larger group of French stragglers who asked for a meeting. Ribault and eight soldiers were led to the site of the slaughter and shown the goods taken from their fort. Ribault offered a large ransom and asked for ships to return his troops to France. Menéndez repeated the same terms given the previous French party—he would accept only an unconditional surrender. That night, 200 of the French withdrew into the wilderness, but Ribault, believing he had some hope of protection, surrendered to the Spanish, turning over weapons, standards, and the seal Coligny had given the colony. The French were bound and led in small groups to an isolated location. The few Catholics, plus a handful of musicians, were removed; the rest were slaughtered.[20]

The adventure of French Florida was over, and the century's French presence in Latin America and the Caribbean was at an end. Ill-fated from the beginning, it suffered from leadership both oppressive and naïve, especially in the lack of skills needed to make the settler colonies agriculturally viable. Historians of Parkman's generation cast it as an unsuccessful struggle of French arms against Spanish arms, but the French were also defeated by their inept relations with local peoples and their failure to grow crops, fish, or raise the livestock required by an enduring settlement. France's attempts to establish colonies in Brazil and Florida were but a bloody footnote to history. According to one French participant,

> Qui veut aller à la Floride,
> Qu'il aille, j'y ai esté.
> Et revenu sec et aride
> Et abbatu de povreté.[21]

> [Those who would go to Florida,
> let them go, I was there.
> And I returned dried out
> and parched and beaten into poverty.]

16TH CENTURY SCIENCE, A NEW HEAVEN AND A NEW EARTH

The geographical discoveries of this century were possible because the moment of Europe's quest for overseas wealth coincided with a technological revolution that brought about improvements in shipbuilding and cartography that made transoceanic voyages possible. New instruments for measuring time, space, and distance were perfected, allowing mariners to plot voyages more accurately than before and to record the results of explorations more precisely. By the end of the 16th century, the world—whose dimensions until then were as much the property of artists as of cartographers—was a known quantity in its broad outlines, and it remained for the next century's mapmakers to correct details, extend coastlines, and trace inland rivers, plains, and natural features.[22]

The spread of European exploration into every part of the world was also made possible through improvements in ship design. Ships circa 1450 to 1550 were small by later standards, often displacing less than from 60 to 70 tons. Originally built for coastal sailing, or for commerce between Europe's Atlantic ports and the Mediterranean, in the 16th century they were modified to accommodate larger cargoes and longer voyages. The basic ship was a combination of the old Celtic cog, with a flat bottom, single mast, and square sail, and a banana-shaped hulk, with improved keels and platforms for warriors. This new ship would be the basic model for both cargo and warships in northern Europe until it was overtaken by new technology a century later.[23] None of these ships was particularly fast, and most were built to defend themselves as well as transport cargo. Some had temporary battlements mounted on bow and stern in wartime, and these features were incorporated into ship design. During the century there were also improvements in ship armaments, and in the placement and construction of sails as well. To the older coastal ships' single mast and sail set on a large spar were added several masts and lateen sails, borrowed from Arab vessels. These triangular sails formed an oblique angle to the mast and were easily maneuverable, allowing quick turning to take advantage of the wind.

Voyagers also profited from Portuguese improvements in the instruments used for measuring and recording space and distance, including the astrolabe and quadrant, both of which allowed ships to take periodic readings of their latitude. When used at sea they could be as much as a degree off, however, and it was not until the invention of the marine chronometer in the 18th century that it was possible to determine longitude accurately. The crude compasses and coastal charts of an earlier era were greatly improved on, but 16th century ships still relied on inexact instruments which, on a long oceanic voyage, could lead to errors of several hundred miles. The compass, acquired from Arab sailors, who obtained it from the Chinese, was widely used, but the few available charts rarely noted the difference between magnetic north and geographic north. This created problems in determining bearings, especially in North American waters, where the difference between geographic and magnetic poles was most pronounced. By the late 15th century manufactured compasses were in general use, employing magnetized needles or circular cards on which compass points were marked. These replaced the magnetic needle set on a wooden float in a bowl of water widely used by Mediterranean and coastal pilots. Time was told by hour glasses, turned each half-hour by crew members, assuming they were awake and watching. The Venetian-made hour glasses were accurate but broke easily. Ferdinand Magellan carried 18 of them on his 1519–1522 circumnavigation of the globe.

The science of cartography evolved during this period as well. Originally, mapmakers' sources included log books, sketches, mariners' accounts, and returning merchants' reports. Conflicting interpretations and differences over details were compounded by the effects of fog, rain, mist, and mirage. Islands, bays, shores, and peninsulas could be merged in vivid if inaccurate accounts if actual measurements were not taken. This caused Verrazzano to report the Cape Hatteras Sound as an open waterway to the west, an error that persisted on European maps for sixty years. The most widely used maps in the early 16th century were variations on medieval ribbon maps, which assumed Jerusalem was at the earth's center, and were based on information from returning pilgrims and crusaders. These maps were oblong pieces of parchment from three to five feet long, 18 to 30 inches deep. Ports and known locations appeared as vertically lettered names along a horizontal line representing the coast. Called portolan maps, these charts were little more than written sailing instructions with short distances calculated and sea courses indicated by wind or compass points. By the century's end, neither the earth's curved surface nor latitudinal bearings had appeared on them. The point in media res from which the future of cartography evolved was the 1569 work of a Flemish mathematician and engraver, Gerhard Mercator. His work incorporated the latest known observations of land and sea and used parallel straight lines to establish both latitude and longitude. The distance between lines was corrected to allow for the earth's sphericity. Although it was not fully accurate, it was a vast improvement on earlier maps.

During a single generation, the Cape of Good Hope had been rounded, the West Indies had been discovered, India and Brazil had been reached by sea, and the Pacific Ocean had been sighted by Vasco Núñez de Balboa. At the same time, the recently discovered sea route to the Far East permanently altered centuries' old patterns of commerce. It was literally a "new heaven and a new earth" created by explorers and political leaders, but in France the impact of these changes came later for reasons unique to French history of this time.

HOW THE FRENCH PERCEIVED THE OVERSEAS WORLD: "THE SEA OF DARKNESS" VERSUS NEW MAPS

The worldview of an earlier age prevailed. That is the dominant impression gathered from looking at French 16th century works on the overseas world. Eyewitness accounts of explorers blend with descriptions of lands beyond Prester John's kingdom, religious polemics with ethnographies. As for the geographical works circulating in France, the contemporary reader, far from being transported back to the high literature of the Renaissance, will observe how terse were most French accounts. We are present at the moment when fact and fiction were being sorted out, when the world of fantasy, drawing understandably from imagined realities beyond France's shores, began to give way to eyewitness observations.

An understanding of how the 16th century French viewed the overseas world must consider the body of geographic knowledge and fantasy accumulated during the Middle Ages, which provides the picture of the world beyond France's shores. At the century's opening, with few exceptions, people generally believed that a Sea of Darkness lay beyond the major oceans' known confines, that the sea boiled in places, and that monsters were as real as fish. At the century's end, among cartographers and mariners at least, the globe's broad outlines were known in forms recognizable to modern geographers. To this picture of the overseas world we must add the few contemporary explorers' accounts and consider how both residual fantasy and recently discovered fact were absorbed into the imaginative writings of this period. What emerges is a sense of how strongly the medieval worldview persisted and how little it was affected by geographical discoveries, except among the explorers themselves and those around them.[24]

At the century's beginning, the French formed their impression of the world outside Europe from three sources: from accounts of pilgrim travelers to the Holy Land, from actual descriptions of voyages, and from classical works, such as Pliny's *Natural History*. Pliny's work, written by a Hellenized Alexandrian c. A.D. 77, exercised an immense influence on subsequent geographical writings. Like many of the French cosmographical works popular in this century, Pliny's work mixed many subjects, ranging from geography to biology, medical information to mineralogy, and focused almost exclusively on the Mediterranean world.

A breakdown of published works for the period indicates the ordering of French geographical interests. There are 80 known books on Turks, 50 on the East Indies, 50 on other countries of Asia including pilgrimage literature of the Holy Land, 40 on the Americas, and 5 on Africa. Although the number of geographical works increased sharply at the century's end, there is a notable decline in books about the New World. In fact, more than twice as many books and ten times as many brochures were published about the Turks, expanded to include Tunisians, Algerians, and Moroccans, than about the two Americas.[25]

Jerusalem Books and Marco Polo's Travels

The most popular geographical works circulating at this time were pilgrim guidebooks to the Holy Land, called Jerusalem Books. Primarily devotional guides, these works assume that Jerusalem is at the universe's center and that devils roam at night on Mount Gilboa. Descriptions of the land are scarce; most information deals with the price of food, places to stay, tips to be given to guardians at the Holy Sepulcher, and accounts of miracles. One such book, *Voyages à Jérusalem*, went through 35 editions during the 16th century. As might be expected, these works ignore the considerable achievement of Arabic geography and science developed independently at this time.

Probably the single volume most widely known to literate audiences is the travel account of the Venetian Marco Polo (1254–1324), who spent 20 years as counselor and diplomat at the court of the emperors of China and, after returning to Europe, was taken prisoner in the Venice-Genoa war. In 1298 he dictated his travel recollections to a fellow prisoner who published them in French. Polo's account, largely a document of commercial intelligence, popularizes the Orient as a source of spices, silks, and precious metals and describes the economic activities of the cities and kingdoms he visited from Persia and India to China. The book fired the imagination of generations of Europeans and contributed more than any other work to creating the idea of the East as a place of untold riches; however, it is disappointing as a political or cultural commentary. It was principally a description of the sources and extent of Eastern wealth as seen by the Western traveler.

Another widely diffused book that helped form French attitudes toward the overseas world is the completely fanciful *Voyage d'outre-mer* by Jean Mandeville, translated into French in 1480. Mandeville, the name adopted by the book's compiler, made a pilgrimage to the Holy Land and claimed to have visited China. Following accounts of Prester John and the wealth of the East, and the customs of Tartars and Chinese, there are stories of men with eyes on each shoulder, multiheaded animals with human voices, and other creatures indistinguishable from those in popular tales of medieval France. Works in this vein were extensive, describing overseas lands inhabited by giants and monsters, fire-breathing creatures, and others with precious stones in place of eyes, a glance from which would kill the onlooker. Such mixtures of fantasy and fact appear in numerous *cosmographies*. In them, a description of a huge lobster that could break the back of a sailor with a single pincer's snap might follow a traveler's account of a trip to Prussia. News of a whale with a human face and teeth the size of an elephant's tusks appear next to a description of an erupting volcano.

The line separating the fantasies of François Rabelais and Amadis de Gaule from works actually classified as geographies is a thin one. In fact, the style adopted by Rabelais (1494–1553) in *Pantagruel* (1547) resembles contemporary geographical accounts. Pantagruel sailed for Cathay via the northwest, possibly following the outline of Cartier's voyages of the previous decade, for Pantagruel visited Canada and encountered a local tribe searching for the Northwest Passage. It is not until the century's end that fact and fantasy about geographical knowledge become different domains. Representative of later, more factual, works is the *Chronologie septénaire* of Palme Cayet, an attempt to chronicle events of importance in Europe, Africa, Asia, and America during the period between 1596 and 1604.[26]

Explorers' Accounts

Actual explorers' accounts circulating in France can be divided into two groups: reports of Portuguese and Spanish voyages and reports of French travels to North and South America. In the former category, the writings of Portuguese and Spanish voyages and Italian mariners were generally circulated in France between 1500 and 1525. The earliest known such volume is an account of the voyages of Amerigo Vespucci, Christopher Columbus, and Miguel and Gaspar Corte Real, the *Paesi Nouamente Retrouati*, which went through 15 editions in seven years. Although Columbus' voyages were of general knowledge to the court and maritime community, printed versions do not appear to have gained wide circulation in France.

The first French geographical work is the *Relations authentiques* of Paulmier de Gonneville, an account of a six-month stay in Brazil in 1503 and 1504 with a long description of the ethnic groups found in the Rio de Janeiro region. Almost 30 years later, in 1529, the next French exploration account appears: Verrazzano's long letter to François I about his 1524 voyage. Verrazzano wrote a clear, concise mariner's report. Cartier's *Bref récit* was published in 1545, but neither work created much interest, except among the maritime community and their backers. Cartier's style (if in fact he was the author) was terse, and his subject matter the explorations around the Gulf of Saint Lawrence and the Saint Lawrence River Valley. Compared to the drama of some Spanish discoveries and the tales of the wealth of China, a seemingly monotonous account of visits to bays, rivers, and inlets separated by unrelieved landscape and uninhabited land failed to arouse much interest.

The century's only other French exploration literature concerns the ill-fated colonies in Brazil and Florida, presented as another forum on which the bloody drama of Europe's religious wars was played out. Printed works are less travel accounts than Catholic or Protestant polemical documents. The most important books about the Brazil colony, one written by a Catholic, the other by a Protestant, are François Thevet's *Singularities de la France Anartique* (1558) and Jean de Lery's *Voyage au Brésil* (1578). Thevet spent only a few months in Brazil, and his lively and credulous account is filled with impressions gained from medieval geographic literature. He wrote through the prism of the time in which he lived, and the world he saw belonged more to the Middle Ages than to modern times, which may explain why an ethnographic account shifts suddenly to reports of a race of giants living elsewhere in Brazil. If Thevet's work, except for its religious content, belongs to the Middle Ages, de Lery's account was written when France was torn by the Wars of Religion, which visibly influenced his comments on Brazil. De Lery lived on the mainland; much of his information on local societies came from Norman merchants long settled there.

In Florida, there were no established French settlers as there were in Brazil. Consequently, the few works, thin on ethnographic details, contain scattered references to friendly or hostile "kings" the French encountered. The two main contemporary works are René de Laudonnière's *Histoire notable de la Floride* (1586) and Nicholas le Challeaux's *Discours de l'histoire de la Floride* (1565). Although Laudonnière was present at the Florida colony's tragic demise, his account is flaccid and unobservant, a poor contrast to Jean Ribault's own version, which was published in English in 1563. The *Discours*, limited almost exclusively to the French-Spanish encounter, fit easily into period French literary warfare against Spain.

The New World excited some interest among French writers, and the fantasy themes of "barbarians" and "noble savages" are the stuff from which future generations of writers developed political and literary commentaries. Likewise the overseas world was understandably an infrequent but significant subject in 16th century visual arts. Albrecht Dürer, in a 1520 trip to Holland, reported seeing a sunburst and some of Montezuma's treasures Cortés had sent from

Mexico for the coronation of Charles V, but such works from the New World were rare and regarded as curios and did not otherwise influence artists. This is probably because artists, working within self-contained classical or Christian traditions, found no place for the overseas world's strange discoveries. The *cabinet des curiosités*, which included bones, fossils, and mineral specimens with drums, bracelets, and artifacts brought back by returning sailors, became a fixture in many wealthy European households at this time. It was also fashionable for wealthy merchants to keep menageries or zoological gardens. Plants from the New World created some interest, and one of the most coveted commodities was a parrot from Brazil.

The Overseas World of Classical Authors

Poet Pierre de Ronsard (1524–1585) and political philosophers Michel Montaigne (1533–1592) and Jean Bodin (1530–1596) are the classical authors who drew most conspicuously on themes from the newly discovered world in their own writings. Ronsard's *Les Iles fortunées* (1553), a long narrative poem, was set overseas in a place of "good cheer," where perfect health, harmony, and government exist. Ronsard describes a world in which the Age of Iron, representing war, will be replaced by a contrasting Age of Gold. In describing this land free of laws, morality, property, and other encumbrances of European civilization, Ronsard used many images supposedly drawn from America. But Ronsard was first of all a neoclassicist who drew his inspiration, not from the New World, but from Ancient Rome, principally the poet Horace. His descriptions came from the stock imagery of classical poetry; the mood and setting of the poems and the people belong to the Loire Valley's gentle landscape, not Florida's swamps or Canada's timber forests. Parenthetically, there is a clear anti-colonial sentiment in Ronsard's poetry. He urged Europeans not to destroy the harmony of indigenous societies with colonies and declared that native peoples would be justified in forcibly opposing colonization.

Like Ronsard, Montaigne, a political philosopher and essayist, described a world of "perfect religion, perfect policy, perfect and complete use of all things." Montaigne, in his celebrated essay "Of the Cannibals" (c. 1580), writes about a Brazil where there is nothing "that is either barbarous or savage, unless men call that barbarous which is not common to them." The work, supposedly drawn from conversations with a houseguest who had spent from 10 to 12 years in Brazil, details Montaigne's vision of Brazilian life and customs. Inhabitants are universally happy, given to dancing all day. Prophets live in the mountains and periodically emerge to make pronouncements. In wars against rival tribes, the Brazilians roast their enemies, which Montaigne found hardly less civil than the Portuguese custom of burying prisoners of war up to their waist and shooting their bodies full of arrows. Of the Brazilians, Montaigne wrote, "We may call these people barbarians, in respect to the rules of reason, but not in respect to ourselves, who in all sorts of barbarity exceed them."[27]

Montaigne wrote when the Wars of Religion had gone into their second decade. It was against a backdrop of his own country's intolerance and cruelty that he saw the need for moderation, rationality, and the virtues of *le bon sauvage*, the good savage, which would provide a benchmark against which future French writers would measure civilizing influences. Montaigne's intention was never simply to portray life overseas. He used accounts of life in the New World to construct a vision of a more peaceful and just society than France knew. At times Montaigne stressed the virtues of a state unaffected by laws, when the good savage predominates; at other times, a darker strain of cruelty, cannibalism, and warfare appear in his picture of these societies. He was never able to reconcile these differences beyond acknowledging that conflict was present even in the most harmonious society.

A contemporary of Montaigne's, Bodin advanced a geography-based theory of national character. For Bodin, the world was divided into temperate zones of thirty degrees latitude radiating north and south from the Equator. Northern zone inhabitants, including Europeans, are dark or blond in color, are strong, active, and youthful in character, but lack wisdom. Southerners are contemplative and religious, cerebral but laconic, thin-blooded "old men," which result in their being more timid and feeble than northerners or temperate zone inhabitants. Bodin believed in the superiority of temperate zone people, the versatile moderate force between extremes. He argued that the blood of the Scythians was full of fiber, as in bears and bulls, and produced strength and audacity. These advantages came partly from their being immigrants, but more so from a proper blending of the elements within themselves. In many ways, Bodin mirrored his time. Possessed with a curiosity for new knowledge, his feet were still planted in the Middle Ages. Bodin, like many contemporaries, also believed in witchcraft and, during much of his adult life, he consulted a friendly spirit before making decisions.

NOTES

1. A. N. Ryan, "France and the Sixteenth Century," in *Maritime History*, vol. 1, *The Age of Discovery*, ed. John B. Hattendorf (Malabar, Fla.: Krieger Publishing, 1998), pp. 279–297.

2. Fernand Braudel, *La Méditerranée et le monde méditerranéen a l'Époque de Philippe II*, vols. 1, 2 (Paris: Armand Colin, 1966); H. G. Koenigsberger and G. L. Mosse, *Europe in the Sixteenth Century* (London: Longmans, 1968), p. 207; C. R. Boxer, *The Portuguese Seaborne Empire, 1415–1825* (New York: Alfred A. Knopf, 1969), pp. 20–24, 56–64; C. R. Boxer, *Four Centuries of Portuguese Expansion, 1415–1825: A Succinct Survey* (Johannesburg: Witwatersrand University Press, 1961); C. R. Boxer, *Race Relations in the Portuguese Empire, 1415–1825* (New York: Oxford University Press, 1963); M. L. Bush, *Renaissance, Reformation and the Outer World, 1450–1600* (New York: Harper Colophon, 1967); J. H. Elliott, *The Old World and the New, 1492–1650* (Cambridge: Cambridge University Press, 1970); Georges Duby and Robert Mandrou, *Histoire*

de la civilisation française, vol. 1, *Moyen Age-XVIe siècle* (Paris: Librarie Armand Colin, 1968).

3. Robert Mandrou, *Introduction à la France moderne, Essai de psychologie historique, 1500–1640* (Paris: Editions Albin Michel, 1961); Eugen Weber, *A Modern History of Europe* (New York: W. W. Norton, 1971); J. H. Elliott, *Europe Divided, 1554–1598* (New York, Harper & Row, 1969); Frank C. Spooner, *The International Economy and Monetary Movements in France, 1493–1725* (Cambridge: Harvard University Press, 1972).

4. James Pritchard, letter, Frederick Quinn, May 13, 1999.

5. Philippe Haudrèse, *L'Empire des rois, 1500–1789* (Paris: Denoël, 1997), pp. 15–58.

6. Charles de la Morandière, *Histoire de la pêche française de la morue dans l'Amérique septentrionale (des origines a 1789)*, vols. 1, 2 (Paris: G.-P. Maisonneuve et Larose, 1962); Harold A. Innes, *The Cod Fisheries, the History of an International Economy* (New Haven, Conn.: Yale University Press, 1940); Pierre Loti, *Pêcheur d'Islande* (Paris: Calmann-Lévy, n.d.); Armel de Wismes, *La vie quotidienne dans les ports bretons au XVIIe et XVIIIe siècle* (Paris: Hachette Littèrature, 1974).

7. de la Morandière, *Histoire de la pêche*, vol. 1, pp. 69–70.

8. Lawrence C. Wroth, *The Voyages of Giovanni da Verrazzano, 1524–1528* (New Haven, Conn.: Yale University Press, 1970), p. 57ff.

9. Ibid., pp. 133–135.

10. Ibid., p. 136.

11. Marcel Trudel, *Histoire de la Nouvelle-France, les vaines tentatives, 1524–1603* (Montréal: FIDES, 1963); Samuel Eliot Morison, *The European Discovery of America, the North American Voyages, A.D. 500–1600* (New York: Oxford University Press, 1971), pp. 339 ff; Justin Winsor, *Georgaphical Discovery in the Interior of North America, Its Historical Relations, 1534–1700* (New York: Cooper Square Publishers, 1970 reprint of 1894 edition).

12. J. Cartier, "Première Relation," in Morison, *The European Discovery of America*, p. 354.

13. Ibid.

14. Francis Parkman, *Pioneers of France in the New World, France and England in North America*, Part First (Boston: Little, Brown, 1910), pp. 208–209.

15. Charles-André Julien, *Les Voyages de découverte et les premiers établissements, XVe-XVIe siècles* (Paris: Presses Universitaires de France, 1948); Carl Ortwin Sauer, *Sixteenth Century North America* (Berkeley: University of California Press, 1971).

16. Julien, *Les Voyages*, pp. 180–184; Silvia Castro Shannon, "Military Outpost or Protestant Refuge: Villegagnon's Expedition to Brazil in 1555," in *Essays in French Colonial History: Proceedings of the 21st Annual Meeting of the French Colonial Historical Society*, ed. A. J. B. Johnston (East Lansing: Michigan State University Press, 1997), pp. 1–15.

17. Hugh Honour, *The New Golden Land, European Images of America from the Discoveries to the Present Time* (New York: Pantheon Books, 1975), p. 63.

18. Parkman, *Pioneers of France*, p. 371.

19. Ibid., pp. 45–47.

20. Ibid., p. 191.

21. A. W. Whitehead, *Gaspard de Coligny, Admiral of France* (London: Methuen, 1904), p. 328.

22. J. H. Parry, *The Age of Reconnaissance* (New York: Mentor Books, 1964), pp. 67–83, 93–96, 115–129; Boies Penrose, *Travel and Discovery in the Renaissance, 1420–1620* (Cambridge: Harvard University Press, 1963).

23. Richard W. Unger, "Ships of the Late Middle Ages," in *Maritime History*, vol. 1, *The Age of Discovery*, ed. John B. Hattendorf (Malabar, Fla.: Krieger Publishing, 1998), pp. 37–39.

24. Geoffrey Atkinson, *La Littérature géographique française de la Renaissance, répertoire bibliographique* (New York: Burt Franklin, 1968, reprint of 1936 edition). Other works by Atkinson include *Les nouveaux horizons de la Renaissance française* (Paris, 1935); *Les relations de voyages du XVIIe siècle et l'évolution des idées* (New York: Burt Franklin, 1971, reprint of 1924 edition); *The Extraordinary Voyage in French Literature Before 1700* (New York: Columbia University Press, 1920); *The Extraordinary Voyage in French Literature from 1700 to 1720*, vol. 2 (New York: Burt Franklin, 1969, reprint of 1922 original). See also Elizabeth Armstrong, *Ronsard and the Age of Gold* (New York: Cambridge University Press, 1968); Gilbert Chinard, *L'Exotisme américain dans la littérature française au XVIe siècle* (Paris: Hachette, 1911); Stefan Lorant, ed., *The New World, the First Pictures of America* (New York: Duell, Sloan and Pearce, 1965); Hugh Honour, *The European Vision of America* (Cleveland: Cleveland Museum of Art, 1975).

25. Atkinson, *Les nouveaux horizons*, pp. 9–10.

26. Stephen Greenblatt, *Marvelous Possessions, the Wonder of the New World* (Chicago: University of Chicago Press, 1991); John F. Moffitt and Santiago Sebastián, *O Brave New World: The European Invention of the American Indian* (Albuquerque: University of New Mexico Press, 1996).

27. Michel Montaigne, *Essays,* trans. Charles Cotton (Electric Renaissance, http://www.idbu.edu).

2

The 17th Century: The Traders' Empire

I am unique on the ocean wave
As my king is in the world.

—Motto of one of Louis XIV's flagships

The 17th century was the century of America for France because France's primary interest was in Canada and the Caribbean. Canada became France's largest possession, but now the small boats full of explorers who earlier sought the Northwest Passage were replaced by wandering fur traders who, by canoe or on foot, traded for beaver and by struggling farmers who lined the Saint Lawrence Valley with settlements hand hewn from the thick forests. By the century's end, traders and missionaries had moved inland beyond the Great Lakes, reached the mouth of the Mississippi River, and proceeded westward toward the Rocky Mountains. In the West Indies, the French struggled against Dutch traders, Spanish and English ships and settlements, pirates and buccaneers, and, as always, the insalubrious tropical climate. At the century's end, the balance sheet was mixed; a small settler colony had been established in Canada, but most of France's trading companies had failed or were failing. France established a presence in a scattering of West Indian islands, of which Martinique and Guadeloupe were then the most prominent, where they had created tobacco plantations that were giving way to sugar plantations, which required slave labor and would be immensely profitable in the future.

Thus, the story of the French Overseas Empire in the 17th century resembles the Empire's history in the previous hundred years. France's overriding internal problems, primarily consolidating royal power, continued through the first half-century, and long, costly continental wars extended across the entire period.

A brief look at French history suggests why the overseas empire fared as it did in the 1600s. Twice France experienced periods when centralized control was strengthened, the monarchy's power was extended, and attention was paid to expanding the navy and the colonies and to improving foreign commerce. But both such times in the ministries of Cardinal Richelieu (1624–1642) and Jean-Baptiste Colbert (1661–1683) coincided with periods of expanded warfare that left France almost bankrupt, with few possibilities of improving its colonial holdings.

During the first half-century France suffered steady inflation, triggered partly by the flow of precious metals into Europe from Spain's American ports. Coinage was debased periodically and France twice devaluated its currency. Equally inhibiting to the French economy's healthy growth was the anticommercial attitude of many nobles, those who laughed knowingly at Molière's *Le Bourgeois Gentilhomme* which ridiculed the pretensions of a merchant who put on courtly airs. Those pursuing careers in commerce were neither socially accepted nor fully welcomed in the centers of political power, despite their wealth and Colbert's efforts to dignify commercial careers. Thus many merchants worked only long enough to purchase a title and estate. A period observer lamented, "Whenever, from the small number of Frenchmen who are engaged in foreign commerce, some one amasses a fortune, which is the very moment when he is the most capable of pursuing foreign trade, he abandons it in order to place his children in some office of state."[1]

Contrary to the picture sometimes presented of the steady rise of the absolutist state, France made only limited progress toward becoming a strong, centralized monarchy even during the reign of Louis XIV. French absolutism existed more in the minds of kings and courtiers than in reality, although the trend was inevitably toward centralization. Numerous towns and provinces claimed special liberties, and more than a dozen separate parliaments and regional law courts limited the king's powers and often declined to register or enforce royal edicts they believed contrary to their interests. Customary law, which evolved from Frankish days, was followed in the north; the south employed written codes traceable to Roman times. Furthermore, France's nascent transportation infrastructure was regionally oriented. Merchants in maritime provinces might more readily trade with Spain, England, or the Low Countries than elsewhere in France. It was cheaper and easier for farmers in France's south to send their grain to Spain and Italy, or for northern growers to ship products by sea to Holland or England than to deliver them to the center of France. Not until the next century did France achieve a reasonably widespread network of interconnecting rivers, canals, and roads. While overseas expansion helped foster national unity in England, just the opposite happened in France where it exacerbated long-standing regional and merchant rivalries.

CARDINAL RICHELIEU, TRADING COMPANIES,
AND "A MODEST AND MOTLEY COLLECTION
OF FIGHTING SHIPS"

The ministries of Richelieu and Colbert were the high points of French overseas expansion during the ancien régime, but while Colbert extended France's
overseas interests, Richelieu's achievements were more modest. Cardinal Richelieu (1585–1642) had ambitious plans to build the French navy and make
France a major colonial power by ringing the world with profitable trading
companies along the Anglo-Dutch model. But, when a balance sheet is drawn,
not on the rhetoric of his hopes, but on his colonial achievements, the results
were that few companies were created and fewer still outlived their sponsor.

Richelieu, during his nearly twenty years as chief minister to Louis XIII, who
reigned from 1610 to 1643, tried to make France Europe's greatest power, to
advance the king's prestige, and to build a kingdom glowing with "luster and
reputation." The heart of Richelieu's overseas strategy was to create several
overseas companies. Richelieu was convinced that the companies would be more
profitable and less difficult to administer than settler colonies. The first of Richelieu's companies was the Company of Morbihan, chartered in 1625 for commerce in Northern Europe and America, but it collapsed a year later, unable to
compete with the contraband trade growing in French port cities. In 1627 the
Company of New France, often called the Company of 100 Associates, was
chartered to trade with New France. Its domains extended from the Arctic Circle
to Florida, from Newfoundland to the Great Lakes, and "as much and as far as
they could extend and make known in his majesty's name." Despite their sweeping mandates and risky prospects, the companies continued to be chartered for
over a century—with names like the Cie de l'Asiento, La Chine, Le Mer du
Sud, and, John Law's, Cie de l'Occident, the largest of the companies before
its demise in the 1720s.[2]

On paper at least, owners were given commercial and territorial monopolies
and crown subventions, but royal money was as hard to come by as profits, and
few of the companies ever declared a dividend. Most pledged the "advancement
of the Catholic, Apostolic, and Roman religion" through converting native populations, but this was window dressing for the pope and France's domestic
Catholic constituency. The overseas companies were ill-fated from the start.
Unlike the more flexible Dutch and English companies, France's were controlled
from Paris. Little was decided without an exchange of correspondence, which
could take more than a year. Moreover, the companies were plagued by inept
and frequently dishonest administrators and by a chronic lack of capital. Possibly
the local administrators could have been more entrepreneurial, but they had very
few resources with which to work. Richelieu, furthermore, unknowingly crippled
the growth of France's overseas commerce when he gave the companies exclusive trading monopolies, which stifled the growth of independent traders.[3]

Aware that French merchant ships were few in the Atlantic, Richelieu created a Council of the Marine in 1624. The French coast was surveyed, maritime charts were prepared, and naval arsenals were built. Virtually autonomous regional admiralties were suppressed in favor of central control, and in 1626 Richelieu named himself "Grand Master, chief, and superintendent general of the navigation and commerce of France." Eventually he increased the royal fleet; more than 90 ships representing 40 thousand tons of displacement were added between 1624 and 1630.[4]

The investments in ships were accompanied by large investments in dockyards, sweeping organizational reforms to bring about bureaucratic efficiency, the creation of a large permanent officer corps, a mercantilistic program to make France as self-sufficient as possible in naval stores and a registration of all seafaring population in order to create an efficient system for naval manning.[5]

When Richelieu died in 1642, a scattering of Caribbean planters were France's best hope for colonial success. There were perhaps 200 French residents in Canada at this time and 7 thousand more in the West Indies. Richelieu encouraged the French to trade in India and West Africa, and the Company of the East occupied the eastern shore of Madagascar and nearby islands, but within a decade these possessions were in English hands.

From 1642 until 1661 and Colbert's ascent to power, French maritime activity declined and the fledging colonies barely survived. Cardinal Mazarin, who ruled France in the manner of his mentor, was preoccupied with civil and continental wars and had little time for overseas matters. In 1646 a French observer complained, "Our merchants are idle, our sailors without employment, our harbors without vessels, and our ships wrecked and stranded upon the beach. . . . Like Diogenes, I might carry a lantern at noontide in our cities and our ports in search of a French merchant."[6]

LOUIS XIV AND COLBERT

No one played a more significant role in the expansion of France overseas in the 17th century than Jean-Baptiste Colbert (1619–1683), Mazarin's successor. For over two decades Colbert almost single-handedly controlled the government's finances, navy, commerce, and colonial affairs. Still, Colbert's efforts to establish a national economy out of various competing regional economies and to increase overseas trade were hard hit by inflation, insurrections, wars with the Dutch and British, and the astronomical expenses of the court of Louis XIV (1638–1715), the Sun King. Colbert also faced formidable structural problems that worked against national unity in France, including long-standing regional interests and the intense desire of established merchants jealously to protect their market fiefdoms. Colbert's strength lay in his closeness to the king. Unoriginal but energetic, he was skilled at seizing the ideas of others but originated few of his own. A work-obsessed person, called a work-ox by contemporaries, Colbert eschewed the life of a Versailles courtier. His personal habits were abstemious, almost ascetic. Humorless, he was called "a man of marble," sometimes *le Nord*.[7]

Colbert's ascendancy coincided with an economic downturn in Europe when governments made an effort to build up strong national economies to foot the bills for large armies, extensive royal households, and growing bureaucracies. Accumulate the largest possible revenues from precious metals and natural resources, export your country's manufactured goods, but import as little as possible from other countries was the theory. As royal power extended gradually the power of craft guilds was replaced by more centralized economic control. Industries were created to employ the poor and produce revenues for their monarchs. Monopoly companies were encouraged at home and abroad to provide their royal patrons with prestige and wealth. Europe was entering a new, more global era. In 1661 Colbert became chief administrator of the royal finances, and for the next decade he held several key ministries, including colonies, commerce, the navy, public works, and agriculture. When Colbert came to office, France was undergoing a depression, wracked by famine, and experiencing the economic chaos following the Thirty Years' War. The government was deeply in debt and lacked adequate records of either income or expenditures.

Colbert's primary economic goal was to pay the king's bills, which soared with Louis' wars, and to give France an independent national economy. His basic plan was simple: export as much as possible at high prices and import only what was necessary at low prices. Like others of his period, Colbert erroneously believed a fixed amount of bullion existed, and one nation gained wealth at another's expense. Foreign commerce thus provided an arena for competition among the European countries. To expand France's access to foreign markets, Colbert built up the French navy, which in 1661 had fallen to some 32 fighting ships. When he came to power, there may have been as many as 20 thousand ships along the coast of Europe or engaged in overseas trade: 16 thousand Dutch, 3 thousand English, and 600 French. Maritime historian Jan Glete calculates the number of French warships in 1663 at 32 and in 1671 at 140.[8] With customary thoroughness, Colbert tried to regulate every aspect of life in France's new navy, including standards of ship construction. He favored functional, unostentatious ships, but some flagships were trimmed with ivory and ebony, and captain's cabins sometimes had azure blue ceilings decorated with gold stars, crowns, and lilies.

To support his expanding fleet, Colbert built docks and shipyards and schools for sailors. An Academy of Sciences was founded, as were a naval observatory and a hydrographic service. A naval atlas, the *Neptune français*, was published long before land maps were readily available elsewhere. The manufacture of sails, spars, and ships' supplies by French companies was encouraged, and by 1683 the French navy had grown to 1,200 officers and 53 thousand sailors. Colbert assigned recruitment quotas to maritime provinces.

Life on board ships was miserable, with harsh discipline including floggings for the least offense. Wet weather meant soaked clothes and bedding, difficulties in making fires to prepare warm food, and rheumatic ailments among crew members. Malaria and yellow fever attacked crews in tropical climates; scurvy was a problem everywhere, as were lice. Ships' food was usually of poor quality, often decaying quickly or being attacked by rats. Crews sometimes ate the ship's leather fixtures. One explorer wrote, "At supper we ate some rats and found them very good."

At the time of Colbert's death in 1683 there were perhaps 500 ships in the French merchant fleet, and the Mediterranean galley fleet had grown as well. Despite these dramatic improvements, the French navy failed to overtake its chief rivals, and after Colbert the number of ships declined and the navy rarely figured in the king's plans.

FRANCE'S OVERSEAS COMPANIES

The heart of the French colonial ambitions rested with its overseas companies, enterprises with names like Compagnie de Cap Vert et du Sénégal, de la Chine, de la Nacelle de Saint-Pierre-Fleur-de-Lysée, des Indes, des Indes Orientales, and du Cap Nord. Richelieu had launched the companies with limited success. Colbert tried more of the same, with no better results. Such companies were always undersubscribed, capital was never fully paid up, and there was no second round of voluntary investments from people of means or the wily coastal merchants who would not invest in projects endorsed by the government they distrusted. Moreover, unlike the British and Dutch companies on which they were supposedly modeled, the French companies suffered from minute regulation of activities by government agents, which stifled local initiatives. Directors were named by the government, not from the merchant community. Equally damaging, their primary purpose was to support the French domestic economy, and they never attracted overseas settlers who would run their own enterprises for profit, selling where they could obtain the best prices, and thus have an incentive to stay in a place and develop its potential resources.

From 1664 on the linchpin of Colbert's overseas strategy was several new trading companies with striking names and sweeping charters aimed at attracting French subscribers. Most, in reality, were little more than creations on paper. The French East and West India companies split most of the world in two. One received "the vast expanse from the Cape of Good Hope eastward to the Straits of Magellan, including all the East Indies, China, Japan, and all the Oriental seas." François Charpentier of the French Academy wrote a lush prospectus on Madagascar, calling it a tropical paradise where heavy rains unveiled veins of gold—"the waters are excellent, the fruits delicious, and without hyperbole the place may be improved into a paradise"—where settlers could recover from the wounds of war and "go boldly under the banner of the invincible Louis."[9]

The flagship company, the French East India Company, was launched with great fanfare. The company's motto was "I shall blossom wherever I am carried." Some of its capital was subscribed by the royal family, and Colbert's agents coerced judges, tax-farmers, *intendants*, local administrators, and others who habitually fed from the public trough to contribute as well. Fatally flawed from its inception, the company switched from being a trading enterprise to a colonizing one, with meager results. It failed to realize a profit during its first 20 years, but it did secure a temporary foothold for France on the Indian subcontinent with settlements in Swat and Pondicherry and an important Indian Ocean base at Madagascar. However, the company was never able to rival its Dutch and English counterparts. Not until 1669 did one of its vessels return directly to France with a cargo. A modern commentator could have been writing in the 17th century in describing the company's plans to settle on Réunion island, later called Bourbon, east of Madagascar in a group of islands called the Mascarenes: "Providence, in its wisdom, had without doubt figured that this island without a name should remain uninhabited. Colbert, in his office, decided differently. Thus the fate of several million men and women was sealed and problems were posed which, even until today, have not found their solution."[10]

NEW FRANCE

Decade by decade the French presence grew in North America which, like the West Indies, was the focal point of France's overseas activities in this century. A late 17th century map of North America would show that France held much of the continent's explored lands. French territory, or so the country's mapmakers drew it, swept from the sub-Arctic to the Mississippi River, from the barren Newfoundland coast to the Rocky Mountains. Its heartland was the 1,500-mile stretch from Newfoundland along the Saint Lawrence River to the Great Lakes. Although France had moved along that river deeply into the interior, its claims were perilously thin, for rarely could France exert effective control more than a short distance on either side of the riverbank. Along this thin line the history of New France centered for the next 150 years. Moving westward through the wide gulf, traders' and settlers' ships entered the Saint Lawrence River, which was several miles wide for long distances, but then narrowed sharply at Québec, whose steep cliffs commanded the further passage inland toward Montréal. Above Montréal the river was filled with rapids and could be navigated only by canoe with overland portages toward the Great Lakes. North of the lakes was the Laurentian Shield, with its rich fur trade and conifer forests filled with thousands of small streams, swamps, and lakes with beaver lodges. Farther west in Illinois and south in the Mississippi lands was territory where the French and British would converge.

Such a map, though it might show the extent of French claims, does little to indicate the fragility of France's North American presence, maintained by the determined struggle of small bands of traders, settlers, administrators, and religious combating the wilderness, native inhabitants, other Europeans, and, at

times, each other. The history of New France in this century can be divided into
two parts: the time of the early settlements and the beginning of the fur trade,
and the post-1663 period when New France became part of the royal domain.[11]

FIRST SETTLEMENTS AND QUÉBEC

In 1604 Pierre Du Gua sieur des Monts and Samuel de Champlain established
a base on the Acadian peninsula from which they hoped to discover the fabled
Northwest Passage to the riches of the East. Although they mapped the North
Atlantic coast from Cape Breton to Cape Cod, the westward water passage to
the Orient eluded them, as it had Jacques Cartier a century earlier.[12]

Champlain returned in 1608 to establish a trading post at Québec, a strategic
location high above the Saint Lawrence River, which was accessible to the fur
trade and was on a direct water route to Europe. The post's first years followed
a familiar pattern: a small company, a cold and deadly winter, a crown monopoly
withdrawn, competition from independent fur traders, and conflict with indigenous peoples. By 1652 fewer than ten of the initial 40 settlers at Trois Rivières
had survived Iroquois attacks; in the same year, 600 Iroquois laid siege to the
post for nine days but were repulsed by a force of 40 defenders, many of them
young boys.[13]

What sorts of people came to New France? French society along the Saint
Lawrence Valley in the 17th century differed from that at home in France in
two distinct ways: warfare with local peoples and New France's geography
uniquely molded the settlers' way of life. Through constant guerrilla combat
many settler-farmers became skilled at woodland warfare, adopting their adversaries' traits of endurance, aggressiveness and brutality in combat, and a hardened attitude toward pain and death.[14]

Louise Dechêne, with a lapidarian's skill, has examined the 17th century
documents that remain to reconstruct a picture of life in the colony's main city,
Montréal, a reflection of colonial life in a microcosm. She concludes, "Canada
was created by merchant capital as an offshoot of metropolitan interests to which
it remained subservient. This reality governed the development of all colonial
societies."[15] Two additional factors helped shape Canada's early growth. First,
its location made it difficult to compete with France or with the American colonies trading in the West Indies. Second, although a market economy was the
engine for a growing French presence in North America, agricultural production
never figured into French plans for expansion. The acquisition of profits from
trade rather than land was a driving force for merchants. The isolated setting
and harsh climate further contributed to the early settlers' independence and
stoicism. Life was an unrelenting struggle to clear the land and establish farms.
The abundance of free land available in North America gave recruiters something to offer persons who, through poverty or lack of inheritance, could never
own land in France. Land grants, as a rule, were not vast. Usually they were
rectangular slices possibly averaging three *arpents* of river footage 30 *arpents*

deep (an *arpent* is roughly 190 feet). Significantly, land was distributed in individually owned parcels, with no provisions to create villages. Thus during raids settlers lacked the central protection provided by a walled or fortified village. Some settlements formed around the main river ports, but attempts made by the crown in the 1670s and 1680s to design villages with fields extending from them like spokes from a wheel met with no success.

Life revolved around clearing the wilderness, farming, and trading for furs. Beyond that, there were the long, cold winters, sometimes lasting from October to May, with little relief from the freezing cold and mind-numbing boredom beyond chores, handicrafts, and constantly feeding fires where draughty, ill-constructed chimneys consumed endless quantities of wood from the vast forests.

The seignieural system of land control, so much a feature of France, caught hold in North America, but not in the West Indies or Acadian Louisiana. Anxious not to create a powerful overseas nobility, the French crown purposely circumscribed landlords' powers. But if landowners in New France were not the powerful figures they were in France, neither were they frontier democrats. Nothing like the New England town council or town meeting was ever a feature of New France, and no municipal corporations existed anywhere in French America. In 1757 a French officer described society in New France:

They are not thrifty and take no care for the future, being too fond of their freedom and their independence. They want to be well thought of and they know how to make the most of themselves. They endure hunger and thirst patiently, many of them having been trained from infancy to imitate Indians, whom, with reason, they hold in high regard. They strive to gain their esteem and to please them. Many of them speak their language, having passed part of their life amongst them at the trading posts.[16]

Dechêne has described a society composed of merchants, administrators, military, religious, indentured servants, and *habitants* (peasants), who figured but marginally in commercial enterprises. "There is a timeless quality about the way they continued to reproduce, generation upon generation, static communities that more or less resembled those that emerged soon after their arrival. The polarization of these two societies, which was already apparent in the 17th century, would dominate this region's subsequent history."[17] It was a society with both modest prospects for upward mobility and real possibilities of downward mobility, especially when the population outgrew possibilities for careers in commerce. Moreover, the crown did not sell offices as it did in France, shutting off another avenue of social ascension. By 1715 "half of the 4,200 inhabitants of the Montreal seigneury resided in the town," which looked like a frontier stockade with walls, gates, and fortifications. Probably the population retained the general lines of the 1681 census; in addition to the military, merchants, and religious, at least half the male population were indentured servants or former indentured servants who had settled there. The town was crowded, streets were muddy, and sanitation was lacking, although the fur trading post aspects of the settlement began to change by the 1720s. Of the volatile society, Dechêne observed, "It seems quite likely that soldiers rather than Indians were the more unruly elements in the seigneury."[18]

THE FUR TRADE

A single activity—the fur trade—dominated New France's economy in the 17th century. It began in the previous century when the French fishermen bartered with indigenous peoples for furs while drying fish. The beaver pelts were used to make hats and to trim clothing, and they were sold in France, England, Holland, Russia, and elsewhere in Europe. Worn and restyled French hats were exported to Spain, where they were again worn and reshaped and sold in Portugal and Brazil. Finally, further worn, shapeless hats were traded by the Portuguese in Africa.

Beaver pelts might weigh as much as a pound and a half. They were finely textured and water repellent, ideal for the broad-brimmed European hats of that day. The best furs, called *castor gras* (greasy beaver), came from the cold regions north of the Saint Lawrence and were hunted during the winter months when the pelt was the thickest. Hunters rubbed the pelts with animal marrow and trimmed them into rectangular shapes. Five to eight such pieces, sewn together with moose sinews, made a robe which hunters wore next to their bodies for over a year until the fur was soft, greased, and ready for use in hats. There may have been as many as 10 million beaver in North America in the early 17th century—10 to 50 per square mile in some places.

FUR FAIRS

Initially, pelts were sold at annual fur fairs held in Montréal, the colony's westernmost settlement. The voyage there was fraught with perils, for the Iroquois lurked along the Ottawa River, a main artery, ready to raid other Indians with canoes full of furs. During the 1650s and 1660s, the possibility of such raids intensified, but in other years large numbers of native peoples and traders gathered from long distances, and often the governor was present, surrounded by clerical and lay attendants. He told the local peoples of their distant father, the French king, and urged them to remain loyal to France, to be at peace with one another, and not to trade with France's rivals. Participants offered the governor samples of their best furs "to open his ears" to favorable trade terms. In turn, the governor gave them gifts of muskets, trinkets, plumed hats, and richly colored clothing. The ceremony ended with a common meal, often a stew made of local corn, containing the meat of bear, moose, beaver, and dogs, flavored with dried fruit. When everyone had eaten, the trading began.

The annual Montréal trade fairs served both a commercial and a political purpose. In addition to exchanging pelts for goods, the meetings reinforced social cohesion for the ensuing year among Indians and French. There was a darker side to the gatherings, however. Sometimes the French wanted gifts of large numbers of pelts from the Indians; this was not alliance building but cupidity; in turn, French traders distributed only token European goods, thus disrupting the delicate patterns of exchange Indian peoples had worked out among themselves and thought they had established with the French. The easy availability of raw brandy resulted in Indians being arrested and held for a ransom of pelts. Quarrels broke out, Indians were beaten, and many returned home, bitter and planning revenge by robbing French traders of their goods and subjecting them to indignities.[19] By the 1680s the annual fur fairs had lost their importance, replaced by the spread of *coureurs de bois*, outlaws who moved about on their own, and *voyageurs*, legal traders and other traders who moved deeper and deeper into the woods. The disruptive effects of the *coureurs de bois* is indicated in a contemporary account:

These *coureurs de bois* will frequently commit a thousand base actions to obtain beaver from the Indians. They follow them to their hunting grounds and do not even give them the time to dry and cure their skins. They endure the jeers, the scorn, and sometimes the blows of the Indians, who are constantly amazed by such a sordid display of greed and by Frenchmen who come so far away at the cost of great hardship and expense to pick up dirty, stinking beaver pelts which they have worn and have discarded.[20]

Within a century, the fur trade had transformed the traditional societies coming in contact with it and had altered patterns of hunting, agriculture, warfare, and the division of work between women and men. Hunting became quicker and easier, more accurate with steel hatchets, knives, and steel-tipped arrows. Easily portable copper or brass cooking pots replaced cumbersome wooden vessels, and steel needles and awls supplanted bone ones, making it easier to sew skins and cloth. Sometimes these metal objects, which revolutionized the forest peoples' lifestyle, were among the goods buried with a chief signifying his power and wealth. Most significantly, once agrarian and hunting peoples became traders. Women assumed responsibility for food gathering because the men were now absent several months a year to participate in the fur trade. At the same time, traditional tastes and values gave way to the gradual attraction of European goods.[21]

A COMPLEX RELATIONSHIP—THE INDIANS AND THE FRENCH

Traditional representations of colonial history depict an enduring French-British rivalry spread over much of the North American continent, both sides supported by silent Indian bands who were stoic, skilled at long marches, and good shots. Actual relationships extending from the period of initial sustained French contact in the early 17th century until the fall of French Canada in 1760 were far more complex and continued under the British until 1814. Around the vast world of the Great Lakes, which the French called *pays d'en haut*, or upper country, there were changing patterns of hostility and accommodation—triggered by the spread of commerce or temporary alliances for warfare against common enemies. The result of such century-long encounters was the forging of a new relationship by Indians and French leaving a distinct imprint on all parties and fashioning a unique civilization in what would become Canada. Such encounters were costly to Indians, including those who became Christians.

Infants succumbed to European viruses and to new foodstuffs that replaced a traditional diet. Women, still responsible for the heavy labor, and often mistreated by husbands they could no longer divorce, began to despair. The need to love and procreate languished, along with the will to live, in these first generations torn between two worlds. "We rarely see the natives age," one governor remarked.[22]

Initially, the meeting of two culturally developed societies, vastly different in organization, language, and interests, was a fractious encounter. Each had to deal with the other with no established protocols; the understandable first result was mutual misunderstanding of one another. The Indians thought the French were demigods, and the French called the Indians savages. Indian life was carefully attuned to nature, the seasons, and the cycles of hunting and planting, and Indian religion was intimately linked with nature. In contrast, the French set out to conquer nature, master and exploit it, and cart off its fruits to another country.[23] As for local populations, "The more advanced Amerindian cultures assimilated more rapidly than the less advanced tribes, but they were also better able to preserve their traditional belief system and social organization," according to Cornelius Jansen, who added that the strains of cultural assimilation were equally strong among those who converted and those who retained traditional lifestyles, including susceptibility to epidemics, widespread alcohol abuse, and altered social roles based on the introduction of new technologies and land use patterns.[24]

Social cohesion was attained among fragmented groups through elaborate gift exchanges and reciprocal marriages, thus making or securing alliances with allies. The calumet (peace pipe) ceremony was the principal device for bringing such disparate people together to make peace and solidify relationships.[25] In Africa, the saying, "the chief is rich, the chief is poor," means that a leader is expected to give generous gifts to important strangers, allies, and clients as a way of demonstrating his own importance and to expand relations with neighboring groups or prevent warfare with others. Thus a constant outflow of gifts was required to maintain political and social stability. For the French, annual gifts were distributed from the king to indigenous leaders, as were gifts when a new governor was named, or when one returned from France. In turn, the chiefs decided who in their retinues or list of potential friends or adversaries merited presents, all with an eye toward creating stability or expanding influence.

THE COMPANY OF NEW FRANCE, 1627–1663

Finally, in 1627, Richelieu chartered the Company of New France, or Company of 100 Associates, to colonize New France. Champlain was not in command, but he was one of the company's main administrators. The company's plan was bold—to send 4 thousand settlers within 15 years and over 200 artisans a year to Canada, excluding foreigners and Protestants. In 1629, however, the English blockaded the Saint Lawrence River and forced the French settlement of fewer than 100 persons to surrender. Although the territory was returned to France a few years later, it was eventually sold to its settlers. Workers could become master artisans by spending time in the territory; settlers who cleared land could become citizens and landowners. Landless French peasants were offered attractive inducements to move to New France, but most stayed home.

Unfortunately for France, at the same time the company was founded, another organization, the Kirke expedition, was privately chartered in Great Britain to occupy Canada and hold a monopoly on its commerce. In the spring of 1628 members of this English-Huguenot company sailed to New France, burned French settlements, captured supply ships, and demanded that the struggling Québec garrison surrender, thus ruining Richelieu's company. The French company sent four ships and 400 settlers, a major undertaking on its part, but they unfortunately sailed into an English fleet and were captured. The English, however, did not follow up their victory and soon departed. The French were left to endure another winter, ill and short of rations. In July 1629 the English returned with three ships and demanded Champlain's surrender. Champlain left Québec as an English prisoner on September 14, 1629, and in 1633, freed but now 66 years old, he returned to make one last attempt to establish a settlement. Old patterns were repeated, and by 1645 the company was fast failing, never having attracted the capital or settlers needed to prosper; what remained of it was sold to members. Conditions at mid-century were as hazardous as they had been at the company's founding. The Iroquois ambushed settlers and traders, the long winters took their toll of lives, and residents talked of abandoning the settlement unless additional help was forthcoming from France. After almost 30 years, there were fewer than 2 thousand settlers in New France. Finally, in 1663, the company's charter was revoked. New France became a royal province.[26]

NEW FRANCE AS A CROWN COLONY

Colbert sent his first governor to New France in 1665. Colbert had many ideas for making the Canadian venture prosper, but an independent governance was not among them. Governors and *intendants* vied with each other in dispatching long reports to the crown, filled with information and interlarded with the trivia and personal invective of rivalries left to fester in isolated posts.

Every aspect of the colony's life was regulated, at least on paper. Since there were no municipal jurisdictions, *intendants* issued regulations for public safety and conduct. Minute regulations governed trade, land use, and the conduct of business, although possibilities of enforcing them were frequently limited. Bakers were supposed to have certain types of bread on sale, and the size, quality, and price of loaves were set by decree:

The bakers of this city [Québec] will always be obliged to have all types of bread on sale in their shops, under pain of a fine of three *livres* for the first offense and of double [this amount] for subsequent ones.

The bread will be of good quality, under pain of confiscation for the benefit of the Hôtel Dieu [hospital] and of an arbitrary fine for the first offense.

Under pain of a fine of one hundred *livres*, half of it payable to the informer and the other half to the poor of the Hôtel Dieu, all persons are forbidden by the Council to bake biscuits except the bakers, on condition that they always have a supply of both white and brown for sale, at a price which will be fixed according to that of wheat. All persons are authorized to mill flour for both the colony's internal and external trade.[27]

This careful regulation of New France was designed to keep it within France's economic control. To this end, Colbert devised a plan to ship fish, grain, and lumber from New France to the French West Indies in return for sugar, rum, and molasses. The plan never worked, however, because the small Canadian colony did not use much sugar and sailing ships to New France were few and fewer still were those that would journey to the West Indies as well. Once more, a structural problem was evident. The obstacles of distance and climate made it impossible for New France to obtain consistent markets. In contrast, the larger New England settlements were active trading partners with New France and the French West Indies. Colbert knew he must increase New France's population for it to become economically viable. Colbert sent approximately 500 men and 150 single women a year to the colony for a few years, paying premiums for large families, bonuses for early marriages, and fines for men who passed 20 and women who passed 16 years of age and remained unmarried, but none of these schemes produced the desired results. By 1666 the colony's population was 5,870. Within a decade it grew impressively to 10 thousand inhabitants, but meanwhile much larger numbers had flocked to the English lands toward the south. At the century's end, the population of England's American colonies was over 200 thousand persons. The numerical differences would loom large in North America's history in the next century.

In retrospect, four contradictions contributed to France's problem: first, French overseas interests competed with Continental demands and lost; second, monopolistic companies vied with individual merchants and ports that wanted free trade, with the companies usually losing; third, missionaries' efforts to settle native populations in one place conflicted with traders' encouraging their moving afield for the fur trade, with the result that few native tribes settled; and fourth, government officials who wanted a permanent settler colony were at odds with traders who sought quick, cheap commercial profits. Each position nullified the other, with the result that France was unable to create the overseas possession it wanted in Canada. Still, the question remains—why did so few French emigrate abroad between 1500 and 1800? Fear of the unknown and hazardous travel conditions are obvious reasons, to which one historian of the French colonies during the ancien régime, James Pritchard, has added the suggestion "that the answer is that French peasants had the most secure land tenure in Europe."[28]

THE CHURCH IN NEW FRANCE

The Roman Catholic Church, spurred by the religious revival sweeping France during the first half of the 17th century, was a significant presence in New France. Several new orders sprang up, and it was not long before they sent members to the wilderness of New France. Protestants rarely were admitted to French overseas lands, and French kings, having suppressed political and religious dissenters at home, did not want centers of opposition to shoot up overseas. An initial question faced missionaries: should they learn local languages, convert the natives, and leave them to profess Christ in their own cultures, or should part of the process be to teach them the French language and French culture as well? The Sulpicians, who were dedicated to the teaching of seminarians, were unyielding:

We believe that they profit from living among us, and not in their own land; that they must be taught our language, that their women must wear skirts and their men hats and pants; that they must adopt French housing; learn animal husbandry, and how to sow wheat and root vegetables; and that they must be able to read and hear mass and be taught the holy rites.[29]

In contrast, the Jesuits were more flexible in their approach. They made an effort to learn local languages and customs, to live among the Indians, and often to isolate them from assimilation into French settlements. In 1625 five Jesuits sailed for New France following an earlier mission that had been captured by the English. The New World was not an easy place for French priests. Their experiences are detailed in reports, called the Jesuit *Relations*, published annually from 1632 to 1673 in France. The Jesuits built their main mission station in the center of Huron lands, at Sainte-Marie, where there was a hospital, chapel, stables, mill, forge, rest house, and four outposts equidistant from the main station. Here they sheltered 9 thousand Huron during the last two years before the mission closed in 1649.[30]

The missionaries' task was difficult. Missionary journals are full of tales of clouds of black flies and mosquitoes, of flea bites and smoke endured in the dark, chimneyless lodges, of heavy, greasy foods that left the stomach unsettled,

and of sitting cross-legged in canoes for days at a time. The "black robes," as
the Indians called them, found themselves stumbling along in heavy cassocks
after quickly moving guides who did not wait for them. Indians enjoyed making
fun of the way missionaries made mistakes in pronouncing their language. In
1634 Father Le Jeune recalled, "One day, when my host had a feast, the guests
made me a sign that I should make them a speech in their language, as they
wanted to laugh; for I pronounce the Savage as a German pronounces French."[31]
Elsewhere he described the rigors of moving about the country with Indian
bands in winter and camping in wooden lodges:

You cannot stand upright in this house, as much on account of its low roof as the suffocating smoke; and consequently you must always lie down, or sit flat upon the ground, the
usual posture of the Savages. When you go out, the cold, the snow, and the danger of getting lost in these great woods drive you in again more quickly than the wind, and keep you
a prisoner in a dungeon which has neither lock nor key.[32]

The Indians originally regarded the Europeans as potentially powerful allies,
semidivine figures, "manitous" who could bring success to the hunt, heal the
sick, and provide a victorious edge in warfare. Although some indigenous peoples did convert to Christianity, the disparity between languages, the lack of
understanding between the cultures, and the real differences between the two
complex belief systems meant that, for some groups, what emerged in the first
decades of contact with the French was a syncretic amalgam of both traditions.
    Jesuits and Indians did not understand each other's beliefs. The Jesuits usually
withheld baptism from indigenous people until they were old or near death as
a way of ensuring against backsliding and apostasy. Consequently, many Huron
associated baptism with death and had no desire for it. Moreover, the Catholic
Mass, with its imagery of a blood sacrifice, was incompletely understood by the
Indians, who viewed it as further evidence of sorcery. Likewise, when a pock
disease epidemic swept Huron lands in the 1630s, many local people attributed
it to the missionaries.
    By mid-century the Church's power (broadened to include other missionary
orders as well as the Jesuits) was impressive, although the lack of clergy for
colonial churches remained a real problem. Most colonists could attend services
once or twice a year at best. Notwithstanding, the Church held perhaps a quarter
of New France's total land grants and controlled all schools as well. It was at
the close of Sunday Mass that public announcements were made to the local
populace, and the latest government decrees were posted on the church doors,
as were instructions to the militia. During the second half of the century, however, the Church's direct political influence gradually diminished, and in 1665
the bishop's right jointly to appoint members to the council was withdrawn.
The Church remained a force to be reckoned with, but not a decisive voice in
affairs of state. Thus, the Jesuits' New Jerusalem was never realized. The missionaries' efforts were often undercut by traders, especially the *coureurs de bois*,

who distributed raw brandy among the tribes and lived freely with native women.

The spirit of the times is suggested in a 1686 episcopal letter written by the bishop of Québec to the governor and his wife advising them to decline invitations for supper "so as to avoid late entertainments, dangerous pastimes, and other unseemly happenings that usually occur at nocturnal banquets and gatherings." Gluttonous meals should be shunned, as should balls and dances:

It is of great importance to the glory of God and the salvation of souls that the governor and his wife, on whose conduct most people will pattern their own, not only firmly refuse to enter houses where people are gathered for balls and dances, but also close their own to this sort of entertainment.

However, since their daughter stands in need of recreation on account of her age and vivacity, she may be permitted a few decent and moderate dances, but only with persons of her own sex and in the presence of her mother as a safeguard against indecent words and songs.[33]

THE WEST INDIES

Picture the West Indies as a long oval, extending nearly 2 thousand miles on a northwest-southeast axis, almost 1,500 miles to the east and west. On the western extremities are the rich lands of Mexico and Central America, under Spanish control. Along the upper arc are the southern borders of North America and the Florida peninsula; at the bottom lies the northern rim of South America. Eastward is the Atlantic Ocean and a string of small islands, including Martinique and Guadeloupe, major players in the French Overseas Empire's 17th and 18th century historical drama. Toward the center was the 30-thousand-square-mile island of Hispaniola, the western part of which came under French control as Saint-Domingue. Off its northern shore was the buccaneer island of Tortuga, within easy striking distance of the Spanish Main. Nearby were Cuba and Jamaica, the principal Spanish and British Caribbean islands, respectively. Two main water routes led to and from the West Indies. Ships from Europe, laden with trading goods and supplies, rode the northeastern trade winds southward across the Atlantic early each year. Later, they returned to Europe, sweeping through the Florida Channel to the north, with the westerlies driving their sails with cargoes of tobacco, coffee, or sugar. It was a rich setting for competition, conflict, and intrigue.

The French were no strangers to the West Indies. Individual French ships had sailed there in the early 16th century. In 1536 the French seized a Spanish galleon off the Cuban coast, drowning its crew. Seven years later, Bayonne corsairs swept into the harbor of Santa Marta, Cuba, and sacked the city, and in 1555 followers of the Huguenot admiral, Gaspard de Coligny, raided Havana. "No peace beyond the line" was a contemporary expression, meaning once a ship had crossed an imaginary line west of the Azores and north of Capricorn, it was on its own and, even if Europe was officially at peace, there was no guarantee of safety when several ships from a nearby island harbor suddenly appeared on the horizon.

Originally, Saint-Christophe was the mother colony, and it remained so until the 1680s. Pierre Belain d'Esnambuc, a smuggler and pirate, who had been sailing in and out of the West Indies on his own missions for over a decade, settled in Saint-Christophe in 1625, where a small number of English had already claimed land. Both parties divided the small island, then obtained confirmation of their actions from their home countries. Richelieu, who called it "the entrance to Peru," helped capitalize the Company of Saint-Christophe. Five hundred colonists were dispatched there, 300 of whom died at sea or shortly after arriving in February 1627. Despite friction with the neighboring English, and a failure to raise food crops, the company extended its explorations to other islands. The French settled in Guadeloupe in 1635, where they immediately entered into five years of warfare with the local Carib population. Martinique was also claimed by France in 1635 by the nimble d'Esnambuc, who by then had seen several colonies starve and fail, and took numerous seeds, plantings, and farm supplies with him. By 1640 there were about a thousand French settlers on the islands, and Martinique was flourishing.[34]

At the same time, sugar was quickly becoming a staple on European tables and a big business for planters, shippers, refiners, and slavers. Colbert, probably overly optimistically, estimated that at mid-century the French Antilles sugar exports amounted to 2 million *livres* in value, and other staples would amount to a million *livres*.[35] Plantations were labor intensive. Workers were needed and livestock were required to provide food, transportation, and power. Dutch and French traders kept pastures in Ireland at this time, where cattle were raised for the West Indies. Many of the struggling smaller tobacco planters switched crops and become "little lords" with large sugar plantations and several hundred slaves. By 1674 over 400 plantations produced possibly 12 million pounds of sugar, which increased to 18 million pounds in 1682.

With the plantation economy came slavery. A prosperous planter needed at least 25 or 30 slaves to work his lands. Indentured servants were costly, and by 1670 their terms were set at 18 months, not long enough to get much work out of them, or so the settlers believed. Carib populations had been decimated by disease and warfare, and neither the original Arawak nor Carib island occupants would do fieldwork and, when forced to work, died in large numbers. By 1700 the French West Indies' population grew to an estimated 44,000 persons: 14 thousand from France and 30 thousand slaves.[36]

THE WEST INDIA COMPANY, 1664–1674

In 1664 Colbert issued letters patent to the West India Company, giving it large concessions in North and South America, Africa, and the West Indies. The company also acquired title to 14 islands, which were sold to individuals, or in the case of Saint-Christophe, to the Knights of Malta. The West India Company, which had a 40-year monopoly, could recruit troops, name its governors, and dispose of its holdings at the end of that period. It was obliged to furnish each new monarch with a crown of gold. The company failed after a decade, having never realized a profit; it was replaced by direct rule by royal government, including a governor, *intendant*, and sovereign council. However, the company was successful in directing French ships to the Antilles, 131 in 1674 compared to only four in 1660.

Plantation owners resisted Colbert's rigid policies, such as the requirement that goods be shipped only on French vessels, which was both costly and unreliable compared to the island-hopping Dutch. Colbert's abrupt barring of Dutch trade from the islands created a period of unrest and rebellion from 1665 to 1670, during which French traders could not satisfy the islands' needs for food or slaves. Consequently, planters could not expand their sugar holdings, and production declined. The French and slave populations of Saint-Christophe dropped from 12,588 (8,120 French; 4,468 slave) in 1671 to 11,570 in 1682. When he ordered island sugar cane to be refined only in France, he induced a decade-long period of economic unrest that lasted until 1680.[37]

Colbert also refused to allow islanders to trade their rum and molasses for two greatly needed items: New England timber and foodstuffs. Opportunity flowed to need, however, and a brisk contraband trade sprung up between the French-owned Caribbean islands and British North America. As land under cultivation in the Caribbean increased and more sugar and rum were available for export, North American colonies proved welcome recipients. In turn, they provided much-needed lumber, livestock, and agricultural products to the islands.

By 1700 there may have been 30 thousand slaves in the French colonies—14,200 in Martinique, 9,000 in Saint-Domingue, and 6,700 in Guadeloupe—compared to 100 thousand in the more populous English colonies. A report on slave life by a Dominican priest in 1667–1671 described the harsh conditions under which slaves lived. Owners were interested in maximizing profits. Slaves were required to work long hours, with little time to grow their own crops. If drought or crop failure affected an island, their conditions worsened accordingly, and thefts of the master's crops increased. Slaves were left to the mercy of their masters, subject to beatings, mutilations, and the rubbing of salt on their wounds. There was no effective appeal for justice, although the Code Noir of 1685 had provisions on paper against brutality. As for the Church, Bishop Bossuet, Louis XIV's court theologian, reasoned that "the Holy Spirit, speaking through Saint Paul, ordered slaves to remain in their condition and . . . did not in any way oblige masters to free them."[38]

R. P. Jean-Baptiste Du Tertre, a Dominican, provides one of the few sketches of slaves' lives in the islands in the 17th century. He recalled an example of theft:

I know a very honest inhabitant of Martinique who dealt with theft in the following manner. Seeing that after several thefts which he had pardoned the thief continued to abuse his good will, he trapped him one day in his pig pen and cut off his ears, without any form of trial, wrapped them in the leaf of a tree and ordered the thief to take them back to his master.[39]

Despite their difficulties, slaves tried to lead lives of their own. They dressed as attractively as their poor means allowed, entertained one another, married, held dances, and sang African songs. Since many different African ethnic groups were represented in the slave population, a Creole language, with elements of French, Spanish, and African dialects, developed.

TORTUGA'S BUCCANEERS

One of the most important French Caribbean concentrations was on the small, turtle-shaped island of Tortuga, off Saint-Domingue's northern coast, located within easy sailing distance of the Florida Channel and several Spanish islands. A magnet for sailors who had jumped ship, escaped bond servants, and the remnants of Protestant sects scattered by Europe's religious wars, it was also a haven for unemployed soldier-adventurers used to a life of warfare and to small tobacco producers being pushed out of the French Antilles as the plantation complex grew during the 1670s and 1680s. Several hundred gathered on the island and soon spilled over to the northern coast. They were called "buccaneers," the Carib name for hunters and traders of the dried, smoked beef produced on the islands and sold to passing ships. Vast herds of wild cattle and hogs roamed freely about northern Saint-Domingue, left there from the previous century's abandoned Spanish settlements.

The buccaneers were a male society; members often formed pairs with the right to inherit from each other. Local laws, called the Custom of the Coast, enforced with dueling and boycotts, did not use French law for precedent, for by common assent the buccaneers were said to have drowned all their former obligations and even lost their names when they passed the tropic of Cancer. The Custom of the Coast covered everything from the division of hunting spoils to the settling of disputes, and cruel punishments were inflicted on erring members. Although Tortuga became an important center for raids on Spanish shipping, initially its occupants' main activities were hunting and selling birds and hides to the Dutch. Sometimes the hunters wandered about the mainland for a year or more before returning with hides to Tortuga, where they could squander a year's worth of profits in a month's drinking time before disappearing in the forests for another long stay. Small hunting bands roamed the woods by day; slept in sheds of sticks, hides, and leaves by night; and dressed in coarse cloth garments, blackened by the blood and grease of long-slain animals. A contemporary account describes their activity:

In the morning, as soon as it begins to get light, the hunters call up their hounds and go into the forest, along the trails where they hope to meet the most bulls. Immediately after they have shot a beast, they take what they call their brandy—that is they suck all the marrow from the bones before it is cold. After this, they flay the beast properly, and one of them takes the hide to their rendezvous. They carry on like this until every man has got a hide; this takes until noon—sometimes later, sometimes sooner, when they all meet together at the rendezvous, if they have bond servants, these stretch out the hides to dry, and prepare the food. There is always meat, for they eat nothing else. Having eaten, every man takes his gun and they go off and shoot horses for sport, or to bring down birds with a single bullet. Or they may shoot at targets for a prize—usually an orange tree, to see who can shoot off the most oranges without damaging them, but only nicking the stem with a single bullet.[40]

As the men turned increasingly from hunting to raiding ships and ports along the main waterways and isolated islands of the Caribbean, the Custom of the Coast was adapted to deal with the disposition of spoils.

The buccaneers were a criminal band. In times of warfare with Spain and England, they were encouraged by the French, but in the intervals of peace no one trusted them. The last time they were used as a French naval auxiliary was to capture the Spanish fortress of Cartagena in 1697. Facing constant opposition from the growing French and British colonies, those buccaneers who did not become planters continued to exist as small pirate bands, raiding freely the shipping of all nations. Finally, they scattered to the Persian Gulf, the Indian Ocean, and the far Pacific. Their final moves were to those places just beyond the borders of the growing European overseas empires, where they led a solitary existence, darting into ports or shipping lanes when they could, and, if not caught and hanged, disappeared quickly, sailing their small craft beyond the confines of any empire.

FRENCH GUIANA

France's oldest continual overseas possession, French Guiana was one of the world's least desirable pieces of real estate. First settled by Rouen traders in 1612, this small malaria-and-swamp land along the northeastern coast of South America was the target of the failed economic dreams of the Compagnie de la Douze Associés in 1652 and the Compagnie de la France Équinoxiale in 1661. France lost this possession briefly to Holland in 1676 but recaptured it a year later. An attempt at colonization made by the Jesuits came to naught with their expulsion in 1762.

From 1763 to 1765 Étienne-François, duc de Choiseul, stung by the loss of Canada, hoped in compensation to establish a successful colony in Guiana. Choiseul and a German banker succeeded in attracting thousands of poor people from all over France and the rest of Europe, as well as Acadians expelled from Nova Scotia. Neither food nor housing awaited the new settlers, who had been drawn mostly from their countries' lower ranks. The idle settlers lacked skills in tropical agriculture and, to pass their time, built theaters, gambling houses,

and cabarets. Yellow fever, typhoid, and famine soon swept through the disorganized bands, killing over 14 thousand persons; 900 returned to France. Twenty
families, whose hopes were placed on a small strip of fertile coastal land where
"the sugar is white as snow and as good or better than that of Brazil," stayed
as settlers, but constant skirmishes with Dutch, English, Spanish, and Portuguese
settlers and traders left Guiana with little peace and almost no economic prospects.

The colony's subsequent history was fraught with problems. From 1852 to
1937, French Guiana was the site of the infamous Devil's Island penal colony,
called "the dry guillotine," where 74 thousand prisoners were kept at various
times, including political prisoners from France, Algeria, and Vietnam. Perhaps
the most famous was Alfred Dreyfus, who was held on Devil's Island from
1895 to 1899. Eventually, the high death toll of the prisoners and guards, plus
adverse public opinion, resulted in the prison colony's being closed and replaced
by New Caledonia, an isolated Pacific island. French Guiana became an overseas
department in 1946. Toward the end of the 20th century, a French space launching site was built at Kourou, the site of the earlier infamous colonial debacle.

THE OVERSEAS WORLD IN THE CREATIVE ARTS

A growing body of literature about overseas societies was published in France
during this century, ranging from the relatively straightforward accounts of sailors and mariners like Champlain to the more polemical reports of Jesuit missionaries. However, it is doubtful if the vast majority of French inhabitants knew
anything about the overseas world or, for that matter, of the world beyond their
villages or farms. The literature sold at village fairs was not about France's
explorations but about saints' lives and adventure tales set in fantasy lands.
Geography books were "reduced to garbled old lists of ancient provinces, augmented by mediaeval names, so that in the reign of Louis XIV 19 out of 20
took no account of the existence of America," Pierre Goubert concluded after a
close study of such works.[41]

Artists and writers did not try for accuracy in their descriptions of indigenous
societies. The world was a backdrop, either to magnify the king and his accom-
plishments or to suggest reforms through the mouths of wise strangers. By mid-
century some writers criticized contemporary French politics and customs by
making observations of the supposedly perfectly operating societies of China
and Persia. Censorship was widespread in France, and publishing was controlled
by the crown, Church, printers' guilds, and the courts. Reform-minded works
could not easily be printed, so Persians, Iroquois, Chinese, and South American
wise elders became the mouthpieces for idyllic through-the-looking-glass
worlds, models of what France should have been. Sometimes such volumes drew
on contemporary travel accounts, and on the folk literature passed on from the
Middle Ages, following an editorial formula that remained in place until after
the French Revolution and the advent of a much freer press in France. A traveler,

generally with a companion, sets out from France and visits a distant land or lands, sometimes touring the world or, in the case of Cyrano de Bergerac, outer space as well. While in distant and exotic climes, the traveler would come upon an ideal state, the opposite of problem-ridden France. Here the climate was good, food and shelter ample, and the lightly clad inhabitants as healthy as bronzed Greek or Roman gods. Rational laws governed the country, inhabitants were tolerant toward one another, and their religion was explained by a stock character who might be called "the wise old man," sometimes an Indian, at other times a Persian, who said that churches, rituals, and dogma were not needed and then expounded a philosophy which, with the spread of scientific thought, was increasingly an appeal to reason.[42]

When they ran out of material, authors added descriptions of shipwrecks, kidnappings, storms at sea, battles with pirates, miraculous escapes, struggles with wild animals, and other tales to keep readers' interests. Such accounts could have been transferred, with few alterations, from one book to another. Representative of such work was *La Terre australe connue*, published in 1676 by Gabriel Foigny, a former Franciscan monk. The protagonist was kidnapped twice and shipwrecked four times within the book's first 50 pages. He reached Australia via Spain, the Congo, and some unknown islands. Giant birds carried him in their claws, and he battled fabulous beasts of the sort occupying French travel works since the Middle Ages. The Australians lived in well-regulated communities without nuclear families and conducted articulate debates and discussions with one another, when not growing remarkable fruits and vegetables. A "good old man" disclosed the societies' beliefs, which closely resemble deism, no surprise considering the intellectual currents of the time, and he condemned Europe's wars and the tyranny of men over women.

When writers addressed France's overseas lands, there was a clear difference between the way in which inhabitants of the Caribbean and inhabitants of New France were described. The islands were enchanted places, free from illness, fertile and temperate in climate, where French inhabitants could learn from the blissful inhabitants' eloquent simplicity. By contrast, settlers in New France lived desolately in the cold, endless forest, amid the presence of famine, disease, vermin, and superstition. Most indigenous peoples were hostile to the French missionaries, which helped account for the numerous reports unfavorable to Native Americans. Moreover, French savants believed that North America had been created after Europe, hence its people, formed after other races, were not a completely developed human species.

Missionary accounts were contradictory. Unconverted people lived in squalor, believed in demons, and behaved violently. By contrast, converts were happy and progressed in moral and material well-being as a result of joining the church. Like other educated French of the period, the Jesuits had read the historians of Greece and Rome, and much of the language describing the native North Americans drew on classical examples. However, if native North Americans were sometimes pictured as a race of lesser ability than the Chinese or Caribbean populations, Africans fared even worse. Few accounts regarded them as anything but inferior creatures to whom the laws of civilization and the hope of betterment did not apply.

ART

Should a visitor to Versailles late in the reign of Louis XIV mount the vast Stairway of the Ambassadors leading to the state apartments, he or she would have seen, above the polished marble columns, four simulated balconies from which people of the known world offered homage to the Sun King. An American Indian stood on one balcony—a muscular, noble figure with features resembling those of a classical sculpture, but graced with a feathered headpiece and armed with a wooden club. Other persons were dressed in the headgear and costumes of contemporary France. What was most striking in these figures is not how accurately they represented life in the world beyond France's shores, but how much they drew, like artists of the previous century, on antiquity interpreted through the prism of contemporary France.

The 17th century visual portrait of the overseas world was reflected in a painting called *America* (circa 1665) by a Low Countries artist, Jan van Kessel. The setting is a European palace in which reddish-hued nearly nude natives dance or lounge about. Only the addition of feathers make young aborigines distinguishable from the cherubs of the time. The walls are covered with statues such as might appear in hundreds of palaces, except that the subject matter is people of the New World, not Greek and Roman gods and athletes. On the walls hang collections of butterflies and insects and paintings of indigenous life. Gaily feathered tropical birds perch here and there, and preserved and live fish, reptiles, and small animals clutter the spacious room, while monkeys explore the contents of an overturned golden vase from which ropes of pearls and thick gold and silver coins pour, as if from a cornucopia.[43] To the idea of antiquity was added that of the curious, exotic, and bizarre, and its contents were the subject matter of numerous French palaces and wealthy merchants' homes.

The theme of the peoples of the world paying homage to the Sun King was central to the art of this era. In June 1662 a three-day tournament was held in the Louvre courtyard where the king appeared as a Roman emperor, his younger brother as a Persian king, and other princes as rulers of Turkey, India, and America. The duc de Guise was the king of America, wearing a headdress of feathers set on a golden helmet. A ballet depicting the American colonies was performed before Louis XIV at Fontainbleau on October 15, 1685. Called *Le Temple de la paix*, it featured inhabitants of the Canadian wilderness and Louisiana singing about the pleasures of being governed by such a powerful and glorious king. "We have crossed the vast bosom of the ocean to render homage to the most powerful of kings." An oft-repeated refrain followed, "Ah! It is sweet to live under his laws."[44]

NOTES

1. Quoted in Stewart L. Mims, *Colbert's West India Policy* (New Haven, Conn.: Yale University Press, 1912), pp. 5–6, from Jean Eon, *Le Commerce honorable* (1646): W. P. Cumming, S. Hillier, D. B. Quinn, and G. Williams, *The Exploration of North America* (New York: G. P. Putnam's Sons, 1974); John Lough, *An Introduction to Seventeenth Century France* (London: Longmans, 1964); Frédéric Mauro, *L'Expansion européenne* (Paris: Presses Universitaire de France, 1967); K. G. Davies, *The North Atlantic World in the Seventeenth Century* (Minneapolis: University of Minnesota Press, 1974).

2. Holden Furber, *Rival Empires of Trade in the Orient, 1600–1800*, vol. II, *Europe and the World in the Age of Expansion* (Minneapolis: University of Minnesota Press, 1976), pp. 201–211.

3. Herbert Ingram Priestly, *France Overseas, a Study of Modern Imperialism* (New York: D. Appleton-Century, 1939), pp. 70–72.

4. Jan Glete, *Navies and Nations*, vol. 1, *Warships, Navies and State Building in Europe and America, 1500–1860*, Stockholm Studies in History (Stockholm: Almquist & Wiksell International, 1993), p. 128; Paul Walden Bamford, *Forests and French Sea Power, 1660–1789* (Toronto: University of Toronto Press, 1956).

5. Glete, *Navies and Nations*, vol. 1, p. 187.

6. Mims, *Colbert's West India Policy*, p. 6.

7. Laurence Bradford Packard, *The Commercial Revolution 1400–1776; Mercantilism, Colbert, Adam Smith* (New York: Henry Holt, 1927); Gerald S. Graham, *Empire of the North Atlantic, the Maritime Struggle for North America* (Toronto: University of Toronto Press, 1950); Pierre Goubert, *Louis XIV and Twenty Million Frenchmen* (New York: Vintage Books, 1970); Fernand Braudel and Ernest Labrousse, *Histoire économique et sociale de la France*, vol. 2, *Des derniers temps de l'âge seigneurial aux préludes de l'âge industriel (1660–1789)* (Paris: Presses Universitaires de France, 1970); Robert Mandrou, *Louis XIV et son temps, 1661–1715* (Paris: Presses Universitaires de France, 1973).

8. Glete, *Navies and Nations*, vol. 1, p. 191.

9. Quoted in Geoffrey Symcox, ed., *War, Diplomacy, and Imperialism, 1618–1763* (New York: Walker, 1974), pp. 263–267, from François Charpentier, *A Discourse Written by a Faithful Subject to His Christian Majesty, Concerning the Establishment of a French Company for the Commerce of the East Indies*, trans. R. L. Estrange (London, 1664); H. P. Bigger, *The Early Trading Companies of New France* (Toronto: University of Toronto, 1901); Eleanor C. Lodge, *Sully, Colbert, and Turgot, a Chapter in French Economic History* (New York: Kennikat Press, 1971, originally published in 1931).

10. André Scherer, *La Réunion* (Paris: P.U.F., Que sais-je?, 1994, 4th ed.), p. 3.

11. Marcel Trudel, *Histoire de la Nouvelle-France*, vol. 2, *Le comptoir, 1604–1627* (Montréal: FIDES, 1966).

12. Andrew Hill Clark, *Acadia, the Geography of Early Nova Scotia to 1760* (Madison: University of Wisconsin Press, 1968).

13. W. L. Grant, *Voyages of Samuel de Champlain, 1604–1618* (New York: Barnes & Noble, 1959); Samuel Eliot Morison, *Samuel de Champlain, Father of New France* (Boston: Little, Brown, 1972).

14. Richard Colebrook Harris, *The Seigneurial System in Early Canada* (Madison: University of Wisconsin Press, 1968); Margaret T. Hodgen, *Early Anthropology in the*

Sixteenth and Seventeenth Centuries (Philadelphia: University of Pennsylvania Press, 1964); Gabriel Sagard-Théodat, *Sagard's Long Journey to the Country of the Hurons* (New York: Greenwood Press, 1968); Bruce G. Trigger, *The Children of Aataentsic, a History of the Huron People to 1660*, 2 vols. (Kingston, Ont.: McGill-Queen's University Press, 1987).

15. Louise Dechêne, *Habitants and Merchants in Seventeenth Century Montreal*, trans. Liana Vardi (Montréal: McGill-Queen's University Press, 1992), p. 280.

16. Quoted in W. J. Eccles, *The Canadian Frontier* (New York: Holt, Rinehardt and Winston, 1969), pp. 91–92, from *Papiers la Pausde, RAPQ, 1931–1932*, p. 67.

17. Dechêne, *Habitants and Merchants*, pp. 284–285.

18. Ibid., pp. 200–203.

19. Richard White, *The Middle Ground, Indians, Empires, and Republics in the Great Lakes Region, 1650–1815* (New York: Cambridge University Press, 1997), pp. 107–108.

20. Quoted in Yves F. Zoltvany, ed., *The French Tradition in America* (New York: Harper & Row, 1969), p. 106, from Denis Riverin, *Historical Memoir to My Lord the Comte de Pontchartrain on the Harmful Results of Having Placed All the Beaver in the Same Hand*, December 12, 1705, Archives nationales, colonies (Paris), série C11 A, vol. 22, ff. 362–364. Translated by the editor.

21. George T. Hunt, *The Wars of the Iroquois, a Study in International Relations* (Madison: University of Wisconsin Press, 1972, reprint of 1940 edition); Yves F. Zoltvany, "New France and the West, 1701–1713," *Canadian Historical Review* 46, no. 4 (1965), pp. 301–322.

22. Dechêne, *Habitants and Merchants*, p. 7.

23. Cornelius J. Jansen, *Friend and Foe: Aspects of French-Amerindian Cultural Contact in the Sixteenth and Seventeenth Centuries* (New York: Columbia University Press, 1976), p. 191.

24. Ibid., p. 196.

25. White, *The Middle Ground*, p. 25.

26. Marcel Trudel, *Histoire de la Nouvelle France, le comptoir, 1604–1627* (Montréal: FIDES, 1966), pp. 435–455.

27. Quoted in Zoltvany, *The French Tradition in America*, pp. 71–74, from Document A: *Jugements et délibérations du Conseil Souverain de la Nouvelle France* (6 vols., Québec, 1883–85), vol. 5, pp. 233–236; Charles Woolsey Cole, *Colbert and a Century of French Mercantilism* (Hamden, Conn.: Archon Books, 1964, originally published in 1939).

28. James Pritchard to Frederick Quinn, letter, April 5, 1999. Also, James Pritchard, "The Demographic Context of Colonial Louisiana's Early Settlement: Population in French America, 1670–1730," *Colonial Louisiana: A Tricentennial Symposium, March 3–6, Biloxi, Mississippi*, March 5, 1999.

29. Quoted in Dechêne, *Habitants and Merchants*, p. 9, from Frontenac, Letter of November 2, 1684, ASSP, doss. 109, doc. 1, item 2.

30. S. R. Mealing, ed., *The Jesuit Relations and Allied Documents, a Selection* (Toronto: McClelland and Stuart, 1963), pp. 22–37; J. H. Kennedy, *Jesuit and Savage in New France* (New Haven, Conn.: Yale University Press, 1950).

31. Ibid., pp. 35–36, from Father Paul le Jeune, *Relation of What Occurred in New France on the Great River St. Lawrence, in the Year One Thousand Six Hundred Thirty-Four*.

32. Ibid., p. 32.

33. Quoted in Zoltvany, *The French Tradition in America*, pp. 81–83, from A. H. Têtu and C. O. Gagnon, eds., *Mandements, lettres pastorales et circulaires des Evêques de Québec, 1659–1887*, 6 vols. (Québec, 1887–90), pp. 169–173.

34. Stewart L. Mims, *Colbert's West India Policy* (New Haven, Conn.: Yale University Press, 1912); Nellis Maynard Crouse, *French Pioneers in the West Indies, 1624–1664* (New York: Columbia University Press, 1965); A. P. Newton, *The European Nations in the West Indies, 1493–1638* (London: A & C Black, 1933).

35. Robin Blackburn, *The Making of New World Slavery, from the Baroque to the Modern, 1492–1800* (New York: Verso, 1998), p. 282.

36. Ibid., pp. 294–295.

37. Mims, *Colbert's West India Policy*, p. 326.

38. Blackburn, *Making of New World Slavery*, p. 291, from *Avertissement aux Protestants*, quoted in Louis Sala-Molins, *Le Code Noir ou le calvaire de Canaan* (Paris: 1987), p. 65.

39. Ibid., p. 288, from R. P. Jean-Baptiste Du Tertre, *Histoire générale des Antilles habitées par les français*, 3 vols., Martinique, 1973 (Paris: 1667–71), vol. 2, p. 494.

40. A. O. Exquemelin, *The Buccaneers of America*, trans. Alexis Brown (Baltimore: Penguin Books, 1969), pp. 54–55.

41. Pierre Goubert, *The Ancien Régime, French Society 1600–1750*, trans. Steve Cox (New York: Harper & Row, 1969), p. 268; Robert Mandrou, *De la culture populaire aux XVIIe et XVIIIe siècles* (Paris: Presses Universitaires de France, 1970); Gilbert Chinard, *L'Amérique et le rêve exotique dans la littérature française au XVIIe et au XVIIIe siècles* (Paris: Hachette, 1913).

42. Geoffroy Atkinson, *Les Relations des voyages du XVIIe siècle et l'évolution des idées* (New York: Burt Franklin, 1971 reprint of 1924 edition); Fredi Chiappelli, ed., Michael J. B. Allen and Robert L. Benson, co-eds., *The First Images of America, the Impact of the New World on the Old*, vols. 1, 2 (Los Angeles: University of California, 1976); Durand Echeverra, *Mirage in the West, a History of the French Image in American Society to 1815* (Princeton, N.J.: Princeton University Press, 1957).

43. Hugh Honour, *The New Golden Land, European Images of America from the Discoveries to the Present Time* (New York: Pantheon Books, 1975), pp. 104–105, 118.

44. Ibid., pp. 93–95.

3

The 18th Century:
The Settlers' Empire

"Damn sugar, damn coffee, damn colonies."

—Napoléon

Much of North America, including the vast expanses of New France and part of the American heartland, belonged to the French Overseas Empire in the 18th century, and from it poured the wealth of the Canadian fur trade. In the West Indies the sugar industry burgeoned and, with it, the demand for African slaves. In East Asia the brief but real prospect of a French India made France a major presence on the subcontinent. By the end of the century, however, France had lost Canada, India, and Saint-Domingue, and the vast Louisiana territory would soon be sold. A handful of small Caribbean islands and African and Asian trading stations were the residual souvenirs of three centuries of overseas activity.

The reasons why France failed to sustain a global empire were clear. France could be a land power or a sea power, but not both simultaneously. Its population was not large, and the French did not want to go abroad. The high costs of a century of warfare and substantial aid to the American Revolution also left France overextended, which contributed to the problems that brought on its own revolution. The French navy again came in second to Britain's and could neither adequately supply nor protect its overseas holdings. Two kings, one regent, and successive revolutionary governments were rarely interested in the world beyond their borders, and perennial antagonism among colonists, coastal merchants, and the crown limited possibilities for overseas expansion. Finally, the minutely regulated overseas trading companies on which the commercial hopes for empire were pinned continued to atrophy. At century's end, little remained but the chimera of empire.

A CENTURY OF WARFARE

The long period from 1689 to 1815 was one of periodic struggle between France and Great Britain, who fought at times on the Continent, at sea, in the Americas, or in India. Seven times during this period fighting moved from sporadic exchanges by local commanders to full-scale combat, and when the global conflict ended in 1815, only traces remained of the French Overseas Empire. The most important early conflict was the War of Spanish Succession (1701–1713), a French-Hapsburg dynastic struggle for control of Spain and its long-established empire. European armies fought on battlefields in India and North America in the first global war of modern times. Overseas lands were part of the stakes, and sea power was significantly employed to defend them and seize opponents' possessions. France's losses were small—the peninsula of Nova Scotia or Acadia—and France ceded control over the profitable Hudson Bay territory to the British, plus Saint Kitts and Newfoundland.[1] Considering that France was greatly overextended, did France lose valuable assets or shed liabilities? The question is not easy to answer, but a strong case can be made that the French negotiators did an admirable job of consolidating a difficult position to their advantage.

The French-British conflict next erupted in North America. Both powers had unresolved territorial claims, and when they moved through the American wilderness toward each other, conflict was inevitable. Location and population favored the British, whose settlements, concentrated along the eastern American seaboard, had easy water communication with one another, good agricultural land, a steady commercial base, and a growing population. By mid-century more than 2 million British settlers lived along America's eastern seaboard. In contrast, the French numbered perhaps 70 thousand persons spread along a wide, thin arc from the Saint Lawrence River through the Great Lakes to the Mississippi River Valley. Only Québec and New Orleans, 1,500 miles apart, were cities of any size. Demography often played a more decisive role than statecraft in the contest for empire, and here France usually came in second place.

The interplay among the French, Native American, and English was not a clash of large armies moving through colored map zones northward or southward. Instead, the woods of eastern North America were alive with small bands of traders and warriors traveling along trade routes and waterways on their own or with allies. Raids, ambushes, and guerrilla warfare were more frequent than larger unit actions. The taking of prisoners and hostages was part of such brutal encounters, as chronicled in John Demos' *The Unredeemed Captive, a Family Story of Early America*, which tells how a seven-year-old daughter of a leading New England divine was kidnapped by the French and Indians, converted to

Catholicism, forgot English and learned Mohawk, and married an Indian. A tenuous family-to-family contact spanning several decades was maintained, but the rupture generated wide shock waves. The book vividly chronicles the intensely personal costs of such warfare.[2]

In the West Indies, France held important sugar islands, including Saint-Domingue, Guadeloupe, and Martinique. The British claimed Jamaica and Barbados. In India, both countries had profitable coastal trading stations and ports along the sea routes to China. Important to France were several Indian Ocean islands and Madagascar, where ships resupplied and plantations were established.

The rivalry between France and England again flared into open warfare in the Seven Years' War (1756–1763). Absurd as it would later appear, in the 1750s French and British leaders focused their imperial struggle on control of the Indian village lands on the Ohio and Wabash rivers. The French governor devised an 18th century "domino theory," which argued that the loss of the Ohio Valley would be followed by the loss of Canada and Louisiana, the French Caribbean, and Spanish Mexico.[3] What emerged in North America was a kaleidoscope of competing interests. The Ohio lands lay on the periphery of both the French Canadian and Louisiana colonies, making attempts at control tenuous from either location. Other Indian groups lived there and the hated British, far from representing a united front, included traders from private companies; the colonies of New York, Pennsylvania, and Virginia; a forest full of independent traders; and the ubiquitous Iroquois.[4] In 1754 the French and Indians defeated George Washington near what is now Pittsburgh, but France was spread too thin. In 1756 Britain moved from frontier skirmishes to an openly declared war on France. British objectives were clear: to seize the rich Newfoundland and Saint Lawrence fisheries and the North Atlantic fur trade. Initially French forces in Canada fought successfully; elsewhere, the English lost Calcutta, and the French army and navy prepared for a channel invasion. France, however, was militarily overextended on the Continent, leaving the British fleet free to move at will on French shipping and overseas colonies. In America in 1758 the British seized Fort Duquesne, a main French inland outpost strategically located at the intersection of three rivers at what is now Pittsburgh.

Next to fall was the large French fortress of Louisbourg, gateway to the Saint Lawrence River. Despite its awesome appearance amid the barren coastal stretches, it contained glaring structural faults. Impressive rows of guns were left unprotected on their flanks or rear, and the seemingly impregnable stone walls were porous and too poorly built to withstand artillery pounding. Within 45 years the fort, designed to control the entrance to a continent, was twice taken and finally destroyed.[5] Louisbourg, the French believed, was impregnable. Sébastien Le Prestre de Vauban (1633–1707), France's celebrated military engineer, already had built a string of successful fortresses along France's borders and coasts. Louisbourg was a massive engineering undertaking, employing thousands of workers over a quarter-century. Although New Englanders originally captured Louisbourg in 1745 and exiled its inhabitants to France, it was returned to France three years later in 1748. In the final conflict with the British in 1758 the seemingly invulnerable fortress fell. Vauban's geometric fortress, displaying the symmetry and austere beauty of French colonial architecture through the centuries, was packed with explosives by British soldiers. When they were finished, only long lines of rubble remained, and the once imposing fortress had been reduced to a suggestion of some prehistoric site.

General Louis-Joseph de Montcalm, the French commander in Canada from 1756 until his death in 1759, was a traditional infantry and cavalry officer, a veteran of many European campaigns who constantly misread the meaning of local events and lacked the skills needed to keep the subtly balanced alliance intact. The combination of a British blockade, a smallpox epidemic, and disgruntled Indian allies resulted in the demise of the French position; its death knell came with France's defeat by the British in 1759.

As in previous centuries, the French were hampered by heavy-handed control from the metropolis. It was not for nothing that Alexis de Tocqueville later said that in New France he saw as through a microscope all the shortcomings of the French administrative system. Detailed regulations governed every aspect of overseas life, from how fires should be kept in settlements to what prices could be charged for goods, from where streets and roads should be placed, to the types of rope used in various ships. It was the presence of such detailed records that allowed the social historian Christopher Moore to reconstruct the lives of magistrates and sailors, marriage partners and fishermen, soldiers and artisans in *Louisbourg Portraits, Life in an Eighteenth-Century Garrison Town*.[6]

France's North American fate was sealed at the Battle of Québec, a large-unit skirmish that lasted barely fifteen minutes. Its effects might be compared to the battle of Dien Bien Phu in the 20th century, for it brought to a close a chapter of empire history. The French defeat at Québec was not foreordained, for France commanded the high terrain and, for once, outnumbered the British troops, roughly 14 thousand to 9 thousand. During the night of September 12–13, 1759, the British brought a large force quickly up a narrow path to a point on the plain before the city's west wall. When a French messenger brought news of the British advance, he was greeted with disbelief. Montcalm rode into town that morning to find the autumn landscape red with 4 thousand British troops massed on the plains. Without waiting for his full forces to assemble, the surprised general ordered an attack, but his panicked troops fired quickly and erratically. The French sustained more than a thousand casualties; the British lost 58 troops and 600 wounded; and both commanders were killed. Sporadic fighting continued until the bitter winter, but the French needed reinforcements to retain Canada, and the minister of marine, preoccupied with Continental conflicts, reportedly replied to repeated requests for assistance, "One does not attempt to save the stables when the house is on fire." Montréal surrendered to the British in September 1760; the Saint Lawrence Valley was then entirely in British hands.[7]

THE PEACE TALKS: "FRANCE COULD BE HAPPY WITHOUT CANADA" (VOLTAIRE)

Much of what France had lost on the battlefield was reclaimed in the subsequent peace talks which culminated in the Treaty of Paris (1763). Britain entered the peace talks at the height of its power. Militarily strong, its commerce with the New World had grown steadily during the war and it seemingly could dictate peace on its terms. France, with a much weaker position, was represented by the shrewd, tenacious duc du Choiseul (1719–1785) who, like the British, wished to end the long and draining conflict but was willing to prolong it should British terms not be acceptable. Choiseul, who had a clear idea of French interests, profited from conducting the negotiations himself. On the British side he faced four inept parliamentarians picked for their friendship with the king. The British had no idea of what they wanted from the negotiations, and they were anxious to conclude the talks as quickly as possible and often quarreled among themselves.

Part of Britain's indecisiveness reflected a sharp debate at home over whether Canada or Guadeloupe should be retained. Canada, it was argued, was large and potentially rich in natural resources, but its inhabitants were given to quarreling with authority, and they were vulnerable to ideas of independence now circulating in the English colonies. But, should Britain keep Guadeloupe, there would be problems there as well. This rich sugar island was more productive than any British West Indies island except Jamaica. If retained, it would probably flood the London sugar market, causing prices to fall and damaging British planters' interests as well. Finally, Britain decided to take Canada instead of Guadeloupe.[8]

This choice was acceptable to Choiseul, who had had long considered the North American colony a liability, and who agreed with Voltaire that "France could be happy without Canada." With Canada went French land claims to North America, excluding Louisiana, which it retained. France otherwise fared well, keeping profitable fishing rights in North America with the small islands of Saint-Pierre and Miguelon off the Newfoundland coast as a base, and its West Indies sugar islands, the most important of which were Saint-Domingue, Martinique, and Guadeloupe. It also retained the slave trading station of Gorée, an island off the West African coast, and some coastal trading posts in India, but gave up its sizable claims to the subcontinent's interior, which could not be protected militarily in any case.

LOUIS XV AND LOUIS XVI

The century's crucial central years were largely a period of decline in French overseas interests under the long reign of Louis XV (1710–1774). Regal in bearing, Louis looked like a king but was not a forceful man. Indecisive and easily bored, he was ill-cast as a national and international leader. As its losses to the British mounted, France gradually abandoned claims to global hegemony. The

British navy grew and British control of the seas became increasingly important in Continental politics. By the time Louis XVI (1754–1793) came to the throne, France's naval problems were acute and major reforms were needed. Louis heeded his ministers' plea to increase the size of the army and the navy, which grew to over 78 ships of the line and nearly 200 other craft, allowing the French navy to have brief superiority over the English during the American Revolution.[9]

In 1776 France moved openly to support the American Revolution, seeing in the conflict an opportunity to tip the balance against England. Muskets, powder, and other supplies were sent to the American insurgents by the French, and during the summer of 1781, French and American commanders designed a bold plan to trap the large British force concentrated at Yorktown. Defeated by the French at sea, and outnumbered by the French and Americans on land, on October 17, 1781, the British asked for terms. Colonial and military historian James Pritchard has written of the strategy of Charles Gravier, comte de Vergennes, Louis XVI's minister and secretary of state for foreign affairs (1774–1787): "The ideological paradox of an absolute monarchy aiding a republican uprising bothered Vergennes not a whit. For him the problem was not the independence of the United States but how France could benefit from intervening in Britain's growing troubles in America."[10] However, in addition to helping America, France faced growing internal problems; interest on the war debt and upkeep of the armed forces required substantial government revenues. The Estates General gathered in 1789 to solve the financial crisis with new taxes but unleashed the French Revolution instead, a consequence of which was a seismic shift in French colonial interests.[11]

LOUISIANA: "DAMN SUGAR, DAMN COFFEE, DAMN COLONIES"

By the 18th century France still claimed over a million square miles of North America in the vast but undefined Louisiana territory, land extending from the fur country of New France to the Gulf of Mexico, including much of the Mississippi River Valley. The French presence was real in the agriculturally rich Illinois Country of the middle Mississippi Valley, with its large number of French settlers. Westward, French claims stretched to the Rocky Mountains.[12]

French interest in Louisiana had begun with René-Robert Cavalier, Sieur de la Salle's explorations of the Mississippi in the 1680s, and the movement of itinerant soldiers and fur traders westward and southward from New France. From 1712 to 1717 Louisiana was held as a private grant from the king by Antoine Crozat, a wealthy businessman. Crozat found it too expensive to keep and sold it to a company, which soon transferred it to the Company of the Indies, which returned it to the crown in 1731, caught up in the speculation of what was later called Law's "Mississippi Bubble." John Law (1671–1729) was a Scottish banker and adviser to the French government, who chartered the Compagnie d'Occident, or Mississippi Company, in 1717 as part of a multifaceted financial system designed to reduce France's immense debts and return handsome profits by purchasing the government's debts in return for shares that would pay dividends based on profits from colonial commerce. The scheme's great weakness was the failure of the colonial companies to realize the needed profits to pay off the debt. Initially, investors were attracted to the company, which promised to grow silk, cotton, timber, and tobacco for export, and its shares soared to 40 times their worth. By 1720, however, they had dropped to half their nominal value; the company was never profitable and soon collapsed. The French government took control of the failing enterprise in 1721 and re-organized it in 1723. In Paris, a satirical song spread with Law's fall:

> Monday I bought stock,
> Tuesday I made millions,
> Wednesday I decorated my house,
> Thursday, I bought a carriage,
> Friday, I went to the ball,
> Saturday, to the poor house.[13]

It was not until the 1720s and 1730s that conditions approached stability for the French residents in Louisiana. Two thousand settlers and 4,000 slaves accounted for about half the population transported by the Company of the Indies. Others had died en route or of diseases after arrival in the New World. By 1726 Louisiana's colonial population included about 1,663 settlers, including 1,385 black slaves and 159 Indian slaves. Through barter with the Indians, the French had acquired adequate foodstuffs to ensure their survival, and other French settlers became farmers, growing grains, livestock, and poultry sufficient to launch a settler economy.

Set 100 miles inland from the coast to avoid hurricanes, New Orleans, the principal port town, was founded in 1717 by Jean Baptiste Le Moyne, Sieur de Bienville, who spent 40 years in Louisiana as French governor. A corrupt but entrepreneurial politician, he used French navy ships to move his own products up and down the lower Mississippi River.

Louisiana society was an amalgam of partly reformed Caribbean pirates and somewhat settled *coureurs de bois*, many of whom, with their Indian wives, built small towns. The land itself was uninviting; if ships made it through pirate-infested waters, shifting sandbars were a menace to ships. Mortality was high in the hot, humid climate. Hurricanes were common; flooding was frequent. One commentator described the isolated, confining life in New Orleans of that epoch: "Of education there was little, of art and literature none. Social gatherings for billiards, dancing, church festivals, and feasting were varied by fishing, boating, and hunting. Gay costumes indicated the modest gradations in society."[14] Police files contain notations like "Here is a true subject for Louisiana" since many of the early settlers came from the flotsam and jetsam of European society: unemployed laborers, deported salt smugglers, and itinerant *colpoteurs* (peddlers) whose habits of moving about the country with small packets of merchandise would launch them on commercial careers.

What developed in these decades was a symbiotic relationship between intruders and indigenous people. The nimble governor, Le Moyne de Bienville, realizing the need for good relations with the populous Choctaw and other peoples, offered them armed protection against invaders and slavers, but continual interplay was exhibited as well between the French and numerous smaller Indian groups, who in turn interacted with one another and with the growing number of African slaves.[15] These African slaves added the final ingredient to the region's volatile social mix. The lower Mississippi Valley has been described as one moving "from slave society to society with slaves."[16]

A SHIFTING NETWORK OF ALLIANCES

A feature of the French presence in Louisiana was a constantly shifting network of alliances with local populations, who in turn made their own political-military-economic ties with one another and with France's European rivals, England and Spain. Louisiana was always a far outpost on the margins of empire for France, rarely having the needed numbers of troops or economic support required to advance French interests. The small French garrisons and trading posts along riverbanks could do little by themselves and depended on a vast web of Indian agents from various tribes to act as traders with the inland areas and to provide foodstuffs for the Europeans' survival. The Indian nations also had their own agendas and often skillfully played one European power off against another.

An additional ingredient in this volatile mix was the spread of European disease, which decimated Native American peoples. Lacking immunity to viruses, thousands of Indians died of smallpox, influenza, measles, cholera, yellow fever, typhus, and dysentery. Slave raids further depleted their numbers. When African slaves began to arrive in considerable numbers, their ranks were depleted by scurvy, caused by the lack of citrus fruits, and other diseases.

By the 1720s the contour of Louisiana's network of Indian trade alliances was firmly established . . . henceforth trade in the Lower Mississippi Valley flowed mainly from the Indian villages around the interior French posts to the Gulf Coast ports of Mobile and New Orleans. . . . The outer limits, or periphery, of this network included the Upper Creeks to the northeast, the Quapaws due north, and the Caddoes to the northwest.[17]

If colonial society was divergent, so were the numerous Indian groups with whom the French interacted. The French established formal alliances and relations with large nearby groups like the Choctaws and Chickasaws, but they also had ongoing relations with possibly 20 different *petites nations* by the 1720s, most of them remnants of once-larger communities decimated by disease or defeated in warfare. The main activity for most such groups was the daily round of providing goods and services to settlers and traders.

Settlers, servants, slaves, and soldiers moved along divergent paths in the evolution of a plantation economy. Contrary to retrospective impressions about race, not all Europeans had equal stakes in the enslavement of Africans or Indians. Most settlers could not afford to purchase slaves; some barely survived their own indentured servitude or military service. Not all slaves were African in origin, and some managed to acquire freedom. And whether African or Indian, slaves fell into a wide range of roles in colonial society.[18]

Equally complex were the demarcations in Indian society. While some came to work as laborers or servants for the French and some became slaves, others worked as free traders, balancing "their political autonomy with their economic interdependency by staying on the margins of colonial society."[19]

Relations between the French and local populations were riddled with tensions. As slaves acquired skills as artisans and replaced French workers, friction resulted. The French were also always on guard against prospects of Indian-black collusion as well, and there were numerous examples of prolonged warfare between the French and Indians, incidents which proved costly to both sides. Four such disputes include the French-Chitimachas encounters of 1706–1718, the French-Natchez hostilities of 1722–1729, the French-Chickasaw wars of 1731–1740, and the French-Choctaw hostilities of 1746–1756. The reasons for each conflict differed but generally included Indians experiencing French encroachments on their best agricultural land, the frustration of populations decimated by the white man's diseases, and periodic food shortages, plus encouragement by European rivals of France, as well as inter-Indian alliances.

One such encounter in the 1720s was between the French and the 3,500-member Natchez. Natchez-French relations were marked by periodic violence and increased bad feelings. The French lured several Natchez, including their leader, the Great Sun, into captivity in retaliation for a Natchez ambush in which five Frenchmen were killed in 1723.

Reflecting on their relationship with the French, the Tattooed Serpent, a high officeholder in traditional Natchez society, remarked bitterly in 1723:

What need did we have of the French? Before them, didn't we live better than we do now? Because we deprive ourselves of a part of our grain, of game and of fish that we killed to share with them. In what, therefore, did we have need of them? Was it for their guns? We used our bows and arrows which sufficed to make us live well. Was it for their white, blue, or red blankets? We did well enough with the skins of buffaloes which are warmer. Our wives worked on these coverlets of feathers for the winter and of the bark of myrtle trees for summer. . . . Finally, before the arrival of the French, we lived like men who know how to do with what they have, whereas today we walk like slaves who do not do what they wish.[20]

Issues came to a head on November 28, 1729, when the Natchez executed a carefully planned raid on several French settlements under the guise of moving out on a large communal hunting party. Between 200 to 300 French were killed in most major plantations and settlements, representing over 10% of the resident

French population. Only women, children, and slaves were spared, and these were taken into captivity. It took the French two months to muster a retaliatory force, and intermittent warfare continued for several years. Finally, the French captured the Natchez leadership, including the last Great Sun, who were sold into captivity in the Caribbean. By the mid-1740s the Natchez had scattered, their nation destroyed.

In 1763 France gave Louisiana to Spain to compensate Spain for aiding France in its recent war with England, during which Spain had fared disastrously and had lost great quantities of shipping and the main port of Havana. Also, as part of the Treaty of Paris (1763) peace negotiations with England, France ceded to England all of its lands east of the Mississippi River. This provided England the land it wanted for the westward expansion of its American colonies beyond the Appalachians. France also retained the Ile d'Orléans (New Orleans), which it had secretly ceded to Spain, plus Guadeloupe and Martinique, which were returned by Britain.

In 1768 Spain outlawed commerce between Louisiana and France and its possessions, abruptly severing the long-established French merchants' trading ties with France's islands in the West Indies. The Spanish decree came at an inflationary time; food prices had doubled, and the value of the colony's currency was in sharp fluctuation. Rebellion broke out among the French planters and merchants in Louisiana, and in 1769 the Spanish sent Alejandio O'Reilly, an Irish soldier of fortune, with 3,600 troops to restore order. O'Reilly talked with enough of the troubled planters to identify the local community's leaders, who were invited to a reception where they were seized.[21]

Toward the north, English settlers continued their steady westward migration. At century's end, 900 thousand Americans had settled beyond the Alleghenies, moving steadily into lands claimed as part of the Louisiana Territory, where only 42 thousand French lived. In the lower Mississippi Valley the death rate among colonists was high, 65% of the white population in the 1720s. In 1726 only about 1,500 settlers and soldiers remained, numbers that would allow the French few possibilities to confront the English or to expand their holdings.[22] The French failure was thus less one of political will than of feeble population numbers. France in this century (as in other centuries) never raised the numbers of settlers needed to compete with the British, nor did most of the French sent overseas desire to remain there.

NAPOLÉON REDUX

France's brief claims to the vast North American territory were revived by Napoléon Bonaparte who, after his defeat in Egypt, hoped to establish a second New France, this time connecting the Caribbean and the Gulf of Mexico with the North American interior. In exchange for Louisiana, he offered Tuscany to Charles IV of Spain who had been looking for a small kingdom for his brother-in-law. Napoléon added six warships to the deal with Spain, and Louisiana again became a French territory. However, Napoléon's plans for the Americas received a fatal blow in 1803, when a large French force sent to retake Saint-Domingue was defeated by the island's ex-slaves and by yellow fever. After learning about the disaster, Napoléon exclaimed, "Damn sugar, damn coffee, damn colonies." His dreams for an American empire died, and within weeks he offered to sell France's Louisiana interests to the United States. Napoléon needed money to finance his Continental wars, and if Louisiana were in American hands, he reasoned, it would strengthen the anti-British forces.[23]

Originally, America sought only to acquire the important port of New Orleans, but France wanted to rid itself of its entire holding, and in April 1803 the United States gained title to land five times the size of continental France. Acting on their own, and without instructions, the American negotiators agreed to pay France $11,250,000, plus assume claims of American citizens against France for an additional $3,750,000. Interest payments increased the total sum to over $27 million before it was entirely paid. At a time when the American national revenues were about $10 million a year, the negotiators were criticized for the folly of their vision and fiscal irresponsibility. Had France retained this territory, the course of French, American, and world history might have evolved differently. The American nation might have been limited to the eastern United States. Would a French Louisiana have stemmed the tide of American migration westward? If so, would the United States have been large enough to play the preponderate role in international affairs it did in later times? History's twists and turns leave many intriguing questions unanswered.

SCIENCE AND INVENTION

French naval architecture led the world for much of this period. French ships of the line, while far fewer than those of the British navy, were often larger and better engineered. Among the nautical innovations employed at this time was replacing the ship's tiller with a more accurate steering wheel. Impressive gains in cartography and engineering went with an expansion of construction in harbors, ports, and naval arsenals. The Academie Royale des Sciences, founded by Louis XIV in 1666, had begun to generate an impressive set of new maps of France and the world. In 1693 it published a corrected map of the coastlines of France and sent observers to Asia, Africa, the West Indies, and elsewhere in Europe to base their charts on actual observations rather than speculation. The new charts were far more accurate than anything previously available because they were based on Gerardus Mercator's projection for the sphericity of the earth, instead of the maps of a flat earth in use since the Middle Ages. Guillaume Delisile produced an accurately and beautifully designed world map in 1700. It left unknown or unsure areas blank and did not fill them in with imaginary embellishments as had been customary until then.[24]

The chief navigational problem facing mariners was determining longitude when a ship had lost sight of land. Latitude could be accurately plotted through the sighting of stars, but longitude for 18th century sailors was strictly a matter of guesswork. An English plan to rectify this was to anchor ship hulks at intervals along main trade routes, but this was never accomplished. In 1715 the French Academy established a prize for the person who discovered a way for ships to measure longitude. The basic problem was finding an instrument to measure the passage of time at sea accurately, from which distance could then be calculated. Sand glasses and water clocks were inaccurate; pendulum clocks were of little use once ships began to move and tilt, and spring-driven clocks were affected by humidity and temperature. It was not until the 1760s that an accurate way of calculating longitude by lunar distance was perfected. The basic instrument employed for sighting the moon was a reflecting octant, with a transparent mirror that could be aligned with the horizon. Simultaneously, a movable mirror reflected the heavenly body onto the first mirror, allowing an observer to calculate longitude from the angle of the horizon and that of the heavenly body. Thus, by the 1760s, it was possible for sailors, with a sextant and set of tables, to calculate longitude with lunar reckoning. Equally significant, in 1761 an English carpenter and clock maker, later known as Longitude Harrison, built a spring-driven watch-type chronometer, which could be used at sea, and which was the most accurate of all instruments for measuring longitude. A French watchmaker, Pierre Le Roy (1717–1785), improved the chronometer by including a device to compensate for variations in temperature. At first, these chronometers were expensive and difficult to make, and conservative mariners resisted their use. However, as designs steadily improved, costs declined, and such chronometers continued in use until radio time signals replaced them in the early 20th century.

FRENCH EXPLORATION OF THE PACIFIC: BOUGAINVILLE AND LA PÉROUSE

Systematic exploration of the Pacific by France and England did not begin until after 1763 and the end of the Seven Years' War. But when a balance sheet is drawn, these were expeditions of scientific interest, and only rarely of imperialistic importance, lively footnotes to the history of European expansion. In 1766 an army colonel and veteran of the Canadian wars, Louis-Antoine de Bougainville (1729–1811), circumnavigated the globe, not an unusual feat at the time; during the same period, Captain James Cook made his worldwide voyages of exploration. Bougainville's two ships, *La Bourdeuse* and *L'Étoile*, left France on November 15, 1766, carrying a naturalist, an astronomer, a surgeon, and a writer on a long, risky trip. A voyager called *L'Étoile* "that hellish den where hatred, insubordination, bad faith, brigandage, cruelty, and all kinds of disorders reign."[25] The ships did not reach Tahiti until April 1768. Bougainville claimed the island for France. His stay was short, only nine days, and he did little to map the island or its harbors. By early June they reached the Great Barrier Reef, beyond which lay Australia, but the ships did not proceed toward the nearby continent, leaving it for the British to claim. Bougainville's voyage was a popular success; his *Voyage autour du monde* was published to acclaim in 1771.

The second widely publicized French Pacific voyage was the scientific exploration of Jean-François de Galaup La Pérouse (1741–c.1788), whose two ships, *Astrolabe* and *Boussole*, set out in 1786 to study the Pacific. To ease their way with local populations, the ships carried medals stamped with the king's effigy and plumed helmets to present to appropriate chiefs, as well as pins, hatchets, bells, combs, a thousand pairs of scissors, and 9 thousand fish hooks.

The explorers visited Russia's Kamchatkan Peninsula, where the inhabitants of the only sizable settlement gathered at a ball in their honor. The governor offered them hunting and fishing trips and opportunities for the scientists to collect specimens. During their long wait, mail for the French party arrived and when news of La Pérouse's promotion to commodore was announced during the ball, the port artillery fired a salvo. La Pérouse sent his Russian interpreter, Barthélemy de Lesseps, son of the French consul general in Saint Petersburg and uncle of the canal builder, across Russia with his accounts of the expedition, saving them for posterity as the author headed south. The rest of the voyage was doom-ridden. The ships sailed south toward Samoa, where more than 20 members of a 60-person landing party were killed or wounded when several hundred Samoans attacked them. Next the French visited the Fiji Islands and Australia in 1788, then headed northeast, where they encountered a hurricane, ran into reefs, and went down between the Solomon Islands and the New Hebrides. Relics of the voyage, such as a ship's stern with markings, were discovered nearly 40 years later. The results of La Pérouse's voyage, like Bougainville's, were of popular literary and some scientific interest, but gave France neither commercial outlets nor new territory. Like their wandering counterparts who planted lead plates or raised stone markers and claimed North America for France, French sailors declared numerous scattered islands as French property, leaving decrees sealed in bottles buried under trees, but these claims were not backed by occupation, and France never became a Pacific power.

THE MASCARENES ISLANDS

East of Madagascar are several islands of strategic importance situated along global shipping lanes. (They would later be called "French pistols aimed at British India.") French ships had visited Bourbon (later Réunion) and Mauritius (later Ile de France) by the middle of the 17th century. Small numbers of settlers (150 in Bourbon in 1678), isolation (company ships visited once every two or three years), and often despotic or ineffectual governors gave the French settlements a precarious existence at best. The Seychelles were added in 1742, at about the same time pirates, chased away from other islands by the English, began settling on Bourbon as planters.

Coffee was introduced in the early 18th century. Of six Arabian plants brought there in 1718, only one survived, but from it sprang the coffee plantations that within a decade were supplying all of France and providing much of the French mocha coffee that made its way around the world. With plantations came slaves, mostly from East Africa, and by 1778 Bourbon's population was 8,800 whites and 37 thousand slaves. A series of tropical storms ruined the coffee plantations between 1806 and 1807 and, in keeping with the times, the island was renamed Ile Bonaparte from 1806 to 1810. Invaded by the English in 1810, it was restored to France in 1815 and became a sugar-producing economy until 1848 when slaves (63 thousand of them) were freed and replaced by low-paid Indian or Chinese workers.

By the middle of the 18th century, Ile de France had become the more important of the two islands. It was graced with an attractive harbor, a strategic location, and a growing spice industry (cinnamon, nutmeg, and vanilla.) In 1767 the always-fragile Compagnie des Indes, nominal owner of the island, was replaced by a crown colony, and by 1788 the population included 4,691 whites and freed slaves and 35,915 slaves. The island was seized by the British in December 1810 with an Anglo-Indian force of 10 thousand troops. The Treaty of Paris (1814–1815) gave Great Britain Ile de France, which became Mauritius, and restored Ile Bourbon to France as part of the final settlement.

FRENCH INDIA

Many people think of India as the jewel in the crown of the British Empire. But there once was a French India, twice the size of France, with a population of 30 million people under its nominal control. Early in the century the entire French claim to the Indian subcontinent was less than 50 acres. British holdings were similarly small, limited largely to Madras, Bombay, Calcutta, and a few small factories elsewhere. The French concentrated on Pondicherry off the southeastern coast with its healthy climate, strategic location, profitable local textile industry and weak local rulers. As a trading base Pondicherry led a precarious existence, with one year's receipts determining the next year's trading stores. It took over a year to exchange messages with France, and local administrators were left to their own devices.[26]

THE DUPLEIX YEARS (1722–1754)

The crucial period of the French presence in India closely followed the rise and later fall of Joseph-François Dupleix in what was now called the Perpetual Company of the Indies, successor to the failed French East India Company. Son of the company's director general, Dupleix joined the enterprise at the age of 18 and spent more than 30 years in India, systematically expanding France's commercial and territorial interests and becoming governor general in 1742. Dupleix was no colonial theorist but a shrewd, energetic trader who heavily committed his own and others' resources into expanding trade between India and the Far East. On his own, he engaged a dozen ships in the Far Eastern trade and made a handsome profit.

At first Dupleix sought neither power nor territory as ends in themselves, but he saw the possibility of vast profits in India for a fairly minimal effort. He believed the best way to assure profits was through alliances with local rulers to secure local territory which would also assure stable revenues from tribute, taxes, and rents. He thus created a string of "protectorates," assigning French resident advisors to each to represent his interests. Dupleix petitioned the company for soldiers, whose upkeep he hoped local rulers would fund, but in Paris the company turned him down and was indignant to learn that Dupleix had already struck out on his own in two local wars.

Generally, Dupleix was careful to keep the company's owners ignorant of his activist policies. Minimizing the serious shortcomings he encountered, and exaggerating successes, he believed that once he succeeded the company would back him. In the meantime, the less said to Paris the better; communications sometimes took over a year to complete via ships' mail. By the late 1740s Dupleix hoped to turn India's southern triangle into a zone of French influence, but the attractive but economically unproductive southern peninsula as a source of potential revenues did not compare with the richer northern Ganges River region claimed by the British.

A resourceful and courageous strategist, Dupleix made three miscalculations that brought about his downfall at the moment success was in sight in the mid-1740s. He seriously underestimated the extent of opposition from the company in Paris. Also, the southern Indian lands he held were devastated by warfare and could never produce the revenues on which Dupleix counted. Finally, Dupleix's constant challenges to the British brought a substantial British military response, which Dupleix did not have resources to counter. He fortified Pondicherry, the main French base, but at the moment conflict with the British broke out in 1743 the company ordered him to cut his military expenses in half. Dupleix was given a small fleet of eight ships harbored at a distant base in Ile de Bourbon, but it did not arrive until September 1746. Dupleix and Mahé de la Bourdonnais, the fleet's admiral, quarreled over strategy. Dupleix wanted the ships to attack the British center at Madras and destroy Pondicherry's rival, but La Bourdonnais preferred to sack the town instead, or claim a high ransom for leaving it untouched. Eventually La Bourdonnais sent his ships to Madras, which they took in three days. Dupleix had promised the city to a native ally in return for previous favors; but La Bourdonnais, on his own, had agreed instead to return it to the English for a suitable ransom. In the end, Dupleix prevailed, and when the admiral returned to Paris, he was briefly jailed for consorting with the enemy.

During the French-British peace talks held at Aix-la-Chapelle in 1749, Madras was returned to England in exchange for the English withdrawal from the Netherlands. The recently concluded peace in India did not last long. This time the issue was dynastic quarrels in two Indian states, one in the southwest, one in the north. The energetic Dupleix backed claimants to both thrones, who promised France territorial and financial concessions. Meanwhile, English traders, alarmed by the French incursions, backed different candidates and warfare followed.

In 1754 the company recalled Dupleix, who had staked his hope on a quick, successful war, but instead found himself in a protracted conflict with the English. The company was always an adjunct to the French navy, which Dupleix refused to acknowledge. The ministry, knowing France was overextended, and refusing to see Dupleix as anything but a reckless adventurer, recalled him. The company proposed a truce with England and an agreement not to interfere in local disputes. They wrote to Dupleix, "Your successes do not prevent us from desiring a state of affairs less brilliant and more peaceful. . . . We want nothing but a few trading stations and some rise in dividends."[27] Dupleix, out of favor, returned to France in 1754 and spent several fruitless years trying to reclaim reimbursement for his substantial personal expenditures of over eight million *livres* on behalf of the company.

THE FALL OF FRENCH INDIA

When the Seven Years' War (1756–1763) broke out, both the British and the French stepped up warfare in India. Such local encounters now were part of a global conflict as national armies and navies expanded from what had once been traders' quarrels. In India, France had the advantage of a large fighting force, more territory, and a web of alliances with local rulers. French strategy was to build a compact domain in the land around Pondicherry, giving up sizable claims to widely scattered lands elsewhere in India. The ambitious French goal was "no more Englishmen in the Peninsula," which they hoped to accomplish without the help of native rulers, whom they found to be crafty and unreliable allies.

A new French commander arrived in India in 1756 with ambitious instructions to expel the English from the subcontinent. The commander, Count Lally Baron de Tollendal, was a firebrand who had none of the sensitivity required to negotiate his way through the delicate political situation in which he had been placed, and he had no skills as an administrator to run the company as a commercial and military instrument. The quick-tempered Lally was soon as detested by native rulers as by his own local troops, who mutinied from time to time for overdue wages. The French placed their hopes on taking Madras, the main British port in southern India. Lally waited until the autumn monsoons of 1759 drove the British fleet from the coast to Bombay, but no support was forthcoming from the French fleet, which had withdrawn to the tranquil safety of distant Ile de France after having lost an encounter to the British. In December 1759, Lally's 750 troops attacked Madras. A two-month French siege resulted in the city's walls being breached. However, on what the French hoped would be the siege's last day, a British naval squadron and a thousand troops arrived and saved Madras.

The French defeat at Madras effectively ended the Indian war. After that, it was only a matter of time before France left India. English control of the seas, a lack of French troops, and the chaotic state of the French holdings left France hopelessly vulnerable. The inept Lally was returned to France and, after a controversial trial, was beheaded.

The French surrendered on January 16, 1761, at Pondicherry, and the British took the remaining French lands; there was no more French India. Several French commercial ports were restored on the Coromandel and Malabar coasts and in Bengal, as part of the settlement ending the Seven Years' War in 1763, but the unsuccessful French trading company was abolished in 1769. A handful of French adventurers remained in India, roaming about the peninsula, trying to make quick fortunes, encouraging a native prince here, training local forces there, and looking toward the never-to-be-realized goal of restoring French India.

WEST INDIES

By 1700 a division of interests was reached between the British and the French in the West Indies which would hold, with few exceptions, throughout the next century. England and France were now the region's two principal European powers. The Dutch remained important as traders but retained only a few scattered posts. Spain, once the region's greatest power, was now on the defensive, with Cuba and Puerto Rico being the twin centers of its diminished power. Spain's presence was otherwise concentrated on the Central and South American mainland.

The West Indies became part of Europe's global wars. Island colonies contributed vast wealth to England and France, but they were scattered, poorly defended, and easy prey to invading fleets or corsairs. The main French possession was Saint-Domingue, the western portion of the island of Hispaniola, settled by France by the 1660s, and often called "the pearl of the Antilles" or "the Eden of the western world." In the Lesser Antilles, the French held Martinique and Guadeloupe. It was not long, however, before the large plantations on Saint-Domingue, which employed slaves and indentured servants, quickly surpassed the small plantations elsewhere in numbers and importance, and Saint-Domingue became the most important island in the West Indies. A fertile tropical setting of 7 thousand plantations, it accounted for 40% of France's foreign trade, and it was the source of two-fifths of the world's sugar production and over half of the world's coffee.[28] In addition, Saint-Domingue accounted for two-thirds of all French exports from the West Indies, a figure surpassing the combined exports of neighboring British and Spanish possessions. According to Herbert S. Klein, "In any one year, well over 600 vessels visited the ports of the island to carry its sugar, coffee, cotton, indigo, and cacao to European consumers."[29]

Such production volumes were only possible because of massive slave labor. "In the 1780s the slave population of Saint-Domingue almost doubled and slave imports averaged 30 thousand per annum in the last years of the decade."[30] This

French possession also held the largest slave population in the West Indies, approximately 460 thousand persons, roughly half the million slaves then being held in this region.

The British, meanwhile, concentrated on Jamaica, captured from Spain in 1655, and in the Lesser Antilles they held Barbados, Antigua, Nevis, and Montserrat. France and Britain divided Saint Kitts, but only until 1703. In 1713 it permanently transferred to Britain. A few other medium-sized islands were unclaimed or in dispute, and hundreds of smaller islands were rarely if ever visited, except by pirates, wandering traders, or ships driven ashore by storms.[31]

Initially, the French came to the Caribbean to raise tobacco, which remained an important export until the 1680s, followed by coffee, and later sugar, which would become the most important of all export crops. Smoking pipes and taking snuff became popular among men in Europe, and the tobacco market spread. Coffee was introduced into Europe in 1644 from Arabia by merchants from Venice and Marsailles. It, too, swept Europe, commanding high prices and transforming social life. Johann Sebastian Bach wrote a *Coffee Cantata*; coffeehouses became gathering places for representatives of different social and economic groups; and fashionable salons served coffee to visiting guests. By 1767 more than 6 million coffee trees had been planted in Martinique and almost as many in Guadeloupe. After 1765 coffee production increased sixfold on Saint-Domingue.

French commerce was additionally favored by the French islands never becoming committed to a monoculture. While sugar emerged as the primary crop, coffee, cotton, and indigo were also important to the French economy. In addition to table and confectionery sugar, the ground cane was used to make rum, molasses, and eau-de-vie, a clear brandy, the production of which was restricted to the *métropole* by Jean-Baptiste Colbert's decree. France had favorable, well-situated land, and the number of French plantations and mills outstripped the British, and the land area the French had under cultivation was double that of the British.[32] Over 100 sugar mills were functioning in Martinique by 1717, 450 by 1740 when the population was estimated at 11,450 whites, 14 thousand free mulattos, and 117,400 slaves. The number of slaves rose steadily on Guadeloupe from 33,903 in 1738 to 91,545 in 1789. By 1789 the population of Saint-Domingue had risen to an estimated 30,826 whites, 27,548 free mulattos, and 465,429 slaves—two-thirds of the French Overseas Empire's slave population. A typical plantation might be 750 square acres in size, and according to Philip Curtin, in a study of slave numbers, "the typical Caribbean sugar plantation had a force of at least 50 slaves—more often 200 or even 300."[33]

Sugar production was a labor-intensive process. The sugar mills required constant maintenance, and slaves quickly became supervisors, coopers, carpenters, masons, and iron workers; other worked as house servants, gardeners, or nurses in the plantation infirmary.[34] Ground had to be cleared and thousands of stalks planted, then cut 12 to 15 months later and the land rotated every three or four years. Cane was hacked down in the field, pulled by animal-driven carts to nearby mills, and ground between rollers turned by oxen or mules. The juice was then boiled in large kettles and became sugar crystals, most of which were shipped to France for refinement, except from Martinique where stubborn planters held out against Colbert. The king's leading minister forbade colonial refineries from completing the final steps in sugar production since he did not want France's overseas possessions to be independent commercial entities competing with the motherland, or to disturb the profitable monopolies of coastal trading houses.

Slaves quickly replaced indentured servants of an earlier era. While slaves cost more initially, they were the planter's possessions for life, and their children belonged to the master as well. A premium was paid by the French government for each slave transported to the New World, and merchants of France's coastal cities were strong supporters of slavery. Abandoning "the Guinea trade," they argued, would cause the loss of all colonial commerce and, even if France outlawed slavery, other countries would move quickly to transport human cargoes from Africa to the West Indies.[35]

THE TRIANGULAR TRADE

The triangular trade—France, Africa, the Antilles, and back—took 15 to 18 months to achieve. It was strongest in its first two links; slave ships rarely returned to Europe with anything approaching full cargoes.[36] The trade began when a slave ship left from one of over ten French ports, the main ones being Nantes, Bordeaux, La Rochelle, and Le Havre. The trade was mostly in the hands of family businesses, since commercial banking was undeveloped in the 18th century. First the ships—3 thousand of them in the 18th century—headed for the West African coast, generally between the Bight of Benin and the Angolan coast, where Africans sold other Africans into slavery with the complicity of local rulers who profited from the trade and in return received woven cloth, trinkets, weapons, and alcohol. If, in the 1680s, a young Gambian male slave was sold for more than five pounds' worth of European goods, that price could have purchased 17 muskets, 200 liters of brandy, or 349 kilograms of wrought iron.[37] Slaves were bought individually after being carefully inspected and, when the boat was tightly loaded, the two-month voyage to the Caribbean began.

The longer the voyage, the higher was the mortality rate among slaves and crew. Usually it was in the 13–15 percent range, but it could go as high as 50% to 75% on longer, more demanding crossings. Ships were small, originally less than 100 tons capacity, 65 feet keel length, 19 feet amidships, 10 feet draft. They were closely packed and sparsely furnished, except for the captain's quarters. Slaves were given water three times a day and two meals a day of rice and beans; crews received hardtack biscuit, salted fish or meat, and wine. Only the major officers ate more varied fare.

The most traumatic moment for the slaves was the time of departure from shore; this was when revolts took place, or protestations were made. A late 17th century French writer observed:

It should be said that the moment one had completed one's trade and loaded the Negroes on the ship, one must set sail. The reason for this is that the slaves have such a great love for their land that they despair to see that they are leaving it forever, and they die from sadness. I have heard merchants who participate in this commerce affirm that more Negroes die before leaving port than during the voyage. Some throw themselves into the sea and others knock their heads against the ship; some hold their breath until they suffocate and others starve themselves.[38]

During the 1730s, the so-called golden age of Saint-Domingue, 374 ships reached the island within seven years, bringing 16 thousand slaves annually, or 110 thousand from 1737 to 1743. Robert Louis Stein, in *The French Slave Trade in the Eighteenth Century*, estimates that from 1737 to 1783 the French sent out approximately 55 slave ships a year, after which the number doubled until the French Revolution.[39] Curtin, in his pioneering 1969 work, *The Atlantic Slave Trade, a Census*, estimates that 1,349,000 slaves were imported into French colonies between 1701 and 1810; 838 thousand arrived on French ships, and the remaining 511 thousand came on British, Dutch, Danish, or North American ships.[40] David Eltis, in *Economic Growth and the Ending of the Transatlantic Slave Trade*, estimates the number of slave arrivals in the Americas between 1781 and 1867 at 23% greater than the numbers used by Curtin. For the period from 1781 to 1800, Eltis calculates the number of slave imports into Saint-Domingue at 384 thousand, and elsewhere in the French Americas, 55 thousand.[41]

THE PROFITABLE RETURN

Of the voyage's end, Stein wrote of one ship, "With one-sixth of its crew dead, with its hold half-empty and with major damage to its structure, it limped into port more a survivor than a conqueror, yet each little vessel which completed the triangle represented a triumph for French business."[42] Profits could be high but risks were real. A French slaver might purchase a slave for 300 *livres* on the African coast and sell him or her for over 600 *livres* in the Antilles, realizing a profit of 100% or more if the ship returned to France loaded with sugar or coffee. However, accurate figures are hard to come by, and Klein's research suggests that profits in the 10% range were more common, as African slave traders were skilled bargainers in human flesh, and island planters were notoriously slow to pay.[43] Also, ships were costly to outfit, slaves died on the Middle Passage cutting profitability, and it was a buyer's market on arrival, for few planters had ready cash and most tried to extend payment terms over several years and even then often reneged on debts.

The value of the two-way trade between France and the West Indies increased steadily from 1784 to 1789. France exported 193 million *livres* worth of products to the islands, an almost 100% increase over the 1762–1776 period. It imported 93,056,000 *livres'* worth of goods, largely sugar, from the islands. In addition to sugar, a lucrative provisioning industry attracted merchants from France.[44]

As they returned home, some planters brought slaves with them, and by 1770 there may have been as many as 4 or 5 thousand such persons in France. Since French law decreed that slaves became free once they touched French soil, many slaves thus gained their freedom, but others had to sue for their liberty, and in some port cities a specialized bar developed to handle such cases. In the 1770s restrictive laws were passed to keep slaves out of France. Interracial marriage was barred, blacks were required to carry identity cards, and those who violated the laws would be returned to the colonies at their owner's expense.[45]

CONTROL BY THE MÉTROPOLE

To control the island trade, the French employed a familiar set of decrees: only France could purchase the island's exports, and only French ships could provision the planters. This position was clearly enunciated in a 1765 set of instructions to the governor of Martinique:

It would be a mistake to consider the colonies as provinces of France merely separated by the sea. They are in reality nothing but commercial establishments. . . . Indeed, the administration of this kingdom strives to use their advantages exclusively for the nation . . . and this is the sole object of their establishment, and they should by all means be abandoned if they cease to fulfill it.[46]

Foreign trade with other countries was specifically prohibited but, as happened elsewhere, France could not maintain exclusive control; the irregularity of French shipping and the growing market in British North America worked against it. Moreover, animosities grew between French merchants and the *métropole* over the control of prices and shipping. Planters could buy and ship cheaply with the Dutch and British, whose ships arrived regularly and whose trading goods were often better than the French could offer. Planters resented France's ban on exporting sugar syrup, molasses, and rum to their homeland, where its importation was forbidden to avoid competition with French brandies. The island planters made repeated arguments that restrictive trade practices harmed rather than helped build French commerce. According to one observer of the period,

It is, indeed more strictly true to say that Bordeaux, Nantes, Le Havre, are more effectively made by the colonies than to say that the colonies are made by the *métropole*. . . . Who, then, ought to be listened to, the colonists or the merchants? Surely the colonists. . . . It ought to suffice to point out that the merchants have mercilessly exploited the colonies and never supplied their needs . . . the colonies ought to be liberated from ruinous explotation and turned over to their own management.[47]

Unable or unwilling to assert their independence, the island settlers solved the problem by engaging in widespread illicit trading, especially with British North America.

LIFE IN THE ISLANDS: "AU PIED DU VÉSUVE"

Social conditions in the islands were complex and problem-ridden. Despite the obvious drawbacks of isolation and limited resources, attempts at cultural life were launched by the French planters, and the African slaves brought their music, dances, and languages as well. The first balloon ascent in the Americas took place in Saint-Domingue in 1784, and during that time at least eight towns had live theaters; the one in Le Cap seated 1,500 people in segregated space. More than twenty Freemasons' lodges existed and there were several literary and scientific clubs. Port-au-Prince had an eleven-person orchestra, and in 1784 Beaumarchais's *The Marriage of Figero* was performed in Saint-Domingue, shortly after its first performance in Paris.[48]

Beneath the surface, however, the scene was an admixture of unrest and boredom, petty jealousies among planters with long periods to stew over them, dependence on slaves yet always a deep fear or suspicion of them. Only 7% of Saint-Domingue's population was white. The Comte de Mirabeau correctly saw white society, greatly outnumbered by others, as being "*au pied du Vésuve.*"[49] Among the French were a handful of government administrators sent from France who quickly established their superiority in relation to the planters. Next were the principal white planters, who lived on vast estates, sometimes entertaining one another lavishly, both as a way of displaying wealth and as a way of warding off the boredom that infected their lives. One planter wrote that "the pleasures of Saint-Domingue are easily counted, a blue sky, and no cold weather. I can name no others." The quarrelsome nature of planter life made for rivalries, jealousies, and bloody arguments about the trespass of slaves and cattle. A contemporary traveler wrote, "You must not be surprised that each owl nests in his hole, and that so little sociability reigns among men who have few or no social qualities."

Initially, plantation homes were of simple construction, designed to take maximum advantage of breezes. Toward the century's end buildings became more elaborate, with facades and trimmings imported from France. A school of local carpentry developed, designed to copy French furniture, but using heavy local woods and without the gilding characteristic of French cabinetry. Many of the most substantial dwellings soon gave the impression of neglect and decay. French cloth mildewed quickly in the tropics, metal rusted in sea air, and insects devoured books and manuscripts. A traveler to the island wrote about coming upon "an elegant carriage drawn by horses or mules of different colors and sizes, with rope for traces, covered with the most filthy of housings, and driven by a postilion bedaubed with gold, and barefoot."[50]

Wealthy planters and their families often came, not from the sea front adventurer class, or landless peasantry induced to go overseas, but from the minor aristocracy who sought to leave the unsettled France of Louis XIV. The island's important offices were held by the planters who returned to France when

they could, and lived ostentatiously if sometimes precariously, fending off merchant creditors and shippers. Many planters did not like living in the islands,
and they returned to France when their fortunes were made, visiting the islands
only when necessary. Initially, the planters worked alongside their indentured
servants and slaves, walking barefoot, and planting sugar cane and coffee trees,
but as their fortunes grew, their lifestyles changed. Instead of dining on wild
boar and bananas, their tables were now set with burgundy and champagne
imported from France, and planters who once ventured out in the noonday sun
now waited on the verandah for sundown and a carriage with comfortable
springs. Planters were surrounded by household slaves, several to wait table,
including "such numbers of waiting-men as cut off the very air," boudoir slaves
to help the owners' wives prepare their coiffure or toilet, and one or two slaves
for each child.

Next in the social order came a class of *petits-blancs*, holders of small estates,
artisans, and shopkeepers, who were resentful of both the wealthy planters and
the slaves and mulattos about them. These planters could afford few slaves and
often had to rely on the work of indentured servants, at least during the first
half-century. Their existence was more precarious than that of the larger planters,
for they had few reserves, and in times of warfare or economic crisis, they were
extremely vulnerable. The instability of their own positions exacerbated the
depths of their resentment of more privileged whites and successful coloreds
and free black people.

Sexual liaisons, at least among the planters and women slaves, were commonplace. A large class of mulattos or colonial-born French and free blacks
soon developed. Unmarried Frenchmen often moved between concubines, who
might greet one another as *matelot*, a buccaneer expression for "mate." Some
married planters kept mulatto concubines in town and passed their idle hours
with their women and a bowl of rum. These women held the island's equivalent
of salons and balls and were the centerpieces of social life. A 1774 census
showed 5 thousand out of 7 thousand free colored women were living as mis-
tresses to white planters or officials. Eventually many of the mulattos were freed
and founded farms of their own. Some became quite wealthy. Forced into the
uplands, they benefited from the coffee plantations that flourished there, but they
had no possibilities of participating directly in governing the islands until the
French Revolution. By the end of the 18th century there were many such free
colored people three or four generations removed from slavery. Many of the
freed slaves had their own plantations or small farms and, by the 1790s, may
have owned a quarter of the colony's plantations and a similar proportion of its
slaves.[51]

SLAVES

The most numerous class of people in the islands were the thousands of
slaves, field slaves and a growing number of household slaves, who were taught

to read, write, keep accounts, and act as overseers, or, in the case of women, who virtually ran the home and brought up the planters' children. In the 1780s, "While the whites and free coloreds each numbered under 40 thousand, the slave population, swelling with imported Blacks, totaled something like 500 thousand."[52] The slaves were imported in crowded ships from Africa and had no prospect of attaining freedom for themselves or for their children. Life expectancy after arrival on the islands has been estimated at seven years. To the shock of separation and dislocation from families must be added the ravages of yellow fever and malaria, as well as hard work with an inadequate or unfamiliar diet in a difficult climate. The slaves were treated cruelly, equally so by whites and their African overseers, and in 1791 they violently revolted and laid waste to most of the northern plantations. Accounts of rapes by slaves, gutted children, boiling oil being poured in ears, and captured blacks being broken on the wheel were commonplace during this time of carnage.[53]

For slaves, the day began at five o'clock when the *commandeur*, the head slave, blew a whistle or cracked a whip, and it continued until sundown, sometimes longer during the season when sugar cane was harvested and had to be processed quickly. Field work generally continued from early morning until eight o'clock, interrupted by a meager breakfast, then work until noon. A two-hour rest period was followed by work until sundown, after which some slaves might be required to feed draft animals or gather firewood before settling down to a simple meal of beans, manioc, and possibly potatoes, rarely with any fish or meat. It was on Sundays and holidays that slaves cultivated their own small gardens, gathered to tell stories, dance, and sing. In commenting on the resilience of the indigenous African culture among the slaves despite the privations of plantation work, Carolyn E. Fick observed that "in addition to the repeated prohibitions against nocturnal gatherings (especially if they included slaves from different plantations), in Saint-Domingue as in all plantation societies throughout the New World, slaves invariably found the energy to dance, and even to travel several miles if necessary for the occasion."[54]

A slave's life was governed, in principal at least, by the 1685 Code Noir. Over 60 articles regulated welfare, punishments, appeals rights, and emancipation, but provisions favorable to the slaves were rarely applied. Masters were prohibited from torturing slaves or dispensing justice on their own, and slaves, in theory, could appeal to the courts against cruel masters, or against being inadequately fed, clothed, or housed. On paper, at least, Creoles and slaves could appeal unjust treatment to the courts, and some Creoles used the judicial process to claim freedom and inheritances of goods and land, but for most persons, especially slaves, access to justice remained only in dreams. Three representative extracts indicate the scope of the Code Noir:

Art. 16. We forbid slaves belonging to different masters to gather together by day or night on pretext of a wedding or anything else either at their masters' residences or elsewhere, and still less on the high roads or in remote places, on pain of corporal punishment not less than whipping or branding; and in case of repeated offenses or more serious circumstances, they may be punished by death, as shall be decided by the judges.

Art. 18. We forbid slaves to sell sugar cane, on any occasion, even with the permission of their masters, on pain of whipping for the slaves, and a fine of ten *livres tournois* for the masters who permit them, and for the purchaser.

Art. 28. We declare that slaves cannot own anything that does not belong to their masters; and anything that is theirs by reason of their labor, or through the liberality of other persons, or for some other reason, under whatever title it may be acquired, is to become the property of their masters, so that the slaves' children, fathers, and mothers, or any relative, whether slave or free, may not claim any share or disposition of it or succession to it; any such dispositions we declare to be null and void, together with any promises and obligations made in that connection, as being the act of persons incapable of disposing or contracting in their own right.[55]

Punishment of captured slaves varied. On one hand, planters did not want to harm good workers. On the other, they did not want the possibilities of revolt to exist. First offenders, or strong workers, might be pardoned or receive a few lashes. A common punishment was keeping the prisoner isolated, with feet held apart between pieces of wood "at the bar." Repeat offenders were chained, given iron collars with spikes, and placed in lightless dungeons. If a slave struck his master and drew blood, the slave could be executed. The theft of horses or cattle was severely punished; the theft of smaller animals or food-stuffs was met with flogging or branding. Fugitives gone a month could have an ear cropped and the fleur-de-lis stamped on a shoulder. Second offenders were branded on another shoulder, and the ligaments were cut at the back of a knee to hamper mobility. The manager of a sugar estate in Saint-Domingue in 1768 wrote;

April 23, 1768. That bad fellow La Trippe—who was a maroon for two years—broke his leg in trying to extricate it from the bar. The only solution was to cut his leg off. He almost died an hour later, by undoing the bandages. Since that time his hands have remained bound, and I have kept him guarded night and day so that he won't die, but will be able to serve as a living example to others.

September 29, 1768 . . . La Trippe . . . seeing that a wooden leg had been fashioned for him so that he might be useful killed himself during the night trying to pull it from the bar.[56]

Many other slaves simply drifted away from plantations, lived in the outskirts for a while, and returned, usually at Christmas or the New Year, sometimes with the parish priest or one of the plantation women who had arranged for a safe return. Slaves were required to be baptized as Catholics and observe Sundays and fast days. They could not marry without their masters' consent. Food was furnished slaves once a week, clothing once a year. Old and ill slaves were their masters' responsibility.

In 1784 there were slight improvements in the slaves' living conditions, and slaves were given Sundays and holidays off and could not work before daylight or after dark, or between twelve and two. Pregnant women worked only from sunrise to late morning, and again from 3 P.M. to a half-hour before sunset. No slave could be clubbed, mutilated, or executed, and the maximum penalty a slave could receive was 40 lashes. French citizenship could be given to ex-slaves who had bought their freedom or been given it. They could own land, bear arms, own slaves, take up any career, marry, and vote. Some inherited large estates from former masters. Others visited Paris and sent their children to France for schooling. The numbers and influence of the former slaves grew each year. The rich southern region of Jérémie was almost entirely owned or inherited by them by the century's end, and probably they owned between one-third and one-fifth of the land and slaves as well.

MAROONS

Bands of escaped slaves wandering about the mountains were part of the islands' populations. Called maroons, or "wild animals," they raided at night, sacked plantations, waylaid travelers, and robbed up to the outskirts of Port-au-Prince. Some were captured; others died in the forests and were replaced by still other escapees. In 1720 possibly a thousand escaped slaves joined their ranks; in 1751 an estimated 3 thousand such persons lived near the Spanish border. Bands do not appear to have been larger than 100 persons; it would be difficult for larger groups to live off the land. Pursuit of fugitives by plantation owners was not easy: the plantation owners were greatly outnumbered, troops were few, the terrain was difficult, and when hunted the fugitives could withdraw increasingly into the densely forested interior. Maroons often lived on the plantations' margins, raiding, not the houses, but crops and cattle, and capturing women slaves. A symbiotic union sometimes was formed between maroons and plantation slaves; the maroons traded fish, game, and stolen objects for plantation-grown manioc, peas, and vegetables. A live-and-let-live attitude often prevailed between plantation owners and fugitives, unless the bands grew large or violent. Bounties were offered for their capture, as high as several hundred pounds of sugar, and sometimes slaves took advantage of the bounties to turn in a maroon.

It is difficult to imagine a more volatile social setting than the one that existed in the sugar islands at this time. All participants were relative newcomers to the land. Tensions were rife, large plantation owners had ample time to brood, small white planters were insecure, mulattos were caught between two worlds, and slaves were angry and oppressed. Compounding tensions, the colony's council passed an ordinance in Saint-Domingue designed to humiliate non-whites, prohibiting them from carrying side arms, swords, and sabers, as symbolic of non-slave status as they were as weapons. Subsequent legislation said non-whites must be indoors by 9 P.M., must not sit in the same section of public gatherings as whites, and must wear clothing of different material and cut than that worn by the whites. Non-whites could not become doctors, lawyers, jewelers, or pharmacists, and they were banned from holding public office. But in 1788, when some slaves who had been subjected to torture by Le Jeune, a coffee planter, appealed to the courts, word of their case spread among the slaves and planters and to France, and Le Jeune was acquitted "for the safety of the colony." In 1778 marriage between the races was forbidden. These increasingly humiliating decrees came at a time when some blacks in the sugar islands were gaining educations and modest economic means. Denying them access to fuller life in local society, even proscribing what they could or could not wear, came at a time when the debate over the rights of persons was broadening in France; in the islands, no resolution of the problem short of violence appeared possible.[57]

THE FRENCH REVOLUTION OVERSEAS

In addition to the upheaval it caused in Europe, the French Revolution quickened the demise of France's 18th century overseas empire.[58] First, it must be said that overseas questions were only of sporadic interest in the revolutionary debates. Only 360 of the more than 50 thousand remaining *cahiers*, the ledgers into which the French inscribed their grievances, raised colonial questions, and these were largely petitions on trading issues, such as the large mercantile and coastal towns wanting to keep foreign competitors out of colonies. On the crucial question of slavery, contrasting views emerged. Arguments about the inhumanity of slavery were voiced, urging either its immediate or gradual abolition. The opposite view held that France's economic health depended on its colonies and, while there were unfortunate aspects to slavery, France would be seriously disrupted by its sudden abolition. The latter position acknowledged slavery's evils but argued the need for a transitional period leading to its abolition. The anti-slavery view was summarized by the Third Estate of Ameins, which called the slave trade "the cause of the most atrocious crimes," adding, "a man cannot, under any title, become the property of another man . . . justice and humanity alike cry out against slavery." Realizing that "a reform of this nature cannot be the work of one day," and that colonies must prosper and the colonists' interests be safeguarded, it charged the deputies "to consider the most suitable means of diminishing the slave trade and of preparing for the abolition of slavery."[59]

Early in the National Assembly's history, two groups formed in support of the two principal opposing viewpoints. Opponents included the Société des Amis des Noirs (1788), whose membership included such well-known figures as the Marquis de Condorcet, Mirabeau, and Robespierre. The Amis, founded with help from British Quakers, never caught hold in France the way comparable abolitionist and emancipation groups did in Great Britain. The Amis had to battle public indifference and a hostile political climate aided by French suspicions that they represented a British attempt to cost France its island colonies and stir up dissension at home. The poorly organized Amis were pitted against the politically powerful and well-financed coastal traders, planters, and urban chambers of commerce, who argued that sugar and coffee represented nearly half of France's annual exports to Europe in the 1780s.

Traditional planters' interests, slave traders, and colonial officials were represented in Paris by the Colonial Committee of the Rue de Provence and the Club of the Hôtel Massiac, two informal coalitions named for the places where the members met. The historian and jurist Moreau de Saint-Mèry, a deputy from Martinique, articulated the sugar planters' viewpoint. The planter bloc elected six deputies to the Paris assembly. Later it increased the number of deputies to 32, 18 of them came from Saint-Domingue.

The issue of who should represent the islands was a complex one. If all persons were created equal, as revolutionary proclamations had it, then should not slaves and mulattos, as well as whites, sit in the legislative body? The Assembly evaded the issue by stating that the islands did not come under the new constitution with its majestic declaration of human rights but remained, instead, overseas possessions, part of the empire. As a compromise, it allowed for individual island assemblies, with the assumption that mulattos would find political expression there. But what the French thought was a compromise triggered open revolt among the people it excluded. Local assemblies formed in Saint-Marc disavowed the French Assembly's work and began legislating on its own. The French called out troops, and violent disorders flared up in the islands.

A subsequent decree giving civic rights to men of property regardless of color angered the disenfranchised because it did not include all their numbers, and it equally enraged the planters, who did not want to see rights extended. They refused to enact it. In two towns, petitioners requesting political rights for free persons of color were killed, and others who raised the issue were threatened. Vague or contradictory news from France exacerbated the situation, and the slave community began to formulate its own ideas about what constituted freedom. Sailors on merchant ships or newly arrived soldiers from France carried news of events at home, and word of a 1789 slave uprising in Martinique spread as well. Revolution was in the air. Meanwhile, after Louis XVI's execution in February 1793, the planters placed Martinique and Guadeloupe under English rule until a new monarch could take the throne. (The British had been a presence in Guadeloupe, which they had captured in 1759 and held for four years. It was seized again in 1794, but this time the British were driven out by Victor Hugues, the French Republican administrator, aided by slaves liberated for that purpose.)

A decree of general emancipation was passed by the Convention on February 4, 1794. The Declaration of Rights, part of the Constitution of 1794, affirmed, "Any man may pledge his time and his services, but he cannot sell himself or be sold; his person is not alienable property," but the declaration was only a statement on paper, and it was revoked within eight years.

Rebellion and violence were now widespread in the islands. The white planters wanted to hold on to their lands and retain enough slaves to make them agriculturally productive; the mulattos had to bear the intolerable frustration of being caught between the rhetoric of freedom they heard from Paris and their actual limited possibilities; and the slaves bitterly realized the hopelessness of their situation. Although the early black revolts occurred within the context of the white-mulatto struggle, by 1791 the whites and mulattos had lost control of the revolt and a general conflagration ensued. The 1791 revolt was widespread among the black slaves, the most numerous group, and one with no prospects of incorporation into island political life. Reprisals by white planters were swift and savage. Slaves were hanged, burned, or broken on the wheel. By October 1791 more than a thousand whites had been killed in riots in Saint-Domingue, and over 200 sugar and 1,200 coffee plantations had been burned, including most of those along the fertile northern coast. Crops had been devastated, leaving both slaves and planters hungry. Many planters left for Louisiana at this time. The English moved quickly into the disturbed islands, supported separatist movements, and hindered French commerce. They held part of Saint-Domingue from 1793 to 1798, often supported by local French planters.

Although slavery had been formally abolished in 1794, it was reinstituted by Napoléon in 1802 and not finally abolished until the Revolution of 1848 when the last parliamentary battle was fought between colonial interests and the abolitionists led by the pamphleteer-journalist Victor Schoelcher (1804–1893), who had made a trip to the Antilles and became undersecretary for colonies in 1848. As a way of replacing slavery, French planters devised a system of "engagements" whereby blacks were contracted for seven to 14 years at low wages. In this way, 10 to 15 thousand blacks were sent to the Antilles in the 1850s and 1860s, but their numbers never approached anything like those in the heyday of the slave traffic, and by now Antilles sugar had largely been replaced by the production of sugar beets in France, an agricultural scheme Napoléon had devised to reduce France's dependency on imported sugar.

THE FRENCH LEAVE SAINT-DOMINGUE

France, occupied with internal disruptions and Continental wars, in the face of a British invasion, named Toussaint Louverture, a black ex-slave, as colonel and commander of the French forces in Saint-Domingue in May 1794. Louverture rallied the black slaves, something a French commander could not do. Well-organized and a superb tactician, he and 4 thousand followers defeated the British in 1798. He took things into his own hands, named himself governor for life, seized the island, and in 1801 promulgated a local constitution. Torn by revolution at home, the French had no forces to restrain him. In January 1802 Napoléon sought to end the warfare by naming his brother-in-law, General Victor-Emmanuel Leclerc, to head a large force designated to bring order to the decade-long chaos in Saint-Domingue. Leclerc was instructed to occupy the coastal towns quickly, wipe out resistance, and take control of the former colony.

Napoléon also told him that all slaves should be returned to their masters. However, after prolonged fighting and heavy losses on both sides, the French struck a deal with Louverture, after which the slave leader retired to his estate. Duped by the French, he was seized and taken to France where he died in a dungeon. Another black leader, Jean-Jacques Dessalines (1758–1806), continued the war against France.[60]

The arrival of French troops on the island coincided with a yellow fever epidemic which decimated the newly arrived forces, and France never regained a military initiative in the West Indies. In fact, only 10 thousand of the 59 thousand troops sent to the island between 1791 and 1803 made it back to France in good health; the rest died, mostly of yellow fever. In September 1803 Leclerc wrote to Bonaparte that the French position was desperate. Soldiers carted their dead to lime pits outside the principal towns. "Since I have been here I have seen nothing but incendiarism, insurrections, deaths and dying; my spirit is exhausted," Leclerc wrote, and his subsequent letters were a plea for additional troops. He died that November.[61] The remaining French troops surrendered to the English, who had backed the former slaves, and were sent home to France. The Republic of Haiti was proclaimed on January 1, 1804.

As conditions in the West Indies grew more unsettled, sentiment in France increased for abandoning the island colonies for possessions closer to home where profitable tropical crops might be grown. Charles-Maurice de Talleyrand (1754–1838), France's future foreign minister, had been an émigré in England and America from 1792 to 1796, where he met many refugees from the sugar islands. Talleyrand wanted to establish new tropical colonies in Egypt and West Africa. In a new departure for France, he argued that colonies should be made attractive for political refugees and "restless men who need projects and unfortunate men who need help," but he avoided allowing potential religious and political dissenters to gather in overseas possessions, as they did in some of the British North American colonies. No specific program of colonization followed Talleyrand's appeal. Saint-Domingue was lost, Louisiana would soon be sold, and the once-widespread French presence in the Americas was reduced to a few small islands.

THE WORLD THE WRITERS SAW: "WARRING OVER A FEW ACRES OF SNOW IN CANADA"

Most major writers of this period made only passing comments on slavery or colonial questions, and even these were from a distinctly *métropole* viewpoint. Writers gathered their information from Paris literary salons, which reflected a society increasingly disillusioned with the ancien régime's excesses.

As many as 130 titles of works about life in China, Turkey, Persia, and—to a lesser extent—the Americas may have been published in 18th century France as essays, novels, comedies, and tragedies. Averaged across the century, less than ten titles a year were published on Oriental themes, and most of them used the overseas world as subject matter to provide a setting for hoped-for reforms in French life. Between 1704 and 1717, the *Thousand and One Nights* appeared in French translation and French writers adapted this form, combining a short tale, travel narratives, satire, or mythical travel accounts. These Oriental tales were employed widely in the first half-century, when censorship was most widespread in France, but when it was relaxed in the century's final decades there was a corresponding decline in the publication of such literature, since it was no longer necessary to convey images of distant countries. Native North Americans who were brought to France appear to have had fairly miserable times. Little effort was made to ascertain exact information about the societies from which they emerged.

Most "overseas" works were blank screens onto which authors projected hoped-for political, economic, and social reforms. The veneer of exotic decor was thin: the shah closely resembled the French monarch, the Persian court was the French court, the imams and fakirs were the Catholic clergy, viziers were ministers, and the presumably Persian issues they discussed differed little from conversation in French salons. The most successful use of the Oriental tale was Montesquieu's (1685–1755) *Persian Letters* (1721). Of noble birth, trained as a jurist, moderate and conciliatory in outlook, Montesquieu delivered his criticisms in mordant satires on French life. His interlocutors were two Persians, Usbek and Rica, who visited France from 1712 to 1720 and, through letters, brought news of Persia and conveyed their impressions of France. French manners and institutions were criticized, as were kings and popes. Montesquieu opposed despotism and suggested a form of utopian government based on reason and equity. No friend of the colonies, he wrote, "The ordinary effect of sending out colonists is to weaken the country from whence they are drawn without populating the lands to which they are sent."[62] He believed climates were responsible for human behavior and suggested that slaves became slaves because of living in a hot climate which weakened their resistance and courage.

However, Montesquieu's interest was not in the overseas world, but in France, and his Orientals were never more than *philosophes* with turbans. He did oppose slavery in general, but he defended it on the West Indies plantations because sugar would be too costly if not cultivated by slaves. Montesquieu mirrored French attitudes in a biting satire which said Africans lacked judgment because they valued a glass necklace over a gold one and "one can hardly conceive that God, who is a very wise being, can have placed a soul, especially a good soul, in a body entirely black . . . small spirits exaggerate too much the injustice done to Africans." His disjointed, elliptical comments on slavery were often delivered as epigrams extolling liberty while defending colonies as economically advantageous to France.[63]

Voltaire (1694–1778) was another major French author who commented on the overseas world, and, as with Montesquieu, the results were mixed. He made some barbed observations about slavery, but his opposition to it was limited to a few ironic observations. Voltaire believed Africans had lower intelligence than

Europeans, and said that slavery existed because blacks sold other blacks into bondage. In *Candide* (1759), which went through 50 editions before the French Revolution, Voltaire described coming upon a mutilated slave in Dutch Guyana, who lacked both a left leg and a right hand. The slave says, "When we are working in the sugar refineries and a finger is lost in the mill, the whole hand is cut off—I have suffered from both these practices. This is the price paid for the sugar you eat in Europe."[64]

A constant critic of the French presence in New France, Voltaire discussed the French-British conflict in New France, "I am like the public, I much prefer peace to Canada and I believe that France could perhaps be happy without Québec."[65] In contrast, Voltaire admired Louisiana, where he had visions of rich cocoa, tobacco, and indigo plantations set in a temperate climate. In his *Essai sur les moeurs* (1756), he stated a preference for Louisiana with "the best climate on earth, in which one can grow tobacco, silk, indigo, a thousand foodstuffs, and make once more advantageous trade with Mexico." As a grace note he added, "If I was young, and in good health, and had not built Ferney, I would establish myself in Louisiana."[66] Coffee and sugar were available in Europe, the author said, because, "We have depopulated America in order to get a land to grow them; we have depopulated Africa in order to get a people to cultivate them." He added, "Those bright-colored garments in which our ladies dress themselves . . . the sugar, coffee, and chocolate used at breakfast, the rouge with which they relieve their pallor; all this the backs of unhappy blacks have prepared for them."[67]

Opposition to slavery grew during this century. Typical of those expressing such sentiment was Bernardin Saint-Pierre, whose *Paul et Virginie* (1788), a tropical romance, was widely read in France. The clearest, most comprehensive antislavery statement came in the *Encyclopédie*, a 17-volume compendium of human knowledge and rational thought edited by Denis Diderot (1713–1784), a *philosophe*, and Jean d'Alembert (1717–1783), a mathematician, who wrote in 1765:

Thus there is not a single one of these hapless souls—who, we maintain, are but slaves— who does not have the right to be declared free, since he has never lost his freedom; since it was impossible for him to lose it; and since neither his ruler nor his father nor anyone else had the right to dispose of his freedom; consequently, the sale of his person is null and void in and of itself: this Negro does not divest himself, indeed cannot under any condition divest himself of his natural rights; he carries them everywhere with him, and he has the right to demand that others allow him to enjoy those rights. Therefore, it is a clear case of inhumanity on the part of the judges in those free countries to which the slave is shipped, not to free the slave instantly by legal declaration, since he is their brother, having a soul like theirs.[68]

AMERICA

A growing body of French literature of the second half-century dealt with America and, like the accounts of China, contained two basically contradictory viewpoints depending on the writer's interests. In one, the land and its inhabitants were physically and mentally inferior to Europe; in the other, America represented a new golden age, a second Syracuse, or a new Athens. Apologists for these two positions were unaware of the opposing viewpoint and never factored it into their own arguments.[69]

Human society will degenerate in America, and the children born there will be physically and intellectually inferior to their European ancestors, suggested Cornelius De Pauw, a Dutch writer widely read in France, in 1768, because the climate of the New World was unfavorable to all forms of life. This long-established idea of geography and climate influencing behavior was popularized in France by Montesquieu in *Esprit des lois* (1748); Diderot gave it space in the *Encyclopédie*. De Pauw's ideas were widely diffused by the *abbé* Thomas Guillaume Raynal in 1772 in one of the century's most influential works, *L'Histoire philosophique et politique des établissements et du commerce des Européens dans les deux Indes*, a comprehensive and condemnatory theory of empire. The book was first published in Amsterdam, which suggests its content was more controversial than what the censorious ancien régime would allow, and it went through 30 editions within a decade. Raynal's canvas was vast—nothing less than a comparison of all of Europe's empires: the established ones of Spain, England, and France; the Dutch and Portuguese examples; and even Prussian and Russian attempts at expansion. The work is thus, on one hand, supportive of French commercial and civilizing efforts, yet condemnatory of colonies for what they did to both the colonizer and the colonized. Two centuries later, such writers as Frantz Fanon and Albert Memmi would make similar arguments.

Raynal's book was a popular success and, following the custom of the time, was reprinted with additional essays, the most celebrated of which, by Diderot, in the final edition (1780, Geneva), considerably surpassed the cautious Raynal in condemning colonialism. According to Diderot, *philosophe* and editor of the *Encyclopédie*, the decline began when the prospective settlers made the decision to migrate in the first place. Abandonment of the civic center, its values, culture, and social identity was the first step toward decline and disintegration. The move abroad was to territory East of Eden. "The greater the distance from the capital," Diderot wrote, "the further the mask of the traveler's identity slips from his face. On the frontier it falls away altogether. . . . Once past the equator, a man is neither English, nor Dutch, nor French. . . . All that he preserves of his homeland are the principles and prejudices which authorize or excuse his conduct."[70]

Diderot, in one of the 18th century's most stinging condemnations of slavery, regarded slavery as the outgrowth of depraved colonial behavior, coming from a climate in which "tyranny, crime, ambition, misery" flourish. Slavery denied the enslaved all hope and left the slaves with the knowledge that, although they were human their humanity would always be denied them, and thus (in his image) they were of little more value than the dogs the Spanish had brought to America.

For Diderot, the forced migrations of so many people destroyed races, depopulated lands, and prejudiced the interest of the oppressors. The destructive act destroyed its perpetrators as well. Finally, the continued presence of slavery left Europeans with a hardness of heart and a lack of compassion which denied them the most important wellsprings of their own civilization. Diderot laid the blame for such racism squarely on the Church. If a biblical explanation were required, the story of Cain and his descendants could provide it. Racism was thus given a scriptural foundation.

The *philosophe* the Marquis de Condorcet (1743–1794) took the argument further, but at the same time, employed the same distinction many contemporaries made between slavery and the slave trade. The slave trade, the massive capture and sale of other human beings, was reprehensible, but slavery was permissible, following the idea from Roman public law that the slave was property and the master had control only over his labor.

In short, Raynal, Diderot, and their contemporaries condemned slavery, but abolishing the institution was a different matter. Their arguments were that the complex, long-established, economically important institution could not be easily dismantled, and they offered no formula for its abolition. It would take revolutionary violence to do that. Thus, Diderot believed that only a "Black Spartacus," whom the Haitians believed to be Toussaint Louverture, was needed to bring about redemptive social change through a violent revolution. Here, again, Fanon and Memmi adopted similar positions in the 1950s during the Algerian crisis.

In contrast to Raynal's negative views of America was the concept of the "noble savage," already extant in earlier travel literature and popularized by Jean-Jacques Rousseau. This concept gained acceptance in the halcyon days of French-American friendship following the American Revolution. Rousseau believed that property, government, and civilization enslaved people, who had previously lived in a blissful state of happiness, well-being, and virtue, of which the life of the American Indian was an example. Voltaire, who otherwise had no time for the colonies, still said in 1734 that a golden age could be found in Pennsylvania. He admired William Penn for purchasing land from the Indians rather than seizing it, and he wrote about a state where native inhabitants and settlers lived peacefully together, where freedom of speech and thought existed, and where the tolerant Quakers lived without priests, rulers, or weapons. As a grace note, Voltaire said he would spend his final days in Pennsylvania were he not subject to violent seasickness.[71] (He made a similar, conditional promise to pass his later years in Louisiana, but remained at home.)

If Penn was popular in France, Benjamin Franklin was accorded celebrity status after the American Revolution. His experiment of drawing electricity down a kite string to a metal key during a storm was hailed as proof of what the new experimental method in the natural sciences might produce. When he arrived in France in 1776, Franklin was greeted by savants and frequenters of salons. *Franklainistes* were numerous among the French and, after the American Revolution, Franklin canes, hats, busts, clocks, and other mementos were widespread. No more skilled propagandist ever worked against the British cause, and no more able public diplomat ever represented America than Franklin, whose works were quickly translated into French, and who embraced Voltaire to the applause of the Academy of Sciences. Franklin spoke of a Philadelphia where workingmen read newspapers at lunch time "and a few good works of philosophy or politics for an hour after dinner." Defenders of the New World were as rhapsodic in their way as the original critics of America, suggesting that "a new Olympus, a new Arcadia, a new Athens, and a new Greece will perhaps give birth on the continent . . . to new Homers."[72]

The period of France's greatest admiration of America was the decade immediately following the American Revolution. Lafayette returned in triumph in 1784, transatlantic trade grew, and many Americans came to live in Paris, including John Paul Jones and the painter John Trumbull. Thomas Jefferson had a wide circle of acquaintances in France and was influential, although never on the scale of Franklin. Between 10 thousand and 25 thousand French royalists and moderates emigrated to America between 1791 and July 1794 when Robespierre was overthrown in the Thermidor counterrevolution. A sharp dropoff in interest in America followed; rhetoric about the second Syracuse disappeared in these violent times. The rude simplicity of the frontier and the boring life of small settlements shocked many French emigrants. What emerged in France in this century was a contradictory and multilayered image of America, depending on the observer and the time. After the French Revolution, there was no longer a need to create verbal utopias to express hoped-for reforms in French society, and the symbol of America as a golden land diminished. In the future, French attitudes continued to reflect two basic viewpoints: that of America as the land of liberty and plenty, and that of America as a new country lacking the maturity and cultural achievement of France.[73]

NOTES

1. Philippe Haudrère, *L'Empire des rois (1500–1789)* (Paris: Denoël, 1997); Howard H. Peckham, *The Colonial Wars, 1689–1762* (Chicago: University of Chicago Press, 1964); Guy Frégault, *Histoire de la Nouvelle-France, le guerre de la conquête, 1754–1760* (Montréal: FIDES, 1975); John Lough, *An Introduction to Eighteenth Century France* (New York: David McKay, 1961); Samuel Eliot Morison, *The Oxford History of the American People* (New York: Oxford University Press, 1965); Frank W. Brecher, *Losing a Continent, France's North American Policy, 1753–1763* (Westport, Conn.: Greenwood Press, 1998).

2. John Demos, *The Unredeemed Captive, a Family Story of Early America* (New York: Random House, Vintage Books, 1995).

3. Richard White, *The Middle Ground, Indians, Empires and Republics in the Great Lakes Region, 1650–1815* (Cambridge: Cambridge University Press, 1997), p. 223.

4. Ibid., p. 224.

5. Peckham, *Colonial Wars*, pp. 97–106, 172; Herbert Ingram Priestly, *France Overseas Through the Old Régime, a Study of European Expansion* (New York: D. Appleton

Century, 1939); John Robert McNeill, *Atlantic Empires of France and Spain, Louisbourg and Havana, 1700–1963* (Chapel Hill: University of North Carolina Press, 1985).

6. Christopher Moore, *Louisbourg Portraits, Life in an Eighteenth-Century Garrison Town* (Toronto: Macmillan, 1982).

7. Peckham, *Colonial Wars*, pp. 185–210; Francis Parkman, *Montcalm and Wolfe: The Decline and Fall of the French Empire in North America* (London: Collier Books, 1969), pp. 489–490; William Bradford Willcox, *Star of Empire, a Study of Britain as a World Power, 1485–1945* (New York: Knopf, 1950).

8. Peckham, *Colonial Wars*, pp. 210–212.

9. D. K. Fieldhouse, *The Colonial Empires from the Eighteenth Century* (New York: Dell Publishing, 1966), pp. 45–49; C.B.A. Behrens, *The Ancien Régime* (New York: Harcourt Brace Jovanovich, 1967), pp. 149–157.

10. James Pritchard, "French Strategy and the American Revolution, a Reappraisal," *U.S. Naval War College Review* 48, no. 4 (Autumn 1994), p. 89.

11. Jonathan R. Dull, *The French Navy and American Independence, a Study of Arms and Diplomacy, 1774–1787* (Princeton, N.J.: Princeton University Press, 1975), pp. 338–344; Claude Manceron, *The Wind from America, 1778–1781*, trans. Nancy Amphoux (New York: Knopf, 1978).

12. Carl J. Ekberg, *French Roots in the Illinois Country: The Mississippi Frontier in Colonial Times* (Chicago: University of Illinois Press, 1998); Alexander de Conde, *This Affair of Louisiana* (Baton Rouge: Louisiana State University Press, 1976); Raphael N. Hamilton, *Marquette's Explorations, the Narratives Reexamined* (Madison: University of Wisconsin Press, 1970).

13. Gail Alexander Buzhardt and Margaret Hawthorne, *Rencontres sur le Mississippi: A French Language Reader of Historical Texts* (Jackson: University of Mississippi Press, 1993), p. 111.

14. Priestly, *France Overseas*, p. 227.

15. Patricia Galloway, *Choctaw Genesis, 1500–1700* (Lincoln: University of Nebraska Press, 1995).

16. Quoted in Ira Berlin, *Many Thousands Gone: The First Two Centuries of Slavery in North America* (Cambridge: Harvard University Press, Belknap Press, 1998), p. 77; Gwendolyn Midlo Hall, *Africans in Colonial Louisiana: The Development of Afro-Creole Culture in the Eighteenth Century* (Baton Rouge: Louisiana State University Press, 1992), p. 14.

17. Daniel H. Usner, Jr., *Indians, Settlers, and Slaves in a Frontier Exchange, the Lower Mississippi Valley Before 1783*, published for the Institute of Early American History and Culture, Williamsburg, Va. (Chapel Hill: University of North Carolina Press, 1992), p. 31.

18. Ibid., p. 45.

19. Ibid.

20. Translation of Patricia Galloway from Simon Le Page du Pratz, *Histoire de la Louisiane*, 1774, vol. 1, Chapter 15, pp. 200–206, collection of the Mississippi Department of Archives and History, in Jim Barnett, *The Natchez Indians* (Natchez: Mississippi Department of Archives and History, 1998), pp. 31–32.

21. De Conde, *This Affair of Louisiana*, pp. 11–14.

22. Berlin, *Many Thousands Gone*, p. 82.

23. E. Wilson Lyon, *Louisiana in French Diplomacy* (Norman: University of Oklahoma Press, 1974 reprint of 1942 edition) pp. 194–207ff.

24. J. H. Parry, *Trade and Dominion, the European Overseas Empires in the Eighteenth Century* (London: Weidenfeld and Nicolson, 1971), pp. 203ff.

25. Quoted in John Dunmore, *French Explorers in the Pacific*, vol. 1, *The Eighteenth Century* (New York: Oxford University Press, 1965), p. 65; E. W. Dahlgren, *Les relations commerciales et maritimes entre La France et les côtes de l'océan pacifique (commencement du XVIIe siècle)* vol. 1. (Paris: Librarie Ancienne Honoré Champion, 1909).

26. Holden Furber, *Rival Empires of Trade in the Orient, 1600–1800*, vol. 2, *Europe and the World in the Age of Expansion* (Minneapolis: University of Minnesota Press, 1976), pp. 203–211; Priestly, *France Overseas*, pp. 170–195; Auguste Toussaint, *History of the Indian Ocean*, trans. June Guicharnau (Chicago: University of Chicago Press, 1961); George Bruce Malleson, *History of the French in India* (London: Longmans, 1868).

27. Priestly, *France Overseas*, pp. 183–186, 194–195.

28. David Patrick Geggus, *Slavery, War, and Revolution: The British Occupation of Saint-Domingue, 1793–1798* (Oxford: Clarendon Press, 1982), pp. 6–7.

29. Herbert S. Klein, *The Atlantic Slave Trade* (Cambridge: Cambridge University Press, 1999), p. 33.

30. David Eltis, *Economic Growth and the Ending of the Transatlantic Slave Trade* (New York: Oxford University Press, 1987), pp. 34, 36.

31. Michel Devèze, *L'Europe et le Monde à la fin du XVIIIe siècle* (Paris: Éditions Albin Michel, 1970), pp. 405–420.

32. Robin Blackburn, *The Making of New World Slavery: From the Baroque to the Modern, 1492–1800* (London: Verso, 1998), p. 432.

33. Philip D. Curtin, *The Tropical Atlantic in the Age of the Slave Trade* (Washington, D.C.: American Historical Association, 1991), p. 7.

34. Gabriel Debien, *Les esclaves aux Antilles Françaises, XVIIe–XVIIIe siècles* (Basse-Terre, Guadeloupe/Fort-de-France, Martinique: Société d'Histoire de la Guadeloupe/Société d'Histoire de la Martinique, 1974), p. 137.

35. David Brion Davis, *The Problem of Slavery in Western Culture* (Ithaca, N.Y.: Cornell University Press, 1970, reprint of 1966 edition); Robert Louis Stein, *The French Slave Trade in the Eighteenth Century, an Old Regime Business* (Madison: University of Wisconsin Press, 1979); Philip D. Curtin, *The Atlantic Slave Trade, a Census* (Madison: University of Wisconsin Press, 1969); Herbert S. Klein, *The Middle Passage, Comparative Studies in the Atlantic Slave Trade* (Princeton, N.J.: Princeton University Press, 1978); Herbert S. Klein, *African Slavery in Latin America and the Caribbean* (New York: Oxford University Press, 1986); David Northrup, ed., *The Atlantic Slave Trade* (Lexington, Mass.: D. C. Heath, 1994); Klein, *The Atlantic Slave Trade*; David Eltis, Stephen D. Behrendt, David Richardson, and Herbert S. Klein, *The Transatlantic Slave Trade, 1562–1867: A Data-base CD-Rom* (New York: Cambridge University Press, 1998).

36. Klein, *Atlantic Slave Trade*, pp. 96–97.

37. Curtin, *Tropical Atlantic*, p. 12.

38. Quoted in Stein, *French Slave Trade*, p. 94, from Jacques Savary, *Le parfait négociant* (Lyon, 1697, 4th ed.), pt. 2, p. 206.

39. Stein, *French Slave Trade*, p. 23.

40. Curtin, *Atlantic Slave Trade*, p. 219; Boubacar Barry, *Senegambia and the Atlantic Slave Trade* (Cambridge: Cambridge University Press, 1998).

41. Eltis, *Economic Growth*, pp. 241–249.

42. Stein, *French Slave Trade*, p. 116.

43. Klein, *Atlantic Slave Trade*, pp. 98–99.

44. Priestly, *France Overseas*, p. 267.

45. Sue Peabody, *"There Are No Slaves in France": The Political Culture of Race and Slavery in the Ancien Régime* (New York: Oxford University Press, 1996).

46. Quoted in Priestly, *France Overseas*, p. 299, from A. Dessales, *Histoire générale des Antilles* (Paris: 1847–1848, V) p. 456.

47. Quoted in Ibid., pp. 298–299, from L. Deschamps, *La question coloniale en France* (Paris, n.d.), p. 316.

48. Blackburn, *Making of New World Slavery*, pp. 450–451; Debien, *Les escalves aux Antilles françaises* (Fort-de-France: Société d'Histoire de la Martinique, 1974); Carolyn E. Fick, *The Making of Haiti: The Saint Domingue Revolution from Below* (Knoxville: University of Tennessee Press, 1990).

49. Quoted in Geggus, *Slavery, War, and Revolution*, p. 1.

50. Quoted in Stephen H. Roberts, *The History of French Colonial Policy, 1870–1925* (Hamden, Conn.: Archon Books, 1963, reprint of 1929 edition) p. 133.

51. Geggus, *Slavery, War, and Revolution*, p. 19.

52. Ibid., p. 23.

53. Gabriel Debien, "Marronage in the French Caribbean," in *Maroon Societies, Rebel Slave Communities in the Americas*, ed. Richard Price (Baltimore: Johns Hopkins University Press, 1979), pp. 107–134; *Études antillaises; XVIIIe siècle* (Paris, Librarie A. Colin, 1956).

54. Fick, *Making of Haiti*, p. 40.

55. Quoted in Geoffrey Symcox, ed., *War, Diplomacy, and Imperialism, 1618–1763* (New York: Walker, 1974), pp. 312–333, from M-L. Moreau de Saint-Méry, *Lois et constitutions des colonies françoises de l'Amérique sous-le-vent*, 5 vols. (Paris, 1785), vol. 1, pp. 414–423, pp. 248–249, 406–407.

56. Quoted in Richard Price, *Maroon Societies, Rebel Slave Communities in the Americas* (Baltimore: Johns Hopkins University Press, 1979), p. 121, from the papers of Galbaud du Fort.

57. Priestly, *France Overseas*, p. 272

58. Jean Martin, *L'Empire renaissant, 1789–1871* (Paris: Denoël, 1987), pp. 17–85; Laurent Dubois, *Les Esclaves de la République, l'histoire oubliée de la première émancipation, 1789–1794* (Paris: Calmann-Lévy, 1998).

59. Priestly, *France Overseas*, pp. 317–318.

60. James G. Leyburn, *The Haitian People* (New Haven, Conn.: Yale University Press, 1955); Robert Debs Heinl, Jr., and Nancy Gordon Heinl, *Written in Blood: The Story of the Haitian People, 1492–1971* (Boston: Houghton Mifflin, 1978); T. Lothrop Stoddard, *The French Revolution in San Domingo* (New York: Houghton Mifflin, 1914).

61. Priestly, *France Oversers*, p. 352.

62. Montesquieu, *Lettres persanes*, quoted in Pierre Pluchon, *Histoire de la colonisation française* (Paris: Fayard, 1991), p. 569.

63. Quoted in Priestly, *France Overseas*, p. 272; Montesquieu, *De l'esprit des lois* (Amsterdam, 1784), livre xv, ch. 5.

64. Voltaire, *Candide* (chapter XIX), in André Lagarde and Laurent Michard, *XVIIIe Siècle, les grands auteurs Français du programme* (Paris: Bordas, 1965), p. 167.

65. Quoted in Pluchon, *Histoire de la colonisation Française*, pp. 228, 360–361.

66. Ibid., p. 361.

67. Quoted in Lagarde and Michard, *XVIIe Siècle*, from Voltaire, "Le Nègre de Surinam," p. 167.

68. Quoted in Davis, *The Problem of Slavery*, p. 416, from *Encyclopédie* (Neuchâtel, 1765), p. 532; Marc Pachter, ed., *Abroad in America: Visitors to the New Nation, 1776–1914* (Reading, Mass.: Addison-Wesley, 1976); Gilbert Malcolm Fess, "The American Revolution in Creative French Literature (1775–1937)," *University of Missouri Studies* 16, no. 2 (194); Henry Vyverberg, *Human Nature, Cultural Diversity, and the French Enlightenment* (New York: Oxford University Press, 1989), pp. 107–112, 116–132.

69. Anthony Pagden, *European Encounters with the New World: From Renaissance to Romanticism* (New Haven, Conn.: Yale University Press, 1997), pp. 141–173.

70. Diderot, quoted in Raynal, 1781, vol. 3, cited in Anthony Pagden, *Lords of All the Worlds, Ideologies of Empire in Spain, Britain and France, c. 1500–c. 1800* (New Haven, Conn.: Yale University Press, 1995), p. 166.

71. Durand Echeverria, *Mirage in the West, a History of the French Image of American Society to 1815*, foreword by Gilbert Chinard (New York: Octagon Books, 1966), pp. 15–19, 129ff; Edith Philips, *The Good Quaker in French Legend* (Philadelphia: University of Pennsylvania Press, 1952); Henry Nash Smith, *Virgin Land: The American West as Symbol and Myth* (Cambridge: Harvard University Press, 1950); Frank Monaghan, *French Travelers in the United States, 1765–1932* (New York: Antiquarian Press, 1961).

72. Quoted in Echeverria, *Mirage in the West*, pp. 29–31; Gilbert Chinard, "Eighteenth Century Theories on America as a Human Habitat," *Proceedings of the American Philosophical Society* 91, no. 1 (1947) pp. 27–47.

73. Hugh Honour, *The New Golden Land, European Images of America from the Discoveries to the Present Time* (New York: Pantheon Books, 1975), pp. 138–159; Marie-Louise Deurenoy, *L'Orient romanesque en France, 1704–1789* (Montréal: Éditions Beauchemin, 1946).

A French stone column placed in Florida by Jean Ribault, head of the brief-lived French colony there (1562–1565). Such stone columns, like lead plates and stone crosses, marked territory claimed by French explorers and colonists. This period illustration shows Athore, an Indian chief, conversing with Jean Ribault, the French commander, while other Florida Indians, having brought gifts of fruit, vegetables, and arrows, venerate the marker column. From Theodore de Bry, *America*, Part I (1591). Pl. VIII, vault, "Signs of Possession," xfE136.B79 v. 1–4. Courtesy of the Bancroft Library, University of California, Berkeley.

Cod fishing in the North Atlantic. *Top:* An early *terre-neuvier* (Newfoundlander) shows fishermen hauling up cod while others clean the fish. A *saleur* (salter) works in the hold. *Bottom:* A *habilleur* (dresser) and a *trancheur* (slicer) cut up the cod, next to a fisherman. All sit in barrels and the fisherman is protected by a windscreen. From Duhamel du Monceau, *Traité général des pêches*, Paris, 1769–1779, 3 vols.

The sugar industry in the West Indies was a source of immense profit for France in the 18th century, requiring extensive slave labor. This 1719 illustration compresses the entire process into a single plate, showing the cut sugar cane being brought to the mill, ground, and boiled. Anxious to preserve a monopoly, the French insisted on shipping the boiled syrup to France for final refinement and export, thus preventing the growth of an independent industry in its island possessions. *La figure des moulins à sucre*, from Anon, *Voyages aux côtes de Guinée et Amérique*, Amsterdam, 1719. © The British Museum.

America was an attractive subject for French artists and artisans of the late 18th century, especially in the period from the American Revolution to the Battle of Yorktown (1781), in which French armed forces played a major role in the British defeat in North America. Benjamin Franklin and William Penn were depicted in busts, clocks, and china. America appears to be an idyllic land in this silk and wool Beauvais tapestry (1789–1791) with its lush tropical setting, stilled cannon, and victorious French and American figures. *America*, Beauvais Tapestry Factory after Jean-Jacques-François Le Barbier the Elder, tapestry of silk and wool. 1789–1791, 144 × 180 inches.

.Victor Schoelcher (1804–1893), politician, journalist, and abolitionist. As Undersecretary of State for Colonies, he was responsible for the decrees of March 4 and April 27, 1848, abolishing slavery in French colonies. Photo courtesy of French Embassy, Washington, D.C.

The good ship *Faidherbe* was named for a leading mid-19th-century French governor and colonist in West Africa. It was lugged, floated, and carried piece by piece for over 120 miles inland in Africa to a Nile tributary in support of Jean-Baptiste Marchand's move on Fashoda (1898) on the banks of the Upper White Nile. The French exposition traveled from the French Congo in 1897 to Fashoda a year later where they met the British heading south, then withdrew under pressure. Fashoda triggered a major French-British confrontation, contributing to the partition of Africa. Image from Bibliothèque nationale de France, Paris.

Abd al Kader (1808–1883) militarily opposed French penetration of Algeria from 1832 until he was captured by the French in 1847 and exiled in France and later Damascus, Syria. Son of a leading traditional leader, Abd al Kader traveled extensively in the Middle East and was an important Islamic religious leader as well as a military figure. He alternated periods of armed conflict with negotiation with the French, and from 1837 to 1839 he divided the land under his control into a modern state with nine provinces. Photo courtesy of French Embassy, Washington, D.C.

French colonial architecture tried to reflect the glories of French civilization. Colonial capitals often contained an elaborate governor's residence, impressive government buildings, carefully laid out streets, and a cathedral. Hanoi Cathedral (1888), built on the ruins of a traditional pagoda, was sometimes criticized for its gaudiness and inappropriateness in a Vietnamese setting. Hanoi Cathedral (1888) postcard.

Watch towers along the Hué River provided the French garrison with an early warning of invading forces. Sentinels used gongs and flags to describe traffic on the river. "Watch Tower on Hué River," drawing by Th. Weber, based on a sketch by Brossard de Corbigny in *Le Tour du Monde*, 1878.

French colonial mule-mounted cavalry, aided by a single-engine reconnaissance aircraft (1920s), head for Taza, a strategic location between the Middle Atlas and Rif mountains in Morocco. Such aircraft, coupled with superior firepower, gave France a military advantage in early-20th-century warfare.

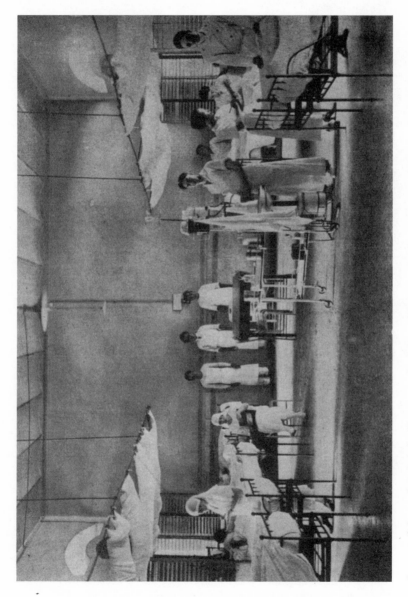

A state-of-the-art hospital for Europeans in Saigon, Vietnam (1930). During the interwar period France tried to improve medical conditions in overseas possessions to make colonies attractive for European settlers and to increase the productivity of local work forces and add to the numbers of potential military recruits. *"Donnez-moi un médecin et je vous renderai un battalion,"* Marshal Lyautey once said (Give me a physician and I will give you back a battalion). From *Le Domaine Colonial Français*, T. 4 (Paris: Les Éditions du Cygne, 1930).

Marshal Louis-Hubert Lyautey, French *résident général* in Morocco (1912–1925), one of the most illustrious colonial figures of the 20th century, served previously in Indochina (1894–1897), Madagascar (1898–1902), and Algeria (1904–1910), and later as *commissaire général* of the 1931 Colonial Exposition. Photo courtesy of French Embassy, Washington, D.C.

The centerpiece of the Colonial Exposition of 1931 was a replica of the Temple at Angkor in the Paris suburb of Vincennes. The French billed themselves as "legitimate heirs of the ancient Khmer civilization." Pavilions from all over the world covered 100 hectares of ground where 8 million visitors from all over Europe sampled Moorish coffee, watched African dancers, and saw exhibits about France's civilizing efforts. From *Le Pèlerin*, May 21, 1931. J.-L. Charmet photo.

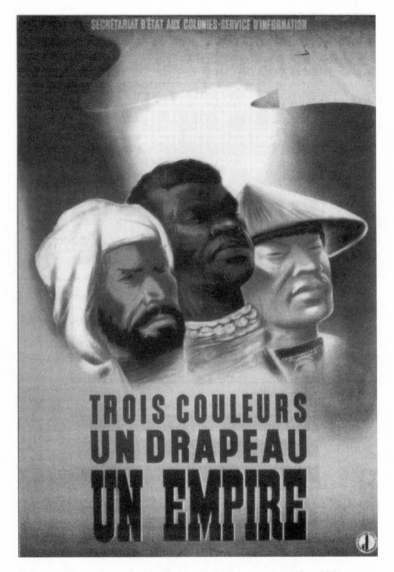

"Three Colors, One Flag, One Empire" is the theme of a 1941 poster issued by the Secretary of State for the Colonies. The overseas world was of interest to French photographers, filmmakers, and graphic designers in the 1930s. During World War II, both sides, Vichy and Free French, attached propaganda importance to France's having an overseas empire that would aid it in its current struggle. Poster by Eric Castel, *Trois couleurs, un drapeau, un empire* (1941), French government poster.

Tirailleurs Sénégalais during World War II. Members of the Senegalese Infantry, a generic term used for African troops, were often forcibly recruited into the French army. During World War I, 136 thousand such troops fought; during World War II, 160 thousand; and in Indochina, from 1947 to 1954, 56 thousand. Photo courtesy of French Embassy, Washington, D.C.

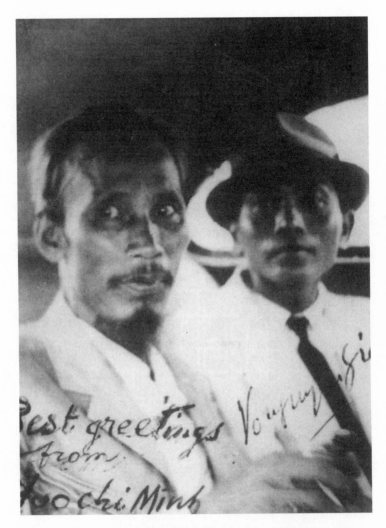

Ho Chi Minh and Vo Nguyen Giap in Hanoi in September 1945. Ho Chi Minh as political leader and Vo Nguyen Giap as military leader engineered the Vietnamese military victory over the French. Ho, who sought American military support, knew about President Franklin D. Roosevelt's opposition to French colonialism, but with Roosevelt's death, such a prospect ended, and Ho, an avid Communist, was actively aided by the Soviet Union and Communist China. Courtesy of Major Allison K. Thomas.

Dien Bien Phu shortly before the French surrender on May 7, 1954. The French commanding officers (shown above) and soldiers had lived on coffee and cigarettes since the battle began on March 13. Monsoon rains and a poor location, surrounded by hills and thick growth, left the 16 thousand troop French garrison surrounded by superior Viet Minh numbers and well-placed artillery. The French loss has been compared to the Japanese defeat of the Russians in 1905. Photo courtesy of Keystone Photo Agency.

"Yes for the New Algeria, Yes for Friendship, Yes for General de Gaulle" (1958). Faced with endless conflict in Algeria, French voters of all political persuasions recalled General Charles de Gaulle to office in 1958. An attempted revolt by army officers and stepped-up military and economic assistance programs in Algeria proved fruitless for France, leading to Algeria's independence in 1962. Poster *Oui pour l'Algérie nouvelle—Oui pour l'amitié—Oui pour de Gaulle*, from l'Association nationale pour le soutien de l'action du général de Gaulle (1958).

Hands raised in victory was a trademark of General de Gaulle's public appearances. In Ft. Lamy, now N'Djamena, Chad, an unknown local artisan crafted small hand bells, or *sonnettes*, for use at overseas French dinner tables in the 1960s. The French ambassador was furious that France's chief of state was satirized this way, and the bells were banished from the marketplace, but vendors kept them not terribly well hidden with their other merchandise. De Gaulle dinner bell (artifact), N'Djamena, Chad, collection of author.

Poet-president Léopold Sédar Senghor of Senegal, a leading African politician of the 20th century. Senghor served in the French army in World War II, was captured by the Germans, and later completed courses in French grammar and literature in Paris, graduating as an *agrégé de grammaire*, passing the highest competitive examination for teachers. An early exponent of *négritude*, a literary movement promoting traditional African and Antillian cultural values, he was equally active in his country's and France's politics, serving as president of Senegal from 1960 to 1980. He was elected to the Académie française in 1969. Photo courtesy of French Embassy, Washington, D.C.

4

The 19th Century:
The Military's and
Missionaries' Empire
(Part I)

"We follow the flag of France, without ever concerning ourselves whose hands hold it."

—Cardinal Lavigerie

The new empire of the early 19th century hung like a necklace from France to the South Pacific via a scattering of Caribbean islands and coastal trading stations in Africa, the Indian Ocean, and along the Indochinese coast. Distances were immense between outposts, European populations were small, and the economic potential of claimed territories was exploited in only the most rudimentary manner. The empire was at its all-time historic low in the century's early years. The Congress of Vienna in 1815 had left France with the Caribbean islands of Martinique and Guadeloupe, the pestilential coastal settlement of French Guiana, the volcanic island of Réunion near Madagascar, fishing rights off Newfoundland, the slivers of islands Saint-Pierre-et-Miquelon, and a few trading posts in Senegal and India. During the century France added new possessions at an uneven rate. If registered along a graph, it would show slight movement during the century's first seven decades, a dramatic rise in conquered territories toward the century's end, and then a drop to virtual inactivity.

In the first period, France established a presence in Algeria in the 1830s and in West Africa and Indochina in the 1850s and 1860s. The pace quickened in the 1880s when the French presence grew in Tunisia and Morocco, French holdings in Indochina were expanded, and more than one-third of the African continent was claimed by France. By the late 1880s the scramble for empire had slowed, and the boundaries of France's overseas lands were set; they now included nearly 11 million square kilometers of land and 50 million overseas inhabitants. Only the temporary addition of several League of Nations mandate territories—Togo, Cameroon, Lebanon and Syria—after World War I changed the shape of France's empire until the post–World War II period and its demise.

Studying the history of these overseas territories during this period is like viewing a series of old newsreel clips; rulers appear briefly on camera, make some obvious gestures, and awkwardly disappear as the camera fades. During the first half-century, from the fall of Napoléon Bonaparte in 1815 until 1848, three mediocre rulers succeeded one another, and overseas acquisitions came by fits and starts. Louis XVIII, Louis XVI's aging brother, restored the Bourbon monarchy in 1815 and paid off France's war debts. Next came Charles X, who tried during his brief reign (1824–1830) to rule as if there had been no revolution. Charles sent French troops into Algeria in 1830 to bolster his failing prestige at home, but opposition remained widespread and the seizure of Algeria did not save the monarch, who then departed for England. Louis-Philippe, the Duke of Orléans, occupied the French throne from 1830 until the Revolution of 1848. A "citizen king," he wore a sober business suit and carried an umbrella instead of a scepter, and he gradually expanded the French presence in Algeria, stirred the pot of Egyptian politics, and backed French expansion in the Pacific islands. He created the French Foreign Legion in 1831, primarily to fight in Algeria. "The Legion was the illegitimate child of the July Revolution, an embarrassment, at once acknowledged and shunned, whose meager patrimony was the right to die for France in the wastes of her empire."[1]

The most important supporter of overseas expansion in this period was the nephew of Napoléon, Louis-Napoléon Bonaparte (1808–1873), who came to power in December 1848 as a president elected by universal suffrage. (He had been sentenced to prison after two armed insurrections, but, dressed as a stone mason, had walked away from his guards.) Capitalizing on the residual nostalgia for his ancestor, he was elected as "the father of the workers" and on vague promises to restore French glory. On December 2, 1851, he consolidated power through a coup d'état, and in 1852 he held a plebiscite and proclaimed France an empire and himself its emperor. Assuming dictatorial powers more extensive than those of his illustrious ancestor, he reigned until his resounding defeat and capture by the Germans in 1870. Notwithstanding his capricious policies and authoritarian personality, his reign, a time of achievement for France, climaxed in the creation of new banks, the growth of foreign trade, the spread of industry and railways, and public works such as Baron Haussmann's sweeping changes of the Paris landscape, which created wide avenues that made it difficult for insurrectionists to erect barricades in the streets.

A slight rise in overseas expansion occurred from 1848 to 1869 when Louis-Napoléon conducted an aggressive but ill-conceived policy of expansionism. Calling himself the "Emperor of the French and the Arabs," and recalling the "light from the East" that drew his famous uncle to Egypt, he encouraged Ferdinand de Lesseps to construct a canal at Suez. Louis also backed French inland incursions in Senegal and the southern part of Vietnam and Cambodia, and he revived the possibility of a joint British-French opening of China to European trade. Desiring to establish a French kingdom in the Americas, Louis sent troops to Mexico when the Mexican president refused to honor his predecessor's debts to France. The Mexicans soundly defeated the French in the battle of Vera Cruz. Next Louis tried to establish a provisional government in Mexico by placing the Archduke Maximilian, brother of Francis Joseph I, Austrian emperor, on the throne in 1861. No aspect of the expedition went well for France, and when the American Civil War ended, the United States invoked its Monroe Doctrine about not permitting outside forces in the Western Hemisphere, and France withdrew, leaving Maximilian undefended. He was defeated quickly, tried, and shot, ending any French dreams of an empire in the Americas.[2]

There were ample internal reasons for France to look only fitfully at overseas questions. If France itself was not internally united, how could it build a coherent overseas empire? According to Eugen Weber, a leading contemporary historian of France, "The famous hexagon can itself be seen as a colonial empire shaped over the centuries: a complex of territories conquered, annexed and integrated in a political and administrative whole, many of them with strongly developed national or regional personalities, some of them with traditions that were specifically un- or anti-French."[3]

French internal history of the 19th century reads like colonial history: authority imposed from without; elaborate development schemes; contempt for the natives, their language, and customs; talk of conquest and civilizing; and armed rebellion in places—the same issues a historian would deal with in Senegal or Vietnam. Overseas possessions did not interest most French citizens, who expected to live and die within their villages' orbits. For many, a stranger from another part of France, should one appear, would be as much a foreigner as a Senegalese or a Vietnamese. Journalists and politicians compared the poor, isolated parts of France to the colonies. Raymond Cartier was to do this with great effect in the middle of 20th century, but as early as 1843 Adolphe Blanqui saw resemblances between the French Alpine provinces and Algeria's Kabylia. The Landes in 1826 was called "our African Sahara," its settlements were *colonies*, "a trackless desert where one needs a compass to find one's way." Public works in one region were compared to those in Tunisia; in another, a writer, noting the construction of a railway line in Africa, exclaimed, "If only they would treat us like Arabs!"[4]

The most traumatic event in France's late 19th century history was the Franco-Prussian War of 1870 which affected every aspect of French life and which was the motor driving French overseas interest for the next generation. French officers, whose only actual military experience had been leading African and Asian bush patrols, were ill-prepared for large-unit warfare. Eighty thousand French troops, led by the emperor, surrendered in September 1870; the total French war losses were 150 thousand dead. Terms like "amputation" and "mutilation" were used to describe France's fate. A Parisian journal was called *La Revanche*, and General Jean Marie Boulanger, a popular demagogue, was called "General Revenge." The difference between sentiment for revenge and colonial expansion was expressed by one French citizen after the war of 1870, "I have lost two sisters and you offer me 20 domestics."[5] War losses and a low birthrate combined to reduce French numbers severely at a time when the populations of Germany and Great Britain grew. French women were urged to help save the French race by creating "an overseas France," especially in light of the dramatic imbalances between French and German birthrates in the post 1870s. Although there were increased demands for women to go abroad, especially as wives of administrators, their roles were carefully circumscribed as teachers, nurses, social workers, or religious.[6]

Once again nature, in the form of population numbers, frustrated French imperial efforts in ways more effective than the machinations of rival prime ministers or chancellors. Comparative population figures and growth rates were disturbing for France. France had 36 million persons in 1875 and 39 million in 1901; Germany grew from 41 to 56 million persons in the same period. Victor Hugo accurately reflected French postwar sentiment when he wrote, "Henceforth there are in Europe two nations which will be formidable, the one because it is victorious, the other because it is vanquished." The scars of France's ruinous defeat at Sedan helped determine French imperial policy for the next generation, and many politicians, writers, and most French citizens believed that reconstruction, revenge, and restoration of national prestige must take place at home. Others thought only a world empire would restore France to its former glory and provide security. The lines were clearly drawn, and the finding prestige at home versus abroad argument would be played and replayed in countless forums over the next decades. France's main line of defense had been moved back to Verdun, within striking distance of Paris, and arguments for the safer "blue line of the Vosges" were widespread. France's main European competitor, other than Germany, was Great Britain, to whom France generally lost out in colonial competition.

The relative sizes of the French and British navies suggest why France came in second best. In the period from 1870 to 1910, the French accounted for only 5% of total world shipping; the British, for 45%. Throughout this time the navy remained central to France's overseas empire; it provided the main transportation routes to the overseas world until the 1930s and the growth of the airlines. After 1870 the French military budget predictably concentrated on rebuilding the army; in 1900, France had 26 naval cruisers under steam to England's 51. Long after iron ships were the norm, France still used wooden frames to reduce its considerable stores of seasoned wood. France emerged with Europe's second-largest navy, but the clear message was that second place counted for nothing in international naval competition. Many French settlements along the African and Asian coasts were picked for their harbors. Saigon was supposed to be a French Gibraltar, and other isolated islands were retained as fueling stops. The naval officer corps, traditionally drawn from those in privileged positions, provided many colonial governors and high ministry officials.

AN EMERGING COLONIAL LOBBY

A colonial lobby, which emerged in France in the 1870s, became a vocal force in French politics. It had a steady base, perhaps 91 out of 576 votes in the Chamber in 1893, not bad for Third Republic politics, but not enough to dominate either. Supporters included the military, missionaries, trading houses with overseas interests, and some legislators seeking revenge against Germany through expanding France's overseas presence. Numerous geographic societies then sprouting up also encouraged imperialist sentiment. More than 12 such societies existed by 1881, claiming 9,500 members. An undeniable euphoria informed their activities; a geographer with Napoléon's mission in Egypt wrote, "We want . . . Africa with the rest of the world to pay its tribute to our industry, to send to our cities overfilled with men its treasures, products. . . . Africa must in its turn fall to modern civilization."[7]

The Paris Geographical Society's president was a former minister of the marine, and by 1881 the society had 2,000 members, many of them highly placed government officials. Each Friday the secretary general, Charles-Jean Maunior, gathered those with colonial interests and visiting officers from the colonies in the back room of a neighborhood eating place, La Petite Vache, following the society's regular meetings. Francis Garnier and Pierre Savorgnon de Brazza, on home leave from Indochina and Equatorial Africa, attended such gatherings, as did most leading colonial administrators. For such persons, geography provided both a scientific and a political basis for overseas explorations and conquests. "Providence has dictated to us the obligation to know the earth and conquer it," French President General Maurice de MacMahon said, and "geography, that science which has inspired such devotion and in the name of which so many victims have been sacrificed, has become the philosophy of the earth."[8]

The most important figure in the colonial bloc was Eugène Étienne (1844–1921), who served as undersecretary for colonies from 1889 to 1893. Étienne's followers called him the "*grand marabout*" and "*Notre Dame des Coloniaux,*" (Our Lady of the Colonials). Born in Oran, and employed by a Marseilles trading house, he worked hard to increase the colonial bloc from 91 to 200 members by 1902. He also successfully established the principle that, in legislative affairs, parliamentary comment on Algerian questions should be reserved for deputies from Algeria, which effectively squelched potential opposition to controversial policies.[9]

Efforts to promote interest in overseas affairs were intense, although the number of promoters was never large. A chair of geography was established at the College of France, and various French chambers of commerce supported the study of commercial geography. Expeditions were commissioned, explorers' accounts printed, prizes for discovery conferred, and conferences held, including an International Congress of Commercial Geography in Paris in 1874. The expanding interest in geography and the overseas world coincided with the growth of mass circulation periodicals, like *Tour du Monde* and *Magazine Pittoresque*, which carried features about overseas life. Several geographical periodicals sprang up, including *L'Année géographique*, *L'Explorateur*, *La Revue des Deux Mondes*, and *Le Journal des Débats*.

The step from scientific to political activity was a short one, and many geographical societies urged France to compete with other European powers through colonization and emigration. Committees for French Africa, Asia, and Morocco launched scientific expeditions and lobbied for roads, hospitals, and public works. The widening geographic interests also supported developmental schemes like the plan of Ferdinand de Lesseps, builder of the Suez Canal, to construct another canal in Central America, and his project to link the Mediterranean and interior of Tunisia through an isthmus and interior sea. Other projects would connect Africa's extremities with continent-crossing railroads and agricultural and transportation schemes seemingly drawn from the pages of author Jules Verne.[10]

If a single work summarized the ideas of French expansionism of the post-1870 period, it was Paul Leroy-Beaulieu's *De la colonisation chez les peuples modernes*, published in 1874, when its author was only 31 years old. Leroy-Beaulieu was an economist for whom two sorts of colonies existed: those to which people emigrated and those in which capital was invested; in other words, colonies of *peuplement* and colonies of *exploitation*. He did not place much emphasis on France's sending great numbers of people overseas, for France did not have a population surplus, the unemployed were not interested in leaving France, and the impact of such colonies on the French economy was minimal. In contrast, exportation of capital was necessary for the country's economic and social progress. Infinite possibilities awaited French investors. Leroy-Beaulieu's language was rhapsodic. "Colonization is the expansive force of a people," he argued. It was "submission of the universe, or a vast part of it to the [French] language, customs, ideas, and laws." Colonization was "one of the most noble spectacles of which man is both agent and witness."[11]

What triggered this statement of French colonial dreams was not the realities of the world overseas, but the aftermath of the recent war with Germany. If France was battered at home, it would find new strength and purpose in foreign lands; if its population was decimated by the war, it would find new troops in zouaves and Senegalese riflemen; and its lack of natural resources at home would be compensated for in rich mines and large plantations abroad. French colonial doctrine in the late 19th century was, above all, a response to the political and psychological climate of post-1870 France.

JULES FERRY

After years of sporadic overseas activity, the time of France's most active overseas expansion occurred in a brief five-year period, from 1880 to 1885,

during the two governments of Jules Ferry who, as prime minister, never expressed a coherent colonial policy or held a clear parliamentary majority. Ferry
was first elected a Republican deputy for Paris in 1869 and soon became a
leader in the Republican party, rising to become minister of foreign affairs and
premier for two action-filled terms: 1880 to 1881 and 1883 to 1885. He allowed
a freer press than had existed before, reduced senatorial terms from life to a
limited number of years, created schools for girls, and made the French educational system nonclerical with mandatory, free primary education.

Tunisia was declared a French protectorate in 1880, shortly after Ferry became
prime minister. During his second ministry, France added most of Indochina
and extended French influence in the Congo and Madagascar. When he arrived
in office, Ferry had little interest in or knowledge of colonial affairs, but he was
an energetic, impulsive improviser. His policies were doled out as *"petits pa-
quets"* (little packages) to the legislature and public, rarely with explanations.
Ferry had only a handful of followers and no desire to expose himself to the
risks of parliamentary debate, a hostile press, or an indifferent public. His
brusque, sarcastic manner brought him political enemies, all of whom cited his
overseas ventures as examples of poor judgment. Issues coalesced in March
1885 when Chinese troops routed a small French unit in Lang-Son, in northern
Vietnam, near the Chinese border. The French commander was seriously
wounded, and his second in command ordered an immediate retreat, abandoning
supplies, artillery, even the brigade chest which had just arrived with the soldiers' pay.[12] Telegraphed reports to Paris were confused. The local commander
said, "I hope that, whatever comes, to be able to defend the delta,"[13] several
days march to the south. Although the incident came to nothing in Indochina,
the tight-lipped prime minister refused to comment on it, and opponents used it
to topple his government. Crowds gathered yelling, "Death to Ferry" and "Ferry
of Tonkin," and he became a lightning rod for anticolonial sentiment. Ferry
finally responded. Blame for the French defeat, he said, belonged not with the
Chinese but with those in the legislature who denied France money to fortify
its overseas defenses. The appeal meant little; Ferry was defeated 306 to 149.
Georges Clemenceau, leader of the opposition, reflected the debate's bitterness,
"There are no more ministers which I have before me, these are those accused
of high treason."[14]

After the debate was over and Ferry was out of office, he enunciated the
French colonial policy he had been advocating in piecemeal fashion in a book
called *Le Tonkin et la Mère-Patrie* (1890) (Tonkin and the Motherland). Ferry's
first appeal was predictably to French economic interests. Colonies, he argued,
would be a source of natural resources and markets. Although he came from
war-ravaged Lorraine, Ferry dismissed any revenge-minded arguments against
Germany. The decisive battles for France's future would be fought elsewhere
than in Europe, he argued, and "Marseilles and Toulon will be defended quite
as much in the China Seas as in the Mediterranean." Ferry played on French
fears of becoming a second-rate power, asking the French what they would think
if the *tricolore* was hauled down in Vietnam and replaced within hours by

another European flag. Reflecting prevalent racial theories, he argued that the "superior races" of the West had both rights and responsibilities toward "inferior" ones. France should employ the benefits of science, culture, and justice to lead local populations from darkness to light, without neglecting the importance of sound economic returns. As late as 1954 François Mitterrand, a minister of France d'outre-mer, proclaimed in *Aux frontières de l'Union française*, "L'oeuvre de Jules Ferry sert d'exemple et de modèle aux initiatives les plus modernes" (The work of Jules Ferry serves as an example and model of the most modern initiatives). But Ferry's *protectorat réformateur* (reforming protectorate) contained no provisions for local leadership to assert itself, let alone dream of independence.[15]

LATE 19TH CENTURY IMPERIALISM

In addition to lingering memories of its defeat by Germany, French overseas expansion in the late 19th century was driven by three forces. First, the ambitions of military officers in scattered outposts of empire led them to want to add to France's glory, or sometimes simply to do what military officers were trained to do: lead troops in combat and conquest. Second, an active Roman Catholic missionary movement sent missionaries abroad and created a favorable climate for overseas missions while publicizing them at home. In 1869 the director of Saigon's Roman Catholic seminary spoke of a "mysterious connection" between Christianity and France, adding, "You wish then that this country might be Christian; once Christian it will be French."[16] Third, a vigorous but loosely organized colonial party could sometimes muster a significant bloc of votes and encourage explorations, geographic societies, and the development of overseas lands. France's late 19th century expansionism proceeded by fits and starts— with considerable opposition—and was neither logical nor inevitable in the course it took. As before, there was no great outpouring of overseas populations because, except for those displaced by the German takeover of Alsace-Lorraine, the French showed no more disposition to move overseas than they had in previous centuries. It was not for nothing that Otto von Bismarck said, "France has colonies but no colonists."

Economic arguments are of limited use in explaining French expansionism. French exports were more significant to the Americas, where France's colonial presence was limited to a few islands, than to Indochina and North Africa, the focal points of a new French overseas presence. French export houses were important in the colonial lobby, but they represented generally small-scale businesses in port towns, and the arguments of their proprietors failed to move a nation. Henri Brunchweg, in his provocative book *Mythes et réalités de l'impérialisme colonial français, 1871–1914*, showed that French exports to the colonies exceeded imports in the last decade of the 19th century and from 1882 to 1886 accounted for less than 6% of the country's total trade figures. This scale of activity suggests profit for some individual traders or companies, but a marginal contribution of overseas possessions to the national economy. Moreover, it was not until the century's end, long after the conquest of Vietnam, that France prepared an economic growth plan for its potentially richest possession.

The acquisition of new lands was generally accepted reluctantly in Paris. Gustave Flaubert echoed a widespread sentiment in his *Dictionaire des idées reçues*, "Colonies: (ours): they pain us when we speak of them."[17] Colonies were expensive luxuries to the parsimonious French who did not want to increase budgets, and there were frequent appeals to make better use of the territories France had already claimed rather than add new possessions. Clemenceau was one outspoken opponent of colonial expansion. His was *la politique du pot au feu*, and the pot's ingredients were strengthening France's army in Europe, liquidating the war debt, and building schools and public works at home. But, while procolonial sentiment was never widespread in France, its proponents had a powerful advantage. They knew that lands once taken would probably never be returned, despite claps of parliamentary thunder.

Politicians railed against the acquisition of territory and its cost to France, but no one ordered the captains and lieutenants to strike the flag and withdraw to their small outposts along the Senegal or Mekong rivers. For their part, some of the military were attracted by the heady vision of restoring France's prestige in the wake of a disastrous war. Besides, there was little activity for an energetic officer in the tropics, especially officers wanting to command troops and engage the enemy. All this took place in the quasi-sacred name of national interest, and the question was not whether there would be confrontations between French agents and local rulers, but when and where they would occur. Once such entanglements took place, a familiar set of requirements came into play—the need for more troops to defend France's interests and the need for prompt, decisive annexation to consolidate France's position, followed by statements of France's political, economic, and social mission in the new territory. A pantheon of French military fired off these arguments from the outposts of empire: Francis Gardiner, Louis-Léon Faidherbe, Louis-Hubert Lyautey, and Joseph-Simon Gallieni, among others. Without such voices from the frontiers, to which those of the Colonial party were added, there never would have been sufficient interest in Paris to lead to the final territorial annexations. The French Overseas Empire thus followed no grand design; its expansion was due to the activities of a distinct minority of vocal figures, mostly military, but supported by missionaries and others with colonial interests, who set the wheels in motion to conquer overseas lands.[18]

An example of the imperialist-on-the spot was Louis Charles de Montigny, the French vice-consul in Shanghai in 1848. Montigny established a French concession where none had previously existed, and he made his residence in a dilapidated native house which he abandoned each spring when the Woosung River flooded. Montigny had close ties with the missionaries, and he allowed them to build a cathedral and a school on the French compound. The size of his consular district appeared limited only by his imagination, and Montigny toured it frequently by junk or sedan chair, confronting local mandarins who had caused the missionaries difficulties. He offered protection to French and native Christians, of whom there may have been 70 thousand, in his consular district. At one point, the enterprising Montigny asked the missionaries to send him several thousand swatches of local cloth in hopes of establishing a trade in fabrics, but there was little support in France for such an initiative, and it soon failed. At times he restrained mobs, scattered robber bands, rescued sailors, and advanced French interests as he interpreted them, unencumbered by directives or superiors.[19]

Another example of a completely local initiative was the annexation of Tahiti and nearby islands in 1843 by Admiral Abel Aubert Dupetit-Thouard and a French squadron, which the French government originally disavowed when they learned of it several months later. The islands' seizure concluded several years of quarreling between French missionaries and the Tahitian queen and her British advisor, whom the admiral had arrested and deported, who was subsequently greeted in England as a hero. By 1847 the incident had lost its value as an irritant between the two countries. The British expressed indignation, the French belatedly offered regrets, but Tahiti remained in French hands. Improvised French adventuring in the East Asian seas came to a temporary halt off the Korean coast in 1847 when two French ships, *La Gloire* and *La Victorieuse*, ran aground with a total of 560 persons while landing a party of missionaries. Both ships were wrecked and their crews were rescued by the British. The French presence in the Pacific at this time thus followed no grand design beyond visceral competition with other powers, especially the British, and the activities of individually adventurous admirals possessed of few resources.

ADMINISTRATION OF THE COLONIES

During much of this century, actual administration of the overseas empire had no sure home within the French government. (Britain had a single secretary for war and the colonies from 1794 to 1854). From 1669 until 1881, the Ministry of the Marine was responsible for overseas possessions, with the brief exception of the period from 1858 to 1860, when Napoléon III created a Ministry of Colonies to employ a relative, and in 1881, when the colonies were briefly transferred to the Ministry of Commerce. By the late 19th century things changed again—three different ministries were now responsible for the overseas empire. The protectorates of Tunisia and Morocco came under the Ministry of Foreign Affairs. Algeria passed from control by the army to the Ministry of the Interior and then became a department of metropolitan France. The Ministry of the Marine administered the protectorates of Laos and Cambodia until a Ministry of Colonies was created in 1894.

Few French people sought careers in the colonies, and the turnover rate among colonial officials was extraordinarily high. Governors averaged a one-year stay at best in Algeria, Vietnam, and Tahiti. Finding competent personnel was difficult. William Cohen, in a comprehensive study of the French Colonial Service, concluded that most colonial officers lacked the personal qualities and professional skills needed to operate successfully in a strange and difficult environment. Few were interested in the lives of local people; most lacked creative ideas on how to advance agriculture, commerce, or education; and depended on directives from France of supposed universal applicability for their marching orders. A few brilliant exceptions stood out—a linguist here, an ethnographer there—but, by and large, the inland administrator was a man "with ten black soldiers under his order and a village of a hundred huts to survey."[20] He moved infrequently about the region, depending on his interpreter for most information about what was transpiring, and he comforted himself with a bottle, a deep chair, and infrequent letters and publications from home.

Many men resorted to keeping concubines, as reflected in a 1902 guide on conduct for French administrators living in Africa, which advised "a temporary union with a well-chosen native woman" for those who lacked the "moral strength to endure two years of absolute continence." According to the author, "Many mysterious dramas of the red Sudan have been provoked by native women: despite their inferior status they succeed in playing their part in all aspects of life, palavers, assemblies, etc., and in influencing the decisions taken there." Africans would have a greater respect for a French administrator who had an African woman living with him, the author argued, and a union with a native woman would be a good way to learn the local language and customs, dispel boredom, and "sometimes prevent him from indulging in alcoholism or sexual debauchery . . . so common in hot countries." When the French officer's tour of duty was ended, the woman was returned to her family with an appropriate dowry to assure her access to a husband. "Former wives of Europeans are in great demand among the Negroes and can generally make very good marriages." There was no provision for the children born out of such temporary unions beyond two schools where "for a modest sum, children of Europeans are brought up and taught manual trades, according to their aptitude."[21]

To remedy the deficiencies in its overseas administrative corps, France created an École Coloniale which by 1900 had turned out 214 graduates. Most of its curriculum was irrelevant to the future administrator's needs. Classical Vietnamese and Cambodian, rather that the vernacular languages, were taught. Courses were based almost entirely on French colonial law and history. Future bush administrators were asked to "describe the financial regime instituted in the Antilles and Réunion by the Senatus Consultus of 1866. Criticize it and discuss the reforms of 1900."[22]

Health problems continued to contribute to the negative image the colonies held for many French military. Although a cure for scurvy had been discovered by the British in the use of citrus fruits, it was not widely used on French ships until late in the century, and no effective cures had yet been found for yellow fever, dysentery, and other tropical illnesses. By the late 1830s French military physicians in Algeria had found that quinine was effective in treating malaria, but the drug was expensive and acceptance of it slow to catch hold. During the 19th century, as in earlier centuries, as many colonists and explorers were killed by disease as by enemy action. Almost all colonies were called "the white man's grave" by overseas French as malaria, dysentery, yellow fever, and other illnesses decimated the numbers of troops and settlers. Although a Scottish naval surgeon, James Lind, showed, in 1753, that citrus juices could cure and prevent scurvy, the disease continued to plague seafarers until well into the next century. An early 19th century French ship's doctor wrote,

Bereft of the most effective remedies, confined in a narrow ship, the plaything of the winds and of the sea, far from any place suitable for us to put into, the sick were multiplying every day. Swellings covered by black scabs appeared on various parts of their bodies. . . . But nothing was more hideous than the appearance of their face: to the leaden complexion of the victims of scurvy was added the prominence of the gums jutting out of the mouth. . . . The sick gave out a fetid smell, which, when you breathe it, seemed to attack the very root of life. I have often felt all my strength ebb away when I approached them. Their state of weakness did not prevent them from retaining the use of all their intellectual faculties, which made them feel all the more cruelly the pangs of despair.[23]

THE INDIGÉNAT

French colonial rule left local peoples with few definable rights. The paternalistic attitude of most administrators was expressed by G. L. Angoulvant, the governor of the Ivory Coast, in 1908:

To make ourselves understood we must totally change the Negro mentality. . . . For a long time yet our subjects must be led to progress despite themselves, as some children are educated despite their reluctance to work. We must play the role of strong, strict parents towards the natives, obtaining through authority what persuasion would not gain. . . . It is desirable to avoid the use of force, but if it is used against us we must not be afraid to use it in our turn. I am determined to teach the natives a very sharp lesson wherever, wearying of our gentleness, they think they can flout our authority.[24]

One of the most dreaded powers in the hands of local administrators was the *indigénat*, a legal code adopted in 1887, but used in Algeria since the 1830s, which allowed colonial administrators arbitrarily to impose fines and prison sentences of up to 15 days without trial. While flogging was specifically excluded, its use was widespread, and some administrators simply applied consecutive sentences without listing them in court records.

The *indigénat* was not part of the regular penal code; much of its content restricted political and economic activity and contained prohibitions against various forms of expression, meetings, and so on and sanctions against those who refused to work on state projects. A colonial administrator, not a judge, both determined the facts and delivered summary judgment, which could include imprisonment, fines, or confiscation of goods. No such extrajudicial proceedings could be used against French citizens. The reach of such ordinances was illustrated by a 1903 decree in Indochina prohibiting "calumnious or offensive statements against French authority, and propagation of false news or lies of a nature that troubles public order. . . . Cries or the use of alarm drums without necessity."[25]

THE MISSIONARIES

In addition to the vigorous efforts made by military officers to expand France's overseas presence, a second active force was the Roman Catholic missionaries and their supporters in France. Protecting a missionary presence drew the French military into Indochina, which became France's most important Asian possession. Despite their substantial differences in outlook, there were many common bonds between the French military and the missionaries. Both shared a common vision of the superiority of French civilization. Léon Gambetta (1838–1882), leader of the radical Republicans, said that "anticlericalism is not for export."[26] Of the cardinal he declared, "His presence in Tunisia is worth an army for France." A French prelate in Vietnam wrote that on seeing the French flag, even "the most fierce mandarins become gentle as lambs."[27] In France, popular missionary publications flourished, accounts of missionary travelers were eagerly awaited, and numerous appeals were made to send troops and support missionaries with money. Between 1816 and 1870, 22 new missionary orders sprang up in France. Charitable and educational groups were founded to care for former slaves, and moneys were collected to liberate indigenous Christians captured by brigands or imprisoned by hostile rulers. Church propaganda also carried vivid tales of French martyrdoms to hostile pagan rulers and triumphs over native superstition. A Lyon missionary publication in 1830 had a press run of 16 thousand copies, and visiting missionaries were popular in pulpits around France. Missionary accounts contained tales of converting people living in fear and "the shadow of death," exposing them to the Christian church and the French flag. As early as 1847, when the number of magazine subscriptions in France was in its infancy, 100 thousand copies of the *Annales de l'Association de la Propagation de la Foi* were circulated, and other missionary publications soon followed.[28]

The missionary presence was typified by the work of Bishop Charles Martial Allemand-Lavigerie, the founder of the African missionary order of the White Fathers. Named bishop of Algeria in 1867, Lavigerie was a prelate who saw the continent as his parish and built churches, schools, and orphanages throughout Africa. History, archeology, and agriculture were his interests, and it was he who brought the muscat grape to North Africa. He told the French military and settlers, "It is you who can open the gates of this immense world and the keys of this sepulcher are here in your hands." Often speaking of Africa as a grave or a sepulcher, he told the 100-some members of his growing order they should try to convert all of Africa, "that almost impenetrable interior whose dark depths are the last hiding place of a brutal barbarism where cannibalism prevails and slavery is in its most degrading forms." His imperial vision is suggested in an 1871 appeal to French refugees from Alsace-Lorraine

at this moment on the roads of France, Switzerland, and Belgium, fleeing your burned homes, your devastated fields, Algeria, an African France, through my voice as bishop, opens its gates and extends its arms to you. Here you will find for you, for your children, for your families, lands more abundant and fertile than those you left in the hands of the invader.[29]

In 1875 he made his headquarters the historic chapel of Saint Louis of Carthage, where a medieval French king, the only French monarch to die abroad, had died in 1270 while returning from a crusade. Lavigerie built a vast basilica and, through his lively imagination, saw himself as the successor of Saint Augustine and was installed eventually as the primate of Africa in the succession of the Carthaginian bishop. Recalling the ancient ties of France and Africa in his numerous fund-raising tours, Lavigerie sometimes cried in the pulpit "as a simple missionary" then passed the collection plate in his cardinal's robes.

A complex, flamboyant personality, skilled as any marshal of France in planning a patriotic ceremony to focus on himself, he devoted constant effort to spreading the faith militantly and to building schools, medical centers, and orphanages, as his motto *"Charitas"* might indicate. In 1872 he consecrated the Moorish-domed basilica of Our Lady of Africa, set on the heights of Algiers, from whose vistas each Sunday ships in the Mediterranean were solemnly blessed. From there he sent missionaries into the far reaches of the Kabylia mountains hoping to find traces of the early Christian church among the Berber populations that had withdrawn there when the Arabs overran Roman North Africa.

The first three priests he sent across the Sahara in 1874 were killed, as were another group of three in 1881. Lavigerie then hired armed guards, dressed in the colorful uniforms of the papal zouaves, to protect his clergy. Lavigerie often quarreled with the French military, for example, when the French administration supported Islamic institutions. Pilgrimages to Mecca were encouraged, crumbling mosques were rebuilt by the French government, and Koranic studies were encouraged. The prelate would have none of this. He called Islam "truly the masterpiece of the evil one."[30] His own priests wore loosely flowing white robes similar to those worn in parts of Africa, and they learned local languages and customs, but they never made any accommodation to local religions or beliefs. Lavigerie had no quarrel with the secular French administration. He said, "We follow the flag of France, without ever concerning ourselves whose hands hold it." His priests were often paid as army chaplains, and the government underwrote some of the expenses of his hospitals, schools, and charitable enterprises at a time when the Church's secular power and educational role was being curbed at home. Although he feuded frequently with the military, Lavigerie was a stickler for protocol, insisting on the 25-gun salute to which his rank entitled him, equivalent to the reception accorded a marshal of France.

The cardinal devoted his final years to combating the slave trade in central and eastern Africa. Plagued with arthritis and rheumatism in a climate conducive to neither, with customary foresight he prepared his tomb in the basilica of Saint Augustine shortly before his death in 1882. He was a leader of the expanding French missionary movement; by 1900, more than two-thirds of the Roman Catholic priests abroad, 4,500 out of 6,500, were from France. "God has chosen France for himself," Lavigerie said, "and reserved [for it] the evangelization of the African continent."[31]

NORTH AFRICA

Algeria was the first North African country to come under French control in the 19th century, followed by Tunisia and Morocco. Until then, the French Mediterranean presence was largely one of coastal traders moving among the port towns. The scale of French activity was not large, and the precarious relationship between European and Arab, Christian and Moslem, had endured with minimal conflict for several centuries. All this changed, however, within a few years. Initially, Egypt was the lodestone that drew the French, but French soldiers and settlers also came to Algeria and Tunisia in the 1830s, and, by century's end to Morocco, altering the relationship from one of sporadic commercial contact to one characterized by sustained hostility and conflict, creating suspicions that endured long after these countries achieved independence in the middle of the 20th century.[32]

ALGERIA

The French conquest of Algeria was a blood-drenched affair. The French faced a hostile population, as well as a religion and a language with which they would make little accommodation. Local peoples resisted French incursions, with guns as long as they could, then passively. Of all of France's overseas holdings, Algeria and Vietnam were the places where French influence penetrated the least.

In 1827, during a dispute, the *dey*, the local ruler, struck the French consul in Algeria on the arm several times with a fly whisk in a confrontation over French nonpayment of a debt to supply grain to Napoléon's Egyptian mission. In 1829 Algerians fired on a French ship flying a truce flag while pursuing pirates in a local harbor. In 1830 France occupied Algeria with over 34 thousand troops. What pushed France into action was a desire to prop up the lackluster regime of Charles X, whose government fell within days after Algiers was taken. As usual, the French were of two minds about the occupation: it was good news for traders from the south of France, but there was general opposition to it in the Chamber. Everyone talked about it a lot, but once presented with a fait accompli, the French government would not repudiate the action. It was easy for France to occupy the principal seaports of Algeria, seize the capital, and dictate terms to local rulers. More complicated was the question of what to do next. Geography did not favor the conquerors, for the country was laterally cut by two mountain ranges; beyond them was the Sahara; between them was a dry, desolate plateau; and before them was the coast, with a thin strip of rich agricultural land, especially around Algiers. France needed a large army to hold the land; local populations were hostile to invaders, there were no roads, mountains were difficult to traverse, and if pursued Algerian bands quickly fled beyond the open borders into Tunisia and Morocco. Neither seeking a full-scale occupation nor wanting to withdraw—since national honor and prestige were at stake—the French let events take their course.[33]

The Algerians declared a jihad in 1832, a holy war led by Abd al Kader, (1808–1883), a young Muslim warrior-scholar who united the Algerian tribes in diplomatic and armed resistance for the next fifteen years. A charismatic figure, he claimed descent from the prophet, Muhammad, had made the hadj, had traveled abroad, and subscribed to French newspapers as a way of following French politics. From his base on the slopes of the Atlas Mountains near Oran, he sent his troops on guerrilla raids all over the country, stringing the French forces out and leaving their small enclaves vulnerable to surprise raids. His troops stuck the heads of slaughtered French troops or settlers on the ends of poles, a grim reminder of war's consequences. Abd al Kader was no reformer. His political goal was constant: a traditional, centralized theocratic state with himself as its unquestioned leader.

In 1837 the French signed a treaty ceding to Abd al Kader the whole of western Algeria, in return for France being allowed vague claims to sovereignty in Africa, plus the city of Oran and its environs and several smaller towns. Abd al Kader wanted his troops to be as well armed as the French and, as part of his negotiations with General Thomas Bugeaud, the French commander in Algeria, obtained 3 thousand modern rifles while negotiating separately with the British for additional arms.[34] Despite the agreement, warfare continued; both sides had negotiated mainly to allow time to improve their positions. At maximum strength, the Algerian leader commanded 50 thousand troops and fought the French to a virtual standstill.

Opposing the Algerian leader was General Bugeaud (1784–1849), "Father" Bugeaud, as his troops called their leader who had risen gradually through the officer ranks.[35] He had suppressed the 1834 popular uprisings in Paris and served as the French commander in Algeria from 1840 to 1847. His policies followed his personal motto, *Ense et arato* (by the sword and the plow). When relations between the French and Abd al Kader broke down, Bugeaud turned to armed conquest. He told the French Chamber, "Yes, in my opinion, the possession of

Algiers is wrong, but since you want to do it . . . you must do it grandly, because that is the only way to obtain some fruit."[36]

Beginning at the coast, Bugeaud and his army of 60 thousand soldiers tried systematically to push the militant Arab and Berber tribes back through *razzias*, a scorched-earth policy of methodically burning and plundering each village in the army's path, wasting the land with famine and destruction. Meanwhile, Abd al Kader's position was weakened by the failure of several important local leaders and independent cities to support him and a disastrously miscalculated frontal attack on much better armed French troops. In 1847 he surrendered. The period of open warfare was over for now at least, although isolated insurrections continued for several years.

OPPOSING SHIPS AND CANNON WITH POEMS AND SONGS

If they could not always win their battles with the French militarily, Algerians, employing a weapon familiar to oppressed people, launched an all out poetic attack against the invaders. As town after town fell, Algerian bards responded with epic poems and songs that worked their way into the folk consciousness of a people and became part of their resistance to the French. Most such poems recalled a golden past, heaped scorn on the infidels, reflected that somehow the invasion was the will of Allah, and ended with assurances that Islam would triumph in the end. Often the laments were bitter:

> O believers, the world has seen with its own eyes
> Their horses tied in our mosques.

Elsewhere:

> Men who were lions now carry the pack-saddle
> . . . we, like beasts of burden,
> Eat grass that grows in the dung heap.

In "Song About the Taking of Algiers," the poet Si Abd al Kader wrote,

> I am grieved, o world, about Algiers!
> The French move on (toward) her
> With troops whose numbers (only) God knows.
> They have come in vessels which cleave the sea;
> It is not a matter of a hundred vessels or two hundred,
> Mathematics does not understand.
> Those who counted wore themselves out;
> O Muslim, you would have said they were a forest!
> They swam ashore;

But the dogs, as soon as they faced the port,
Saw the cannons aiming at them,
And they went toward Sidi-Farruj.[37]

For several decades, warfare was intense. When Alexis de Tocqueville visited Algeria in 1841 he observed, "We have made Muslim society far more miserable, disorganized, ignorant and barbarous than ever it was before it knew us."[38] Bugeaud's program of "military colonization" forced local populations out of their lands and replaced them with European settlers. The policy met with only limited success, for the French once again were not eager to settle in a hostile, disease-ridden land. Some French said, "Algeria is a rock without water, a place where only air is found, and even that is bad." By 1880 possibly half the European rural population of 119 thousand small-scale farmers, artisans, and traders were Spaniards, Italians, and Maltese.[39]

Brutality was a constant feature of the French presence. In 1845 a French force trapped 500 Algerian men, women, and children in the Dahra caves, where they kept fanning fires burning at the cave's entrance, suffocating the prisoners to death. Despite protests in Europe, the French commander, Pélissier de Retnaud, rose to increasingly high positions and finally became the governor-general of Algeria. The French troops sent to Africa were not a commendable lot. The long-standing practice of conscripts being allowed to buy their way out of military service by providing substitutes helped diminish the quality of troops. When jails were cleared criminals were allowed to join military labor units such as the *bataillon d'Afrique*. The French Foreign Legion, founded in 1831, was based from 1845 on south of Oran at Sidi-bel-Abbés. It eventually became an elite multinational fighting force and was sent wherever it was needed to help hold the empire together.

Faced with the French intrusion, indigenous Algerian leaders had difficult choices about how to respond. Some waited cautiously, others tried frontal attacks with little success, and still others fled beyond the battle zones to the apparent safety of Tunisia or deeper into the Sahara. According to Julia A. Clancy-Smith, "The single most representative response . . . was a wait-and-see position, an expression of bet hedging, which conferred considerable room for political manipulation and maneuvering."[40] Another dramatic but unsuccessful response was that of the Mahdi (redeemer), the militant putative descendent of the Prophet who, in a time of crisis, would raise up an army to overthrow the infidel and usher in a time of peace. The important Madhist uprising that took place in 1849 was mercilessly put down by 8 thousand French troops after a two-month siege. The village of Za atsha, southwest of Constantine, was razed; its inhabitants were killed; and the head of the Mahdi, Bu Ziyan, was cut off and displayed on a pole as a warning to other potential insurrectionists. It had just the opposite effect, however, for the martyr gained in death a stature beyond what he had attained in life and he became the subject of praise songs and poems, part of the collective folklore of resistance common to repressed peoples.

The seemingly isolated encounter had wider repercussions among the French. It resulted in the deaths of more than 1,500, many of them from cholera; detracted resources from the hoped-for Kabylia campaign; and convinced many French in Algeria of a widespread "Sufi menace."[41]

In 1863 France articulated a misnamed "Algeria for the Algerians" policy of mixed land exploitation. The concept, championed by Napoléon III, came from the writings of a mulatto intellectual and convert to Islam, Ismaïl Urbain, born of a Marseilles wine merchant and a Guyanese woman, and married to an Algerian. The emperor declared, "Algeria is not a colony properly speaking, but an Arab kingdom; the natives like the settlers have an equal right to our protection, and I am equally the emperor of the Arabs as of the French."[42] The formula adopted by the emperor, which was systematically violated, was to leave most agricultural lands with the Algerians; the Europeans would concentrate on mining and industry and receive no more free land, and the Algerians' rights to the land they held would be recognized. However, the new decrees allowed Algerians to sell communally owned lands to the French, which they soon did, often staying to work for the French as laborers and thus contributing to the disintegration of local society. Within a 14-year period, the French acquired 377 million hectares of the country's most productive farm and forest land for 37 million francs. By 1872 Algeria's population was estimated at 2,416,000 of whom 250 thousand were Europeans.

Several French regimes conducted expansionist policies in Algeria. Charles X originally sent troops there in 1830; Louis-Philippe, who followed with additional soldiers, was succeeded by Napoléon III, whose fascination with the Arab world emulated that of the original Napoléon, his more prominent ancestor. Napoléon III was possessed of what the 1911 edition of the *Encyclopedia Britannica* (vol. XIX, p. 211) called a "grave and dreamy character." More to the point, he was given to dramatic, impetuous gestures in overseas policy, hoping to find the glory there that eluded him at home. In addition to other initiatives in Algeria in 1856 he agreed to send a popular French magician, Robert Houdin (1805–1871), for a tour of troubled regions to demonstrate a greater power than that claimed by local marabouts and potential Mahdi leaders. Posing as an inventor and scientist in the imperial service, Houdin enjoyed a brief success. He used the now-harnessed electromagnetic energy in some of his tricks to humiliate Arabs and glorify France. This brief incident serves as the point of departure for a later novel, Brian Moore's *The Magician's Wife*, which relates the ragged incongruities of the French imperial temperament in overseas settings.[43]

"THE CEMETERIES ARE THE ONLY COLONIES THAT CONTINUALLY PROSPER IN ALGERIA"

It was not until 1879, almost a half-century after the arrival of the first French people, that the peoples between the sea and desert were brought under French control, but at a high cost of troops and colonists killed by hostile action or disease that caused the French to remark, "The cemeteries are the only colonies that continually prosper in Algeria." Later a caustic observer said the price of colonization was that each settler in Algeria "is seated on four dead bodies, guarded by two soldiers." Establishing civilian settlements in Algeria was further impeded by the occupation's military character. The French army, which controlled the administration of Algeria from the time of the initial conquest until the army's defeat in the Franco-Prussian War 40 years later, always viewed the settlers with suspicion. Civilian colonists were systematically excluded from political power, and resident army officers created their own policy, ignoring directives from Paris. When Bugeaud received orders not to move on Kabylia, he said the instructions arrived too late and his troops were already in the field. Success, he added, would reflect on the government in Paris; if the expedition failed, and Bugeaud was confident it would not, he would personally accept the blame. Despite an infusion of French troops, Algerian opposition continued. In 1864 an insurrection broke out south of Oran which lasted for several years, as did another in the Kabylia in 1871. Many French settlers were massacred in a jihad, and new insurrections occurred in Oran from 1881 to 1884.

Until 1879, when a civil administration was installed, France governed through the widespread use of locally recruited troops, chiefs, and councils who reported directly to army commanders. The linchpin of these local administrations were the *bureaux arabes* originally staffed by military linguists who translated French orders into Arabic for local populations. These French soldiers were charged with knowing local customs and political and other personalities, and they traveled extensively throughout their regions to raise taxes and control the activities of local chiefs. They soon became the central units of French military control in Algeria, disdainful of the populations they sought to know, and they were equally hostile and independent toward bureaucrats in France.

French policy as well was to co-opt local institutions, but the result was satisfactory neither for France nor for the subjugated peoples. In Algeria, the local judiciary, the *qadi*, were state appointed with the endorsement of Muslim religious leaders. Under the French, the delicate balance that had sustained the indigenous legal system was altered. In traditional society jurists worked patiently for consensus in dispute resolution, for the litigants must live together, often in a small town, after the case was concluded. This system was disturbed by an appeals process to French courts, which was costly. Moreover, local petitioners did not know French law, nor did the French appointed as judges understand the dynamics of the long-functioning local legal system. Not that the local system was monolithic; its members contained both reformers and reactionaries, but neither had leverage before the wide-reaching French authority. With the progressive loss of power, the *qadi* lost their Islamic religious tie as well; in the popular image, they were pictured as takers of bribes, drinkers of alcohol, and hopelessly entangled in the minutiae of French laws, decrees, and regulations.[44]

In 1881 the administration of Algeria changed yet again, and several different cabinet ministers became responsible for Algerian affairs falling within their jurisdiction. One of the administration's first moves was to force native Algerians out of 400 thousand hectares of rich coastal land between Algiers and Constantine under the pretext of putting down a rebellion. The administration's response to the political and human problems caused by this massive dislocation was an official's remark, "We shall forget their existence." Some of the new land was offered to Alsatians and Lorrainers who moved as village units to help assuage their losses in the recent war with Germany. As was true in Vietnam and Senegal, French citizenship was offered to Algerians, but only a few hundred took it, for the gulf between the two cultures was wide. With the fall of France in 1870, its settlers in Algeria wanted to be assimilated as part of the motherland and not be treated as a separate Arab kingdom. A decree to this effect, which was executed in France in October 1870, provoked a local uprising which was brutally put down. In 1896 France reversed the system of "attaching" Algerian departments directly to French ones, and the governor-general, largely a ceremonial figure until now, was given virtual control of the country's administration.[45]

How did Algerians react to French penetration? In addition to the fight or flight options, religious and lineage leaders resorted to more subtle strung-out forms of political accommodation and religious-cultural resistance, such as seen in the lives of Shaykh Muhammad (b. Abd al Qasim, 1823–1897) and his daughter and successor, Lalla Zaynab (c. 1850–1904), a devoutly religious and forceful woman leader. (Such forms of resistance are common to deeply committed religious groups facing strong opposition, as was the case with Roman Catholic recusants in Elizabethan England or Church of England loyalists under Cromwell.) Sidi Muhammad was a Muslim holy man who declined French offices, subsidies, medals, and other signs of collaboration, but constantly welcomed French officials, writers, and artists to his extensive and important *zawiya* (Sufi educational and religious center) 200 kilometers south of Algiers. His followers numbered in the thousands, and wherever he traveled, crowds came to seek his *baraka* (blessing), as they would that of his daughter. Outwardly cooperative with France, the Muslim leader was left largely alone to run his religious establishment, which grew in numbers and influence. At his death, Zaynab continued as an adroit manager of the large estates and as a spiritual teacher and healer.[46]

TUNISIA: "THE TUNISIAN PEAR IS RIPE FOR PICKING"

If the Ottoman Empire was the sick man of Europe in this century, its Tunisian satrapy was among its least healthy members. Aware of the French-Algerian conflict, and anticipating impending trouble with France, the Tunisian rulers had outlawed corsairsing, and in 1857 it became the first Moslem state to grant a constitution to the people. However, corruption and a costly modernization program, which included installation of a telegraph line and rebuilding an aqueduct at Carthage, left Tunisia's finances in chaos. The local army of 10 thousand, whose main activity was armed tax collection, was a constant drain on finances. In 1869 the British, French, and Italians created a financial commission to bring the Turkish provinces' chaotic finances into order. France had a telecommunications monopoly and the largest single agricultural project in North Africa, a 96-thousand-hectare development in what had once been known as the granary and wine cellar of the Roman Empire. France's interests were represented by "Bey Villet," an autocratic French administrator whose influence soon extended far beyond his financial commission.[47]

France had no desire to become further involved in Tunisian affairs—it had only 200 citizens there—but when Italy, which had 20 thousand settlers, appeared ready to intervene in Tunisian affairs, France ordered part of its Algerian army across the border, using as a reason the uprising of unruly local tribes. France claimed that in the decade before 1881 more than 2,600 raids crossing the Algerian-Tunisian frontier had occurred, and in 1881 Ferry, during his first term as prime minister, asked for funds for an expedition to subdue rebellious border tribes. Léon Gambetta, his successor from November 1881 to January 1882, declared that France's goal was to gain reparations, to take a large belt of territory as a precaution for the future, sign a treaty, and then retire.

There was much opposition to the move on Tunisia in the Chamber. Some deputies argued that every franc spent overseas represented a further withdrawal from the Rhine and an insult to the dead of 1870. Ferry was called *"Le Tunisien,"* a term of derision. Once they arrived, however, it was apparent to the French that only an extended occupation would allow completion of the "pacification" process and protect their commercial interests. A protectorate treaty was declared in 1881, which secured the bey's dynasty and gave France control over Tunisia's external affairs and most of its internal governance as well, including financial and military affairs. Within a few months more than 120 thousand Tunisians had fled toward Libya, and a jihad was declared against the Christian invaders, which took six months to put down. In suppressing it, France occupied all of Tunisia, including the sacred city of Kairouan, sometimes called the Mecca of North Africa. Thus what originally was viewed by France as a quick and relatively simple operation became a permanent and costly occupation, bringing down the first Ferry government. Lang-Son in Vietnam brought down his second government four years later.

Bismarck encouraged the French move on Tunis. Well aware of French bitterness over their losses to Germany, at the Berlin Congress of 1878 he suggested France find compensation for the loss of Metz and Strasbourg in Tunisia, Morocco, Egypt, or Greece. In 1879 he told the French, "The Tunisian pear is ripe for picking." The protectorate was realized following two agreements with France: the Treaty of Kassar Said of May 21, 1881, in which the Bey of Tunis ceded to France the "voluntary limitation" of external sovereignty for "a temporary but indefinite period"; and an agreement, two years later, the La Marsa Convention, competed the turnover of power to France. The bey also agreed to institute financial, judicial, and administrative reforms. Although legally a protectorate, Tunisia was often pointed to by colonial advocates as a "model colony," less cumbersome and expensive to administer than Algeria. In reality, any distinctions between the two were sharply blurred by century's end. The overwhelming fact in both cases was the presence of a large number of French troops and administrators controlling most aspects of the country's life and active or passive local opposition to their presence.[48]

MOROCCO: "A MOSAIC OF MOSLEM PEOPLES AND TRIBES, OF ARAB AND BERBER LANGUAGES"

In politically fragmented Morocco, independent towns, autonomous regions, and ruling families all were contending for power. The country was a theocratic state, with a sultan as its nominal spiritual and temporal leader. More than 300 provincial *caïds* provided the backbone of administration in the countryside. Poorly paid, they siphoned off generous portions of the royal tax collections for themselves. The army had declined to perhaps 7 thousand troops by the late 19th century, and the troops lived largely off the land. Many of the troops were Bedouins who served only for land grants and tax exemptions.

Most sultans were weak rulers, faced with revolts and a virtual state of anarchy. Louis-Hubert Lyautey, the military commander who became France's *résident général* in the early 20th century, saw Morocco as a mosaic of Moslem peoples and tribes, of Arab and Berber languages, some of whom obeyed a central power, and others of whom were independent. Internally, Morocco's 19th century is the history of conflict between the sultan and his inadequate forces, who controlled perhaps half the population of 5 million persons and one-third of the land, and strong, unruly tribes, long opposed to the ruling dynasty, including Berber tribes of the Atlas and Rif mountains who had only scorn for the country's nominal rulers but lacked the power and central organization needed to challenge them.[49]

French, British, and Spanish traders had long been active in Morocco. During the 1850s and 1860s, Moroccans exchanged rights to collect customs and legal jurisdiction over Europeans for trade agreements, from which they never really benefited. Once Tunisia came under French control in 1881, French military and colonial lobbyists increased their calls for Morocco's conquest. The sultan, Moulay Hassan (1873–1894), attempted some of the reforms Morocco needed for political stability, but most ended disastrously. He tried to stabilize the currency and modernize the army and royal bureaucracy, but everyone with a vested interest from tax collectors to members of the royal household opposed his program, veiling their self-interest in appeals to Islamic law and tradition. The sultan had also run up large debts with French banks, which negotiated the right to send French agents to collect up to 60% of Moroccan customs receipts as debt payments. European incursions brought matching Moroccan resistance in the countryside, much of it sporadic and disorganized, and in Fez, a center of traditional Islamic learning, leaders urged the sultan to replace French advisors with Muslim Turks.

The sultan's death in 1894 and the regent's death six years later precipitated a crisis. Moulay Abd el Aziz, heir to the throne, was intelligent but impulsive, often indecisive in his dealings with ministers and subjects. His entourage included several British adventurers and a Scottish *caïd*, Sir Harry Maclean, who had spent 25 years in Morocco as a military adviser and commander of the royal army. The monarch's faddish interest in modernization earned him the ire of Islamic traditionalists. Mechanical toys filled the palace, along with phonographs, billiard tables, and cameras, abandoned after being used a short while. The new sultan introduced tax reforms, abolishing traditional levies for a single tax on all agricultural products and animals. Provincial administrators received regular salaries and were deprived of tax-collecting duties, thus removing a favored source of income. As they had done with the previous sultan, those with vested interests in maintaining the old system argued the proposed reforms violated Koranic law. The sweeping reform proposals stirred up the population, but the weak ruler let conditions fester and neither withdrew the reforms nor pressed for their realization. Chaos was compounded by indecision.

Meanwhile, an itinerant prophet, known to the people as Bou Hamara, the Man on the Ass, traveled about the country, preaching revolt, denouncing the new taxes, and passing himself off as an elder brother of a sultan who had been unjustly deprived of his inheritance. He successfully stirred up the dissident tribes, and when the sultan sent an army against him, it was defeated, and the ruler was forced into exile. Bou Hamara, however, could not capitalize on the situation, for his own supporters were poorly organized and only loosely committed to him. He was captured in 1909, brought in a cage to Fez, and executed. The uprising had lasted seven years.[50]

The Moroccan empire's disintegration coincided with the general scramble for African colonies. Despite a growing desire to move into Morocco, France could not do so without risking conflict with other European powers, which had similar designs. Spain had long-established enclaves in Mililla, Ceuta, and elsewhere on the Atlantic coast. Across the straits from Tangier was the British base in Gibraltar, and Britain's share of Morocco's trade was double France's at that time. More than a thousand British traders resided in Morocco, carrying on an active sea trade with firms in London, Liverpool, and elsewhere in exchange for hides, cloth, and cereals. British advisers were close to the sultan and dangled the possibility of a large loan for public works before the monarch. France resented the growing British influence, having already lost to the British in Egypt and at Fashoda. The French army prepared for a military operation in Morocco and told the sultan that any further British inroads would result in an immediate French response. Engaged in the Boer War and with few allies in Europe, the British were vulnerable in 1902. The two countries thus began negotiations which resulted in the colonial settlement of 1904 and ended two centuries of overseas rivalry.

Morocco and Egypt were two pivotal points in the settlement. The British virtually ceded Morocco to France in turn for withdrawal of the French presence from Egypt, where France had maintained numerous advisers and merchants since Napoleonic times. France would be allowed to enter Morocco without British opposition, Tangier would become an independent city, and Spain maintained its enclaves. Germany made a vain attempt to drive a wedge between the British and the French when the kaiser visited Tangier in 1905 to demonstrate German interest, and Germany offered a plan which one observer said would give the British "strategic" Morocco, Germany "economic" Morocco, and the French "picturesque" Morocco. The Germans never followed up on their initial probings, but the British and French moved quickly to consolidate their positions.

Once established in Morocco, it was not long before France demanded control of the sultan's police, banking, and publics works administrations. The French presence kept escalating. In 1907, following the murder of nine European workers at the port of Casablanca, France occupied that large coastal city. In 1911 the French army moved decisively to suppress a widespread revolt around Fez in opposition to tax collection. A year later a French protectorate, similar to that in force in Tunisia, was declared over Morocco.

NOTES

1. Douglas Porch, *The French Foreign Legion: A Complete History of the Legendary Fighting Force* (New York: HarperPerennial, 1991), p. 5.

2. Nancy Nichols Barker, *The French Experience in Mexico, 1821–1961* (Chapel Hill: University of North Carolina Press, 1979).

3. Eugen Weber, *Peasants into Frenchmen: The Modernization of Rural France, 1870–1914* (Stanford, Calif.: Stanford University Press, 1976), p. 485; Pierre Guillaume, *Le monde colonial, XIXe-XXe siècle* (Paris: Armand Colin, 1994); D. W. Brogan, *The Development of Modern France (1870–1939)* (London: Hamish Hamilton, 1963); J. M. Thompson, *Louis Napoleon and the Second Empire* (New York: W. W. Norton, 1995).

4. Weber, *Peasants into Frenchmen*, p. 489.

5. Jacques Thobie, "La France coloniale de 1870 à 1914," in *Histoire de la France coloniale des origines à 1914*, ed. Jean Myer, Jean Tarrade, Annie-Ray Goldzeigeur, and Jacque Thobie (Paris: Armand Colin, 1991), p. 617.

6. Jacques Thobie, "Le bilan colonial en 1914," in Jacques Thobie, Gilbert Meynier, Catherine Coquery-Vidrovitch, and Charles-Robert Ageron, eds., *Histoire de la France coloniale, 1914–1990* (Paris: Armand Colin, 1990), pp. 27, 300–301.

7. Quoted in William B. Cohen, *The French Encounter with Africans, White Response to Blacks, 1530–1990* (Bloomington: Indiana University Press, 1980), p. 265, from Bulletin de la Société de Géographie, 2 (1924) p. 240; Stuart Michael Persell, *The French Colonial Lobby, 1889–1938* (Stanford, Calif.: Hoover Institution Press, 1983).

8. Quoted in Raoul Girardet, *L'Idée coloniale en France, 1871–1962* (Paris: Table Ronde, 1979), p. 33.

9. Gilbert Comte, *L'Empire triomphant, 1971–1936*, vol. 1, *Afrique occidentale et équatoriale* (Paris: Denoël, 1988), pp. 35–39, 47ff.

10. Henri Brunchweg, *Mythes et réalités de l'impérialisme colonial français, 1871– 1914* (Paris: Librarie Armand Colin, 1960), pp. 105–134; Cohen, *French Encounter*, pp. 243–245.

11. Paul Leroy-Beaulieu, *De la colonisation chez les peuples modernes* (Paris: Guillaumin, 1874), pp. 605–606.

12. Porch, *French Foreign Legion*, pp. 232–234.

13. Annie Rey-Goldzeigeur, "La France coloniale de 1830 à 1870," in Jean Meyer, Jean Tarrade, Annie-Rey Goldzeigeur, and Jacques Thobie, eds., *Histoire de la France coloniale des origines à 1914* (Paris: Armand Colin, 1991), p. 610.

14. Girardet, *L'Idée coloniale*, pp. 67ff.

15. Charles-Robert Ageron, "De l'Empire à la dislocation de l'Union française," in *Histoire de la France coloniale, 1914–1990*, ed. Jacques Thobie, Gilbert Meynier, Catherine Coquery-Vidrovitch, and Charles-Robert Ageron (Paris: Armand Colin, 1990), p. 404.

16. Quoted in Milton E. Osborne, *The French Presence in Cochinchina and Cambodia, Rule and Response (1859–1905)* (Ithaca, N.Y.: Cornell University Press, 1969), p. 42.

17. Girardet, *L'Idée coloniale*, p. 4.

18. Charles-Andres Julien, *Les techniciens de la colonisation (XIXe-XXe siècles)* (Paris: Presses Universitaires de France, 1947); Alf Andrew Heggoy and John M. Harr, *The Military in Imperial History: The French Connection* (New York: Garland Publishing, 1984).

19. John F. Caddy, *The Roots of French Imperialism in Eastern Asia* (Ithaca, N.Y.: Cornell University Press, 1967), pp. 73–93 passim.

20. William B. Cohen, *Rulers of Empire: The French Colonial Service in Africa* (Palo Alto, Calif.: Stanford University Press, 1971), p. 41.

21. D. Bardot, *Guide Practique de l'Européen dans l'Afrique Occidentale* (Paris: n.p., 1902), pp. 328–331, quoted in John D. Hargreaves, *France and West Africa: An Anthology of Historical Documents* (New York: Macmillan, 1969), pp. 207–209.

22. Quoted in Cohen, *Rulers of Empire*, p. 42.

23. John Dunmore, *French Explorers in the Pacific*, vol. II, *The Nineteenth Century* (New York: Oxford University Press, 1965), pp. 41–42, quoted in R. Bouvier and E. Maynial, *Une aventure dans les mers australes* (Paris: n.p., 1992), pp. 165–166.

24. G. L. Angoulvant, *La Pacification de la Côte d'Ivoire*, General Instructions, November 26, 1908 (Paris: n.p., 1916), pp. 60–67, quoted in Hargreaves, *France and West Africa*, pp. 202–204.

25. Guillaume, *Le monde colonial*, p. 146.

26. Jeremy Murray-Brown, *Faith and the Flag: The Opening of Africa* (Boston: George Allen & Unwin, 1977), pp. 174–201; Girardet, *L'Idée coloniale*, pp. 32–37.

27. Girardet, *L'Idée coloniale*, p. 35.

28. Ibid., p. 37.

29. Murray-Brown, *Faith and Flag*, p. 181.

30. Murray-Brown, *Faith and Flag*, p. 188.

31. Ageron, "De l'Empire," pp. 563–564.

32. Jean Martin, *L'Empire Triomphant, 1871–1936*, vol. 2, *Maghreb, Indochine, Madagascar, îles et comptoirs* (Paris: Denoël, 1990), pp. 47–183.

33. Charles-Robert Ageron, *Modern Algeria: A History from 1830 to the Present*, trans. Michael Brett (Trenton, N.J.: Africa World, 1991); V. G. Kierman, *Colonial Em-

pires and Armies, 1815–1960 (Montréal: McGill-Queen's University Press, 1982 and 1998), pp. 73–76; Julia Clancy-Smith, "Islam, Gender and Identities in the Making of French Algeria, 1830–1962," in *Domesticating the Empire: Race, Gender, and Family Life in French and Dutch Colonialism*, ed. Julia Clancy-Smith and Frances Gouda (Charlottesville: University of Virginia Press, 1998), pp. 154–174.

34. David R. Headrick, *The Tools of Empire: Technology and European Imperialism in the Nineteenth Century* (New York: Oxford University Press, 1981), p. 92.

35. Porch, *French Foreign Legion*, pp. 70–89.

36. Guillaume, *Le monde colonial*, p. 27.

37. Alf Andrew Heggoy, *The French Conquest of Algiers, 1830: An Algerian Oral Tradition* (Athens: Ohio University Center for International Studies, Africa Studies Program, 1986), pp. 3–8, 20–23. The poem "Song About the Taking of Algiers" by Si Abd al Kader is from E. Daumas, *Moeurs et coutumes de l'Algérie: Tell, Kabylie, Sahara* (Paris: Hachette et Cie, 1853) pp. 130–144.

38. Quoted in Ageron, *Modern Algeria*, p. 21.

39. Ibid., p. 59.

40. Julia A. Clancy-Smith, *Rebel and Saint, Muslim Notables, Populist Protest Colonial Encounters (Algeria and Tunisia, 1800–1904)* (Berkeley: University of California Press, 1997), p. 71.

41. Ibid., p. 117.

42. Guillaume, *Le monde colonial*, p. 28.

43. Brian Moore, *The Magician's Wife* (New York: Dutton, a William Abrahams Book, 1998).

44. Allan Christelow, *Muslim Law Courts and the French Colonial State in Algeria* (Princeton, N.J.: Princeton University Press, 1985), pp. 262–265.

45. Ageron, *Modern Algeria*, pp. 47ff; David Prochaska, *Making Algeria French: Colonialism in Bône, 1870–1920* (Cambridge: Cambridge University Press, 1990).

46. Clancy-Smith, *Rebel and Saint*, pp. 218–245.

47. Martin, *L'Empire Triomphant*, pp. 85–95.

48. Ibid., pp. 96–107.

49. Edmund Burke III, *Prelude to Protectorate in Morocco, Precolonial Protest and Resistance, 1860–1912* (Chicago: University of Chicago Press, 1976); William A. Hoisington, Jr., *Lyautey and the French Conquest of Morocco* (New York: St. Martin's Press, 1995).

50. Douglas Porch, *The Conquest of Morocco* (New York: Knopf, 1983), pp. 95–96, 98–107, 205–208.

5

The 19th Century: The Military's and Missionaries' Empire (Part II)

INDOCHINA

France's East Asian colonial presence is directly traceable to the recrudescence of Roman Catholicism in France during the post-Napoleonic period, part of the backlash against the political radicalism and intellectual rationalism of a revolutionary age. This resurgence of religious interest was fueled by widespread nostalgia for the Church and the monarchy as they supposedly once were, and for the Gallican Church to assert its overseas role as the "eldest daughter of Rome." By appealing to the religious revival's followers, politicians of the right hoped to strengthen their position and stem the growing tides of republicanism and socialism. Defeated in recent wars with Britain, the new French monarchy was held suspect by Europe's traditional rulers for accepting a king, Louis XVIII (reign 1814–1824), whom they said plucked his crown from the gutter after a street brawl, and whose country was a nesting ground for socialists and radicals. Anxious to improve his lot, Louis championed the Church, restoring the two missionary groups most active in the Far East, the Société des Missions Étrangères and the Lazarist Society. The Paris Seminary, which became a center for overseas missionary work, was reopened in 1823, and a missionary group, l'Oeuvre pour la Propagation de la Foi, followed.[1]

The French presence in Vietnam actually began in the late 18th century. In 1772 a French bishop and dabbler in local politics, Pigneau de Behaine, backed Nguyen Anh, one of the claimants to the throne. In 1787 the bishop took the pretender's son with him to Paris, where he persuaded the government to provide his client with over a thousand French-trained troops from India. In turn, the

French government received commercial concessions, including control over the large harbor at Tourane and the offshore island of Poulo Condore. Nguyen Anh successfully conquered the southernmost part of Vietnam and hoped to seize the entire country. Pigneau plunged enthusiastically into the fray, and soon he and several followers were named court mandarins. They helped build a royal army and navy, created a currency, organized a civil administration, and advised the ruler on foreign and domestic policy. The bishop, wounded while leading the royal troops in an assault, died in 1799. By now, however, France was wracked by Revolution, and the French religious and commercial presence in Vietnam languished.[2]

In 1839 the Vatican responded to the favorable new climate in France by awarding it a significant missionary role in Asia, thus limiting Portugal's centuries-old claim to exclusive missionary rights, which until then had been protected by papal bull. Several important Chinese vicarates were given to the Society of Foreign Missions, and in 1850 the successor to the Portuguese bishop of Beijing was a French Lazarist. By 1848, 58 members of the Jesuit order were active in China, often dressing and living like Chinese, despite disease and hostile climate. Zealous and hard-working, the French missionaries moved quickly to the interior of East Asia whenever there were opportunities, paying little attention to the vagaries and formalities of international politics. In China, the missionaries were generally tolerated; in Vietnam and Korea they were often persecuted.

The missionaries' numbers grew—from 75 between 1859 and 1868, to 135 between 1870 and 1880, to 136 between 1881 and 1890. By 1904 in Tonkin there were four bishops, 105 missionaries, and 32 nuns of the Order of Saint Paul of Chartres and three cloistered Carmelites. Where possible, the missionaries' strategy was to gather converts in Christian villages. Here the priest was the central figure and often the only European presence.

Many such missionaries learned local dialects, lived in the only cement house in the village, and mandarin-like, represented both a temporal and a spiritual authority. Around them clustered the mission school, the medical dispensary, a small convent for the nuns, possibly an orphanage, and homes for native catechists.[3] Charles Meyer has described the priest's role:

They expected everything from him. Not only to be the spiritual guide who brings the good news and presides at liturgies. In the true Confucian sense of the term, he should be *the Father* who protects against the colonial administration, mandarins and pirates, dispenses justice and arbitrates differences, chastises and pardons, gives work orders for the general interest, and preserves peace and prosperity for the community of which he has charge.[4]

Opposing the growing French presence was a carefully structured, culturally self-contained society of long duration. The office of Vietnamese emperor was modeled on the Chinese one—a son of heaven who spent most of his time secluded in the imperial city of Hue, itself suggesting the forbidden palace of

Beijing. Here the emperor, surrounded by mandarin advisors, ruled by dictates that depended heavily on Confucian precedents. The state was highly centralized; its bureaucracy had nine orders of mandarins subservient to the emperor. Military castes, religious hierarchies, or wealthy landowners were never allowed to form groups that might threaten the royal court; all political power rested ultimately with the emperor. Next came an elaborate system of provincial governors, prefects, subprefects, cantons, and hamlets. The Vietnamese saying that "the emperor's power stops at the hamlet's gate" meant that day-to-day life in the country operated independently of the semidivine figure at the top. French officials originally misunderstood the system, believing the Vietnamese hamlet resembled a French village, with a similar mayor and council, but this was not the case. In Vietnam, there were two categories of notables: the greater, usually wealthy landowners who made decisions; and the lesser, who carried out the decisions and from whom the administrator or mayor was chosen but with no powers of his own. Under the French, these mayors were responsible for tax collection, recruiting for work gangs, and acting as a conduit for orders, and they were given responsibilities that never would have been given them in traditional society.

The Vietnamese monarchy, except for Nguyen Anh's attempt to use the bishop, never voluntarily cooperated with the French. A continual line of militant resistance to outside domination existed throughout Vietnamese history, traceable before the earliest days of the French incursions to Vietnamese opposition to the dominant Chinese presence emanating from across Vietnam's northern border. Although 19th century anti-French resistance movements were supported by the mandarins, the latters' goals were retrogressive and traditional, aimed at restoring Confucian practices and holding on to their own comfortable sinecures.

As in Algeria, the Vietnamese resisted the French intrusion at all levels. Times had changed by mid-century, and no longer were the missionaries kingmakers and court favorites. Mistrust and suspicion had set in. Christians were strangers in the land in Vietnam; they represented perhaps 20 thousand persons out of a population of 2 million in the period before the French occupation. Persecutions were frequent, and a French priest of the 1840s wrote about being moved about among Christian homes under cover of darkness lest his hosts attract reprisals. Minh Mang (reign 1820–1841) rid the country of all French advisers; during his monarchy seven missionaries were executed, as were numerous native Catholics, who were accused of stirring rebellion against the emperor. Thieu Tri (reign 1841–1847) expelled more missionaries. The French responded by shelling Tourane harbor in 1847, and French Catholics increasingly called for military intervention, declaring that the xenophobic emperor Tu Duc (reign 1847–1883) forbade all expressions of Christianity and threatened to execute indigenous and European priests. In 1848 Tu Duc proclaimed,

The religion of Gia To [Jesus Christ] already forbidden by the kings Minh Mang and Thieu Tri is a perverse religion, for in that religion they do not respect the cult of the ancestors, they close the eyes of the dying to use a magical water which serves to fascinate people, and further they commit other superstitious and abominable acts. In consequence, the European masters who are the most culpable should be thrown in the sea with a stone around their neck.[5]

Minh Mang ordered his mandarins to force the Christians "in their presence, to trample the cross underfoot." During the 1850s as many as 25 Europeans and 300 Vietnamese priests and 30 thousand Christians had been killed in persecutions in the previous 12 years. The blood of the martyrs would be the seed from which the colony grew.[6]

On November 25, 1857, Napoléon III, having heard the missionaries' protests of persecutions, sent a naval squadron to redress their grievances. Napoléon had recently received complaints about the emperor Tu Duc. The missionaries complained that Catholics had suffered persecutions for over 26 years and the infrequent visits of French gunboats had left the mandarins angry but unconquered. It was time now, they argued, to replace the emperor with a pro-Christian ruler who would protect missionaries and Christians and agree to commercial treaties. A French expeditionary force arrived the following August. They were instructed to seize the port of Tourane to guarantee any accord reached with the Hue government, to demand indemnification for the loss of French lives and property, and to receive assurances that the French would receive better treatment in the future.

ADMIRAL VERSUS BISHOP

However, delays in the fleet's assembling meant the August 31 arrival gave the French invaders less than three months before the start of the long tropical rainy season. Monseigneur Pellerin, who had worked hard to persuade Napoléon III of the expedition's importance, returned to Vietnam with a fleet of 14 French ships, commanded by Admiral Charles Rigault de Genouilly. Although admiral and bishop stood amicably on the bridge of the admiral's flagship, they soon became bitter adversaries. The French breached the flimsy harbor defenses and landing parties went ashore. The main Vietnamese force, estimated at between 7 thousand and 8 thousand troops, gathered west of the city. After the landing was accomplished, the French waited. The Vietnamese did not counterattack, and the debilitating heat and humidity began to take their toll of the invaders. Dysentery, malaria, cholera, and other tropical diseases quickly decimated the French ranks. Slight wounds turned gangrenous, resulting in amputations performed by unqualified field surgeons. Almost 100 persons died monthly from disease during the worst period of the French stay at Tourane.

By mid-October the heavy rains came and lasted several months. Missionaries had predicted a popular uprising of Christians and Vietnamese who disliked the emperor, as well as a grateful populace to help the French build fortifications, but that did not happen. The cautious Vietnamese avoided the foreigners, and soon the army's main concern was finding shelter, building hospitals, and keeping dry. The Vietnamese did not directly engage the French but built strong fortifications close to the French lines and waited.

As their situation deteriorated, tempers flared between the admiral and the bishop. The admiral was angered by the local peoples' hostility to the French and said that the missionaries had painted a too-rosy picture of an easy conquest. The missionaries argued that the French military was too cautious, a simple landing was not enough, and something more dramatic was needed, like capturing the capital of Hue and replacing the emperor with a pro-Christian successor. Hue was only a short distance from the harbor at Tourane. Had the French moved on the imperial city shortly after arriving, while it remained undefended, they probably could have taken it. However, they lacked the shallow-draft boats needed to move up the Perfumed River to the royal city, which was left unchallenged.

In early February 1859, Admiral Genouilly left part of his force at Tourane and sailed with most of his troops southward to Saigon, a small southern port city, where he hoped for a consolation victory. By mid-month he had seized the city and, with it, a quantity of firearms, powder, and sufficient rice to feed several thousand troops for a year. Leaving a small garrison behind, he returned north where the situation had worsened. Disease had reduced full companies to skeleton forces of from 20 to 30 soldiers. Cemeteries were often too small for the number of cadavers, and common graves were widely used. Funeral services were brief; commemorations for the dead, few.

Meanwhile, the Vietnamese remained unyielding. Local populations were hostile to the European invaders, and in June the admiral began negotiations with the Hue government which led to a complete withdrawal from Tourane. When the Vietnamese prolonged the talks, he abandoned demands for a land base, religious liberty for missionaries and indigenous Christians, and commercial privileges. Some of Genouilly's greatly reduced forces were withdrawn for an Anglo-French expedition in China; disease swept the remaining ranks. The last French troops left on March 22, 1860.

SAIGON: "WHERE THE LARGE HOSPITAL IS ALWAYS FULL AND THE LARGE CATHEDRAL IS ALWAYS EMPTY"

The French, however, remained in Saigon. Here they were in a relatively favorable position, with a force of 800 troops, many of them Senegalese. Eventually the force was increased to 4 thousand soldiers, including 2 thousand French troops. By June 1861 Saigon and three adjoining provinces were conquered and emperor Tu Duc was forced to conclude a peace. He was now in less favorable circumstances than before. By occupying Saigon the French had cut off his major rice supply, and a serious rebellion broke out in the north with another contender for the throne. The French, in a position of strength for the first time, made demands they were unable to secure earlier. They also asked for a sizable monetary indemnity and commercial concessions, including open-ing the port of Tourane to French traders.

However, the French troops still had to combat both hostile peoples and disease. Figures for illness and death were high, and Saigon became known as a city "where the large hospital is always full and the large cathedral is always empty."[7] Of the 3,500 troops who landed in 1861, 347 soon died and 371 were medically evacuated. Another 2,774 visited the main Saigon medical compound; 170 of them died, and 371 were evacuated. Dysentery, which accounted for 43.5% of the fatalities in 1862, was the main killer; from 15% to 30% of the remaining deaths came from mosquito-borne diseases, followed by cholera and typhoid. Hospitals of that era were considered annexes of cemeteries rather than as places of healing. Medical evacuation ships made up to ten voyages a year between France and Saigon in the 1870s, and fatalities were numerous aboard the ships as well.[8]

Meanwhile, local populations practiced forms of active and passive resis-tance—an ambush here, a food delivery not made elsewhere, and cultural re-sistance in the form of songs, long narrative poems, and folk tales seemingly about mythical characters, dogs, ants, lice, crabs, and mosquitoes that were, in reality, the French or those who collaborated with them.

Notable among the resistance figures was Truong Dinh (1820–1864), a south-ern regimental commander in the royal army and a skilled organizer married to a wealthy, land-owning wife. Truong and his locally recruited soldiers fought harassing actions, confronting the French in places, then withdrawing inland. Malaria, he declared, was a "special ally" to help compensate for superior French armaments.[9] Despite superior knowledge of the terrain and language, Truong Dinh's forces were overwhelmed by greater French numbers and firepower and weakened by a devastating famine in 1864. Finally, the resistance leader was betrayed by a former associate, Cong Tan, who later became a prefect in the colonial administration. At Cong Tan's death, a nationalist poet, Nguyen Van Lac, encountered the funeral cortege, part of the elaborate local burial ritual, and wrote these bitter lines, an elegy-in-reverse called "The Floating Dog's Corpse,"

> In life you snatched meek rabbits and listened to them squeak in pain,
> In death your rotting carcass drifts down the river,
> The colors on your hide jumbled yet still clear,
> The smell infamous and penetrating to the core.
> Only a gang of shrimps lingers as a cortege,
> Bustling to greet the circling crows and falcons.
> Along comes the wind and the splash of a wave,
> See how your bones and flesh scatter.[10]

THE NEXT PHASE: "WE WILL WORK
ON THE MANDARINS"

After the 1860s the importance of the missionaries to French East Asian policy diminished; they became one voice among many in colonial affairs. Once the French were established, the next task was building an administrative system. Admiral Louis Adolph Bonard filled even the most obscure provincial posts with French clerks. The principal regional administrators, called inspectors of native affairs, were responsible for justice, taxation, and civil administration in units of roughly 20 thousand people. Bonard's successor, Admiral Pierre Paul Marie de la Grandière had no respect for native institutions. In 1865 he stated, "We will work on the mandarins, and if the fruit does not fall by itself, we will shake the tree."[11]

Although the admirals never did prepare a specific plan for the colony's development, their goal was to secure a "land forever French, open to the civilization, the riches, and the fertile ideas of Europe, which will radiate over neighboring countries."[12] De la Grandière, on his own and with no instructions from Paris, annexed the three provinces west of the Mekong River, using as a pretext the suppression of an anti-French uprising. All of Cochin China, the southern part of Vietnam, was now under French control, and it was formally declared a colony. (Traditional Vietnam was divided into three parts—Tonkin, Annam, and Conchin, corresponding to north, central, and south.)

One of Bonard's initiatives had been to replace the Chinese characters in the Vietnamese script with the missionaries' Latinized alphabet, *quôc-ngu*, or national language. While most administrators vehemently opposed the use of Chinese characters as a visible affront to French culture and civilizing efforts, a few argued it was more logical for the handful of French administrators to learn Vietnamese than for millions of local people to acquire a new language. Some French administrators believed that *quôc-ngu* was a bastard language, one not suitable for effectively translating traditional concepts or for providing an adequate substitute for French. Since *quôc-ngu* originated with the missionaries, its early literature was catechisms and saints' lives, and since Catholics were the first people who learned it, they became the government's clerks and interpreters.

A monthly official journal was begun in Saigon in 1865 to print decrees and agricultural or commercial information in *quôc-ngu*. A contemporary French source said the journal should "recount the lives of the great men of France, give anecdotes taken from picturesque magazines or from children's journals, so as to give the natives an appreciation of our character in its most noble expressions . . . and to satisfy the passion which they have for reading." By 1869 six schools in Saigon taught French and by 1870 small provincial schools taught *quôc-ngu* to more than 5 thousand persons, often using provincial interpreters as teachers. Some of the schools competed with missionary establishments, which caused friction, and frequently children of the poorer families were sent to fill the village's school quota, as traditional ruling elites continued to value Confucian education, which endured until that generation of Confucian teachers died out. Teaching at government schools was accomplished by rote memorization; one administrator said the children were like parrots who had learned to read and write.[13]

FRENCH EXPANSION

In the mid-1860s the French began explorations of the Mekong River, seeking a water route to the inland China trade. The expedition was led by Doudart de Largée, who established the French protectorate over Cambodia, and Francis Garnier, a former naval officer, now employed as a civil administrator. After discovering the Mekong did not offer a navigable waterway to the sources of the China trade, Garnier, an adventurer-imperialist with a short but meteoric career, planned to explore the Red River delta to the north. His published report of the Mekong explorations attracted wide attention in France, and Garnier used the book to urge France to assert its national greatness and commit enough troops and money overseas to rival the English globally. Seeing himself as a second Dupleix, Garnier wanted France to build in Indochina the empire it had lost in India. Garnier respected traditional Chinese culture, but he was an enthusiastic supporter of France's civilizing mission: France "has received from Providence a higher mission, that of emancipation, of bringing into the light and into liberty the races and peoples still enslaved by ignorance and despotism."[14]

In 1873 Garnier was asked by Admiral Marie Jules Dupré, Cochin China's governor-general, to help take Hanoi. Dupré wanted to use a Vietnamese request to expel a French arms smuggler as an excuse for intervention. He would send a small force to Hanoi for that purpose and, finding it threatened by coastal black flag pirates and the Chinese, would establish a protectorate under a clause in the 1862 treaty and seize the citadel and coastal provinces until an agreement justifying their takeover could be concluded. The admiral asked the French government for permission to carry out his project and in September received a brief telegraphic reply, saying only he should do nothing to expose France to dangerous complications. Since this was not a flat refusal, Dupré pressed on, and with three small vessels and 60 troops led by Garnier, set out to take Hanoi. Finding the city's defenses weak, he declared the Red River open for trade and stormed the citadel on November 20. Garnier's swiftly rising career ended on December 21, 1873, while he was working on treaty details with the Vietnamese at Hanoi. A group of coastal black flag pirates attacked the citadel and were quickly routed, but Garnier pursued them and was killed, along with several members of the French party.[15]

Garnier's rapid gains were wiped out by a colleague who was sent to complete the negotiations. In contrast to the activist Garnier, P.-L.-F. Philastre was a scholar-administrator who had translated the lengthy Gia-Long legal code from

Chinese characters into French. An inspector of native affairs and director of the Office of Native Justice, he was one of a handful of colonial administrators to question sharply some French colonial practices, such as trying to impose French legal norms on Vietnamese society. Noting the Vietnamese peoples' armed resistance to the French, Philastre argued that while France claimed to respect the traditions of a conquered people, "We pitilessly violate these customs and institutions." Notwithstanding, he believed the French presence was necessary "to raise up the Annamite people from the state of moral degradation into which they have fallen."[16]

Philastre denounced Garnier's conquests as unwarranted aggression, withdrew the small French force from Hanoi, and sought no concessions in return. As soon as news of the unilateral French withdrawal spread, several hundred Christian villages around Hanoi were burned, and French settlers in Saigon became angry at Philastre. The retreat, however, was supported by the ministry, for the overenthusiastic Garnier had clearly exceeded his instructions. The final treaty, signed on March 15, 1874, established a resident French consul, with a guard force at Hue. Other articles established Christianity and opened Hanoi and several other ports to commerce, which the French were powerless at that time to enforce. The Franco-Prussian war had just ended, and France had no troops to send to Vietnam. It was not until 1883, when a French force of 250 soldiers was defeated in a skirmish with the Vietnamese, that the French Chamber voted funds for Tonkin's conquest. French troops bombarded Hue, unaware that the Emperor Tu Duc had died a few weeks earlier, and on August 25, 1883, the court mandarins signed a treaty making both Tonkin and Annam French protectorates. Laos was taken a decade later, under the pretext that it was land controlled by Vietnam, the same tenuous argument used to justify the French seizure of Cambodia.

JOSEPH-SIMON GALLIENI AND THE *TACHE D'HUILE*

Joseph-Simon Gallieni (1849–1916), who had served previously in the Sudan, was stationed in Indochina from 1892 to 1895, assigned by the governor-general, J.-L. de Lannesan, to the Haut-Tonkin region, where unrest was substantial, no clear authority was evident, and piracy was widespread. Gallieni was a conventional secular Republican in political views and an action-oriented field commander rather than a theorist.[17] Success was measured in numbers of opponents brought under control and in the quantity of roads, bridges, markets, schools, and medical dispensaries built locally. Gallieni belonged to a small band of Third Republic commanders, many of them self-contained and ascetic in demeanor, who, after going abroad, quickly became impatient with policy vacillation and with the slow communication with France. They often took action locally, believing that was what commanders were trained to do.

Gallieni arrived in 1892, followed in 1894 by an admirer, Louis-Hubert Lyautey, and soon he had secured for himself complete control of military and civilian affairs and launched a carefully planned and coordinated frontal attack on the insurgents. Next he began pacification of the region, preparing cartographic and ethnographic maps; building an infrastructure of roads, bridges, markets, schools, and dispensaries; and dismissing corrupt mandarins who had a stranglehold on local populations. Gallieni called this carefully coordinated military and social strategy the *tache d'huile*, the oil spot. Start out and carefully secure a hundred such bases and you are on your way to conquering a country, or so the argument went. Gallieni also developed a technique that would gain widespread currency in Vietnam in later times: the fortified village. Once a village was brought under government control, and its leadership was secure and loyal to France, Gallieni distributed arms to the villagers, as he had in the Sudan. Some French military objected vocally to the plan, but Gallieni saw it as an effective way to build trust with local populations. His basic idea, much of which came from another colonial administrator, Colonel Théophile Pennequin, was simple. France would always be a minority population in a colonial setting; therefore, it should rule through local power structures. Keep them intact, co-opt them, and reward their leaders. The fatal flaw in such a policy is that it fails to take into account local resistance, which was strong in places like the Sudan, Indochina, Madagascar, and the Maghreb. When that happened, France's response was military conquest or, eventually, withdrawal.

The Vietnamese state at this time was a client of the Chinese emperor; the Vietnamese emperor's royal insignia was known as "the lesser dragon," containing one less claw than that of the Chinese emperor, and when they met, the Vietnamese sovereign went on foot the final distance to pay homage to his Chinese counterpart. Thus when the Chinese signed the second Treaty of Tien Tsin with France, abandoning Vietnam to French control, the Vietnamese mandarins had either to accept becoming a French protectorate, with a stinging loss of face, or ask their traditional Chinese patrons to revisit their policy.[18] The king fled the capital on July 5, 1885, a symbolic act with two significant implications. First, by vacating the royal palace at Hue and moving into the countryside, the royal presence gave legitimacy to active resistance against the French. Second, with the throne empty but with the king alive, any collaborationist monarch the French might back would always be seen as a usurper.

FRENCH-VIETNAMESE RELATIONS: "YOUR COUNTRY BELONGS TO THE WESTERN SEAS, OURS TO THE SEA OF THE EAST"

Many Vietnamese closest to the French came from the Roman Catholic converts, once the converts were sure France was not planning to withdrew. The quality of this first group of Vietnamese clerks, militia, hospital orderlies, and interpreters did not satisfy the French, who knew that the trained mandarins, on whom the traditional administration depended, had departed for the north, taking their tax and census records with them. A contemporary French administrator said that most of the current local employees were "catechists sacked by their bishops for misconduct, who under a Latin (Christian) name presented a summary of the deception, the prevarication, and the corruption of Asia." More impressive to the French were such figures as Tran Ba Loc who rose to significant advisory positions in the administration. A product of mission schools, Loc had moved with his family into a zone of French control shortly after the French occupied Cochin China. He joined the newly formed French militia and helped put down anti-French and anti-Catholic elements. Late in life Loc expressed his esteem, for France, "If I have served France to this day, it has been so as to be able to cover the object of my affections with the shadow of my influence."[19]

Another Vietnamese who occupied a significant position in the local administration was Pétrus Truong Vinh Ky, a graduate of mission schools with a gift for languages. He began to work for the French administration in 1860, a relationship that lasted 40 years as teacher, editor, interpreter, and, in the 1870s, a political counselor to the French. In his writings Ky, whom one administrator called "the most Frenchified Annamite we have," presented Vietnam as a disinherited country, whose Chinese political and cultural tradition left it atrophied, unable to function as a modern state. His preference for French instead of mandarin rule was expressed in a poem written in the 1870s describing the French presence as a wind or a flood destroying the tree of traditional culture. It concluded,

> Let us offer homage to the striking powers of the French;
> Let us make our farewells to the Fatherland and unite with the French.[20]

After 1881 French citizenship was offered to Vietnamese who could read or write French, or who had earned major military decorations. The application process was long and difficult, and some Vietnamese were confused by the requirement that new citizens adopt a French family name; in Vietnamese usage, the extended family's name was the first name listed. Often fewer than three persons applied each year, and many of these were former soldiers, clerks, telegraph operators, and military hospital orderlies. Like Algerians, many Vietnamese of means and influence, such as Ky, saw little value in having French citizenship. By 1906 there were only 254 naturalized French citizens in Cochin China, including Chinese and Europeans living in Saigon.

Widespread opposition to French culture also existed. The Vietnamese knew they had a long history and a proud Confucian past they believed superior to that offered by France's civilizing mission. A number of Vietnamese challenged the French, such as the blind poet Nguyen Dinh Chieu, who encouraged opposition to the French through his verses. A broader-based resistance movement flared up in central Vietnam from 1885 to 1888, and guerrilla warfare was encouraged there by the scholar-nationalist Phan Dinh Phung until his death in 1895. Secret societies and syncretic religious movements became surrogate nationalistic groups. As early as 1862, a remarkable document was circulated in

Go Cong, a province south of Saigon, that in argument and tone summarized the shape Vietnamese opposition to foreign powers would assume over the next century. "Just as the horse and the buffalo differ between themselves" so the Vietnamese and the French differ, it argued, adding that the Vietnamese would pay a ransom for their territory, make commercial concessions, but ultimately, "your country belongs to the Western seas, ours to the sea of the East.... If you insist on bringing fire and the sword amongst us, disorder will last for a long time.... When we lack everything, we will take branches for flags and sticks to arm our soldiers. How then will you be able to live in the middle of us?"[21]

By the late 19th century a Herodian elite of wealthy or educated Vietnamese emerged, fully trusted by neither the French nor their own people. Do Huu Phuong was a wealthy Saigon businessman who extended generous hospitality to the resident French, wore European clothes, visited France four times, and frequented the Café de la Paix. A Vietnamese poem, "The International Exposition," described officials on leave gathering there: "One meets the mandarin Do Huu Phuong, and Bonner is seated there chatting."[22] Two of Do's sons became officers in the French forces; two others were administrators in Cochin China. While a small number of Vietnamese rose to positions of wealth or local responsibility under the French, sustained resistance to the European presence endured throughout most of the 19th and 20th centuries. The French were never really welcomed by the majority of Vietnamese. Like Algerians, the Vietnamese were part of an ancient culture, with its own language, religion, and political system, and they viewed Europeans as intruders.

THE DOUMER YEARS: INCREASED CENTRAL CONTROL

Although France claimed Vietnam, it never developed any consistent policy toward it until the administration of Paul Doumer as governor-general (1897–1902). Doumer, who later became president of France, removed all power from the mandarins, placed a puppet emperor on the throne, put down the vestiges of armed opposition, and established direct French rule in every aspect of the administration. His economic and social policies, like the administrative structure he devised, lasted with minor modifications throughout Vietnam's colonial period. Consolidating the economic resources of the entire region under French control, he built roads, railroads, canals, bridges, and harbors to make the country economically viable. Anxious that Vietnam pay a major portion of the total costs of his programs, he taxed the lucrative opium, alcohol, and salt commerce for money to fund his extensive public works projects. Doumer was not interested in indigenous economic development, but in realizing quick profits for France through exporting raw materials and natural resources, including rice, rubber, coal, and other minerals. According to Doumer, "With the empire modernized, the new Indochina can reach a prosperity and a glory about which the ancestors of our present subjects could not have dared dream."[23]

CAMBODIA: "YOUR PROTECTION IS THE CREMATION OF THE MONARCHY"

When the French explored the Mekong River they became interested in nearby Cambodia. The Mekong, another river which Europeans thought would lead to the riches of China, crossed Cambodia, a once-powerful state of perhaps one million persons that was now a vassal to two expanding powers, Vietnam and Siam (Thailand). In 1811, when the Cambodian king asked the Vietnamese for support in putting down a rebellious brother, Vietnam took advantage of the invitation to intervene in Cambodian affairs.

In 1863 France declared a protectorate over Cambodia, which Norodom, the Cambodian emperor (1860–1904), was powerless to resist, as he had just ended an extended period of intrafamily warfare. France would guard Cambodia from external attack, help keep internal order, and affirm the king's sovereignty. In return, Catholic missionaries and French traders would be protected, a French representative would be appointed to the Cambodian court, and France would take over the country's foreign affairs. The protectorate's legal justification, thin as it may have been, was that Vietnam historically claimed suzerainty over Cambodia, and France, having now established a protectorate over part of Vietnam, was entitled to assume control over Cambodia as well. Traditional rule was by a god-king who symbolized the nation but whose actual powers were limited. So divine was the king that once, when he fell from a carriage in Phnom Penh, he was left unaided until a European assisted him—no Cambodian would dare touch the royal personage. Although the king's control over his immediate court was unlimited, his actual power did not always extend over family members or outlying provinces, and dynastic feuds were a conspicuous feature of traditional politics. The country was a small, rural, agrarian state, with provinces administered by governors named by the monarch. In addition to peasants, the population included hereditary slaves, war captives, and persons temporarily sold into serfdom for nonpayment of debts. Among Cambodians, the king was always regarded as a living symbol of the nation, while in Vietnam the monarch was a more distant figure, isolated at the court, and usually associated with a particular dynasty.[24]

Initial French control in Cambodia was tenuous. "From the 1860s to the 1890s, Cambodia had been dominated by a loose-knit group of gunslingers, missionaries, adventurers, and carpetbaggers interested in furthering their own military, religious, or commercial gain under a figurehead French government," an Australian historian has noted.[25] Tension was endemic between the French, who did not have enough troops to dictate policy totally, and Norodom, who lacked the power to challenge the French directly and resorted to unending stratagems of confusion and delay. Norodom's throne was coveted by two half brothers: Sisowath, an opportunist whom the French encouraged periodically, and Si Votha, whom Norodom had exiled to a modest court in an isolated province. Norodom liked French brandy, smoked opium, and suffered from gout and later from cancer. He liked dancing, long banquets, and the glitter of court life. When the king traveled, it was by a caravan of 200 elephants, plus cavalry, carriages, and followers on foot. However, the king was no mere hedonist. He had keen political sensibilities and was a shrewd negotiator and, within the limits of possibilities open to him, skillfully waged defensive resistance against the French for more than 40 years.

From at least 1874 on, the French prepared contingency plans for the succession when Norodom should die of ill health, something they anticipated for the next three decades while the king continued in power. Kingship should pass to a son of the present ruler; nevertheless, the French exploited the possibilities of succession with the pliant Sisowath, but they made no final commitment to him. They had justifiable reservations about the extent of support he could command. Si Votha, the other half brother and a perennial usurper, gathered supporters in the Upper Mekong and besieged a provincial capital. Norodom needed help to put down the rebels. French aid came but with a steep price. The French let rebellion foment, then offered support providing Norodom would eliminate the powers of most ranking members of the royal household, abolish slavery, and institute a council of state with a French adviser with political power independent of the king. A weakened Norodom had no choice but to accept these demands, but in an effort to counterbalance them held secret talks with the Spanish consul in Saigon, which the French soon discovered and stopped.

Within a few years the French were collecting taxes on the sale of opium and alcohol in Cambodia, and Charles Thomson, the governor, proposed taking over all other tax collection. If Norodom would not yield power, Thomson suggested, France would regard the protectorate as applying "less to the person of the king than to the kingdom of Cambodia," a thinly veiled suggestion they would depose him. Norodom replied he, but not the French, had faithfully observed the 1863 treaty of friendship and protection, and there was no reason to modify it. Moreover, turning over the national customs service to the French would visibly cripple royal authority in the public view. On June 17, 1884, Thomson arrived at the palace at dawn, while three gunboats stood ready in the harbor, and presented the king with an ultimatum to accept a set of administrative, judicial, financial, and commercial reforms, including stationing French officials in the provinces to control the administration. Norodom had no choice but to accept the ultimatum, although he did write a letter of protest to the French government in Paris.[26]

By the following January widespread revolts had broken out against the French, with at least the palace's tacit support. French reports speak of armed bands moving about the country, recruiting troops, taxing the population, and burning houses of pro-French Cambodians. Intermittent warfare continued for two years. The Cambodians could not dislodge the French from their forts, but the latter were powerless to advance. More than 4 thousand French troops put down the uprising, and in 1886 the French offered enough concessions to end the hostilities, such as reducing the number of French officers in each province from eight to four. By 1892, however, the tax collection was entirely in French hands, and five years later the French resident chaired the council of ministers. Aged and in ill health, Norodom had done his best to delay the French from taking over his kingdom. It was not for nothing he told them, "Your protection is the cremation of the monarchy."[27]

* * *

Just as a moat separated the French quarter from Cambodians in Phnom Penh, the French were supposed to maintain rigidly separate space from the natives, keeping distinctly European in their habits and furnishings. Spoken and unspoken protocols kept indigenous peoples in their place. Cambodians were ridiculed for adopting European dress, and women were discouraged from learning French. Underlying the French desire to keep indigenous peoples separate were an implicit desire to assert the superiority of French culture and a fear of miscegenation that underlay many such social taboos. Viewed in such a perspective, sexual encounters risked corrupting the white race. The realities of Cambodian society would have been different from what most French perceived them to be; in traditional Cambodian society, women were both entrepreneurs and significant economic forces, as would be expected in a matrilineal society. "The gangland of Cambodia was remade in their [French] hands as a docile, female creature," Penny Edwards concluded, adding, "The gentle, serene, and feminine facade of colonial literature and iconography belies decades of banditry in the vast Cambodian hinterland beyond the narrow frontiers of European enclaves."[28]

LAOS

The French seizure of Laos was another example of the activities of an energetic local official striking off on his own. In this case, Auguste Pavie, a former military officer, post office employee, and explorer, traversed much of the country in 1889 and wrote a treaty in which neighboring Siam agreed to respect the status of Laos. In 1892 France proposed dividing much of what remained in Southeast Asia with Great Britain. France wanted all the land east of the Mekong River, which would include much of Laos. This was unacceptable to the British, for it threatened their commercial interests in Siam, but France, on its own, sent troops and gunboats toward Bangkok in 1893. When the Siamese fired on the French ships, the French presented them with an ultimatum to cede the territory east of the Mekong in return for the former Cambodian provinces of Angkor and Battambang. The British were unwilling to intervene in the dispute, as their overriding foreign affairs interest at this time was protecting their Suez holdings. France thus acquired Laos and, in 1896, signed an agreement with Britain acknowledging these border changes and reaffirming Siam's independence, completing the partition of Southeast Asia. In 1897 Laos became part of the Government-General of Indochina.[29] What emerged was called the Indochina Union (1887–1945), a shaky amalgam of the protectorate of Cambodia and Laos, the old colony of Cochin China, and the new one of Tonkin, split off from Annam, which remained a protectorate in name only.

PACIFIC TERRITORIES

French explorations of the Pacific were decidedly less important in the 19th than in the 18th century. They were triggered by the Anglo-French rivalry and a quest for new naval bases in East Asia. However, the vast Pacific and the weak state of the French navy meant that competition there was doomed from the start. No James Cook emerged from among the French explorers. Jean-François de Galaup La Pérouse might have been a comparable figure, but he perished before his return to France, and his various successors made botanical and cartographical but rarely political contributions to the advancement of French interests. France's Pacific possessions were concentrated in two groups of islands, the Society Islands in Polynesia and Melanesia, where France established a penal colony in New Caledonia in 1853. While France's Pacific territories were spread out over a wide area, the French Pacific presence was never large, and these territories existed mainly outside the mainstream of 19th century European political life.[30]

Tahiti, a Polynesian island known to most Europeans from the paintings of Paul Gauguin (1848–1903), was acquired in 1842, as was the nearby Marquesas island group. An Anglo-French agreement of 1847 gave France protectorates over these islands, although rights to other islands acquired by French naval officers were rejected by the conference, and both Britain and France agreed to stay out of several other island groups as a way of avoiding conflict. France sent 15 governors to Tahiti in 36 years. Many of them were officers otherwise unassignable and represented the dregs of such talent as was available for overseas postings. The protectorate became a full-fledged annexation in 1880 and the Society, Marquesas, Austral, Tuamotu, and Gambier islands became the Etablissements Français d'Océanie (French Oceanic Establishments), or EFO.

New Caledonia, a cigar-shaped island twice the size of Corsica, was very different from the exotic Tahiti. Whereas Tahiti was verdant and tropical, New Caledonia, in Melanesia, was harsh and forbidding. It was claimed for France in 1843 by French missionaries and later was designated a penal colony by Louis Napoléon, replacing French Guiana whose hostile climate killed both convicts and administrators. Approximately 7 thousand convicts eventually lived there at any given time working New Caledonia's nickel and cobalt mines or engaged in agricultural labor. Often assigned as groups of 15 or 30 on road gangs, some were chained together like oxen. Those whose conduct was acceptable to the authorities were given small parcels of land, or were allowed to work part-time for freed convicts. From 1863 to 1897, 21,630 convicts had been sent to the islands; more than 7 thousand died, and only 4,684 were freed or escaped.[31]

Beginning in 1872, political offenders were sent to the island as forced colonists. After 1885 persons classed as vagabonds, incorrigibles, or criminals with a certain number of convictions over the past decade were sent there as a way of removing undesirables from France. On New Caledonia they could work, but most remained as disgruntled in New Caledonia as they had been in France. The experiment lasted only a decade and involved fewer than 3 thousand people. Other convicts called them *pièces du Chili* (coins from Chili), a reference to the glittering counterfeit coins widely circulating in Pacific commerce at the time. Convicts, once freed, had no desire to settle on the grim island. Mine owners preferred to pay higher salaries to emigrants who were more productive than convicts. Finally, the convicts were not transformed into good citizens. France abandoned its penal colony experiment as a failure; after 1897, no new convicts were sent to the island.

MADAGASCAR AND THE *POLITIQUE DES RACES*

"O you who come here, read this warning. It will be profitable for you, for yours, and for your life; watch out for the inhabitants." This warning was left behind in French and Portuguese in 1653 by one of many French sailors who departed Madagascar. It might equally apply to most French voyagers visiting the island from the early 16th century to the late 19th century, for the seemingly attractive Indian Ocean island off the African coast had more perils than assets for the French. The island's numerous ethnic groups, mostly of Malayo-Polynesian origin, fought lengthy wars with each other and were continually hostile to the French as well. Moreover, the hot and humid tropical climate of the coastal lowlands was fatal in an era when tropical illnesses could easily result in a high fatality rate of those infected.[32]

Although it was the world's fourth largest island, Madagascar always belonged to the outer edges of empire. It did not offer the riches of India and East Asia, nor was it directly located on one of the great sailing routes. Madagascar was difficult to penetrate, with a rocky coastline, few harbors, and a mountainous interior on its eastern shore. For several centuries the French concentrated their presence on a small southeastern coastal port, which they named Fort Dauphin, which had a good harbor but did not conveniently lead to the interior. Madagascar also failed to develop because France vacillated between leaving it for trading bases, offering beef and rice to feed passing ships, or developing extensive settler colonies as they had done in the West Indies. The result was neither course was effectively pursued, and the island's trade and politics languished.[33] It was never easy to find French settlers who wanted to go to Madagascar in any numbers, nor were the Malagasy people welcoming. The soil was such that traditional plantation crops like sugar cane and coffee could not be profitably grown. Madagascar's isolated location also mitigated against its being a main supplier of the American slave markets.

For over three centuries it was by no means certain that French contact with Madagascar would lead to colonization. French trading ships of the 16th century visited the island, and in 1642 the Compagnie des Indes Orientales attempted to establish a settlement there, which failed in 1665, when the island was formally claimed for France. It was abandoned nine years later. During the late 17th and early 18th centuries, the island became a haven for pirates driven from the West Indies. At one time, French, British, and American pirates formed a short-lived International Republic of Libertalia; for the pirates, Madagascar's scattered small coastal harbors were within reach of the two profitable trade routes, the India–East Asia route and the Gulf of Oman. Captain Kidd operated from Madagascar until he was caught and executed in 1701. The number of French living there was never large; at times, there were fewer than 50 at Fort Dauphin, and some expeditions from France contained fewer than 60 persons. In 1717 fewer than 900 Europeans resided on the island.

By the early 19th century the Merina people, whose name means "those from the country where one can see far," who occupied the central highlands, consolidated their political kingdom, with Tananarive as its capital. The numerically and culturally dominant Merina were expansionist minded. One of their kings declared, "The sea will be the boundary of my rice field."[34] The British, based on nearby Mauritius which they gained at the end of the Napoleonic wars, gave weapons and provided advisers to the Merina ruler, Radama I (reign 1810– 1826), whom they recognized as the king of Madagascar, thus preempting any claims the French might later make based on their own relations with coastal tribes. The London Missionary Society arrived in 1818, and the missionaries established schools and a printing press, were active among the Merina elite, and created a written language. French claims to Madagascar were not seriously revived until the 1880s. The French and Merina fought from 1883 to 1885, a conflict that ended in a military standoff and a treaty. France would represent Madagascar in its foreign relations, a French resident with a military escort was installed at Tananarive, and the French were ceded Diego-Suarez, one of the world's largest deep water harbors, on the island's northern tip.

A tense period followed, in which a band of 2 thousand Malagasy rebels killed a French-appointed Merina governor. When the French then tried to impose a protectorate, warfare ensued intermittently until 1894, when the French Chamber voted funds for an expedition and in December sent a force of 15 thousand including Algerians and Hausa troops, plus a regiment composed of soldiers from all over France selected by lottery to show the undertaking's national character. Illness yet again took its toll. At one time only 20 soldiers had been killed in combat, but over 6 thousand, including a thousand of the new regiment or half its combat troops, had been killed by disease, mostly malaria. Twelve ships were needed to return the sick to France. Philip Curtin calls the expedition "the worst . . . medical failure of any military campaign in the European conquest of Africa."[35] Tananarive was occupied in September 1895 and annexed as a French colony in 1896. Two hostile prime ministers were put to death, and Queen Ranavalona was exiled to Algeria.

From 1896 to 1905 General Joseph-Simon Gallieni, who had served previously in the Sudan and Vietnam, served as the island's military and civil governor.[36] Gallieni put down scattered insurrections and broke the political hold of the Merina people over the country not only by removing the ruler, but also by pursuing Gallieni's *politique des races*, by which the French ruled through chiefs appointed for each ethnic group, who in turn governed their own people. Gallieni unilaterally abolished the royal house, a decision later affirmed by the Chamber, once they learned of it. Domestic slavery, affecting perhaps one-third of the island's inhabitants, was outlawed, and the Malagasy traditional water festival was replaced by Bastille Day as a national holiday. Gallieni introduced the military strategy of the oil spot, which he had used in Indochina, the *tache d'huile*, which became a staple of subsequent French colonial administration. Under the oil spot concept, frontiers were expanded only when the regions behind them were secured. Local populations would be governed, food supplies assured, schools built, and medical services provided. Small military posts, linked by roads, were established to assure security. A single commander was in charge of all military and civil affairs at each post, district, and regional level, which were linked through a chain of command to the governor-general. The use of flying columns was eliminated, as was moving about the countryside, raiding at random, burning villages, or conducting summary executions at an officer's whim.[37]

Gallieni, unlike many other French commanders, urged his subalterns to learn local customs and people. He told them, "Work so that your subjects will only tremble at the thought of your departure."[38] To carry out his work, Gallieni had 7 thousand troops, most of whom were concentrated in the central highlands. By 1897 effective opposition to the French had all but ceased. There was another widespread rebellion in 1904, but it was put down. When Gallieni left in 1905 Madagascar was considered "pacified" by the French.

AFRICA: FILLING OUT THE MAP

The European presence in Africa changed radically in the early 19th century after the trans-Atlantic slave trade of the past three centuries ended, replaced in a relatively brief period by a trade in ivory, gold, tropical woods, and vegetable oils. The French slave trade never had the dramatic ending of the English trade; its demise was gradual, not abrupt. The Danes were the first to prohibit slave commerce in 1792, but British leadership gave global impetus to abolish it. The rise of abolitionist sentiment coincided with the revolution in France; the Convention abolished it in 1794, but by then the effects of the British naval blockade and the actions of the Convention's local representative in Saint-Domingue who outlawed it had brought it to a temporary end. Napoléon restored slavery in

1802, but British insistence resulted in France's reluctantly declaring slavery's abolition in 1814–1815. Slavery was finally outlawed by the French in 1848, but resourceful French planters devised a series of "engagement" contracts which differed little from slavery. British pressure finally brought the nefarious commerce to an end. While both British and French navies participated in the slave patrols, in West Africa the initiative generally was with the British, who had a large navy and a well-organized antislavery lobby. In the early 1840s, a British antislavery patrol intercepted a ship carrying a French trader licensed by the governor of Senegal to purchase slaves. After that, recruitment for African garrisons under conditions close to slavery continued until the century's end, but the indentured soldiers were conveyed by French military ships to avoid embarrassing incidents like the one cited above.[39]

The center of French West African activity was Senegal, which was compared to the Nile Valley by some French politicians. In 1818 a plan was announced to settle a thousand French colonists there; forts, plantations, and gold mines were envisioned, and vast commerce with the interior was dangled as a further attraction. Little came of the appeals; the French, as always, had no enthusiasm for emigration. Africans did not welcome the French, cheap labor was not forthcoming, and it would take longer than anyone would have dreamed to make the colony productive.[40]

By mid-century Saint-Louis was a town of 15 thousand persons, 300 of them European. Its commerce in groundnuts multiplied from 10 million francs in value in 1849 to 37 million in 1866. Trade was mostly in the hands of African coastal merchants long associated with the French. However, the French soon sought to remove these intermediaries by sending their own African agents up-river. There they encountered skilled Moorish traders who played the ancient traders' game of encouraging competition between the agents and the intermediaries in order to strengthen their own power. Thus the upcountry traders steadily expanded their influence as the French sought to widen theirs.[41]

The French also moved inland in West Africa. René Caillié, a former officer's servant in Senegal, reached Timbuktu with a caravan of itinerant Dioula traders in 1828. For over 10 years Caillié had planned to visit this important Islamic holy city, also the desert terminus of the trans-Saharan trade in gold, ivory, salt, and slaves. He studied Arabic and disguised himself as an Egyptian Muslim returning to his country via Senegal after being captured, so his story went, by Napoléon's forces in Egypt and then taken to West Africa. Caillié spent two months in the holy city, interlarding his travel notes between pages of the Koran. Eventually he crossed the Sahara by caravan, arrived penniless in Morocco, and sought out a French consul with his story, which he published in France.

The French presence spread southward along the West African coast as well; from 1839 to 1842, France concluded treaties with chiefs along the West African coast, giving France interests in the Gabon, Ivory Coast, and Guinea. At the same time, the French reoccupied their abandoned fort in Wydah, Dahomey, and a treaty of commerce and friendship was concluded with Ghèzo, the king of Dahomey. In Guinea conflict broke out between French traders and coastal tribes in 1839; the French military intervened, and by 1849 French rule had been established over that part of the coast.[42]

LOUIS FAIDHERBE AND EXPANSION IN SENEGAL

It was Louis Faidherbe, 36, a French engineering officer with Algerian service, who greatly expanded France's presence in Senegal during two tours as governor, from 1854 to 1861, and from 1863 to 1865. Previously 37 colonial administrators had followed one another in quick succession. Didactic and authoritarian in temperament, Faidherbe was also hardworking and inventive; not only did he launch numerous new programs, but he stayed in Senegal long enough to see many of them substantially realized. Drawing on his Algerian experience, Faidherbe recruited a local militia, established the rudiments of a school system including a school for interpreter-clerks, started public works programs, and established an administration to control the newly conquered lands, which were divided into a number of *arrondissements*, each such district with its own French *commandant*, who was responsible for keeping the peace and encouraging commerce. Eventually a three-tiered level of local administration evolved which, with minor modifications, served as the basis of French control of Africa for the next century. In addition to the French administrators, there were also numerous local chiefs. Those who effectively carried out French orders, recruited workers, or collected taxes were retained. Those who were considered recalcitrant or incompetent were removed.

Faidherbe conquered much of the interior, built roads, founded schools, and in 1857 recruited the first battalion of the Tirailleurs Sénégalais (Senegalese Infantry) who would make a major contribution to the French war effort in the next century. The Tirailleurs Sénégalias actually came from many parts of West Africa. Most of them were slave-soldiers, a long-established African reality; with conquests, they were allowed to capture household slaves, wives, and booty. Although their numbers included 500 troops in 1857, they rose steadily to 8,400 at century's end. Recruitment was a mixed bag; the European leadership was not strong, drawn often from soldiers on penal duty. Originally, many of the soldiers were bought from chiefs, a practice officially stopped in 1848, but continued informally until 1882, after which the Tirailleurs' ranks contained forcibly recruited African peasants and prisoners of war, plus regularly recruited African mercenaries. As demands for the Tirailleurs increased (they were stationed elsewhere in Africa, Madagascar, and Indochina), the recruitment circle widened, both inland and along the West Coast of Africa.[43]

Unlike in Algeria, where French settlers had already staked out the best land, Faidherbe did not want Senegal to become a settler colony, and he issued a governmental edict to that effect in 1859. Self-governing municipalities were created in 1872 in Saint-Louis and Dakar-Gorée, governed by French municipal law instead of colonial decrees. Rufisque and the city of Dakar were soon given similar status, and these four became the "four old communes." Inhabitants of these communes were citizens rather than subjects of France; they sent a deputy to the French parliament and elected their own local municipal officers.

On the coast, Faidherbe actively supported French traders, something not true of most of his predecessors, and he established a small number of coastal forts. Gradually the French trade with the West Coast of Africa grew. Faidherbe's administration fortunately coincided with a time of growing European demand for vegetable oils, which were used in the manufacture of candles and soap. Senegalese farmers, whose dry, sandy soil was ideal for groundnut production, could grow a cash crop with little difficulty, and the colony enjoyed a prosperous time. Less successful would be the determined French efforts to grow cotton in the interior.[44]

THE MOVE INLAND AND ISLAMIC OPPOSITION

As he moved inland, Faidherbe confronted a powerful, well-organized Islamic state led by El Hadj Omar, who controlled an empire stretching from the Senegal River Valley to Timbuktu. The question was whether to attempt an all-out military conquest or reach accommodation with Omar and his 20-thousand-soldier army. There were ample precedents for a French attack, but it would be costly, French troops were few in numbers and confined largely to the coast, and Omar could evade the French in the vast empty lands of the pre-Sahara for years if necessary. Faidherbe chose to negotiate with him and establish a boundary delineating their spheres of influence to the satisfaction of both parties.[45]

Faidherbe still wanted to find a water route to the vast Niger region, and from 1863 to 1866 he engaged Lieutenant Eugène Mage, a member of the Senegal administration, to lead a mission to the Niger to explore possibilities of future cooperation with Omar in opening up the territory to trade. Faidherbe wanted Mage to see if France could establish a string of trading posts and forts at intervals linking the upper Senegal with the upper Niger, hoping thus to divert inland trade to the French-controlled route. The Islamic leaders drove a stiff bargain, wanting modern arms, including howitzers, which the French were unwilling to provide. Faidherbe wanted to build several forts beyond the previously established limits, but he received a vague reply. Faidherbe left Senegal in 1865 and, without his leadership, plans to penetrate the Niger region languished.[46]

After its defeat by Germany in 1870, the French hoped to find in Africa what it had lost in Europe and to open a vast territory to French commerce. Holding territory and establishing local administrations would come later. The move inland began through small-unit actions launched during the dry season. A French commander and subalterns led several hundred African troops to provision scattered inland posts and deliver mail to isolated garrisons, castigate enemies, and sign treaties. A total force of from 400 to 700 troops was aided by superior firepower. The recently invented magazine rifle had been introduced to the French army, and most units had a few machine guns as well, and a light artillery piece to knock down walls and doors. As always, disease was the silent presence accompanying many expeditions. Malaria was widespread, as were yellow fever and dysentery. One French force lost 49% of its European strength to yellow fever in a two-month period in 1879; a similar devastating epidemic came again in 1881. "In a crowded urban setting, like that on the island towns of Saint-Louis and Gorée, almost all of the non-immune population would be infected, and 50 to 70 percent of those infected would die."[47]

In 1878 the colonial administration revived the idea of moving a substantial force inland in Senegal, this time under Faidherbe's successor, Captain Joseph-Simon Gallieni, later a French proconsul in Indochina and Madagascar. Gallieni, 30, was a brusque and energetic military officer. Impatient at being limited to the Senegal River Valley, and having no information on the interior more current than Mage's decade-old account of his travels, he set out in October 1878 to bring the Sudan under French control beginning a quarter-century-long effort to subdue the large, mobile, and well-armed indigenous groups of the Sahelian region south of the Sahara. In 1880 Gallieni, lacking forces needed for a conquest, negotiated an agreement with Ahamadou, one of the regional leaders. Again, the French found the African's terms unacceptable. The Africans wanted four pieces of artillery and a thousand flintlocks, plus evacuation of French forts already built in lands claimed by Ahamadou and a provision that any administrators named by the French to the region be African Muslims. France, in turn, would be given exclusive rights to establish trading posts, build roads, and create communication links between Senegal and the Niger, though specifically restrained from building military posts there. At one point, Ahamadou's chief negotiator declared, "We like the French but we do not trust them. They, on the other hand, trust us, but do not like us."

In 1881 the French sent a new mission to the interior, this one under Dr. Jean-Marie Bayol, an army surgeon, who had accompanied Gallieni to Bamako. On the way, Bayol induced various local leaders to make their marks on letters that placed the vast Futa Jalon region under French protection and limited commerce there to French traders. In 1882, as the French moved southward, they collided with the Dyula trader and warrior Samori Touré (c. 1830–1900), who was extending his power gradually north of the Niger River. Ahamadou, son of El Hadj Omar, and head of the Ségou Empire, would not join with his rival, Samori, to challenge the French, seeing himself as a third force between two competitors. Major Louis Archinard in 1890, acting on purely personal responsibility, pursued Samori and attempted to eliminate him rather than negotiate commercial or political concessions. Samori moved slowly eastward from the Upper Niger toward the Middle Volta, destroying crops in his wake, so his pursuers would find the way increasingly difficult. He was not captured until 1898 by which time the French had occupied the whole of the Western Sudan.

These extensive but largely unrelated conquests by several French military leaders over three decades led to the acquisition of a vast empire in the interior of Africa. At the same time, from the Congo, the French sent expeditions northward to meet their West African counterparts at Lake Chad and edged toward the Upper Nile by way of the Ubangi, as another force moved southward from Algeria. Between 1879 and 1883, France reached the Upper Niger and followed the river up to Timbuktu in 1893. They moved toward the Mossi lands of the Upper Volta three years later when Captain Gustave Binger completed a two-year journey through the Upper Volta and the Ivory Coast, the last significant French exploration of sub-Saharan Africa. By then France occupied the whole Western Sudan. France originally had no plans to seize this vast expanse of desert land, but traders, explorers, and armed skirmishes led to deepening entanglements with Moslem theocracies in the interior. By the mid-1890s France's West African empire was three times the size of Britain's, although much of it was what Lord Salisbury called "light soil," and what Joost Van Vollenhoven, a French governor-general of later times, called "a lunar landscape." It remained now for France to link its various appendages of land; briefly, the vision of a French empire, bounded by the Atlantic, Mediterranean, and Indian oceans glittered like a mirage.

Despite these visions in the field, French politicians at home still had little enthusiasm for territorial expansion, but they were not willing to repudiate the local conquests popular with the vocal colonial lobby. Richard L. Roberts, describing the personal decision of a French field commander to advance beyond the boundaries delineated in his marching orders and establish a fort at Bamako, Mali, in 1893, wrote, "Officers refined the principle of not accepting orders when they did not fit their interests. Insubordination, when it brought desired results, was rewarded. For bringing the French to Bamako in the face of orders to the contrary, Desbordes himself was promoted to colonel."[48]

The next question was finding the considerable sums needed to administer the new lands with soldiers, district officers, and revenue-producing crops. The short-lived years of drum-and-trumpet expansion gave way to a longer, less colorful era in which the overriding goal was to turn the conquered lands into economically productive colonies.

THE CONGO

When Leopold II of Belgium began staking out his immense Congo Free State, the French moved more modestly into the Congo. Savorgnan de Brazza, an Italian-born French naval officer, headed up the Ogooué River on France's behalf and by September 1882 had reached the site of the future Brazzaville, where he obtained the ruler of the Bateke peoples' signature on a treaty, ceding his hereditary rights to France, and agreeing to allow a military post to be built along the river. Brazza hoisted the flag and posted his Senegalese sergeant as a guard. Brazza returned to France a popular hero, accounts of his exploits were carried in the popular press, and his treaty was applauded by the Chamber. In March 1883 he returned to the Congo, this time as leader of a small, well-financed expedition—fewer than 15 officers until the 1890s—and Brazza was told France would not indefinitely support a period of costly exploration.[49]

GABON, DAHOMEY, AND OTHER WEST AFRICAN POSSESSIONS

France also secured a presence elsewhere on the West African coast, including the Guinea Coast and the Ivory Coast followed by inland incursions that brought the Upper Volta, Mali, and the Niger nominally under its control. At the same time, France extended its presence into what would become known as French Equatorial Africa (AEF), often called "the Cinderella of Empire," including Gabon, the Congo, Chad, and Oubangui-Chari, which later became the Central African Republic. Gabon, rich in tropical woods, originally was seen as the French counterpart of Liberia and Sierra Leone: a place to settle slaves liberated by French antislavery patrols. Libreville was founded in 1849 by Admiral Edmond Bouët-Willaumez. By 1865 the colony had 1,800 new inhabitants, including 100 Europeans.[50]

No overall strategic plan governed France's imperial claims in Africa. It was like a scientific experiment in which certain ingredients were placed in proximity, conditions were right, and unpredictable growth followed. Much of France's African expansion was the result of initiatives undertaken by local military and colonial figures who set their sights on conquests. Many were officers of the same generation who knew there were vocal supporters of empire at home and that parliamentarians would not rebuff their efforts. One such local agent was Victor Règis, a Marseilles trader, who acquired the region south from the Ivory Coast to Dahomey for France after a 30-year effort. Règis built a successful palm oil business and continually sought French naval and military support to compel African intermediaries to trade with him on more favorable terms. Règis moved about the coastal region from 1840 until 1856, when he concentrated on the palm oil trade near Dahomey. He flew the French flag at the coastal fort of Wydah and told the Dahomians he was the emperor's agent. After obtaining a near monopoly of the palm oil trade, and a string of coastal trading concessions, in 1868 his representatives signed a treaty giving France Cotonou and its surrounding region. In April 1883 the French raised the flag on Porto-Novo and at several nearby ports, and in 1893 the Kingdom of Dahomey was claimed by France as part of its African empire.

EGYPT: "EUROPE IS A MOLEHILL, WE MUST GO TO THE EAST; ALL GREAT GLORY HAS ALWAYS BEEN ACQUIRED THERE"

By the late 18th century, when it appeared France might lose its Caribbean sugar islands, Egypt became the likely target for a new colony. Much nearer to

France than the West Indies, it supposedly would be a gateway to India and Africa, and it appeared to have a climate suitable for growing tropical products. France had centuries-old ties with Egypt; relations went back to at least 1536 when François I made an alliance with Suleiman the Magnificent, the Sublime Port, the Turkish ruler who controlled Egypt. France had a consul general in Cairo, as well as consuls in Alexandria and Rosetta, the main ports, and a small resident merchant community. France always cast a covetous eye on Egypt; in 1769 the duc de Choiseul wanted to acquire it as a way of replacing France's American colonies if they were lost. In the late 18th century the Ottoman Empire once again appeared on the verge of collapse, and the fertile Nile Valley seemed waiting only for France to claim it. According to one account, "The flax, the sugar-cane, and vegetables of all kinds sprout up, almost without culture, cucumbers and nearly 20 species of melons, melting sweet, and most healthy adorn the banks and rivulets."[51]

Napoléon was fascinated with the Levant, and as the English presence grew in the Mediterranean and the prospect of the English seizing the Cape of Good Hope became real, he moved to occupy Egypt, as a way to India. He reportedly said, "Europe is a molehill. We must go to the East; all great glory has always been acquired there." His flag ship was named *L'Orient* and his forces were called the Army of the Orient. In June 1798 the 28-year-old Napoléon set out with an army of almost 30 thousand soldiers, 300 slow transport ships, and an escort fleet of 72 ships to take Malta and Egypt, which he did within a few months. However, in August the British, who had barely missed capturing Napoléon sailing from Malta, destroyed the French fleet sheltered in a bay near Alexandria, leaving the emperor stranded in Egypt and giving the British undisputed control of the Mediterranean. Impulsively, Napoléon ordered his troops north toward Syria, where they met fierce opposition at every point, plus bubonic plague. The number of effective troops was reduced from 30 thousand to 12 thousand in several months. The French held on to Egypt for the next three and a half years, suffering severe losses from disease and drought. This was primarily a military occupation, and France never realized its hopes to build large sugar plantations, resettle colonists from the West Indies, and extend a trading empire from Egypt to India. Still, Napoléon continued to build a colony and introduce the elements of what would become a French *mission civilisatrice*.

It was mainly smoke and mirrors, however. An Egyptian Institute was created to study local history, art, and customs and, although it carried out impressive scientific studies, its main purpose was to advise the French government how to control Egyptian society expeditiously. Napoléon originally ordered French troops to respect local people and property, but the order was incompletely observed. The emperor wore an Egyptian mullah's robe over his military uniform for the traditional Feast of the Inundation of the Nile. In addition to ordering a complete legal and administrative overhaul, he devised schemes for purifying Nile water, brewing local beer, creating French cafés and gardens, and installing streetlights. The French set up a press with Arabic characters, purloined from the Vatican during a recent Italian expedition, and printed propaganda broadsides saying their intention was to protect the interests of "God, his prophet, and the Koran," but when he levied a tax on mosque properties and razed the historic al-Azhar mosque to give his gun batteries a better angle, Moslem clerics declared a jihad against the French and relations received an irreparable blow. A large-scale revolt against the new property taxes took place in Cairo in 1798, and Napoléon ordered prisoners beheaded and persons caught with arms to have their throats cut on the spot and their bodies thrown into the Nile. Tired of his adventure in the Orient after a year, Napoléon sailed for France in August 1799, again barely missing the English fleet.[52]

With his subsequent fall, French interest in Egypt diminished and the French presence withered. This chapter of France's Egyptian intervention ended for France in 1802 when the British and French signed an agreement that neither would occupy Egypt. Napoléon, as was often the case, had the last word. A skilled propagandist, he commissioned or inspired massive paintings with titles like *The Battle of Nazareth* (1801) and *General Bonaparte Visiting the Pesthouse at Jaffa* (1804) by Antonine-Jean Gros and *Bonaparte Pardoning the Rebels in Cairo* (1808) by Pierre-Narcisse Guérin, creating an illusion of victory on canvas in the Louvre and at Versailles never actually achieved on the ground in the Levant.[53]

If most French artists and writers presented the Egyptian expedition as a triumph for Napoléon, the Egyptian view was one of both fascination for European military success, science, and technology, and disgust at French cultural hypocrisy and injustice in their dealings with native peoples. Rare are the local chronicles of European invasions in any society, but one survives in the *Tarikh muddat al-Fransis bi Misr* by the Egyptian historian Abd al Rahman al Jabarti (1753–1825 or 1826).[54] The *Muddat* (1798) covers the first seven months of the French invasion, a period in which the basic themes of the Egyptian-French encounter were enunciated: large-scale warfare, the establishment of local government (*diwan*) advisory councils, and a determined Egyptian resistance to the French presence. Jabarti's work is a day-by-day chronicle of Egyptian-French encounters describing topics as diverse as large-scale riots, raids on Egyptian houses where guns and gold were confiscated, and disputes over keeping street lamps lit at night. Assembling information in traditional chronicle style, the author devoted an opening section to the original French occupation proclamation widely disseminated in Arabic "In the name of God, the Merciful, the Compassionate. . . . On behalf of the French Republic." He spent several pages picking apart its grammatical and theological errors "incoherent words and vulgar constructions . . . put into this miserable letter." In this passage the Egyptian writer described local response to Napoléon's effort to turn the annual blessing of the Nile into a French festival:

On Friday the fifth, coinciding with the . . . twelfth month of the Coptic calendar, the blessed Nile reached its full flood and the French leader gave orders to make the usual

preparations and decorate . . . a number of ships and galleons. They called upon the people to go outside and to stroll along the Nile . . . as was customary demanding this in
spite of what had suddenly come upon them, as for example, poll-taxes, unrelenting
demands, looting of homes, harassing women and girls, arresting and imprisoning them,
and making financial settlements which exceeded all bounds. [The French Chief-of-Staff]
sent instructions to . . . the Shaykhs who were members of the Council and high officials
. . . to present themselves the next morning. He rode forth with them accompanied by
his procession, decorations, troops, drums and pipes, to the palace of Qantarat al-Sadd,
and the dam was cut in their presence. Then they celebrated with fireworks and shooting
of cannons until the waters flowed in the canal [of Cairo], then [the French Chief-of-
Staff] rode with those accompanying him and returned to his house. And not a single
person went out that night for pleasure excursions in boats as was customary except for
Shami Christians, Copts, Europeans with their wives, and a few idlers who went as
onlookers in the morning, broken-hearted and despondent.[55]

THE SUEZ CANAL AND AÏDA

France's latent interest in Egypt was revived again in 1854 when the former
French consul and engineer Ferdinand de Lesseps obtained permission to cut a
canal across the Isthmus of Suez from Said Pasha (reign 1854–1863), who had
recently become khedive in a coup. French colonial publicists argued that the
shortened distance to the Far East would allow France to make Saigon a second
Singapore or Shanghai, thus rivaling British interests in the Far East. The
French-run Compagnie Universelle du Canal Maritime de Suez had a 99-year
lease on the canal with Louis Napoléon and Said Pasha as major shareholders.
Work started in 1859, but it took ten rather than the planned six years to compete. At first as many as 20 thousand Egyptian workers hand dug the canal,
carting dirt away in baskets, and were provided with fresh water by 3 thousand
camels and donkeys, but in 1864 the work was speeded through the use of
steam shovels. The canal was opened in 1869 by the wife of Napoléon III with
a fanfare, including the first production of Giuseppe Verdi's *Aïda*, commissioned
by Khedive Ismaïl for 150 thousand gold francs. The canal was 100 miles long,
but it was only 20 feet deep and 190 feet wide on the surface. Between 1870
and 1884, more than 3 thousand ships were grounded in its narrow channel.[56]

The Suez Canal became the main artery for the European-Asian trade, but
the British, not the French, were its chief users. French hopes were shattered by
the disastrous Franco-Prussian war, leaving the canal's possibilities as an instrument of French Asian policy untouched. Annual interest payments on the
canal debt soared to $25 million, surpassing the original debt, and the Egyptian
ruler sold his share to the British in 1875. Meanwhile, the Egyptian economy
continued in a free fall, resulting in a joint French-British effort to collect revenues and run the government. A British participant observed that Egypt "must
have been an earthly paradise for all who had money to lend at usurious rates
of interest, or third-rate goods of which they wished to dispose at first-rate
prices." During the century's final decades, Egyptian hostility toward the Euro-

pean intrusion mounted. At one point a jihad was declared, as in other North African states, and the British sent naval forces to Alexandria. The French Chamber, arguing that France had enough problems to deal with at home, refused to vote funds for an expedition, and European power in Egypt shifted to the British. France was enraged at losing out in what was regarded as a French preserve, "the glory of the east" of Napoléon's day, but France would never again be a coequal or full partner with the British in Egypt, although it could be a substantial irritant there and elsewhere. As Egypt paid its debt and established its own institutions, French influence waned.

THE SCRAMBLE

By the century's end almost all of Africa had been claimed by European powers, the result of a scramble for territory that created its own momentum like a cyclone spinning across part of the continent. Nothing was preordained about the European acquisitions of the 1880s and 1890s, nor was there any economic logic to the European powers' actions. Germany's entry into the gradually evolving colonial competition was the wild card needed to turn the rivalries into an outright race. Bismarck, following the Franco-Prussian war, wanted to deflect French-German questions to the colonial rather than the domestic arena. Germany also engaged in a flurry of overseas activity, sending explorers along the southwestern coastline of Africa as Hamburg traders moved about the coast of Cameroon collecting signed treaties while the Germans claimed Togoland, parts of East Africa, and several Pacific islands, including Samoa and New Guinea.

In 1884 and 1885 the European powers met for nearly six months in Berlin at Bismarck's invitation to settle the Congo question. Before other powers arrived, France and Germany agreed to recognize the Congo Free State, which gave the other countries little choice but to follow suit. France, on its own, had reached an agreement to take over King Leopold's vast state should its costs outstrip his resources. Bismarck endorsed the handful of East African treaties collected by a German adventurer, Karl Peters, in East Africa. In a few years, Africa was partitioned among the European powers. No sooner was an area claimed than the partitioners began to look elsewhere. One of the most striking features of the partition was the lack of African involvement in it. Decisions were reached at cabinet meetings or in European country houses, often using incomplete or inaccurate maps to carve up unexplored regions. The image sometimes used of the process was that of a steeplechase over terrain with no certain boundaries.

It cannot be claimed that commerce was the engine driving this scramble. The expansion coincided with a depression in world trade that lasted from 1874 to 1896, during which the price of a ton of palm oil dropped from $250 to as low as $100, and the price of other African agricultural products sank as well. Some European traders headed inland, but Africa still remained of marginal economic importance to Europe, both before and after the great scramble. In fact, most European commerce was with other European countries, or with established markets in the Americas or Asia. French trade in Africa remained largely the activity of a few coastal merchants from Marseilles and elsewhere. It was not until long after Africa's division was completed that the first small flow of French private and governmental investment began to reach it.

FASHODA: A POLITICAL OPÉRA-BOUFFE IN THE MAKING

An obscure outpost in the southern Sudan, 400 miles south of Khartoum, was at the scramble's epicenter. The Sudan was the geographic zone lying between the Sahara and Africa's equatorial regions, parts of which were claimed by both France and England, and into which both countries were moving. Jean-Baptiste Marchand, a young French soldier-explorer, took from 1896 to 1898 to travel from the French Congo to Fashoda, leading a small band of African troops and, at times, 175 dugout canoes paddled by 2 thousand locally recruited villagers. Laboriously they carried 45 thousand kilograms of provisions, including boats and champagne, plus a small steamer, the *Faidherbe*, moved piece by piece inland. Its large boiler was rolled across logs for hundreds of miles through tropical forests, and the hull was floated along rivers or carried on wheels for reassembly when the French reached the Nile. Marchand wanted to annex territory informally as he made his way northward toward the Nile. It was not a military mission; its status was quasi-official, for Marchand was on leave from the West African service at the time. A French occupation of the Sudan, he reasoned, would remove some sting from the British takeover of Egypt and give France some negotiating cards to play in future dealings with the British. The Sudan represented unexplored territory for France, whose only possessions in this part of Africa were two small bases in Somaliland that protected the Suez Canal's southern entrance. As the French were moving toward Egypt, the British headed southward, conquering the Sudan and routing local religious and military leaders in bloody battles. A French column reached the Upper Nile town of Fashoda, once an important Egyptian provincial capital, in February 1898 where a Russian colonel with the French forces planted the *tricolore* and departed when Marchand's small contingent arrived a few weeks later.

On September 19 a large British force, headed by General Horatio Herbert Kitchener, also appeared; a standoff ensued, and the situation unfolded like the plot of a period dime novel. General Kitchener spoke to Captain Marchand in labored French, admired the gardens the French had planted in the desolate spot, and left some newspapers filled with reports of the Dreyfus affair. The French had been out of touch with Paris for eight months and were forced to use the British telegraph for their communication home. To the British, Marchand recalled the alleged words of the French foreign minister when the expedition was first envisioned, "You are going to fire a pistol shot on the Nile; we accept all its consequences." A compromise was struck on the spot. The French flag would remain flying over the isolated fort, Kitchener would raise the Egyptian flag over an outlying desert installation, and both units would refer the problem to their respective governments for solution. Marchand then withdrew from Fashoda in October on instructions from his government. France did not want an open clash with Britain, since it needed British support against Germany. On the other hand, Britain regarded Marchand's wanderings through the Sudan as a deliberate provocation, probing the southern flank of British Nile possessions.[57]

What was originally a confrontation between field commanders became a full-blown international crisis. The conflict in France was fueled by a number of highly placed military and civilian officers below the cabinet level who were both expansionist minded and anti-English. In the spring of 1899 the British and French governments, meeting in London and Paris, worked out an agreement to resolve the standoff. France kept its extensive new acquisitions west of the Nile River watershed but had no presence in the Nile Valley or northeastern Africa. French hopes of a land belt all the way across Africa were thwarted; only the port of Djibouti and tiny French Somaliland remained to recall such dreams. A crisis had been defused, and despite quickly escalating rhetoric neither side would make Fashoda a cause for war. The British, stung by the recent failure of the Jameson raid in South Africa, would not go to war in the Sudan. It was bad timing all around for France. If Marchand had taken one instead of two years to reach Fashoda, leaving the useless *Faidherbe* behind on some freshwater lake, he might have found it with no British soldiers within striking distance, for it was not until 1898 that Kitchener had the troops needed to move south. It is difficult not to agree with Kitchener when he called Marchand's adventure "more worthy of an *opéra-bouffe* than of the outcome of the maturely considered plans of a great government."[58]

SCIENCE AND TECHNOLOGY

Numerous scientific and technological innovations aided French colonial expansion late in this century, although their full effects were not immediately felt. The development of antimalarial drugs, such as quinine, and other medical and hygienic practices meant that settlers had a better chance of surviving in pestilential climates. Steel ships with greatly improved steam engines were larger, swifter, and more comfortable than earlier vessels, and the use of the screw propeller by the late 1830s made them much faster than earlier models. Shipping lines like the government-subsidized Messageries Maritimes allowed for faster travel through the Indian Ocean to Indochina and China.[59]

Improved engineering practices allowed the easier building of roads, railroads, and ports. The spread of electricity soon led to international cable communication, and a small group of badly underfunded specialists promoted better agricultural practices and zoological and botanical gardens. The debate in France between pure and applied science always ended in favor of applied science.

Astronomers, hydrographers, and meteorologists were sent abroad to map lands and provide armies and colonists with more accurate information on the land and seas around them. There was nothing altruistic in these scientific advances being used in the service of the overseas empire. Science was but one more arrow in the quiver of imperialism, a way of retaining and expanding power, making life more bearable for the Europeans, and keeping indigenous populations under control or healthy and productive to advance colonial commerce.[60]

In 1870, after a string of unsuccessful efforts, France hired a British commercial company to lay a cable from Marseilles to Bône in Algeria. France followed with government-sponsored cables to Algiers, Oran, Bizerte, Tunis, and Tunisia. As French politicians dithered, a handful of visionary proponents argued for the country's own investment in a global overseas cable network, but opponents used well-rehearsed arguments that the investment was too costly and the country had more pressing domestic needs. Asian and African connections were made therefore through British firms like India Rubber, Gutta-Percha, and Telegraph Works. Through substantial investment, the British had seized the lead in the underwater cable field, which proved to be a profound irritant to France for the next half-century and more. France had to pay high costs to use the British facilities and limit its own efforts to making short connections from its own possessions to British lines. This gave the British a monopoly on the flow of information, plus political and intelligence-gathering advantages. Since the British employed only British citizens as telegraph clerks, they could easily track French commercial and military shipping from ports like Dakar and Saigon. When in 1893 the French delivered an ultimatum to Siam, the French government's instructions to its local representative were not delivered until after the British government had read them—one of many such episodes. It was not until 1913, after buying out some British companies and making an ill-timed commercial arrangement with the Germans, that France could communicate by cable with all its African possessions. Indochina was reached via a Danish cable crossing Russia and China. "France relied on the kindness of strangers," a historian of technology soberly concluded.[61]

Conquest and communication were aided in other ways as well. Shortly after the French conquest of Algeria, an optical semaphore signal system was established, and it was eventually supplemented by an electrical telegraph line. A separate post office was not created until 1860, and by 1920 the country was covered by 720 post and telegraph offices, a more intensive spread than in any other French overseas possession. Only Indochina came close with 222 offices at century's end, 425 by the early 1920s. In West Africa, some coastal cities, such as Dakar and Libreville, could be reached fairly easily by cable and mail by the 1880s, but it was not until 1912 that reliable telegraph lines had been constructed from the coast to Fort Lamy, Chad, just in time to be supplanted by the wireless radio.[62]

France's colonial advancement in this century was also aided by improvements in the design of weapons. By 1866 the French military had decided on the *Chassepot*, a bolt-action rifle that fired up to six times a minute, as their basic infantry weapon, though it leaked hot gases and had to be held at arm's length. Within a generation it was replaced by quicker, lighter, more accurate rifles. By 1907 the *fusil colonial*, which had seen service in the Sudan, was the basic rifle issued to all colonial troops and was the prototype of the rifle used by French infantry in World War I. Smokeless powder was a French invention of the 1880s, allowing soldiers to fire without disclosing their position. Machine guns and light howitzers or cannons that could easily knock down walls of fortified towns gave colonial forces a decided advantage in firepower.[63]

From the 1850s on, there was growing French interest in colonial flora and fauna, much of it centered on small but active institutions such as the Société Zoologique d'Acclimation and the Société d'Anthropologie. The Musée Social, from 1894 to 1931, sought vainly to promote social reform in the colonies through decentralized voluntary mutual aid societies that would bring colonizer and colonized, rich and poor, together for social betterment.[64] From the time of the first explorations and the *cabinets des curiosités* through the various colonial expositions, plants and animals were collected and displayed in Paris and a few provincial cities. Scientific studies were undertaken and botanical gardens were created in places like Saigon and Libreville, including two dozen of them in Algeria. By the century's end, a fledging colonial agricultural program was in place. However, as French commercial companies grew, they hired their own agronomists to work on rubber, tea, rice, and coffee plantations. Such employees often traveled abroad and studied the techniques of British, Italian, and American researchers to improve their own products.[65]

Followers of the research scientist, microbiologist, and immunologist Louis Pasteur (1822–1895) created overseas Instituts Pasteur which both advanced French colonial interests and contributed to the reduction of some diseases. A navy physician, Albert Calmette, studied sleeping sickness in Africa and created a laboratory for the preparation of smallpox and rabies vaccines in Saigon. Alexandre Yersin, a Swiss-born scientist, created a second Pasteur Institute in Nha Trang, where he conducted experiments on tropical plants and introduced the rubber tree to Indochina. Charles Nicolle, an eventual Nobel Prize winner, headed the Pasteur Institute in Tunis, where his research on parasites and their transmission by lice led to prophylactic measures that sharply curbed the spread of the disease.[66]

THE WORLD AS THEY PERCEIVED IT: ORIENTALISM

Throughout the first half century, up until the war of 1870, when France was left with the wounds of war, images of the world overseas, often called "Orientalism," were widely employed by French artists and writers. Their prototypes were the epic canvases of Gros of Napoléon's campaign in Egypt and Palestine. There had always been a French attraction for the Orient, Asia Minor, the Holy Land, and Constantinople. As France moved into Algiers in the 1830s and the travel literature of North Africa and Asia Minor became more widespread, the taste for so-called Oriental themes grew in France. Homes with chinoiseries and *turqueries* now added memorabilia from North Africa to their collections, such as brass plates and archeological samples from Carthage.

Paintings like Théodore Chassériau's *La Toilette d'Esther* (1841), Eugène Delacroix's *Femmes d'Alger* (1834), and Jean-Dominique Inges' *Bain Turc* (1862) show naked or thinly veiled white women guarded in Oriental harems, leading indolent, languid lives, displaying what Théophile Gautier called, "*le mystère, le silence et l'étouffement du sérail*" (the mystery, silence, and smoth-ering of the seraglio). Most of these paintings depicted jewel caskets, vials of perfume, a hookah, and odalisques leaning against stuffed cushions or seated on thick rugs, all in the murky, diffused light of a North African interior. Such art played to racial stereotypes, an East filled with mystery and beauty, a land of plenty with vulnerable light-skinned women subjugated by cruel, dark-skinned warriors or chiefs. Nations no less than individuals projected their visions of race, class, creed, and politics on fictional screens called colonies.[67]

During the 19th century French writers and artists were both fascinated by the lure of the overseas world but remained aloof from it, as did the French in Loti's books. If the French writers of an earlier age described harmonious so-cieties ruled by wise emperors, many authors of the post-1870 period saw an edenic world overseas whose exorcism contrasted with a defeated France. In such escapist literature, the overseas world provided a backdrop against which to project the stresses of a war-torn world and find their resolution in fantasy.

The contradictions in French analysis of overseas possessions is reflected in contrasting imagery used by French politicians, government officials, and writers to describe France's overseas possessions. After 1870 Marianne, symbol of France, was both strongly maternal and warlike, sheltering and a resolute de-fender of her sons and daughters, armed with a shield and coifed with a helmet. Next are the colonial males, tall, erect, and in control, exuding political deter-mination and phallic energy. Then there are the colonies, feminine, receptive vessels of the advancing colonial presence. In a discussion of the imagery of the French in Cambodia, Penny Edwards wrote, "Matronly métropole, virile colo-nizer, and nymphlike colony were joined in a conceptual triangle which privi-leged French manhood as the vital link between the raw earth of the colony and the bright hearth of the homeland."[68] Cambodia was among the most feminine of the French overseas possessions, as portrayed in such colonial literature, art, and photography. The French seized on the traditional Cambodian *apsara*, a lithe, delicate celestial dancer and liminal figure, the intermediary between the king and heaven, and a reflection of eternal beauty. In colonial expositions she was pictured as subservient, kneeling and bearing gifts of native produce to the mil-itant Marianne. There was a darker side to the sexual imagery as well, reflected in colonial novels and in the burgeoning turn-of-the-century postcard industry. Here Cambodian women differed little from the Vietnamese *congaï* (concu-bines), scheming sexual objects possessed of an arcane knowledge of their culture which they would share with their French lovers, but not capable of the maternal and feminine responses of French women.[69]

JULES VERNE

Popular sentiment about the overseas world was reflected in the works of Jules Verne, who sometimes published two books a year from 1863 until the century's end. "Pure Jules Verne" is how Lyautey once described a development project in Indochina, adding, "Of course it is Jules Verne. For 20 years the people who march forward have been doing nothing else but Jules Verne."[70] Verne's first published work of scientific and political fantasy was *Five Weeks in a Balloon* (1863), in which a celebrated eccentric British explorer, Dr. Samuel Fergusson, crosses Africa by balloon from east to west, beginning in Zanzibar. Fergusson flew with a traveling companion and straight man, Kennedy, a big game hunter and luxury-loving hedonist straight from central casting. The pair almost die of thirst in the desert and flee "the fierce bandits of Al Hadji" as their balloon slowly loses gas on the Senegal River's banks in land held by hostile warriors. The fortunate party manage their landing at a conveniently located French military post in the Upper Senegal minutes ahead of angry pursuers. Verne's explorers in other books visited Tunisia and West Africa, battled with el Hadj Omar in the Sudan, tried to end the slave trade, witnessed the Taiping rebellion and the American Civil War, saw the Australian and New Zealand gold rushes, and were with Napoléon at Acre.

Like the writers of the extraordinary voyages of the 16th century, Verne built a fantasy world to mirror what he wanted to say about France. While he was considerably less critical of French politics and customs than his predecessors, he still commented on French political attitudes. His characters admired independence movements in Hungary, Greece, and Iceland, but Africa and Asia were clearly far from being ready for independence. At times he extolled France's civilizing mission; at others, he had reservations about the spread of progress because it might cause the original peoples of Australia and North America to disappear. "Perhaps, one day the Arabs will be annihilated by French colonization," one of his voyagers ruefully remarked.

Flat contradictions abound in the viewpoints Verne expressed about life abroad, discrepancies mirrored in French attitudes as well. Verne's purpose was to sell books, not to construct a philosophical system; racism and sympathy for indigenous peoples are interwoven throughout his work. Sometimes America is a land of boundless opportunity; at others, it is a competing imperialist power. Respect for Chinese mandarin-like sagacity is mixed with hints of the yellow peril. There are "good" savages in North America, such as the noble Thalcave in *The Children of Captain Grant* (1868). Tall, splendidly attired in fox skins, Thalcave brings to mind one of Montaigne's indigenous philosophers. The native North American describes his people, "The most perfect equality reigns among them . . . they are of good moral character and they have a highly developed family feeling." Not all indigenous people got such high marks; natives of Northern Siberia, Melanesia, and Africans are reported to be "nasty creatures" or "horrible animals."

Ironically, although most of Verne's works had overseas settings, he rarely wrote about French colonies as such. His attitude toward them was ambivalent. Sometimes he suggested that they destroyed traditional societies, but that was the price paid for advancing civilization. Vietnam was not mentioned, and France's Pacific Island territories were described only in passing. One work, *The Invasion of the Sea* (1905), set in Tunisia, contained plans like those advanced at the time to create inland lakes and canals irrigated by the sea. Verne criticized the French policy of confining the Tuaregs of southern Tunisia to regions that would destroy their cattle raising, small-scale commerce, and agriculture. Hadjar, the rebellious Tuareg leader, resisted valiantly for a while, but was eventually defeated by the French. Verne directed his sharpest criticism toward the British. The Indian mutiny of 1857 was the focus of his novel *The Steam House* (1880), in which the British killed thousands of noncombatants. Several badly outnumbered guerrilla bands continued to fight the British from camps hidden in the foothills of the Himalayas, and he vividly portrayed the forced movement of populations, the disease, and the plundering. It almost seems that Verne lifted his plots from the popular press. His finger was always on the pulse of French readers, and he both reflected and helped shape their perceptions of the world beyond their borders, as fanciful and contradictory a place as it had been in centuries past.

PIERRE LOTI

No French author of the late 19th century wrote more about the overseas world than Julien Viaud, a Breton mariner, who spent 42 years in the French navy, writing travel accounts and novels under the name Pierre Loti. Loti came from the port town of Rochefort and traveled to Turkey, Senegal, the Orient, Morocco, and Egypt. His exotic fictional works included *Aziyadé* (1879), set in Turkey; *Rarahu*, a Polynesian idyll, which was published as *Le Mariage de Loti* (1880); *Le Roman d'un spahi* (1881), about life in Senegal; and *Madame Chrysanthème* (1887), set in Japan. His most famous works, *Mon frère Yves* (1883) and *Pêcheur d'Islande* (1886), were Breton sea stories. Although his books were extremely popular, with scenes of music hall humor and picture magazine exotica tumbling on one another in rapid succession, they said surprisingly little about life abroad. Loti's work belonged to post-1870 escapist literature. His heroes were handsome sailors torn between duty to country on one hand and exotic tropical pleasures on the other, caught between abstinence and absinthe. Loti's characters were as primitive as those of Gaugin's paintings; the similarity between the two artists extended to the power of their brooding landscapes as well. Loti's tropics were melancholy places, backdrops against which a distinctly French *mal du monde* was acted out. Characters were powerless to resist a cruel fate and found neither peace nor victory in their struggles. Instead, a grim fatalism was at work in the world. Loti was neither pro- nor anti-colonialist. Powerful, arrogant, European men and vulnerable, indigenous women are drawn together in impossible relationships. The women kill themselves after being left by their European lovers, who return disconsolately to their native lands or are killed in battle or drowned at sea.[71] It is a racist world that lacks happy endings.

Loti's *Le Roman d'un spahi* went through 150 editions and was responsible for his election, at age 41, to the Académie Française in place of Émile Zola. The novel describes a melancholy encounter of cultures set in Senegal, where a young French officer, Jean Payel, is sent to join a Spahi regiment of local soldiers. Coming from the mountainous Cevennes region, he leaves his childhood sweetheart and aging parents behind and falls for Cora, a mulatto "of Spanish pallor," while still maintaining his "homesickness for his native mountains, his village, and the cottage of his old people."[72] Next Jean takes up with Fatou, a slave girl, who follows him inland when the regiment is finally activated to march against Boubaker-Sègou, "the great Negro chief." Jean is wounded in a pitched battle and eventually dies in the savanna. Fatou buries their child alive in the sand beside him, takes poison, and leaves herself as prey for circling vultures.

In *Mariage de Loti*, a handsome young ensign is sent to Tahiti, something he has dreamed about since childhood. The mysterious island paradise exists in a timeless state, as a world of innocence. The voyager is given a new name, Loti, to emphasize his new life. In this setting of ripe fruits, slowly circling butterflies, and pervasive strong perfumes, Loti finds a young Maori girl, Rarahu, with whom he passes the hours, bathing in a secret pool. Rarahu is afflicted when a tuberculosis epidemic hits the island. Loti's temporary marriage ends, and he leaves the island. Rarahu, like his other heroines, dies.

In short, the overseas world for this century's French artists and writers offered both attractions and repulsions, as Loti's books suggest. The trauma of the 1870 war with Germany loomed large in the national consciousness, and exotic, sun-filled gardens graced by lithe maidens provided a momentary escape from the frustrations of a defeated nation.

NOTES

1. John F. Cady, *The Roots of French Imperialism in Eastern Asia* (Ithaca, N.Y.: Cornell University Press, 1967), pp. 18–22.

2. D. G. E. Hall, *A History of South-East Asia* (London: Macmillan, 1964), pp. 608–629.

3. Charles Meyer, *La vie quotidienne des français en Indochine, 1860–1910* (Paris: Hachette, 1985), pp. 240–244.

4. Ibid., p. 244.

5. Ibid., pp. 53–54.

6. Milton E. Osborne, *The French Presence in Cochinchina and Cambodia, 1895–1905* (Ithaca, N.Y.: Cornell University Press, 1969) pp. 15–18.

7. Meyer, *La vie quotidienne*, p. 72.

8. Ibid., pp. 99–104.

9. David G. Marr, *Vietnamese Anticolonialism, 1885–1925* (Berkeley: University of California Press, 1980, reprint of 1971 edition), p. 33.

10. Ibid., p. 38.

11. Osborne, *The French Presence*, p. 61.

12. Ibid., p. 38.

13. Ibid., pp. 89–100.

14. J. Valette, "L'expédition de Francis Garnier au Tonkin," in *Revue d'histoire moderne et contemporaine* 16 (April 1969) (Paris: Armand Colin), pp. 189–220.

15. Cady, *Roots of French Imperialism*, pp. 275–293 passim.

16. Osborne, *The French Presence*, pp. 45–46, 81–82, 146ff.

17. Paul Rabinow, *French Modern, Norms and Forms of the Social Environment* (Cambridge: MIT Press, 1989), pp. 142–162.

18. Ibid., pp. 145–146.

19. Osborne, *The French Presence*, p. 70.

20. Ibid., pp. 66, 95–100, 133–140, 264.

21. Ibid., pp. 303–304.

22. Ibid., p. 131.

23. Ibid., pp. 50, 51–52.

24. Ibid., pp. 175–258.

25. Penny Edwards, "Womanizing Indochina: Fiction, Nation, and Cohabitation in Colonial Cambodia, 1890–1930," in *Domesticating the Empire: Race, Gender, and Family Life in French and Dutch Colonialism*, ed. Julia Clancy-Smith and Frances Gouda (Charlottesville: University of Virginia Press, 1998), p. 117.

26. Osborne, *The French Presence*, pp. 206–211.

27. Ibid., p. 230.

28. Edwards, "Womanizing Indochina," p. 129.

29. Hall, *History of South-East Asia*, pp. 415–421, 643, 826–836.

30. John Dunmore, *French Explorers in the Pacific*, vol. 2, *The Nineteenth Century* (New York: Oxford University Press, 1969).

31. Robert Aldrich, *Greater France: A History of French Overseas Expansion* (New York: St. Martin's Press, 1996), pp. 71, 146–147, 192, 218–219.

32. Hubert Deschamps, *Histoire de Madagascar* (Paris: Éditions Berger-Levrault, 1965).

33. Phares M. Mutibwa, *The Malagasy and the Europeans, Madagascar's Foreign Relations, 1861–1895* (Atlantic Heights, N.J.: Humanities Press, 1974).

34. Jean Martin, *L'Empire triomphant, 1871–1936, II Maghreb, Indochine, Madagascar, Iles et comptoirs* (Paris: Denoël, 1990), pp. 271–309.

35. Philip Curtin, *Disease and Empire: The Health of European Troops in the Conquest of Africa* (Cambridge: Cambridge University Press, 1998), p. 177.

36. Virgil L. Matthew, Jr., "Joseph-Simon Gallieni (1849–1916)," in *African Proconsuls, European Governors in Africa*, ed. L. H. Gann and Peter Duignan (New York: Free Press, 1978), pp. 92–100.

37. Deschamps, *Histoire de Madagascar*, pp. 237–247.

38. Jacques Thobie, "La France coloniale de 1970 à 1914," in Jean Meyer, Jean Tarrade, Annie Rey-Goldzeiguer, and Jacques Thobie, eds., *Histoire de La France coloniale des origines à 1914* (Paris: Armand Colin, 1991), p. 671.

39. Myron Echenberg, "Slaves into Soldiers: Social Origins of the *Tirailleurs Séné-galais*," in *Africans in Bondage: Studies in Slavery and the Slave Trade*, ed. Paul E. Lovejoy (Madison: University of Wisconsin, African Studies Program, 1986), p. 314.

40. Jean Martin, *L'Empire renaissant, 1789–1871* (Paris: Denoël, 1987), pp. 213–232.

41. Charlotte A. Quinn, *Mandingo Kingdoms of the Senegambia: Traditionalism, Islam, and European Expansion* (Evanston, Ill.: Northwestern University Press, 1972).

42. John D. Hargreaves, *Prelude to the Partition of West Africa* (London: Macmillan, 1963).

43. Echenberg, "Slaves into Soldiers," pp. 311–316.

44. Richard L. Roberts, *Two Worlds of Cotton: Colonialism and the Regional Economy in the French Soudan, 1800–1946* (Stanford, Calif.: Stanford University Press, 1996).

45. Gilbert Comte, *L'Empire Triomphant, 1871–1936*, vol. I, *Afrique Occidentale et Équatoriale* (Paris: Denoël, 1988), pp. 51–80; Jacques Richard-Molard, *Afrique Occidentale Française* (Paris: Berger Levrault, 1956).

46. Jean Martin, *L'Empire renaissant*, pp. 213–232; A. S. Kanya-Forstner, *The Conquest of the Western Sudan: A Study in French Military Imperialism* (Cambridge: Cambridge University Press, 1969).

47. Curtin, *Disease and Empire*, pp. 79, 83.

48. Richard L. Roberts, *Warriors, Merchants, and Slaves: The State and the Economy in the Middle Niger Valley, 1700–1914* (Stanford, Calif.: Stanford University Press, 1987), p. 139.

49. R. E. Robinson and J. Gallagher, "The Partition of Africa," in *The New Cambridge Modern History*, vol. 11, *Material Progress and World-Wide Problems, 1870–1898* (Cambridge: Cambridge University Press, 1962), pp. 593–640; Prosser Gifford and William Roger Louis, eds., *France and Britain in Africa: Imperial Rivalry and Colonial Rule* (New Haven, Conn.: Yale University Press, 1971).

50. Timothy C. Weiskel, *French Colonial Rule and the Baule Peoples: Resistance and Collaboration, 1889–1911* (New York: Oxford University Press, 1980).

51. Carl Ludwig Lokke, *France and the Colonial Question: A Study of Contemporary French Opinion, 1763–1801* (New York: Columbia University Press, 1932), pp. 96–97.

52. Annie Rey-Goldzeiguer, "La France coloniale de 1930 à 1870," in *Histoire de la France coloniale des origines à 1914*, ed. Jean Meyer, Jean Tarrade, Annie Rey-Goldzeiguer, and Jacques Thobie (Paris: Armand Colin, 1991), pp. 444–447, 460–461, 478–479, 573–591; David S. Landes, *Bankers and Pashas: International Finance and Economic Imperialism in Egypt* (New York: Harper & Row, 1958); Alan Schom, *Napoleon Bonaparte* (New York: HarperCollins, 1996).

53. Todd Porterfield, *The Allure of Empire: Art in the Service of French Imperialism, 1789–1836* (Princeton, N.J.: Princeton University Press, 1998), pp. 43–79.

54. *Napoleon in Egypt, Al-Jabarti's Chronicle of the French Occupation, 1798*, trans. Shmuel Moreh (New York: Markus Wiener Publishing, 1995), pp. 24–33.

55. Ibid., p. 49.

56. Daniel R. Headrick, *The Tentacles of Progress: Technology, Transfer in the Age of Imperialism, 1850–1940* (New York: Oxford University Press, 1988), p. 200.

57. Edward W. Said, *Culture and Imperialism* (New York: Knopf, 1993), pp. 111–125.

58. David Levering Lewis, *The Race to Fashoda: European Colonialism and African Resistance in the Scramble for Africa* (New York: Weidenfeld & Nicholson, 1987), pp. 222–226.

59. Headrick, *Tentacles of Progress*, p. 174.

60. Lewis Pyenson, *Civilizing Mission: Exact Sciences and French Overseas Expansion, 1830–1940* (Baltimore: Johns Hopkins University Press, 1993), pp. 59–97.

61. Headrick, *Tentacles of Progress*, pp. 15–19, 117–119.

62. Ibid., p. 124.

63. Ibid., pp. 96–102.

64. Janet R. Horne, "In Pursuit of Greater France: Visions of Empire Among Musée Social Reformers, 1894–1931," in *Domesticating the Empire: Race, Gender, and Family Life in French and Dutch Colonialism*, ed. Julia Clancy-Smith and Frances Gouda (Charlottesville: University of Virginia Press, 1998), pp. 21–42.

65. Michael A. Osborne, *Nature, the Exotic, and the Science of French Colonialism* (Bloomington: Indiana University Press, 1994), p. 174; Headrick, *Tentacles of Progress*, pp. 228–231.

66. Patrice Debré, *Louis Pasteur*, trans. Elborg Forster (Baltimore: Johns Hopkins University Press, 1998), pp. 484–491.

67. Edward W. Said, *Orientalism* (New York: Vintage Books, 1979); Angela Chia-Yi Pao, *The Orient of the Boulevards: Exoticism, Empire, and Nineteenth-Century French Theater* (Philadelphia: University of Pennsylvania Press, 1997); Porterfield, *The Allure of Empire*.

68. Edwards, "Womanizing Indochina," p. 109.

69. Ibid., p. 116.

70. Quoted in William B. Cohen, *The French Encounter with Africans, White Response to Blacks, 1530–1880* (Bloomington: Indiana University Press, 1980), p. 281; *Lettres du Tonkin et Madagascar*, vol. 1 (Paris: 1920), p. 224.

71. Aldrich, *Greater France*, p. 241.

72. Tzvetan Todorov, *On Human Destiny, Nationalism, Racism, and Exoticism in French Thought* (Cambridge: Cambridge University Press, 1993), p. 319.

6

The 20th Century: The Expanding Empire

"The colonies . . . I didn't know there were so many of them."
—Étienne Clémentel, Minister of Colonies, 1905

Although the French Overseas Empire reached its apogee in the 20th century, this expansion set in motion the very forces that eventually caused its dissolution. The impact of two world wars, persistent armed resistance in Vietnam and Algeria, and the gradual rise of nationalism were the ingredients that challenged the Empire's existence. Add to that the growth of trade unions, the emergence of educated elites in the overseas territories, the influence of the United Nations, and the changing attitude of French political parties toward colonial issues, all of which contributed to the Empire's demise. The genie was out of the bottle by 1945, and despite efforts to hold the Empire together by political and military means, it failed to survive. By 1962 the French Overseas Empire was no more, although French proconsuls continued their presence in Africa, supporting client states favorable to France, sending in troops on occasion, and trying to preserve French commercial interests in overseas markets.[1]

France began the 20th century in an enviable position with the world's second largest colonial empire, embracing over 10 million square kilometers and nearly 100 million people, counting the *métropole*. After World War I it added League of Nations mandate territories in Togo, Cameroon, Syria, and Lebanon. On paper, at least, the future looked bright. In 1905 the new minister of colonies, Étienne Clémentel, could look at a world map and say, "The colonies . . . I didn't know there were so many of them."[2] As before, overseas possessions were the responsibility of three different ministries. Algeria, with 5 million people, was a department of France and came under a governor-general who reported to the minister of the interior. The neighboring states of Morocco and Tunisia, both French protectorates, were each governed by a resident general who reported to the Ministry of Foreign Affairs. The rest of the Empire was responsible to a small Ministry of Colonies, which, although created in 1894, lacked a clear mandate and adequate personnel. For good measure, colonial troops reported to the Ministry of War. The absurdity of such divided administration was exemplified in 1913 when French troops in West Africa attacked southern Mauritania at the same time other French soldiers operating from Morocco pursued a different, more conciliatory policy at the instructions of *résident général* Louis-Hubert Lyautey.

ASSIMILATION VERSUS ASSOCIATION

The divided colonial administrative structure reflected divisions in French politics about the place of colonies. Should colonial peoples be *assimilated* into France proper, or should they be *associated* with France in an autonomous, federated state that would perhaps one day lead to their being independent nations? The question was debated for decades, often in a lively fashion, but never answered until too late. Because France was a Latin country, so the assimilationist argument went, the structure Rome devised to hold its far-flung empire together should be the model of colonial administration employed by France. At a minimum, assimilation could mean political-legal representation of an overseas possession in metropolitan government and exporting the homeland's political and administrative institutions abroad, including uniform taxation, educational policies, military obligations, and rights of citizens. It was on this latter point, sometimes called the "assimilation of the natives," that French colonial doctrine frequently stumbled.[3]

Arthur Girault, a former colonial official and a theorist of assimilation wrote,

The man whom we deny being first in his country because it is a colony must be offered in exchange the possibility to be Number One in our country. The people whom we want to forbid from having local patriotism must be inoculated with love of the common country, the cult of Empire.[4]

Partisans of assimilation wanted French education extended to the colonies, French laws to apply equally everywhere, and French administrative structures to be replicated overseas. But the extent of overseas political participation always ended at a roadblock. If the Empire claimed millions of people, how would they be represented in the legislature? Certainly this was not possible by direct or proportional vote. (As late as 1936 there were fewer than 500 thousand French voters living abroad—only a handful were non-whites.) The assimilationist doctrine gave with one hand and withheld with the other.

The case for association was made in 1907 by Émile Démaret, the inspector of colonies, who stated that "because the empire is not populated by people of the same race, speaking the same language, having the same customs, a federalist system is superior to all other systems because it applies to all nations at all times and can unite very different peoples."[5] For followers of this school, especially toward the century's middle years, the role of colonial policy was to launch colonies, as children are raised to grow into maturity on their own, and later to live as independent nations, but with economic and emotional ties to the homeland. The unanswered question about association with France and indirect rule was—what if the people didn't want to participate? Lyautey, best known of the proconsuls, was a leading proponent of the associationist viewpoint, but it was easy to do so when French troops had ruthlessly put down any opposition in their way. As a colonial theorist, Lyautey was a case apart—an assimilationist in practice, an associationist in theory. Of his work in Morocco, Lyautey once said, *"Nous avons l'administration directe dans le peau"* (We have direct administration in our skin). No closet democrat, Lyautey subjugated unruly tribes first, then learned about their language, history, and culture. In Morocco he worked through local leaders; his *politique des grands caïds* gave the *caïds* power to run the administration, collect taxes, supervise the police force, and direct local courts, powers which many grossly abused. As a result, the system was widely resented among the people who were supposed to be grateful for the French presence.[6]

The divided nature of colonial policy was mirrored in a patchwork of local applications. In Indochina, rigid centralization characterized the French presence; no attempt was made to work through traditional mandarins, who were held suspect. In Morocco, Lyautey encouraged local clan leaders, and in Rabat he built the European town separate from the Muslim *médina*, which he wanted to preserve intact (but which then became overcrowded, as there was no place for it to expand).

The broader debate on colonial policy took many forms and was never satisfactorily resolved. Should indigenous customs, languages, laws, and belief systems be encouraged, or should they be suppressed and replaced by French ones? Was the indigenous inhabitant a *bon sauvage* or a potential cannibal? How far should France go in educating local peoples? Would they be eternally grateful, or soon want independence? "To instruct our subjects is to one day make them our equals, tomorrow our masters," a colonial official warned. *"Parler en français, c'est penser en français"* (To speak French is to think in French)[7] the opposite saying went, but that could be dangerous, opening subject peoples to French internal political and economic debates which colonial administrators did not care to export. For example, was it wise to teach local peoples about French history? One African independence leader recalled years later the eye-opening experience of learning how Vercingétorix beat the Romans and suggested that Africans could do the same with France. Strong voices opposed colonial participation in French politics, arguing that colonial deputies, black or white, would be fraudulently elected and should have no role in questioning cabinet ministers or bringing down or constructing a government. The alternative point of view, one that carried the day only after World War II, was that it was wrong to exclude some of France's most loyal indigenous defenders from the political process. If an empire was to be an empire, that must be reflected in its political structure; otherwise, how could overseas populations be expected to remain loyal to France?

Opposing association and assimilation were those who argued that France came first and why bother about overseas? Local interests were a powerful magnet in France, as Eugen Weber's study *Peasants into Frenchmen, 1870–1914* demonstrates, and most peasants and their elected representatives preferred a bridge, road, or railroad in the home district to one in Africa or Asia. Opponents of colonial expansion declared, *"Après avoir conquis les colonies il nous reste à conquérir la France"* (After having conquered the colonies it remains for us to conquer France). Such "charity begins at home" arguments were mirrored in parliamentary debates over how much economic aid France should allocate to former colonies versus how much it should spend on projects at home.[8] A wise practitioner with long experience in Africa, Robert Delavignette, later director of political affairs in the Overseas Ministry, wrote, "Assimilation *or* Association? In fact one does not have to make an unconditional choice. Assimilation *and* Association, the two formulas are often combined; the dosage of each varies with the practitioner's dexterity and the temperature of events."[9]

LOUIS-HUBERT LYAUTEY, MARÉCHAL DE FRANCE: A CASE APART

One way to approach the evolution of French colonial policy in the early 20th century is to study the activities of a leading figure who represents, in a microcosm, both its most laudable aspirations and its shortcomings. Louis-Hubert Lyautey, French *résident général* in Morocco from 1912 to 1925, stands alongside General Charles de Gaulle as one of the two most important figures in French 20th century colonial policy. Lyautey (1854–1934) grew up in an aristocratic family. His father was a highly placed government engineer.[10] Although he was a political conservative, Lyautey's interests as a military officer moved from church and crown to the colonies. A trip to Rome and Algeria imbued him with an idea of the symmetry of Roman imperial urbanism, and like many such travelers, he was smitten with the sights and smells of the Orient, as depicted in Delacroix and Flaubert and a hundred less skilled artists and writers. While abroad, he carefully constructed the personal space in which he lived with objects gathered while stationed in Algeria or Indochina. Lyautey called his setting a "home," using the English word. (He also spoke of his carefully selected young staff officers in English as being "the right man in the right place.") The setting is worth dwelling on, for Lyautey for much of his career walked a tightrope between French and local cultures. While despising French business entrepreneurs and settlers, his abiding fixation was with social Catholicism and political conservatism, although he was not a conventional believer or political ideologue. More than any other colonial figure, he supported research about overseas countries and encouraged his subalterns to understand local cultures as a means of controlling local peoples more effectively. Lyautey spoke Arabic and spent many hours while assigned to Algeria (1904–1910) listening to local court cases, a useful way of providing a snapshot of life in any society. He was one of the few colonial administrators who extolled the value of tradition, as long as it posed no threat to French political, military, or economic aims. Lyautey's native affairs officers were required to study Arabic and Berber, plus the ethnography of the peoples with whom they were stationed.

Lyautey became the first French *résident général* of Morocco in 1912. He spent the next 13 years there, except for a brief, turbulent tour as minister of war in 1917. Military pacification was the order of the day when the marshal arrived at his new command. Resistance to the European takeover was sharp among Moroccans. A holy war was declared, and a general uprising flared up when word of the protectorate was announced. The sultan's troops mutinied and killed their French officers. Twenty thousand Berbers poured out of the Rif and Middle Atlas Mountains toward Fez. Armed Moroccan cavalry made numerous raids on the French. Eventually the Moroccans were repulsed, but the country was not free of armed clashes for almost two years, a time of "digestion," as Lyautey put it, before the French were firmly established. Military control was always a main, albeit sometimes unpublicized, theme of his administration, and the final failure to achieve it brought down Lyautey, who was replaced by Marshal Philippe Pétain in 1925.

A stickler for observing the minutiae of royal court protocol and a protector of traditional Moroccan cities, Lyautey was also a supporter of the Islamic center at the Quarawiyyne University in Fez and of the ensconced Berber rulers in the High Atlas. "Vex not tradition, leave custom be,"[11] he said. Find the natural ruling class that exists in each society and make common cause with its leaders, linking their interests to France's.

A careful crafter of his own legend, Lyautey was also a promoter of French and indigenous art and culture. The setting where he held court and conducted business was a sumptuous *Résidence Général*, a setting for *Thousand and One Nights*. Filmmakers were invited to Morocco for shoots, and the marshal obligingly provided interviews and logistical support from the army. Lyautey soon translated his policy goals into urban planning. He summoned Henri Prost, a young French urban planner who spent a decade in Morocco and drew up master plans for nine cities, and a bevy of talented young French architects of the École des Beaux-Arts who were anxious to build their reputations. The imposing results were wide boulevards, some leading to local or French monuments; striking government buildings, employing Arab design motifs, including courts and railway stations; and spacious villas for the leaders of the French community. Far less impressive were the crowded spaces designated for Moroccans. The crucial

issue of proper sanitation, water and sewage, and other public works, such as
hospitals and schools, were ignored in Prost's planning. Finally, there was no
provision for the city's future growth, and within a few years, the land beyond
the carefully constructed city was filled with *bidonvilles*, the makeshift shacks
that were the product of urban drift.[12]

While Lyautey's personality, cultural interests, and interest in urban planning
have always attracted interest, he was first and foremost a soldier, and ultimately
he lost his position for failing to bring the Berber leader Abd el Krim (1882–
1963) under control.[13] Operating from a Spanish-administered section of the Rif
mountains, Abd el Krim wanted nothing less than an independent Berber nation.
In the wake of World War I, France's troop reserves were depleted, and the
reinforcements Lyautey asked for did not arrive. On April 11, 1925, the Berber
leader attacked French positions. Pétain, as head of the French army, and urged
on by politicians of the left, came to Morocco to review Lyautey's plans for
putting down the rebellious Berbers. Without telling Lyautey, he met with the
Spanish prime minister, in whose territory the Berbers were based, and he devised an alternative battle plan to that proposed by Lyautey. "There is not
enough room for both Lyautey and me in Morocco," Pétain supposedly said,
and when Lyautey learned of the new plan and was simultaneously denied the
additional troops he requested, he resigned on September 25, 1925.

The end of the Lyautey era came swiftly. The marshal's policies were abandoned after his departure, and harsher military pacification continued until 1932.
Moroccan sharpshooters on horseback were no match for heavy artillery, war
planes, tanks, machine guns, and an economic blockade. By May 1926 the
Berber leader and his forces were defeated. The Moroccan protectorate was now
a military occupation. French settlers arrived in greater numbers, attracted by
Morocco's rich farm lands. Simultaneously, the growth of factories and commercial establishments meant that any prospects for Arab and Berber political
autonomy had withered. The race for land and influence pushed the Berbers
into an alliance with other Arab populations in joint opposition to France, ex-
acerbating the disintegration of traditional society and sowing the seed of future
nationalistic politics.

Lyautey's later years were spent cultivating his legend. Like Jeanne d'Arc,
Lyautey came from Lorraine. In the 1930s, Lyautey, dean of French colonial
figures, was likened by his admirers to France's heroine who defended the country in its darkest hour, especially in the period between his dismissal from his
proconsular role in Morocco in 1925 and his death in 1934. He busied himself
from 1927 to 1931 with plans for the Colonial Exposition, of which he was
commissaire général. His myth was carefully promoted by followers on both
the right and left. André Maurois published a biography, *Lyautey* (1931), that
went through multiple editions. Lyautey wrote a preface to a book about Jeanne,
which was dedicated to him, "To Marshal Lyautey whose magnificent colonial
work grew under the sign of good Lorraine." Both figures, the book emphasized,
exemplified the region's virtues, faith, and hard work, and as Jeanne had upheld

the nation and revived the faith of its weak dauphin, Lyautey could give new faith and energy to tired republicans. For Jeanne, the external enemy was England; for Lyautey, Germany. Jeanne never left the little Hexagon; Lyautey's career traversed most points of the Great Hexagon. Later France's 20th century political and military leader Charles de Gaulle picked the Cross of Lorraine for his military movement and political party.[14]

THE COLONIAL PARTY

The most vocal advocates of overseas expansion were the Colonial party, an enthusiastic minority—heirs to the colonial lobby tradition of the 19th century—spread across party lines. It included 42 deputies in 1892; its numbers rose to 200 in 1902, and it was the second largest voting bloc in the National Assembly after the agriculturalists. The lobby was supported by about 60 organizations, a handful of journals, and a devout following in ministries and trading companies. Journalists called it *le parti où l'on dine*, for much of its business was conducted at dinners where returning explorers and colonial officials spoke. Committees were formed for Africa, Asia, Madagascar, and Morocco, which sponsored lectures at the Sorbonne and in lycées and offered prizes for the best writings on colonial subjects. Colonial questions rarely interested French intellectuals or politicians, and colonial lobby leadership was limited to the same handful of persons who appeared over and over as sponsors of each others' dinners and lectures. Membership in colonial societies was sparse. The 12 principal colonial societies boasted 10 thousand members in 1900, although they were outnumbered by the 88 thousand members of the Deutsche Kolonialgesellschaft.[15]

The Colonial party and its followers enjoyed a brief revival after World War I. It was, however, a case of rounding up the usual suspects, ex-colonial *fonctionnaires*, business executives with overseas ties, and a handful of journalists, academics, and parliamentarians. Their vision of *la mentalité impériale* and *la plus grande France* never fired the imagination of the masses, who were focused on reconstruction and economic recovery at home. The party remained a vestige of an earlier era, a creature of the age of banquets. It opposed the political participation of overseas peoples, later rejected Vietnamese and Algerian demands for independence as being contrary to French strategic interests, and argued the necessity of retaining forced work requirements in Africa and Madagascar as an economic measure.[16]

WHO WORKED FOR THE EMPIRE?

The texture of French-colonial relations changed markedly as growing numbers of local peoples worked their way into the French overseas administration. Some started as domestic servants, hospital orderlies, or messengers. Those who learned French and adapted to European ways became clerks and interpreters, a choice post in overseas societies. An interpreter was a gatekeeper to the French administrators, many of whom shaped their understanding of local politics from what interpreters told them. Often those most attracted to working for the French in Africa were not chiefs or their first-born heirs, but younger sons who would inherit nothing and lacked career prospects beyond hunting or farming. Learning French and working for the administration provided their ticket to a future. The number of French was always proportionately high in colonial administrations. There were 14 French workers in the Phnom Penh post office alone in 1910. By comparison, the much larger Singapore post office under British rule had only eight English employees. By 1914 there were approximately 12 thousand indigenous workers to 4 thousand French *fonctionnaires* in Indochina. After World War I, numbers of French officials serving in the overseas possessions declined sharply, and indigenous workers were given increasingly responsible roles in the colonial administration.[17]

Bernard Fall, an American writer living in Vietnam in the 1950s, quotes an often-cited figure that in 1925 the British in India governed a country of 325 million people with 4,898 European civil servants while the French administered 30 million Indochinese with 5 thousand civil servants. He recalled "seeing one last French white policeman directing traffic in the streets of Hanoi as late as September 1953—a menial job no British colonial governor would have permitted a white man to do even a hundred years ago."[18]

LABOR POLICIES

By 1935 there may have been 179 thousand African wage earners in French West Africa, in addition to 59 thousand seasonal migrant workers, a little over 1.5% of the estimated total population. A basic question for French policy makers was should Africans be forced to work for planters and on public works projects because they were slow and unskilled, or should the rudiments of socialist-inspired wage and hour legislation be accorded them? Meanwhile, forced labor recruitment existed unchecked in West Africa, although verbal opposition to it was growing. Bush administrators were given quotas of recruits to furnish to private companies on the coast or for government programs. As in Algeria and Morocco, French settlers sought the quick removal of reform-minded colonial officials and blocked attempts made by labor inspectors to curb abuses. One young inspector compared forced labor recruitment to slavery, the difference being the labor contracts were for six months at a time. French colonial governors dodged pointed International Labor Organization (ILO) questionnaires about forced recruitment and complained of the high costs any sudden shift in labor practices would entail, pleaded for a gradualist approach, and argued that the administration was the workers' best ally. It was not until 1937 and the Popular Front that France ratified the International Labor Convention with reservations.[19]

WHO WERE THE OVERSEAS FRENCH?

One the eve of World War I, 700 thousand French lived abroad in colonies, 500 thousand of them in Algeria alone. Tunisia has been described as "an Italian colony administered by France for the profit of the local Jewish merchants."[20] In 1911 its population was 88,180 Italians, 46 thousand French, and 11 thousand Maltese citizens. In Morocco, the European population shot up from 9,890 persons in 1911 to 48,555 in 1914. Fifty-three percent of the population was French; the rest, Spanish and Italian. In Indochina only 24 thousand French lived among 16 million indigenous peoples.[21]

The linchpins of the overseas French presence were the colonial administrators, many of whom were of mediocre quality, and their presence was a mixed blessing for local peoples. William Cohen's ground-breaking institutional study shows that the Colonial School founded to train these officers had graduated 555 persons by 1914, about 20% of the overseas administrators. Many graduates were not impressive, however, for the school lacked the prestige of France's more established schools. Between 1908 and 1914, the Colonial School averaged only 71 candidates for 28 places. Numbers increased later as colonial posts expanded—326 candidates in 1937, 620 in 1944, 900 in 1946—but overseas careers attracted the interest of talented young French students only in the Empire's final years.[22] Many overseas French were minor functionaries who had been stuck in poor-paying jobs at home with no possibilities of advancement. A few, however, were energetic and just administrators, while a handful produced important scientific and historical studies. Robert Delavignette, for example, was one such colonial administrator who came to head the Colonial School in Paris and was a theoretician of empire. In *Freedom and Authority in French West Africa*, he wrote ecstatically about the small city on the hill, the *Cercle*, and its *Commandant* as dispenser of justice, collector of taxes, builder of schools and dispensaries, supporter of missionaries and traders, and promoter of the good life for people who lived under its control.[23] Delavignette wrote:

It was the physical environment of my first post which brought home to me the distinctive character of our colonial administration in its most characteristic form—that of a *Cercle Commandant*.... [The English translator could have used the more accurate term, *Commandant du Cercle*.] At Zinder there were two towns, the European and the African, or rather the colonial and the native; and between the two, at almost equal distance from each, stood the office of the *Cercle*, a dwelling unique of its kind. Our colonial city was lined with symmetrical buildings which served both as offices and residences.... The man who really personified the *Cercle* was the Commandant, and he was not a civil servant like us. He was not a specialist in any branch of administration, nor was he lost in an academic theory of administration in general. He was the Chief of a clearly defined country called Damaragam, and Chief in everything that concerned the country ... he had his own special nickname: "Thief-Purger." And it was not only in court that he purged the country of its rogues and vagabonds, but on tour, when he would give a good dressing-down in private to the *zarki* who was cheating the villages over tax money. This was his way also with certain colonials who traded secretly in coin and cattle.[24]

French West Africa had 118 *cercles*, 2,200 cantons, and 48 thousand listed villages spread out over 4.5 million square kilometers holding 20 million persons. This meant administrators—*broussards*, or "men of the bush" as they were often called—spent much of their time on a daily round of building roads, supervising public works, presiding over local courts, and settling property disputes. Most administrators did not leave long shadows, departing for a new post after two years (with home leave after a year abroad). Not many learned the languages and customs of the people they governed. In 1908, only 54 of 220 administrators in Indochina could get by in the local language, as did three of 100 judges and six of 350 postal and telephone workers. The missionaries did a much better job of learning languages, all the better to prepare local peoples for conversion to Christianity.

In 1897 a society was formed to send women to the colonies, but it lasted only a few years. In its first year it sent more than 400 women overseas—68 teachers, 78 seamstresses, and a number of cooks, maids, and unemployed women. One of its purposes was to send educated single women from France who had not chosen traditional bourgeois roles to the colonies where they would find eligible male partners, contribute to stabilizing and enhancing the French presence overseas, and help defeat the English.[25]

Still, not many French women went abroad. French women living in the colonies were mostly wives of administrators, along with nuns and a few nurses and teachers who received salaries three to four times less than those of male counterparts. Alice L. Conklin noted that in West Africa with improved hygienic conditions during the 20th century and the arrival of more administrators' wives, "Older forms of racial intermingling, both sexual and social, were discouraged, and administrators did not tour their districts as frequently as before. Entertaining other Europeans became an important priority, while concubinage and prostitution, previously tolerated, were now frowned upon."[26] Overseas life was difficult for French women, especially in Islamic countries where they were supposed to be virtually invisible. The few career possibilities, isolation, and lack of medical, social, and cultural advantages worked against them. Notwithstanding, a few women developed careers abroad. Dr. Françoise Legey, for example, directed medical clinics in Algeria and Morocco that treated several thousand patients annually in the early 20th century.[27]

ECONOMY

The colonies were never the principal destination for French exports. During the pre–World War I period, French exports to Russia and Latin America considerably outstripped those to the Empire.[28] Notwithstanding, its overseas possessions were an important market for French business houses, especially those in coastal cities cultivating a colonial trade. Algeria was the lodestone, absorbing 60% of France's overseas exports in 1913 and furnishing France with 40% of its colonial imports. Wine, cereals, and live animals were exchanged in France for cotton cloth, clothes, tools, metal objects, and sugar. Automobile imports in 1913 reached almost 26 million francs. Tunisia and Morocco were also attractive markets. Fifty-four percent of Tunisian commerce was with France and the Empire, 45% for Morocco, whose agreeable climate and proximity to France helped spark a building boom. Newspapers compared the attraction of Morocco to the French to that of the eastern Americans to the western states. Ports, railroad lines, and public buildings went up in quick succession in the Maghreb states. From 1911 to 1913 importation of wood increased five-fold from France, from 9 thousand to nearly 45 thousand tons, and imports of steel, coal, and cement were similarly large.

In Indochina, the French hold was weaker. While Indochina absorbed 16% of French export capital in 1916, trade with France represented only 19% of Indochina's gross trade figures. Rice was the big export item to France with 66% of local production destined for the *métropole*, but most Vietnamese trade was with other Asian countries. The Bank of Indochina, which controlled local economic activity, preferred to deal with China and India, both easier to reach.

The immediate years before World War I were a time of gradual commercial expansion in the French possessions overall; 156 companies registered to conduct overseas trade, 69 of them in North Africa, 36 in Africa, 29 in Indochina. Successful firms made profits as high as 32% a year for mining companies, 25% for commercial companies, and 14% for financial institutions. A few did even better. The Compagnie des Mines d'Ouasta et de Mesloula, which mined Algerian zinc, lead, and copper, earned profits of 123%; the Société des Charbonnages du Tonkin, whose coal supplies were extracted from Ha Lag Bay, consistently gained profits as high as 84%. A leading African trading company such as CFAO realized a 41% annual profit in the "golden years" before World War I and the Great Depression. An investor who bought 500 francs worth of CFAO stock in the late 1890s would realize a dividend of 8.5% at the century's end and 22% in 1914. French overseas investment was concentrated on Morocco and Algeria and, to a lesser extent, Indochina (16%) and Africa (18%).[29]

At this time Africa, sometimes called "the Cinderella of the Empire," had a largely barter economy, exchanging palm oil, groundnuts, and rubber for cotton, sugar, salt, and metal products such as knives and cooking instruments. The agents of economic activity in Africa were a number of established French trading houses from Bordeaux, Marseilles, and Paris, usually based in large warehouses near a principal port with smaller trading stations scattered along key land or water routes to the interior. A handful of French coastal traders were supplemented during the century by a growing number of Greek and Lebanese merchants and many Africans who ran small shops in towns or led trading caravans to the interior. When caravans arrived, members were usually given a gift by the French commercial station manager, a *Sankiriba* (literally "taking off of sandals"), a package of food such as rice and biscuits, some tobacco, sugar, and salt, and a few pieces of printed cotton, the value proportional to the worth of goods transported by the caravan.

Finally, investment in the overseas territories was made by the government throughout the 20th century. The economic historian Jacques Marseille suggests that of the over 25 million francs invested in the French Overseas Empire through 1958, three quarters of the funds were government monies, principally in the form of budgetary credits or equipment purchases. Only one quarter came from the private sector. On the other hand, in the pre-1914 period near-parity existed between private and public sector investments. By 1958 a 1:5 private–government ratio prevailed.[30]

WORLD WAR I, THE COLONIAL CONTRIBUTION

France remained politically and economically fragile after the Franco-Prussian War and its position did not improve as World War I approached. "Pour sauver une petite France, il faut avoir une grande France" ("To save a small France there must be a greater France") was an oft-expressed sentiment by those hoping to encourage imperial ventures. A new war loomed, France's birth rates remained lower than other European countries; its population grew only about 3% between 1900–1939, while Germany's grew at 36%. As war approached, France turned to its *Force noir*, mainly troops from Senegal and elsewhere in Africa. The French believed a vast army of loyal subjects would sail to Europe and give their lives on the front lines for *la patrie*. General Charles Mangin, in enthusiastic but completely fanciful language, wrote in 1910, "The black troops give us not only numbers; they are composed of career soldiers, used to privation and danger, having seen the firing line in such a way as no others in Europe have seen it; they have precisely the qualities needed for a long modern war: hardiness, endurance, tenacity, an instinct for combat, an absence of nervousness, and an incomparable power as shock troops."[31] Paris newspapers fantasized about the impact a Malagasy corps of warriors mounted on small local oxen would have on German troops; "These are small oxen that move with great agility and nervousness. Will we see one day at our front a charge of small oxen from Madagascar?"[32] Racism in the popular press was muted for the war's duration and there were paeans to the loyalty of our "Muslim brothers" and "indigenous compatriots." "All this, we will not forget," the French kept saying, although memories faded quickly. France presented itself as the defender of Islam, organizing pilgrimages to Mecca for loyal chiefs. A Paris mosque was built in 1926, Moorish cafes and restaurants multiplied, couscous and méchoui were added to French menus.

The total number of colonial conscripts was over 800 thousand soldiers, non-combatants, and defense workers. Colonial casualties included over 78 thousand dead, 15% of the 1.4 million French losses, the largest number of them Senegalese, which included men from many parts of West Africa, and Algerians.[33]

The French historian Marc Michel calculated that over 30 thousand of the 134 thousand Africans sent to France were killed or died of war-related illnesses.[34] Colonial troops were thrown into the front lines and were among the first killed and wounded. The black troops had no previous exposure to large-unit European trench warfare. Casualties were heavy among front line colonial troops, especially in 1914, and many were replaced by young African men recruited in haste, people transplanted from rural settings and tropical climates to winter combat conditions. Many suffered from illness; measles, unknown in Africa, decimated entire units while respiratory ailments were common. In 1917, 13.7% of the Senegalese infantry died from pulmonary illnesses.

The Senegalese troops were supposed to be part of a "warrior race" and German propaganda accused them of terrible atrocities, but in reality they adapted poorly to modern mass warfare and generally served as canon fodder on the front lines in places like Verdun and Somme, where they suffered terrible losses. The Vietnamese were called "excessively nervous" and 5 thousand were given work as truck drivers, considered a safe occupation. A contemporary account described them as, "without muscular force, timid, beaten down by the least challenge, short in stature, looking like children." A West Indian writer reflected on the war experience, "Men left singing, they came back with frozen feet. They left laughing, they came back without lungs, gangrened from mustard gas. They left with a valiant heart, they came back pelted with bits of shrapnel. . . . And they would just stand there, counting their lice, bathing their scabies with vinegar, without a penny for pension, and without strength for odd jobs."[35]

Indochina and Algeria were given quotas of troops to raise. In Algeria *caïds* were told to recruit *bal çayf* (by the sword). African chiefs received 10 to 30 francs for each recruit delivered. In some places, military recruiters surrounded villages and took all able-bodied men; in others, recruitment quotas were filled with the short, the under-aged, and the sick. In this way, at least 90 percent of the recruits presented in the Ivory Coast were disqualified. Individuals inflicted injuries on themselves to avoid conscription, such as having all teeth pulled or trigger fingers chopped off, and many fled to the mountains or the bush.

Desertions were widespread and passive resistance endemic. When some men refused to fight, General Ferdinand Foch ordered one soldier in every 10 summarily executed in a Tunisian company in the Flemish sector on December 15, 1914. Villages not cooperating in recruitment drives were burned. Reluctant to give up sons to leave their country and die, parents accompanied offspring to barracks, singing traditional funeral songs or Muslim chants for the dead. Despite numerous appeals to oppose joining the conflict, there was never widespread public resistance to conscription. Resistance was often an extension of traditional unrest in places like the Fouta-Djalon in West Africa, the Kabylia in Algeria, and in the south of Madagascar, or fighting between clans, or between traditional chiefs and their enemies, between those who had power and those who wanted it.[36]

Funds were raised for the war effort at home and abroad through mutual aid societies, balls, and parties. The Martiniquais writer Patrick Chamoiseau, with a touch of pepper, described one elderly islander's contribution:

Each Saturday, clothed in beautiful linens, . . . with a senator's step he would go to the Bouillè Barracks where he would ask to be shown to the commander. He would be introduced into a room which smelled like a stable. There, some chief with a mustache, reddened by mosquitoes, would exclaim, "Oh here comes the child of the Fatherland." . . . he took his money with an embrace. . . . Esternone would leave proud, duty accomplished, and saluting each soldier by clicking his heels, *Vuve la Fouance my friends*![37]

RACISM: "CORRUPTING OUR BLOOD"

Although they were recruited for what France regarded as a noble cause and were sped to the front lines, colonial troops never were treated as equals of the French. Few could rise above the rank of lieutenant, and if a French man and an overseas officer were of equal rank, the latter must obey the former. Convalescent leaves of overseas troops with French families were forbidden, as they risked "corrupting our blood." Restrictions were less severe for lighter-skinned troops from the Maghreb, some of whom married French women. Not much changed with the war as far as racial stereotypes were concerned. All colonial peoples were treated as inferior to the French, reflected in everything from legal decrees to cartoons. Maghrebians, called *Sidis*, were supposedly lazy, vindictive, tubercular, and sexually obsessed. Africans remained *grands enfants* in the *bon sauvage* tradition.[38]

CIVILIAN WORKERS

In addition to the soldiers, numerous civilians from the colonies found their way to France, many staying on after the war, sending salaries back to Algeria, Indochina, or Africa. On the war's eve, 15 thousand Algerians worked in France; by 1918 the number may have been 119 thousand. The number of Algerians would rise exponentially in future years and remain a source of friction between the two countries. Workers had no rights, were subject to police surveillance, and could be summarily deported. Often they were lodged in crude barracks lacking proper sanitation or crowded into small rooms in workers' suburbs around Paris, facing boredom, poverty, separation from families, and conflicts with other ethnic groups. Food was monotonous, always rice for Asians, mutton for Algerians. Rates of sickness and death were high; meningitis and typhoid epidemics produced a 4% mortality rate among French workers, 13% among Algerians, 20% among Vietnamese. Wages were low—five francs a day would have been a decent salary in 1918—with 30% deducted for food.[39]

Unlike the Algerians, the Vietnamese preferred to stay at home in Vietnam where the number of salaried workers reached 220 thousand by 1930. Vietnamese workers, especially miners and those in textile factories where working conditions were poor, were among the early trade unionists. South Vietnam possessed numerous affluent absentee landlords, *diên chu*, many of whom made their money renting farms to other Vietnamese who could not afford the higher interest rates charged by Chinese or Indian speculators. Many upper-class Vietnamese adopted a lifestyle comparable to the French administrators and business officials. Their children were often educated in France, they wore French clothes, built French villas, taught their cooks to make *bifsteak chateaubriand*, bought automobiles and sometimes airplanes. They were as ruthless toward their social and economic inferiors as the foreign money lenders had been.

By contrast the Vietnamese peasantry, who lived a precarious existence in the best of times, suffered from French land seizures, tax systems, agricultural policies which took little account of the delicate fabric of traditional life, and forced large-scale public works, such as the building on the roads, canals, and plantations in what until then had been a rice-growing peasant economy. In the 1860s the French government seized land and made it easily available to French citizens. By the 1930s large chunks of the best rice growing land were in French hands, including 104 thousand hectares (one hectare = 2.47 acres) in Tonkin, 168,400 hectares in Annam, and 606,500 hectares in Cochin China.[40] Peasants, whose life was harsh, became tenant farmers, sharecroppers, and agricultural wage laborers. Tenant farmers often had to pay as much as half their gross income, plus the expenses of cultivation of the land, to the land's owner. The French government levied heavy taxes including a head tax for each male, a rice wine tax, and a land tax collected by corrupt local "contractors." Peasants were forced to borrow money for seeds, often from Chinese or Indian money lenders at interest rates of 10 to 20% a month or 120 to 240 percent annually. Some peasants formed cooperatives for burials and weddings and a "pig association" for families wishing to commemorate their ancestors during the Lunar New Year, but groups like this were not widespread and provided only modest responses to nodal events like birth, marriage, and death.

A microcosmic study of a North Vietnamese village near the Red River northwest of Hanoi reflects many of the colonial encounter's broader themes. During the late 1980s Hy V. Luong, a Vietnamese anthropologist living in Canada, conducted oral interviews and historical research in the village of Son Duong, reconstructing the life of an isolated village under French and later Democratic Republic of Vietnam rule. Son Duong had as tumultuous history as any village on the German-French border. Beginning during the years of effective French occupation in the 1890s, the village opposed the French presence. At that time Chinese troops, imported by the Vietnamese court to fight the French, turned on the villagers, massacring 300 of them. In the 1930s the village was burned by the French for supporting the abortive Yen-Bay uprising. One inhabitant was guillotined and 19 were sent to penal colonies, including to French Guiana. Following World War II, as the rise of the Viet Minh spread through the Red River delta, the village was bombed four times by the French, once with napalm. The history of Son Duong was one of constant active and passive resistance, intermittent raids, assassinations, propaganda campaigns by both sides, and harsh countermeasures by the French, to no lasting avail. The observation of a resident French observer in the 1880s could have been as easily uttered sixty years later, "In all the villages there exists two mayors, one with real power and collecting taxes for the rebels; the other a puppet mayor, an official working for the French government and lying to the latter from dawn to dusk."[41]

THE POST–WORLD WAR I PERIOD: A NEW OPTIC

Slowly and incompletely the seeds of a new world order were being sown in the French overseas territories during the century, a tectonic shift in how peoples interacted politically and attitudinally. Its elements included the disparity between what France upheld as ideals and what it practiced abroad, the emergence of a free press and educated local élites who often studied or worked in France, a nascent awareness of independence movements around the world, and discontent with the ossification of local societies.

When the war was over, *anciens combattants* who had tasted the fresh air of freedom and liked it did not want to return to Africa to be under the thumb of native chiefs and colonial administrators. They had pride in their uniforms, often adorned with combat decorations, including the *Légion d'Honneur*. For their war service they were given land and access to jobs in the colonial administration. War veterans were excluded from work gangs and the dreaded *indigénat* did not apply to them. It was inevitable that changes in attitudes brought about by the war would lead to political activity.[42]

Deputies from the Antilles and Senegal joined a vocal bloc in the French Parliament pushing for reforms, others called for greater attention to human rights, citing repressions and the brutality of individual colonial officials. The war had reduced by at least 25% the number of French administrators in the colonies, and over 50% the number of troops. Schools closed, hospitals operated with skeletal forces, and medical research projects were terminated. Literate indigenous people took over as teachers, minor administrators, and clerks.

PARIS TO SAIGON IN 92 HOURS! (1937)

Changing modes of communication also affected the Empire. Distances shortened as communications became more rapid. In 1934 the first automobile crossed the Sahara; in 1935 Paris-Dakar could be reached in 14 hours by air; in 1937 the Paris-Saigon direct flight took 92 hours. Regular, often weekly air mail now arrived in most parts of the Empire, and the telegraph was expanding, followed by the wireless radio. Hanoi could be reached in a remarkable 5 ½ days by propeller-driven plane. Antoine de Saint-Exupéry was a pilot on the West African route, delivering bags of mail to isolated colonial outposts and describing the experience in his works *Vol de Nuit* and *Courrier Sud*.

In August 1924 radio transmissions became possible between France and

Saigon, using a 1,250 kilowatt transmitter and an antenna whose wires covered 72 hectares of Vietnamese countryside, a prodigious engineering feat for the time. (In 1911 Governor-General Albert Sarraut had ordered the equipment for a radiotelegraphical service, which made it as far as the docks of Marsailles when World War I broke out; then the army rerouted it for domestic use at Lyons.) Within a decade, Indochina had large transmitters in Hanoi and Saigon for local use, and 14 smaller ones spread about the country.[43] By 1939 the number of wireless radio receptors throughout the Empire rose from 500 thousand to 5.5 million. The old isolation was ended, a new era in communications had begun. French magazines were distributed in huge quantities. By 1930 radio reports told French listeners about overseas life. Vacation camps for metropolitan French were organized in the colonies, and "colonial weeks" were held in various parts of France. Robert Delavignette described the changes:

The plane which links Paris to Dakar in less than 30 hours finds at the airport of Ouahkam the same kind of airfield as le Bourget. The cranes at the docks, whether African or European, look like gigantic sea-horses. The same diadem of electric lights glitters at night on the brow of the town, whether the town is white or black. The same radio blares the world's news to the Senegalese jeweler and to his fellows in Paris.[44]

THE 1920s: ECONOMIC AND MEDICAL ADVANCES

Albert Sarraut, former governor-general of Indochina and minister of colonies, submitted an ambitious blueprint for postwar colonial development to the Chamber of Deputies in 1921. The heart of his proposal was the development in overseas possessions of a needed infrastructure of ports, roads, railroads, telegraph and telephone lines, water systems, public buildings, tropical medical research centers, hospitals, and a network of schools. Projects would be paid for by loans from the French government with money forthcoming from German war reparations. Benefits from the development plan would soon make repayment of such loans feasible. However, Sarraut had the ill fortune to present his plan during the 1920–1921 economic downswing, and it went nowhere. Sarraut's catalogue of colonial prospects was published in *La Mise en valeur des colonies françaises* (1923), followed by the more sober *Grandeur et servitude coloniales* (1931), which laid out the difficulties France faced in holding its colonial empire together.[45]

Nonetheless, little economic future awaited its colonies, France realized, unless health and educational conditions were improved. France's primary concern was for the health of French citizens overseas, then for a healthy, productive, local workforce. Tuberculosis and respiratory diseases, malaria, yellow fever, measles, sleeping sickness, and other tropical diseases were still rampant. Deaths from malaria were responsible for perhaps a quarter of the French deaths in Indochina in 1939. Hospitals, clinics, and dispensaries were almost nonexistent, sanitation conditions primitive, health and sanitary education virtually unknown.

Malnutrition was endemic everywhere among indigenous populations, and medical analysis rarely focused on childhood diseases, some of which, like measles, could be fatal.

During the century improvements were made slowly but surely. Indigenous medical assistants were trained and vaccination teams dispensed about the countryside giving injections against diseases. An anti-leprosy research and treatment institute was established in Bamako, Maili (1931) and another to combat eye diseases played important roles in reducing tropical illnesses in francophone Africa, making the countries more habitable for Europeans and Africans. Tropical medicine specialists like Dr. Eugène Jamot in Cameroon organized programs against sleeping sickness and trained hundreds of Cameroonian workers to spread out through nearby countries to combat typanosomiasis and sleeping sickness. Figures like Jamot were deeply respected in traditional societies and medical doctors were valued by French administrators as agents of French expansion. Lyautey once observed, "The role of the doctor as agent of penetration, of attraction, and of pacification is a most solidly established fact."[46]

Malaria and other fevers, dysentery, which could be fatal, intestinal parasites, yaws and other skin diseases all made accepting an overseas assignment a risk for members of the colonial service. Heat, humidity, debilitating climates, and the absence of refrigeration, which meant no way of preserving foods, further complicated colonial lives. Delavignette said that "records of deaths among retired officials show a figure 17 years below the average in France." He described a picture of colonial society where in 1929 in West Africa among 16 thousand Europeans, 5,241 were hospitalized for a total of 89,291 days. It was

a collection of sick men: the obese, carrying before them toad-like bellies, contrasted with the living skeletons, fleshless from fever or drained by dysentery; the liver cases, their eyes by turn dulled or too bright, bowed by that inner gnawing; the nervous types, who, the moment they are back from leave, wilt under the burden of work and see no way to lighten it.[47]

EDUCATION: "FRANCE WANTS THE LITTLE ARABS TO BE AS WELL INSTRUCTED AS THE LITTLE FRENCH"

Part of the *mise en valeur*, the "putting into value" development program was building schools in the colonies. Most teachers and school administrators came from France initially. Teaching French and enough skills to work in an office, shop, or a trade were the system's goals. Advanced education was not encouraged until the 1930s and 1940s, for the French did not want a class of highly educated indigenous professionals challenging them politically at every turn. One consequence of this policy was that many of Africa's future leaders were products of Roman Catholic seminaries where they obtained a solid education but who told the priests in charge they had found other callings when the time came to study for ordination.

France's most extensive colonial educational system was in Vietnam. The old mandarin educational structure was abolished and French teachers were recruited. By 1930 there were 378 thousand children in school. Studies in *quôc ngu*, a latinized version of the Vietnamese alphabet, were encouraged in village schools. A university opened in Hanoi, the best such institution in the entire empire, and schools for veterinarians, agricultural workers, public works, and fine arts were created. Gradually, France realized that for its administration to work, it must have increasingly skilled indigenous collaborators. A handful of such people were chosen to study in France or at specialized schools in Africa or Indochina.

In Africa, primary schools were built in many places, with possibly 37 thousand pupils studying by 1930 in French West Africa, 10% of them girls. In Madagascar, 185 thousand pupils, a third of them female, attended primary school. In Algeria, primary education for children of both sexes rose only to 8% by 1931. Student numbers in other schools were not large either; the total of high school students rose from 386 in 1914 to 776 in 1930. After 100 years of French presence, less than 100 Algerians were certified as teachers of higher education and as late as 1939 only 89 Algerians were enrolled in the local university, out of 1,856 students. A popular French school text, *L'Histoire de France* by Ernest Lavisse, contained a section about "a school in Algeria." Arab and French pupils were kept in separate sections; students read:

Among the pupils, you see some dressed like you. Those are the little French. The others wear a white *burnous*. Those are the little Arabs. The teachers are French. They teach the little French and the little Arabs what you learn in school. The Arabs are good little students. They learn as much as the little French. They also do good homework. France wants the little Arabs to be as well instructed as the little French. That proves that our France is good and generous to the people who submit to her.

This widely used elementary school textbook reflected the epoch's racial and political attitudes toward the overseas world. A section of its chapter on colonial conquests discusses "the goodness of France," illustrated with a dramatic period engraving of three French colonials in impeccable uniforms set in the middle of an isolated African village. The *tricolore* is unfurled and on the ground a freed slave reclines as a French officer loosens his shackles. On one side, cowering slaves wait for their freedom, on the other freed captives dance joyfully. The caption reads: "Slavery is an abominable thing. That is why France does not want there to be slavery in the lands she possesses." The French 19th century explorer Pierre Savorgnan de Brazza is shown coming to the land and planting the flag, "which says that the land belongs to France." One day a band of slaves is marched by, but Brazza says, "Everywhere where there is the French flag there should be no slaves." French soldiers liberate the slaves, "That proves once more that France is good and generous to the people who submit to her."[48]

Education thus both inculcated French values in indigenous peoples and was a way of controlling them. A writer from Martinique, Patrick Chamoiseau, described the process of learning French in his autobiographical novel *School Days*, where children whose native language was Creole learn the French language and French values, while their own cultural tradition is the subject of mockery. The youth concluded:

Each of us tried hard to keep a watch on himself. The children began to laugh at those who couldn't manage a decent *u* or *r*. Opening your mouth had become a risky business. You had to listen closely . . . translate everything into French, and prevent your natural pronunciation from spoiling these new sounds. A dreadfully tall order.[49]

At one point the teacher comments, "Who can construct a sentence for me to illustrate the arrival of spring by evoking a flight of swallows over the snow-capped church tower of your village? No one? Gracious me!"[50] The teacher, like the student, was from the Antilles and tried as hard as any French grammarian to speak perfectly, pronouncing French words "clearly and emphatically, in accordance with some deeply felt rhythm. . . . Dialogues allowed him to assume a variety of accents, delivered through teeth like tweezers; bursting an invisible mold, he transformed himself like protean clay into a Provençal peasant, a solitary miller, a knight of the Round Table. When the paragraph was finished, he closed his eyes to contemplate with his mind's eye the solemn procession of what he had just read."[51]

AFRICA IN TRANSITION

The 1920s were a difficult time for indigenous African rulers. Instead of respecting traditional forms of social organization, the French used chiefs to recruit troops for warfare, workers for local road gangs, and to collect taxes. If local chiefs would not or could not fulfill their quotas, often they were replaced by other "chiefs" who had no lineage standing or by returned *anciens combattants* who followed French orders but had no place in traditional ruling hierarchies. This was a difficult period economically in parts of French-controlled Africa. Many tribes depended on single-crop agriculture and trade was often in the hands of foreigners or other African groups specializing in inland commerce. Prices were generally low, and crops were vulnerable to drought or excessive rainfall. As plantations were staked out in choice agricultural land, transhument populations migrated to increasingly less productive places.

This was also the beginning of marked urban drift. Rural people abandoned life in the countryside to seek employment in growing cities like Dakar, Abidjan, Douala, and Brazzaville. In fact, most were better off in their own villages; the towns offered a handful of jobs for skilled, literate clerks, but only subsistence wages for cooks, house boys, and guardians. Lodging was hard to come by, disease rampant. Upper Voltans said, "Le travail de l'homme blanc mange les hommes" (The white man's work devours people).

THE WINDS OF CHANGE: "THEY ARE CELEBRATING THE FIRST CENTENNIAL OF FRENCH ALGERIA; THEY WILL NOT CELEBRATE THE SECOND"

Two new world revolutions emerged in World War I's aftermath, one incorporating the ideas of Marx and Lenin and the other those of Woodrow Wilson. The Russian Revolution was seen as an example by colonial peoples. An imperialist regime had been overturned by the working class, they believed, and the promise of a classless future awaited them. Russian communists made some effort at encouraging national revolutions, but always with the proviso that they should lead to Moscow-controlled communist movements. Marxist-Leninist ideas were in the air, but communists were only one of many contributors to the rise of nationalist sentiment in the French Overseas Empire. Publications like *L'Action coloniale, Continents*, and *Le Libéré* and various ethnic leagues and associations examined nationalist issues. From the churning milieu of such groups, two emerged in leadership roles: the Intercolonial Union, with its journal *Le Paria*, led by Ho Chi Minh, and the *Comité de défense de la race nègre* (CDRN), led by the Senegalese *ancien combattant* and self-taught communist Lamine Senghor. Both groups were outspoken against colonial injustices, which they believed could only be solved by independence. Future nationalists and independence figures from different countries began to make contact with one another. The best-known alumnus of the French communist movement was Ho Chi Minh, a skilled organizer and articulate journalist. After attending party congresses in Moscow and elsewhere, he emerged as a leading voice of Asian communism.

The ideas of Woodrow Wilson also reached the colonies, especially his Fourteen Points plan and his pleas for the self-determination of subject peoples. Wilson never mentioned France's colonies, but Algerian and Vietnamese intellectuals were quick to make the connection between freedom for peoples subjected to German and Austro-Hungarian domination and their own situation. The League of Nations also became an anticolonial voice. Although the French treated mandate territories like colonies, their inhabitants knew that one day their status must be resolved and they would not be incorporated into France as colonies. In 1930 the International Labor Organization, after several years' debate and opposition from colonial economic interests, adopted a convention suppressing forced work in colonies. Although France was not a signatory to the convention, it issued a parallel decree in August 1930 greatly modifying conditions for forced work.[52]

Another influence was the largely anglophone Pan African Congress movement, meeting in Paris (1919), London (1921 and 1923), and New York (1927). A French counterpart was formed in 1921 by the Martinique socialist deputy Gratien Candace, but it never moved beyond being a debating club of black francophone socialists. More active was the Universal League to Defend the Black Race, led by the Dahomeian Kojo Tovalou Houennou, who had been inspired by Marcus Garvey. At the same time, indigenous intellectuals in

France's North African possessions learned of the recent example of Kemal Ataturk, who overthrew Turkey's decadent rulers and established a modern state.

In the context of postwar anticolonial ferment, liberation movements emerged in Indochina, the Maghreb, and the Near East, but less so in Africa, where they would become more pronounced after World War II. In France, anticolonialism increasingly became a theme of left-wing politicians. However, they did not support independence for subject peoples, offering only criticism that France was not fulfilling its role in carrying out a *mission civilisatrice* and was mistreating subject peoples. Military repression was swift, as during the Syrian and Moroccan uprisings, in 1929 when troops in Brazzaville fired on demonstrators who wanted the power to vote, and when Vietnamese soldiers mutinied in Yen-Bay garrison in 1930. Such brutal actions helped galvanize anti-French sentiment against which no political countervaccine was ever discovered.

French officials of the 1920s were aware of the rise of these movements; police agents kept meticulous records on indigenous organizations and duly recorded their discussions and resolutions, but no one ever came up with policies to solve the real problems they raised. In fact, faced with such challenges, French colonial policy became less creative and more rigid. Local leaders who publicly urged Algerian representation in the French Parliament were severely curbed and the *indigénat* was reinstated there until 1927.

Ironically, at a time when independence movements were growing in Algeria, France chose to commemorate the 100th anniversary of its 1830 arrival with a colonial exhibition. Troops staged a reenactment of the original landing wearing 19th century military uniforms; monuments were erected commemorating the original French landing and honoring the *colons* whose farms were the backbone of the French presence and its most conservative political voices. At the time a saying circulating through Algeria noted, "They are celebrating the first centennial of French Algeria; they will not celebrate the second."

Few would have given any credence to this apocalyptic message. The Empire was at its apogee. With the addition of the League of Nations mandates in Africa and the Middle East, its territory was the most extensive it would ever be, and through commerce, a transportation infrastructure, and investment, France had plans to tighten its hold on overseas possessions everywhere. Yet internal forces within the colonies and external influences had begun to weaken the Empire's foundations. The cracks would not be fully visible for a quarter-century, when they would be too great to be easily repaired.

CAMEROON AND TOGO

Although the League of Nations awarded Cameroon, German Togoland, Syria, and Lebanon to France as mandate territories at the end of World War I, their status always was ambiguous. France treated them like any other colony, but always there was the prospect for inhabitants that some day they would be independent.

LIFE IN A MANDATE TERRITORY: CAMEROON

Colonial policy in Cameroon was reflected in relations between the French and the Beti, an important rain forest ethnic group living near Yaounde, the Cameroonian capital. After their return to Cameroon in 1920 (they had left the country with the Germans in 1918), the Beti chiefs were sent to the mountain city of Dschang, where they supervised road building crews. The French did not trust them but found their replacements inept. In December 1921 the French recalled Charles Atangana to Yaounde as *Chef Superiéur* of the Ewondo and Bane, two Beti groups living near Yaounde. His organizational skills were needed for the road, railroad, and public building programs, and to set up a tax-collecting system for which chiefs like Atangana received payment from the French. It was never easy work; as elsewhere in francophone Africa, the Beti resisted paying taxes and working on road gangs, and other chiefs, seeing there was money to be made in tax collecting, wanted to cut into Atangana's territory.

The darkest period for the Beti, and for Africans living between the coast and the interior, was between 1922–1927 when the French completed an inland railroad, already begun by the Germans. Food was poor for workers, hours long, and wages low, on a route through notoriously difficult terrain. In 1923 there were 3,121 conscripts and only 423 volunteers among the African railroad workers. The African attitude toward the French can be ascertained through folk songs employed by the work gangs, utilizing one of the few forms of protest available to the disenfranchised. While railroad songs in many western countries were festive and upbeat, the Beti songs were laced with bitterness. The person on a horse in this song would probably be a French forced labor recruiter, since the Beti, whose lands were inhabited by the tste-tste fly, did not have horses.

Drum Message Signaling the Arrival of Work Gang Recruiters

A horseman crosses the country.
He will stop all the men. All.
When you walk on the road,
Do so with measured and cautious step;
No one should forget the bush.
Heroes of the wars, do you not know the
Caves, hein?
Move quickly.

Song About the Work Gangs

The tom-tom beats at Yaounde,
The tom-tom which will ruin this country.
The tom-tom of the work gangs.
What does it say?
It says clear out,
Leave your possessions for Chief——.
Get out!

The tom-tom beats at Yaounde.
Tell my mother and father,
And tell my mother to save me some food.
He! My brother, will I survive the work gang?

A French report, required annually since Cameroon was a League of Nations mandate territory, states, "One is happily impressed by the sight of the workers, rhythmically working to the cadence of traditional chants, ready to smile at the least word of encouragement."[53] The French military engineers would not have known that in the following song the "happy workers" described their French supervisors as biting dogs:

Railroad Workers' Song Greeting the White Man
Hey, get away from that dog.
That small dog, the mean one.
That dog is very mean.
He has taken my manioc,
He has taken my meat.
He has bitten me on the leg,
He has bitten my buttocks.
My brothers, let me hear you!
[Refrain and chorus:] Hey, get away from that dog.

It is difficult to estimate mortality and illness figures among the railroad workers, but an annual French government report required by the League of Nations suggested that, of the 4 to 5 thousand persons working on the railroad each year, approximately 400 died, 1,500 were released for medical reasons, and 3,600 received medical attention.[54]

If railroad construction was costly in human lives in Cameroon, it was even more so in the Congo, where the French built a line not far from a Belgian one. The 400-kilometer connection between the capital at Brazzaville and the Pointe-Noire port on the Atlantic Ocean took from 1921 to 1934 to complete. More than 16 thousand of the 127,250 conscripts rounded up from wide distances for the work died.[55]

SYRIA AND LEBANON

African resistance to French League of Nations mandate implementation was largely passive and sporadic, but in Syria and Lebanon, the French faced constant active resistance. As part of the World War I peace settlement, France had been given Syria and Lebanon as mandate territories; Great Britain claimed Iraq and Palestine. It was acknowledged these were temporary mandates that ultimately would lead to independence, something the subject peoples pushed for relentlessly until independence was achieved. France had a long history of contacts with the Middle East; trading posts and consulates had existed there since at least 1535, and France enjoyed special status as protector of the Christian holy places. The French also developed cordial ties with Maronite Christians in Lebanon, backing them against the Turks several times in the 19th century. In 1913, when Arab nationalists decided to hold a congress, they picked Paris as the venue.[56]

Despite these historic Arab ties, the French had few friends in postwar Syria. France initiated a presence in Syria in August 1920 when General Henri Eugène Gouraud marched on Damascus and deposed King Faisal. As soon as the pro-British Faisal was removed, Gouraud divided the country into several competing regions. In Lebanon, one of the regions, the French enjoyed some success. A slight Christian majority there looked to France for protection. The French attempted a short-lived constitutional experiment there, but soon France's high commissioner took full effective power and a Maronite Christian president was balanced off against a Sunni Moslem prime minister.

Other colonized states may have resented the French presence, but few had the power to do anything significant about it in the interwar period. Syria was the exception. The French *divide et imperia* policy was bitterly resented by the Druse people who revolted in 1925. This triggered a parliamentary panic in France comparable to that experienced during the last century's Lang-Son affair in Indochina. French authorities arrested a delegation of 31 Druse chiefs who went to Damascus to protest the occupying power's policies. French forces were in turn besieged for over two months, and a rescue column ambushed. Finally, the uprising was brutally put down. Crowded Damascus was bombarded by artillery, and the French used airplanes against civilian targets.

The territorial assembly was dissolved in 1930 for demanding reunification of the country and control of its armed forces and foreign policy and for not recognizing the French presence in its constitution. Despite France's best efforts, a core of nationalist deputies consistently demanded the mandate be replaced by a Franco-Syrian bilateral treaty. Negotiations took several years. When the treaty was signed on September 9, 1936, it included a provision that France would sponsor Syria for League of Nations membership as an independent country within three years. A Lebanese treaty, a virtual duplicate of the Syrian draft accord, was concluded on November 13, 1936. However, rising Syrian and Lebanese hopes turned into bitter disappointment when the French Assembly refused to ratify the documents negotiated by its representatives. The Popular Front government had fallen in Paris, and a right-of-center coalition would not liquidate its important Middle Eastern holdings in the face of rising German and Italian militarism.

During World War II, Syria and Lebanon were under Vichy control. Active German propaganda stirred up anti-French sentiment in the Middle East and North Africa. "Hajj" Hitler was presented as a liberator, and French political officers reported that swastikas were being sewn together in Damascus souks. Members of the French local administration refused to support General de

Gaulle's Free French. However when, in May 1941, the French high commissioner allowed German war planes to land and refuel on Syrian territory, the British used this as a pretext to invade Syria, accompanied by elements of the Free French forces. After a month's fighting, Vichy troops sued for peace, and Syria and Lebanon were placed under the British Middle East Command. Prodded by the British, the Free French declared their intention to end the mandate and give Syria and Lebanon their independence. The process stalled because the French wanted a guaranteed privileged position, something the Syrians and Lebanese would not grant. General de Gaulle objected to free elections and refused to transfer governmental powers to the new states. This only intensified the demands of nationalists, who chafed under the French power to countermand legislative decrees passed by the local assembly, the presence of press censors, and the overabundance of French advisers and *Services Spéciaux* intelligence officers.

Independence of both countries came, not from direct French action, but by an endgame. In May 1945 negotiations were scheduled to resume on treaty arrangements, but the French preempted them by dispatching troops to Beirut. Strikes and riots followed in Syria and Lebanon. The British intervened when Prime Minister Winston Churchill asked General de Gaulle to order his troops to return to their barracks, which de Gaulle did in the face of impending British military action. On June 21, 1945, Syria and Lebanon issued a joint declaration taking over their customs services, until now run by the French, and dismissing all French people in government positions. France formally agreed to the transfer on July 7, after which several countries recognized the independence of Syria and Lebanon. The two new states became members of the United Nations in San Francisco. The only remaining issue was the withdrawal of French troops, which was accomplished in Syria in September 1946 and in Lebanon in December. The mandate was over. Some French observers spoke of the loss of Syria and Lebanon as a "new Fashoda." Colonized peoples saw it differently. Syrians widely distributed a black book on *Les Atrocités françaises*. Arab and African peoples read with horror about the aerial and artillery bombardments of civilian populations. Many interpreted them as a desperate act by a power with diminished world influence. In Indochina, news of the independence of Syria and Lebanon arrived at the moment when France was trying to restore its hold on the colony.[57]

THE OVERSEAS WORLD OF WRITERS AND ARTISTS

During the early 20th century there was an outpouring of travel accounts, adventure novels, and geographical studies about the overseas world. Most of these works were of no lasting literary value, but they made engrossing reading. Often the theme was the gift of civilization brought by a young French officer. Ernest Psichari, in *Terres de soleil et de sommeil* (1908), wrote of his African experience:

I contemplated this virgin land, not as the country of the Bayas, but as France. . . . I was proud to guard within myself that little lamp of heroism . . . to find, rolled up in my soul, a bit of the ancient passion of the ruler and conqueror. . . . We came here to do a little good for these accursed lands. But we also came to do good for ourselves. We hope that the great adventure will serve our moral health, our perfection. Africa is one of the last refuges of the national energy.[58]

The early 20th century also brought a proliferation of illustrated magazines for which colonial adventure stories were a staple. In addition to those for adults, like *Journal des Débats* and *La Quinzaine coloniale*, there were publications for children, such as *Le Petit Français illustré* and *Le Journal de la jeunesse*, with accounts of defeating Oriental pirates, avoiding African ambushes, or out-smarting wily Arabs. Children's books, like the *Tin Tin* series, carried similar stories. Catholic missionary journals, including *La Semaine de Suzette* for girls, extolled the work of missionaries. The spread of printing and photography and the advent of airmail allowed a flood of colonial postcards to be produced all over the Empire. A single photographer working in Dakar made more than 6 thousand photographs of French West Africa between 1900 and 1925.[59] The photographer's subjects had no names and the postcards presented a romantic "through the looking glass" picture of the overseas world, one of colonial stereo-types, with efficient conquerors in carefully pressed uniforms, heroic mission-aries and doctors, colorful markets, harbors and railroads, costumed natives, bare-breasted women in seductive harem poses, exotic landscapes, colonial buildings, and smiling children in small rural schools.

Close similarities existed between the overseas world the French perceived in this century and in earlier times. All the old racial stereotypes were there— crafty mandarins, fierce Arabs, and *bon sauvage* Africans. Costumes changed as fashions changed through the centuries, but not the subjects' fundamental character. The colonial expositions resembled entertainments choreographed for French kings centuries earlier. In 1906 a section of Marseilles harbor became a Phoenician city, and representatives of Africa and Asia and two Tuaregs arrived in canoes to swear allegiance to France, leaving gifts of ivory, groundnuts, and exotic fruits.

Sexual issues, always a topic in French-indigenous relations, were rarely dis-cussed openly. In 1931 an administrator in the Vietnamese educational service, Eugène Pujarniscle, published *La Littérature coloniale*, which surveyed sexual themes in colonial literature. Two-thirds of the colonial novels about Indochina or Africa dealt with liaisons between white colonial males and local women. For French men, the local contacts were "with women, not ladies," and in the Orient, most indigenous women had only the status and temporary benefits ac-corded as love objects of European men.[60]

A distinct strain of anticolonial literature emerged in the 1920s, but the au-dience remained largely the intellectual left. André Gide denounced recruitment conditions in *Voyage au Congo* (1927) and forced labor in *Retour du Tchad*

(1929). Louis-Ferdinand Céline won the Renaudot prize in 1932 for his *Voyage au bout de la nuit*, which portrayed the decadence of African and colonial society as he saw it during his work as a commercial agent in Cameroon. Another widely known work about the overseas world was André Malraux's *La Condition humaine*, a Eurocentric romantic novel about the Chinese revolution, which won the Goncourt prize in 1933. Malraux was an enigmatic figure. At age 23 he headed an archeological expedition to Cambodia, from which *La Voie royale* (The Royal Way) (1930) emerged to critical acclaim. Malraux and his colleagues, however, not only conducted archeological studies but also systematically looted ancient Angkor temples, and they were arrested. Familiar arguments—the temple was in ruins, it was already looted, and Malraux was rescuing what remained—were raised at the trial in Saigon. The prosecutor argued it was not Malraux's to rescue, and the shipments violated explicit French and Cambodia law on the preservation of historic artifacts. A three-year prison sentence was reduced by an appeals court to a one-year suspended sentence. Although Malraux positioned himself as a champion of antifascism and anticolonialism, he remained silent on the Algerian question as de Gaulle's minister of culture and, when in 1947 Ho Chi Minh visited Paris, Malraux refused to meet him. In the end, the Indochina he portrayed was a world of the French intellectual left with the Orient as a backdrop.

Even as distinguished an author as André Gide was not free from the crude paternalism of other French authors. His writings suggest that North Africans belonged to some sort of higher civilization but that black Africans were more complacent in the *bon sauvage* tradition. An indigenous literature also grew up and found a place in France. Jean-Price Mars, a Haitian psychiatrist and folklorist; Jean-Joseph Rabèarivolo, a Malagasy poet; and an African writer, Bokary Diallo, who wrote *Force-Bontè* (1926), a novel about French-African relations, are some of the early indigenous authors whose works attracted attention.

During the 1930s several Vietnamses social realist journalists described the strains of urban life and colonial contact in works such as Tam Lang's *I Pulled a Rickshaw* (1932), Vu Trong Phung's *Household Servant* (1936), Nguyen Cong Hong's autobiographical *Days of Childhood* (1938), and *Mud and Stagnant Water* (1938) by Hoang Dao, a former judge of the French colonial court. In a chapter called "Christmas Night" Nguyen Hong describes the French officials arriving first in the cathedral to be seated in pews with cushions, after which the Vietnamese elite, "people with power and wealth," are seated; then church ushers drop their arms and "a wave of ragged unkempt people surged in."[61]

FILM: FROM *LES FILS DU SOLEIL* TO *INDOCHINE*

For a war-weary country, books and films about the colonial world created "mirages of exile" (Jean-Renaud), allowing brief escape from the realities of contemporary France. The works showed no more of the real life of colonies and their people than did comparable literature of earlier centuries. The perspective was always that of the conqueror toward the conquered, the bearer of civilization toward primitive peoples. Deserts were places of mystery and romance, interrupted for periodic successful raids on fleeing bandit gangs, or liaisons with local women French officers would never see again. French Foreign Legion films proliferated with titles like *Les Fils du soleil* and *Sous le ciel d'Orient*. The 1930s was not a good time for the army's image at home, but it was polished with innumerable victories by tough Foreign Legion troops in films like *Le Sergent X* (1931) and *Légion d'Honneur* (1937) in which one officer observes, "The desert unites us, women separate us." In most such films, warring tribes were quickly subdued by *militaires des music-halls* who rarely fired a shot. Films created a fantasy world where it was possible to conquer without bloodshed; if war clouds formed in Europe, there were battles to be won on the silver screen.[62]

In the film *Itto* (1934), named for a Berber woman of the High Atlas, Berber actors were used, and a stab was made at ethnographic authenticity as interpreted by Lyautey's native affairs officers. Shortly before the closing battle scene, where Itto dies on the barricades and the High Atlas Berbers submit to France, Itto turns her baby over to the French doctor's wife, who suckles it and her own child, a symbolic act no film watcher could fail to comprehend.[63]

A survey of French films of the 1930s shows that out of 1,305 productions, only 85 were set elsewhere than in France, including 17 in Morocco, ten in the Sahara, and seven each in Algeria and Tunisia. Titles like *La Sultane de l'amour* (The Sultan of Love) and *Le Sang d'Allah* (Allah's Blood) suggest the romantic subject matter of many. European actors were used almost exclusively. The principal roles were central casting's idea of cunning Arabs and sultry native women. *Occident* (1918) was remade in 1928 and 1938. Early versions had the young officer, son of a powerful *colon*, marrying an illiterate but beautiful Moslem girl whose family he had killed in a cannonade. However, by 1938, the hero came from France, not Algeria, and the beautiful *évoluée* was now a Sorbonne student whose parents were slain by a local bandit chief, not the French army. North Africans were largely restricted to crowd scenes, or cameo appearances as jugglers, snake charmers, camel drivers, and native musicians, roles not easily played by French actors.

The films serve as barometers of French relations with overseas possessions. If films of the 1930s peeled the cover off the complex attraction-repulsion relationship between France and its colonial peoples, political topics were still taboo. It was not until the 1990s that a film like *Indochine* raised the full panoply of cross-cultural issues: sex, politics, economics, injustice, exploitation, war, and colonialism. Catherine Deneuve as Elaine, the narrator, symbolizes Marianne, France. She adopts Camille, an orphaned princess who represents Vietnam. Their tangled relationship over the remainder of this costly epic film was the story of France's relationship with Indochina. Elaine both successfully manages her late husband's commercial interests and mixes with the leadership of French and Vietnamese society. Camille bears the child of a handsome young French naval officer. Rejecting a place in traditional Vietnamese or colonial society, she sides with the emerging Communist movement. As "the Red Princess" she is condemned to life imprisonment in the Poulo-Condore penal colony for the murder of a French officer, but she is liberated during a Popular Front amnesty. Dressed in a cadre uniform, she rejects her silk-clad French stepmother, who is left to raise the child of two cultures. The film ends at the Geneva Peace Conference of 1954 where Camille is part of the Vietnamese delegation. Her child, who is with Elaine, wants to see his birth mother, but he is refused. He turns to Elaine with the provocative line, *"Ma mère, c'est toi"* (You are my mother)— an ending tailored to a French and international audience. The film underlines the political, cultural, and sexual bond that the French believed existed between the two countries.

THE FAMOUS COLONIAL EXPOSITION OF 1931

There were expositions before and after it, but none like the Colonial Exposition of 1931. In planning since before World War I, the Colonial Exposition became a reality in Vincennes, a Paris suburb. Subway Line 8 was extended, and improvements were made to 110 hectares of ground. Palm trees were planted at the entrance, and la Grande Avenue des Colonies Françaises was flanked with red, white, and blue lighting. A tranquil suburb became a city of 400 thousand persons between May and November 1931 and received more than 8 million visitors, most of them from Paris and the provinces, and a million persons from elsewhere in Europe. A squadron of Africa *saphis* saluted the chief of state on his arrival, while a wedge of Paris police pedaled their service bicycles in quiet unison to accompany the president. Marshal Lyautey, in full dress uniform, opened the Colonial Exposition and conferred a specially cast medal on President Gaston Doumergue, who recalled his days as a young magistrate in Indochina.[64]

A reconstructed temple from Angkor was the Colonial Exposition's centerpiece. Architects had journeyed to Cambodia to make measurements and moldings of its elaborate carvings. Around it radiated architectural souvenirs from the colonial world: pagodas, tents, and African huts. Native artisans wove fabrics, pounded on copper, carved wood, and cooked local foods. The temple from Angkor, larger than the imposing basilica of Sacré-Coeur à Montmartre, was bathed at night by the light of 144 projectors, each with a 1,000-watt bulb, a technical feat for that time. Fifteen hundred Africans, contracted for the duration of the exposition, built and rebuilt native villages, potters made plates, weavers wove, and copper workers created their wares. Near the craft shops were *cafés maures* (Moorish cafés) where visitors sipped exotic beverages. A steady program of international music and dance was offered, as were rides on camels and in canoes, artisans from Africa and Asia, water and light shows on the lake, theatrical evenings, lectures, and discussions for schoolchildren. "The colonial exposition will be the beginning of a new era in the history of humanity," pronounced the president of Paris' municipal council during the exposition's closing banquet, which 1,200 persons attended. Another banquet was held by the Estates General of Feminism to coincide with a congress on the place of women in the colonies. More than 150 women used the Colonial Exhibition as a springboard to discuss such issues as improving the rights of working women, more equitable salaries, professional accreditation, and equitable retirement benefits, especially for women engaged in colonial careers, such as teachers, nurses, and social workers.[65]

France constructed a monument to colonial troops, and Catholic and Protestant missionary work was extolled—the sites were located side by side. Catholics stressed *"La conquête du monde par la Croix"* (the conquest of the world by the cross) with statues of martyrs and examples of Christian art replacing traditional "fetishes." The more matter-of-fact Protestants featured the medical and educational work of the Société des Missions évangéliques, founded in Paris in 1822. Other displays showed the economic progress and products of colonialism: coal and phosphate from mines in Tunisia and Indochina, wheat, rice, rubber, cocoa and coffee, plus manufactured products. Albert Sarraut, whose *Grandeur et servitude coloniales* came out in 1931, extolled "the holy alliance of colonizing peoples."[66]

"The empire is the result of a perspective and policies that were part of France through all its history," declared Paul Reynaud, the colonial minister, in his inaugural speech at the exposition's permanent palace, adding, "Everyone should taste what it is like to be a citizen of Greater France, those from the five parts of the world." The exposition's sponsors extolled *un rayonnement moral incomparable* coming from Marshal Lyautey, adding, "Colonization is the essential vehicle of civilization." Brochures, posters, dioramas, speeches, and each building's architecture orchestrated a unified message: the moral, civilizing triumph of the French colonial presence.

Neither Germany nor Spain were represented at the exposition, both having lost their colonial possessions, nor was Great Britain, France's rival and the greatest of the colonial powers. The United States produced a replica of George Washington's home at Mount Vernon. The Portuguese exhibit's theme was "pioneers in the predominance of the white race." Fascist Italy reproduced a large basilica from Tripolitania, now Lybia, to show how Benito Mussolini's Italy echoed Rome's grandeur. Lyautey, whose taste ran toward the monumental, called it "the union of strength and beauty."[67]

The Palais des Colonies, which became a museum, and a zoo were permanent reminders of the event as were two striking Bamoun and Bamileke buildings from Cameroon which became an international Buddhist center. The palais' facade was the 1930s equivalent of the great entrance to Versailles, where overseas peoples saluted the Sun King. Surrounding the entrance was a bas-relief crowded with plants, animals, and native peoples turned, in the words of the official report, toward "the exuberant power of our young empire filled with riches and power." Carved by a contemporary sculptor, Alfred Janniot, the bas-relief featured allegorical figures of Abundance, Peace, Liberty, and the Sun, plus colonial goods arriving by ships at France's main ports and at le Bourget airport. The scene differed little from the Golden Age in Ronsard's *Les Isles fortunées* four centuries earlier, with graceful, muscular men and lithe native women at work or play, surrounded by playful animals and abundant fields and forests. Nature and humanity lived in harmonic symbiosis, free of war, ambushes, the *corvée* (work gangs), taxes, and other signs of racial or political friction. Rooms decorated with Berber weavings and Indochinese carvings and the Salon Lyautey filled with native furniture were all designed to show an orderly world of pacification, organization, and administration, with economic progress, cultural vibrancy, and achievements in education and public health.[68]

The exposition's perspective was paternalistic from the top down; its racial attitudes were no more subtle than those in *Tin Tin* and the rest of the popular press. An ethnologist attached to the exposition spoke of the evolved white races of North Africa and the less-developed Negro peoples of Africa and Asia. Racism with a scientific veneer informed every aspect of the event.[69]

The Colonial Exposition was the most pronounced concentration of art and architecture in the service of colonial politics of the 20th century, but in reality the French Overseas Empire created a total institutional image from the palatial residence in Rabat to distant outposts in Africa or Asia. A generation of architects like Henri Prost and Ernest Hébrard continued what Baron Haussman had begun in the Paris of Napoléon III, building new cities to showcase France's power and prestige. In places like Hanoi and Saigon, Rabat and Casablanca, Zinder and My Tho, spacious boulevards radiated to all points of the compass, as did the Empire. Streets were named for French towns, regions, or heroes. Spacious public gardens were framed by wide roads, comfortable villas filled the European section, and—most imposing of all—the residency, the true seat of power where France's representative lived and worked, loomed over the rest. Even in ruins it was striking, as Robert Delavignette recalled when happening upon an abandoned African residency:

[It] was a dwelling of crude brick and adobe like all those which the administrators got the villages to put up for them from the common clay of the country in the old days of the Niger and the Upper Volta. Sometimes their position in the plain is marked by a group of trees lining the approach as to a castle. But their finest site is on a sandy dune, a laterite knoll or the edge of a geological fault, where they dominate the sweep of thorny steppe. . . . They are all alike in their fortified but hospitable air, in their interior geometry which I always find restful to the mind, and in the secret harmony which unites them with the country and with our art.[70]

The Colonial Exposition, the great symbol of France's overseas empire, coincided with the Great Depression and the rise of nationalist movements. While the joys of colonialism were being celebrated in song and dance, prices for colonial products were falling, unemployment and social unrest were mounting, and armed resistance was spreading. The brief euphoria of the 1920s soon gave way to the gloom of the 1930s. The political process in France was slow to function, it lacked inspiring leaders, and it was riddled with corruption. There was also the specter of a rearming Germany at the border, and a divided, dispirited France was not sure what to do. In such a setting, illusions such as a Colonial Exposition were welcome. It was a vast mirage whose shimmering message was that however bad things were at home, there was hope abroad with fresh troops coming to the rescue and markets waiting just beyond the horizon.

THE GREAT DEPRESSION HITS THE COLONIES

When the Great Depression struck, France's first reaction was to circle the wagons around its possessions through restrictive tariffs equally applicable to foreign merchandise entering the *métropole* or overseas possessions. Economic shock waves extending from the Depression hit differently in different places and were less severe in non-cash economies. Tunisian cloth exports, which represented a growing industrial base and a positive balance of trade for Tunisia, lost over 80% of the market to cheaper French imports. The drop in prices for tropical products resulted in misery for peasants throughout the Empire, and since French banks would not extend them credit, many sold their possessions and were forced to borrow money at usurious rates from local moneylenders. Yet, the picture was not completely negative. In West Africa, the number of European-held bank accounts declined following the Depression as many French people packed up and headed home, but the number of deposits in African names increased considerably, although their sums were not comparable to those of the French. During this time there was solid growth in coffee production in the Ivory Coast, cocoa in Cameroon, bananas in Guinea, and cotton in other regions. In Indochina, the situation was less favorable since a decline in agricultural production, primarily of rice, corresponded with an increase in population, as high as a 50% increase in the populous Red River delta near Hanoi. The strain on resources, exacerbated by famine in 1931, helped create a receptive climate for the growing Communist movement. The gulf between rich and poor widened as more peasants lost their land and income and as the small class of affluent merchants and landowners grew. In Tunisia, peasants were driven out of the fertile coastal land and were driven into the harsh interior. In Algeria, wealthy *colons* bought up the land of Algerian fellahs and *petit blancs* at fire-sale prices. This was a time of growing urban drift, when the disenfranchised who did not move farther into the interior came to towns, trying their luck at any job that might come available, living in the first generation of *bidonvilles*, so-named for the metal containers from which fragile housing was constructed. All over the Empire, what were once small administrative or commercial centers kept growing: Tunis, Casablanca, Rabat, Dakar, Conakry, Saigon, and even inland posts like Niamey and Ouagadougou.[71]

ECONOMIC PLANS FOR THE 1930s

During the 1930s French imperial planners, confident of their colonies' economic future, unfolded numerous elaborate economic plans, resembling the
grandiose schemes for the colonial companies of Richelieu's and Colbert's era,
but with a difference. This time they were the products of technicians' planning,
the work of engineers, agriculturists, and colonial administrators; nevertheless,
they didn't fare much better than those of their predecessors. Some improvements to the infrastructure took place—ports, roads, and railroads were built—
but France's economy was at its most vulnerable. With war clouds forming,
neither government loans nor private investments were adequate to realize the
hoped-for development of overseas possessions.

The first interwar development plan came from Edmond Giscard d'Estaing,
an ex–inspector of finances with close ties to the business community. The 1931
document called attention to the lack of modern banking resources in Africa,
especially the lack of credit to sustain the import-export trade in primary products, and the absence of a transportation infrastructure. The report focused on
what could be done to advance French business interests. It recommended easier
access to credits for French merchants, but there was no discussion of improvements to benefit Africans.[72]

In 1934 an Economic Conference for France and Overseas convened, occa-
sioned by the growing colonial debt. Along lines proposed earlier by former
Minister of Colonies Albert Sarraut, the conference's goal was to realize "an
imperial economic plan destined to allow the colonies to be globally competitive." This would require large sums of money; its fruits in Africa would be a
trans-Saharan railroad, another railroad from Douala on the Cameroon coast to
Chad in the interior, and an extensive agricultural program in the Niger region.

Although the companies of Colbert's time were to be largely privately funded,
those of the Popular Front era were to be financed and run by the government
because of the reluctance of French investors to bankroll overseas investments.
Unlike the d'Estaing plan, this one envisioned new indigenous schools and improved medical facilities. The cost was estimated to be 11 billion francs, double
the cost of the original Sarraut plan, payable over 14 years, 30% of it from the
colonies, the rest from France. The plan never gained any broad-based support
and consequently went nowhere.

In June 1936 France tried again, this time through a conference of colonial
governors-general. Colonial officials, with interests broader than those of the
business community, wanted to launch a broad-based program moving considerably beyond strengthening export markets. Components included building local industries to sell cement in Africa and export it elsewhere, encouraging
agricultural cooperatives, and decentralizing economic control to respond to local needs and opportunities. Such plans led to a sharp debate between traditional
French commercial interests, who wanted to protect the status quo, and colonial
administrators, who wanted to engage local peoples as the principal agents of
development as well as its beneficiaries.

In the end, no plans for widespread colonial industrial development were ever realized. French officials were nervous about what might happen if an industrial proletariat was created overseas, though a brewery here or a power-generating station there were acceptable. Morocco was one exception. By 1935 over 800 factories had been built, representing a capital investment of over 1.5 billion francs and employing 67 thousand workers, 4 thousand of them Europeans. They cultivated tobacco, caught and canned sardines, and drilled for oil. Earlier, France had invested heavily in construction, mining, and electrification in Morocco, hoping to create "a little French California."

In 1936 the Popular Front government appointed a commission to review the political and economic state of France's colonies and recommend a reform plan to benefit both France and the indigenous peoples. Various overseas French groups sent communications that read like the *cahiers des doléances* of the French Revolution. The commission included Henri Guernut, the president of the League of Human Rights, as its head. Charles-André Julien, Robert Delavignette, and Hubert Deschamps, respected scholars or colonial administrators, were members as well, as briefly was André Gide, a native of Algeria. However, the commission was slow to organize, and before it was fully launched, the Popular Front had collapsed, and the commission ended its life with few achievements.

THE STAGNANT HEXAGON AND THE POPULAR FRONT, 1936–1937

A word must be said here about France's internal politics, which helps explain why, once again, the needs of the Empire got short shrift. Forty different governments existed during the 20-year interwar period, five alone in 1933. After the wounds of war were somewhat healed in the 1920s, a series of coalition governments formed and reformed, generally led by the conservative right, although from 1924 to 1926 the radical socialists patched together a short-lived government. Communists and fascists were more numerous and certainly louder than ever before. In 1936 a Popular Front combining radical socialists, socialists, and communists held power for over a year. It was led by Léon Blum, a reform-minded socialist, who created what he called "a French New Deal." Modest industrial growth, a rise in wages, and an increase in consumer spending were not enough, however, to turn the corner on France's severe problems. Although the Popular Front had few reforms to show for its efforts, such ones as it realized were important for the future shape of French colonial history.[73] It declared an amnesty for political prisoners in Vietnam, negotiated an end to mandate rule in Syria and Lebanon, made it easier for students and workers to obtain passports for France, and replaced particularly brutal bush administrators in several places.[74]

Under the Popular Front, steps were taken to reduce forced work in the colonies. In Indochina, peasants were required to spend five days a year on non-paying work gangs; in French Equatorial Africa, it was ten days for all males between ages 18 and 60. In Indochina, a system of forced work for pay was forbidden but continued informally for several years. In both Indochina and Africa, forced work for private firms was forbidden in principle but widespread in practice. Expanding rubber plantations in Indochina and coffee and cocoa plantations in West Africa required steady streams of cheap labor. In the Ivory Coast, conditions were so harsh that Mossi workers from the Upper Volta often fled into the nearby Gold Coast for protection.

Africans were allowed to strike, and some made it through the thicket of French administrative regulations and formed nascent trade unions, such as the Syndicat des Ouvriers du Bâtiment de Dakar and the union of Employées du Commerce de l'Industrie et des Banques. By 1938 more than 40 unions had formed in Senegal, 30 of them in Dakar. Hesitant and short lived as the Popular Front reforms were, they allowed Africans to become more familiar with the world of organized work and afforded them some possibilities to improve their lot. The strike and collective bargaining were in their infancy, but both would become increasingly important after World War II. The Popular Front also revived the *Service d'inspection du travail* in overseas possessions. Employers and government officials feared such an independent agency that could levy fines on offenders and correct working conditions on the spot. With the Popular Front's demise, and with strong opposition from entrenched *colons*, the service lost its autonomy until after World War II.[75]

TURNING THE POLITICAL TIDE, FIRST RIPPLES

At its apogee, when it included the League of Nations mandates, the French Overseas Empire encompassed over 12 million square kilometers, and 65 million overseas persons, but never more than 1,475,000 overseas French. "Certainly France had a colonial empire, but she was not ready to be an Empire," a historian of the period noted.[76] France was never sure what to do with its empire, but overseas politicians forced the issue. Gradually, the idea of political self-government, or autonomy for colonies, surfaced. First raised by socialists in the 1920s, it never was with the idea of independence in mind, but with vague talk of indigenous participation in the political process. "Our ideas have attained the maximum of generosity and liberality comparable with the mores of the period," is how the government put it in 1935. Ferhat Abbas, a leading Algerian intellectual and politician, said that his country had decided "to definitely align our future with that of the French effort in our country . . . [but] without freedom for indigenous people, there never will be a durable French Africa." A movement to apply domestic social reforms to the colonies grew, including demands for an eight-hour day, paid vacations, and improved working conditions. There was sentiment to construct more rural dispensaries, to add to the number of roving vaccination teams, and to build more rural schools. The goal was basic literacy and workers' skills, education to prepare "good peasants and rural artisans . . . [rather] than Black or Yellow degree holders."[77]

Except in Indochina and the Middle East, nationalist sentiment among over-seas peoples was still unformed in the 1930s. It was not until the decade's end that radical movements took hold: communism in Vietnam and nationalist move-ments among the North Africans, like the Destour (constitution) party among the Tunisians and the Jeunes Marocains in Morocco. Nevertheless, the numbers of politically articulate nationalists were few; their movements were carefully tracked by the police; and their publications were quickly censured or sup-pressed. Much of the agitation came from students and workers in France. Co-lonial officials were reluctant to allow indigenous students to study in France, believing they would easily fall prey to radical ideas. Student numbers were consequently small: 1,500 Vietnamese in 1930, six of whom held government scholarships; 200 from the Maghreb, largely Tunisians in 1932; and about 20 Africans and Malagasy, whose numbers rose to 60 in 1941. Most students were the offspring of well-to-do Vietnamese mandarins or landowners, or Moroccan or Tunisian bourgeoisie and provincial merchants, like the Bourguiba family.

The French Communist party, skilled at calling attention to colonial excesses in the 1920s, during the 1930s aligned itself increasingly with the Soviet Union, which switched from support of nationalist movements to building Communist parties directly linked to Moscow. The Communist movement in Vietnam was the most advanced one overseas, and it benefited from assistance of the Parti Communiste Française (PCF). Other nascent movements were left to fend for themselves, including that of Tiemoko Garan Kouyaté, a young African teacher, who founded an Institut d'études marxistes in Marseilles to politicize the African port workers there, and who was an early proponent of creating a federation of French overseas territories aligned to France in a power-sharing arrangement. Kouyaté's organizational attempts in Paris and Dakar, however, were frustrated by French authorities. He was one of the most outspoken nationalists of his generation, but it was as a French soldier that he fell to German fire in 1942.[78]

By 1947 the French Communists had renounced classic Leninist anticoloni-alism in favor of retaining France's colonial possessions. Most French Com-munists were French before they were Communist, something that angered militant overseas nationalists. Also, while the workers of the world were sup-posed to unite, the French working class was notoriously chauvinistic and insular in outlook. Communist rhetoric at times was interchangeable with Gaullist rhet-oric, as when Communists expressed concern for maintaining *la grandeur fran-çaise*. French Communists were anxious to keep America out of the French Empire. They believed that if the colonies became free, the United States would move quickly to bring them under its wing. The party supported traditional French nationalistic policies during both the Vietnamese conflict and the 1947 Madagascar insurgency. However, when France signed an agreement in 1951 allowing America to build five air bases in Morocco, the French Communist party switched to support for the independence of Morocco and Tunisia, and Madagascar became, according to Communist propaganda, "the island drowned in blood."

THE RISE OF RESISTANCE MOVEMENTS

All over the colonial empire, nationalist movements were taking shape, and armed resistance was emerging. The Empire was officially "pacified" on paper by 1930, but it would have been unwise to travel unarmed through the Rif Mountains, large stretches of Central Africa, and parts of Vietnam. In 1927 and 1928 the Bayas people of Central Africa were violently put down, and in 1934 Moroccan Berbers were surrounded by 25 French-led armed battalions, 14 thousand locally recruited troops, artillery units, and airplanes that easily spotted troops moving on horseback. The independence-minded Berbers were strafed and bombed.

Encouraged by Vietnamese communists, a local Vietnamese infantry unit mutinied near Hanoi at Yen-Bay in 1931. Peasant revolts, strikes among local plantation workers, and the formation of local soviets throughout the countryside followed. France, reacting quickly and violently, sent in the Foreign Legion and arrested more than 10 thousand people, but the spread of ideas was not stopped by bullets. France put forward a vague plan for a *collaboration franco-annamite*, possibly creating *États associés*, but not independence. Vietnamese opposition continued to grow.

Nationalism was more complex in the Maghreb, and the rise of nationalist sentiment was slower to form than in Vietnam. Even a local leader like Tunisia's Habib Bourguiba, imprisoned for his political activity, still spoke of the "indissoluble union between France and Tunisia"[79] in the pre–World War II period. In Morocco, the presence of a hereditary monarch complicated matters, but *évolués* in the university city of Fez contributed to the growing Jeune Marocain movement, which announced reform demands including a constitutional monarchy and a parliament. Moroccan dock workers in Casablanca struck and marched on the palace. France responded by putting down the demonstrations, arresting their leaders, deporting some, and introducing widespread press censorship. On May 30, 1930, the French *résident général* issued a *dahir* (decree) freeing 700 thousand Berbers from the sultan's rule, on the grounds that the Berbers were not an Islamic people. Protest followed throughout the Islamic world. Moroccan nationalists demanded an end to Catholic propaganda in their country, suppression of the interior passports used to control people's movements, and institution of Moslem legal codes as the law of the land.

Algeria was part of France, administered by the minister of interior. By the late 1930s Algerians were asking why all the country's inhabitants were not enjoying the same rights as French citizens. Increasingly colonial governors saw the need for accommodation and devised formulas they hoped would be acceptable, but the *colons* would have none of it. A former governor-general, Maurice Viollette, was removed at the *colons'* behest in 1927 for being a partisan of reforms. One of his proposals was to extend voting rights to 21 thousand Algerians, principally civil servants, former military, and degree holders, as France had done earlier in parts of Senegal. Both sides were enflamed by the proposal; for Muslims, accepting French citizenship required renouncing parts of the Koran contrary to French law, notably rejecting polygamy and sections of the *sharia*. The voice of the *colons* was the Abbé Lambert, a deputy from Oran, who declared, "We will never support a proposal that allows a village, small as it may be, to have an Arab mayor." At the same time, Monseigneur Durand of Oran declared, "Yes, that God has given us places overseas with the indigenous to be but one in the folds of France's flag, so dear to Christ." Viollette reminded his detractors, "Be on your guard. Native Algerians, through your fault without doubt, do not yet have a country; they are seeking one. They are asking you for France. Give it to them or, without it, they will make another [country]."[80]

One French group studying the question of local rights proposed extending the vote to a small electoral college of 2,700 carefully chosen Algerians who would elect a handful of Algerian parliamentarians. The report coincided with the celebration of the *glorieux centenaire de l'Algérie française*, April 15, 1930, and was summarily dismissed. "There are symbolic dates. Later is sometimes too late," observed Henri Guernut, head of a parliamentary commission charged with studying overseas problems.[81] The *colons* were unyielding. Their lack of accommodation to the complex, hostile political situation they faced can be seen in their approach to the 1931 Colonial Exposition where the Algerian display featured a fountain of a bubbling red liquid and the caption, "Le vin, c'est l'avenir de l'Algérie" (Wine, it is Algeria's future).

Frustrated by roadblocks at every turn, Algerians formed or joined political parties or vented their growing anger by rejecting assimilation and advocating emancipation. No one had a concrete plan for what would happen next or a strategy; what existed was a country peopled by politically aware persons with broken hopes and frustrated aspirations. The bitterness of Algerians met the stubbornness of the French who had come to regard the land as their own. When it came two decades later, the final confrontation would be a bloody one.

NATIONALISM IN AFRICA AND ASIA

Nationalism was less pronounced in sub-Saharan Africa. The region was vast, communication was poor, and most people lived at barely a subsistence level. Some Africans accepted the French presence with fatalism—"The world is a camp; a camp is not a home; so many others, before the French, pitched their tents and went on their way." Modest reforms had been launched in Senegal, and Africans living in the four communes around Dakar could vote as French citizens in contested elections. Trade unionism was rising among dock and industrial workers, who struck or protested for better working conditions, such as the eight-hour day and a safer working environment. A school created in 1930 and named after Governor William Ponty became a center for training several generations of elite African politicians and civil servants, many of whom became leaders in the independence movement. Blaise Diagne, a Senegalese, served in parliament from 1914 until his death in 1934. Diagne recruited thousands of soldiers for France, and after the war he became undersecretary for colonies, the first African to hold a cabinet position in France. When elections took place in the autumn of 1945, Lamine Guèye, who sponsored a bill granting citizenship to all inhabitants of the French Union, and Léopold Sédar Senghor, a war veteran and professor of French grammar, were elected to represent Senegal in the French legislature.

In Dahomey, sometimes called "Africa's Latin Quarter," widespread nationalist sentiment was voiced by the local intellectual elite, government secretaries, interpreters, postal and hospital workers, and a sizable number of Creoles, who were successful in the palm oil and other businesses, lived like Europeans, sent their children to French schools, and became the country's doctors, lawyers, pharmacists, and professionals. At least 14 newspapers existed in the small country in the early 1930s. One, *La Voix de Dahomey* (circulation 2 thousand copies) reported on most sensitive political questions of the time, including abuses of the *indigénat*. Its prudent slogan was *"Ni révoltés ni révolutionnaires, mais des serviteurs de la France"* (Neither rebels nor revolutionaries, but servants of France), but French colonial officials were highly suspicious of it. The paper's leaders were arrested on the vague charge of having a "pernicious effect on the indigenous masses," and, after a long trial, were fined one franc. (By the time the trial ended in June 1936, the Popular Front was in power in France, and the climate was favorable to accommodating some indigenous political interests.) Dahomian leaders took great satisfaction in their victory, but it led to no mass protest movement or political agitation. When war came a few years later, the small Dahomian elite, a few thousand persons at most, rallied to the French cause.[82]

Vietnamese nationalism was long established and deep seated. Long resistance or accommodation to the neighboring Chinese had exposed the Vietnamese to external cultures backed by arms. Thus, as French influence spread and increasing numbers of Vietnamese learned French and worked for the administration, forms of cultural resistance existed alongside the growth of nationalist political movements. Throughout the period of French occupation, Vietnamese nationalists promoted the study of ancient and modern heroes from the Trung Sisters, who rebelled against the Chinese in A.D. 40–42, to numerous more recent figures, such as Phan Boi Chau (1867–1940), a resistance figure of poor scholar-gentry ancestry.[83] The 1920s marked a time of growing resentment among a generation of Vietnamese civil servants, students, interpreters, and small merchants. Faced with growing taxes and stymied by the lack of educational and career opportunities, they had to endure the arrogance and anger of French soldiers and bureaucrats. For many, Marxism, with its promise of a classless society, was an attraction, as was Japan, a haven for Asian reformists and an inspiration for its anti-Western success in the Russo-Japanese War of 1904–1905.

The Vietnamese were also united by a sense of ethnic salvation, or *cuu quoc*, springing from losing one's country *mat nuoc*, both the physical land and its soul. The Vietnamese were driven by an intense, culturally enveloping motivation few French understood. Phan Chu Trinh, an early 20th century observer of Vietnamese society, was a sharp critic of mandarin corruption and an astute observer of inequities in French-Vietnamese relations. More a loner than a political activist, he described local tensions in a letter to Governor General Paul Beau (1902–1908):

The French have been in Vietnam for some time, have seen the greediness of the mandarins, the ignorance of the people, the corruption of the culture, and have concluded sneeringly that the Vietnamese have no sense of national identity. So, when they print articles in their papers or talk among themselves, they all show dislike and disdain for the Vietnamese, considering them savages, comparing them with pigs and cows, unwilling to let them become equals, and even afraid that getting close will be polluting.[84]

The Empire's days were drawing to a close as French and Vietnamese alike were drawn into the movement of events neither could fully control.

NOTES

1. Raoul Girardet, *L'Idée coloniale en France, 1871–1962* (Paris: La Table Ronde, 1972); Prosser Gifford and William Roger Louis, eds., *France and Britain in Africa* (New Haven, Conn.: Yale University Press, 1971); John Chipman, *French Power in Africa* (London: Blackwell, 1989); Raymond F. Betts, *Uncertain Dimension: Western Overseas Empires in the Twentieth Century* (Minneapolis: University of Minnesota Press, 1985); Raymond F. Betts, *France and Decolonization, 1900–1960* (New York: St. Martin's Press, 1991); Charles-Robert Ageron, ed., *Les Chemins de la décolonisation de l'empire français* (Paris: Centre National de la Recherche Scientifique, 1986); Jean Ganiage, Hubert Deschamps, and Odette Guitard, *L'Afrique au XXe siècle* (Paris: Sirey, 1966); G. Wesley Johnson, ed., *Double Impact: France and Africa in the Age of Imperialism* (Westport, Conn.: Greenwood Press, 1985); Denise Bouche, *Histoire de la colonisation française*, vol. 2 (Paris: Fayard, 1991); Eugen Weber, *The Hollow Years: France in the 1930s* (London: Sinclair-Stevenson, 1995); Alice L. Conklin, *A Mission to Civilize: The Republican Idea of Empire in France and West Africa 1895–1930* (Stanford, Calif.: Stanford University Press, 1997).

2. Jacques Thobie, "Le bilan coloniale en 1914," in Jacques Thobie, Gilbert Meynier, Catherine Coquery-Vidrovitch, and Charles-Robert Ageron, eds., *Histoire de la France coloniale, 1914–1990* (Paris: Armand Colin, 1990), p. 5.

3. Martin Deming Lewis, "One Hundred Million Frenchmen: The 'Assimilation' Theory in French Colonial Policy," *Comparative Studies in Society and History* 4 (The Hague: Mouton, 1961–1962), pp. 129–153.

4. Arthur Girault, *Principes de colonisation et de législation coloniale*, vol. 1, 1894, p. 107, quoted in Thobie, "Le bilan coloniale en 1914," pp. 14–15.

5. From Émile Démaret, "De l'idée fédérative dans une organization coloniale," quoted in Thobie et al., eds., *Histoire de la France coloniale*, p. 16.

6. Thobie, "Le bilan coloniale en 1914," p. 18.

7. Thobie, "Le bilan coloniale en 1914," p. 34.

8. Eugen Weber, *Peasants into Frenchmen; The Modernization of Rural France, 1870–1914* (Stanford, Calif.: Stanford University Press, 1976), pp. 485–493.

9. Robert Delavignette, *Freedom and Authority in French West Africa* (London: Frank Cass, 1968), p. 49.

10. Paul Rabinow, *French Modern: Norms and Forms of the Social Environment* (Cambridge: MIT Press, 1989), pp. 104–125, 278–319.

11. Ibid., p. 285.

12. Gwendolyn Wright, *The Politics of Design in French Colonial Urbanism* (Chicago: University of Chicago Press, 1991), pp. 85–160; Gwendolyn Wright, "Tradition in the Service of Modernity: Architecture and Urbanism in French Colonial Policy, 1900–1930," in *Tensions of Empire: Colonial Cultures in a Bourgeois World*, ed. Frederick Cooper and Ann Laura Stoler (Berkeley: University of California Press, 1997), pp. 322–345.

13. Douglas Porch, *The French Foreign Legion: A Complete History of the Legendary Fighting Force* (New York: HarperPerennial, 1991), pp. 396–406.

14. Thobie et al., eds., *Histoire de la France Coloniale*, pp. 164–165.

15. Ibid., p. 568.

16. Ibid., pp. 39–42; L. Abrams and D. J. Miller, "Who Were the French Colonists? A Reassessment of the Parti Colonial, 1890–1914," *Historical Journal* 19, no. 3 (1976), pp. 689–726.

17. Thobie, "Le bilan coloniale en 1914," pp. 30–33.

18. Bernard B. Fall, *The Two Vietnams: A Political and Military Analysis* (New York: Frederick A. Praeger, 1963), pp. 35–36.

19. Frederick Cooper, *Decolonization and African Society: The Labor Question in French and British Africa* (New York: Cambridge University Press, 1996), pp. 36–43.

20. Thobie, "Le bilan coloniale en 1914," p. 30.

21. Ibid.

22. Ibid., p. 31.

23. William B. Cohen, "Robert Delavignette: The Gentle Ruler (1897–1976)," in *African Proconsuls, European Governors in Africa*, eds. L. H. Gann and Peter Duignan (New York: Free Press, 1978), pp. 185–195.

24. Robert Delavignette, *Freedom and Authority in French West Africa*, translation of *Service Africain* (London: Frank Cass & Co., 1968), pp. 6–7.

25. Thobie, "Le bilan coloniale en 1914," p. 27; Janet R. Horne, "In Pursuit of Greater France: Visions of Empire among Musée Social Reformers, 1894–1931," in *Domesticating the Empire: Race, Gender, and Family Life in French and Dutch Colonialism*, eds. Julia Clancy-Smith and Frances Gouda (Charlottesville: University of Virginia Press, 1998), pp. 36–37.

26. Alice L. Conklin, "Redefining 'Frenchness': Citizenship, Race Regeneration, and Imperial Motherhood in France and West Africa, 1914–40," in *Domesticating the Empire: Race, Gender, and Family Life in French and Dutch Colonialism*, eds. Julia Clancy-Smith and Frances Gouda (Charlottesville: University of Virginia Press, 1998), p. 70.

27. Robert Aldrich, *Greater France, a History of French Overseas Expansion* (New York: St. Martin's Press, 1996), pp. 156–158; Julia A. Clancy-Smith, *Rebel and Saint, Muslim Notables, Populist Protest, Colonial Encounters (Algeria and Tunisia, 1800–1904)* (Berkeley: University of California Press, 1997), pp. 245–249.

28. Quoted in Pierre Guillaume, *Le Monde Colonial, XIXe-XXe siècle*, 2d ed. (Paris: Armand Colin, 1994), pp. 251–252.

29. Thobie, "Le bilan coloniale en 1914," pp. 56–58.

30. Ibid., pp. 57–62.

31. Ibid., p. 67; Leonard V. Smith, *Between Mutiny and Obedience, the Case of the French Fifth Infantry Division During World War I* (Princeton, N.J.: Princeton University Press, 1994), p. 104.

32. Gilbert Meynier, "La France coloniale de 1914 á 1931," in Thobie et al., eds, *Histoire de la France coloniale*, p. 75.

33. Jean Martin, *Lexique de la colonisation française* (Paris: Dalloz, 1988), p. 190.

34. Guillaume, *Le Monde Colonial*, p. 115.

35. Meynier, "La France coloniale," pp. 102–109; Patrick Chamoiseau, *Texaco*, trans. Rose-Myriam Réjouis and Val Vinokurou (New York: Alfred A. Knopf, 1997), pp. 189–190.

36. Meynier, "La France coloniale," pp. 74–84.

37. Chamoiseau, *Texaco*, p. 191.

38. Meynier, "La France coloniale," p. 110.

39. Ibid., pp. 109–112.

40. Ngo Vinh Long, *Before the Revolution, the Vietnamese Peasants under the French* (New York: Columbia University Press, 1991 reprint), pp. 14–15, 44–45, 84–85, 138–141.

41. Quoted in Hy V. Luong, *Revolution in the Village, Tradition and Transformation in North Vietnam, 1925–1988* (Honolulu: University of Hawaii Press, 1992), p. 40.

42. Meynier, "La France coloniale," pp. 124–127.

43. David R. Headrick, *The Tentacles of Power, Technology Transfer in the Age of Imperialism, 1850–1940* (New York: Oxford University Press, 1988) p. 135.

44. Delavignette, *Freedom and Authority*, p. 141.

45. Meynier, "La France coloniale," pp. 136–139.

46. Anne Marcovich, "French Colonial Medicine and Colonial Rule: Algeria and Indochina," in *Disease, Medicine and Empire: Perspectives on Western Medicine and the Experience of European Expansion*, ed. Roy Macleod and Milton Lewis (London: Routledge, 1988), pp. 103–117.

47. Delavignette, *Freedom and Authority*, p. 27.

48. Thobie, "Le bilan coloniale en 1914," pp. 45–47.

49. Patrick Chamoiseau, *School Days*, trans. Linda Coverdale (Lincoln: University of Nebraska Press, 1997), pp. 62–63.

50. Ibid., p. 72.

51. Ibid., p. 114.

52. Meynier, "La France coloniale," pp. 112–119.

53. *Rapport Annuel du Gouvernement français sur l'administration sous mandat des territoires du Cameroun pour l'année 1923* (Paris, 1924), pp. 75–79.

54. Frederick Quinn, *Changes in Beti Society—1887–1960*, Ph.D. dissertation, University of California at Los Angeles, 1970, pp. 142–145.

55. Robert Aldrich, *Greater France, A History of French Overseas Expansion* (New York: St. Martin's Press, 1996), pp. 175–76.

56. Philip S. Khoury, *Syria and the French Mandate: The Politics of Arab Nationalism, 1920–1945* (Princeton, N.J.: Princeton University Press, 1987); Meynier, "La France coloniale," pp. 102–105; Matthew Burrows, " '*Mission Civilisatrice*': French Cul-

tural Policy in the Middle East, 1860–1914," *Historical Journal* 29, no. 1 (1986), pp. 109–135.

57. Robert-Charles Ageron, "De l'Empire à la dislocation de l'Union française (1939–1956)," in *Histoire de la France coloniale*, ed. Jacques Thobie et al. (Paris: Armand Colin, 1990), pp. 337–338.

58. Thobie, "Le bilan coloniale," p. 43.

59. Ibid., p. 47.

60. Meynier, "Le France coloniale," pp. 173–179.

61. Nguyen Hong, "Days of Childhood," in *The Light of the Capital: Three Modern Vietnamese Classics*, ed. Greg Lockhardt and Monique Lockhardt (Oxford: Oxford University Press, 1996), p. 191.

62. Catherine Coquery-Vidrovitch, "La Colonisation française 1931–1939," in *Histoire de la France coloniale*, ed. Jacques Thobie et al. (Paris: Armand Colin, 1990), pp. 305–308; Dina Sherzer, ed., *Cinema, Colonialism, Postcolonialism: Perspectives from the French and Francophone World* (Austin: University of Texas Press, 1996); Porch, *French Foreign Legion*, pp. 428–440.

63. David H. Slavin, "French Colonial Film Before and After *Itto*: From Berber Myth to Race War," *French Historical Studies* 21, no. 1 (Winter 1998), p. 141.

64. Catherine Hodeir and Michel Pierre, *L'Exposition coloniale* (Paris: Editions Complexe, 1991), p. 12.

65. Janet R. Home, "In Pursuit of Greater France: Visions of Empire Among Musée Social Reformers, 1894–1931," in *Domesticating the Empire: Race, Gender, and Family Life in French and Dutch Colonialism*, ed. Julia Clancy-Smith and Francis Gouda (Charlottesville: University of Virginia Press, 1998), pp. 41–42.

66. Coquery-Vidrovitch, "La Colonisation française," pp. 213–225; Panivong Norindr, *Phantasmic Indochina* (Durham, N.C.: Duke University Press, 1996); Pascal Blanchard and Armelle Chatelier, *Images et colonies* (Paris: Syros, 1993).

67. Hodeir and Pierre, *L'Exposition coloniale*, p. 64.

68. Wright, *Politics of Design*; Betts, *Uncertain Dimensions*.

69. Coquery-Vidrovitch, "La Colonisation française," pp. 213–303.

70. Delavignette, *Freedom and Authority*, p. 67.

71. Coquery-Vidrovitch, "La Colonisation française," pp. 234–240.

72. Ibid., pp. 245–252.

73. Tony Chafer and Amanda Sackur, eds., *French Colonial Empire and the Popular Front: Hope and Disillusion* (New York: St. Martin's Press, 1999), pp. 1–29.

74. Coquery-Vidrovitch, "La Colonisation française," pp. 259–266.

75. Cooper, *Decolonization and African Society*, p. 92.

76. Ageron, "De l'Empire à la dislocation," p. 312.

77. Ibid., pp. 260–265.

78. Ibid., pp. 281–284.

79. Coquery-Vidrovitch, "La Colonisation française," p. 273.

80. Thobie, "Le bilan coloniale," pp. 275–276.

81. Coquery-Vidrovitch, "La Colonisation française," pp. 275–276.

82. Ibid., pp. 277–280.

83. David G. Marr, *Vietnamese Anticolonialism, 1885–1925* (Berkeley: University of California Press, 1971), pp. 83–86.

84. Quoted in Ibid., p. 161.

7

The 20th Century:
The Receding Empire

"Les colonies, c'est fini! Il faut faire autre chose." (The colonies are finished!
One must do other things.)
— President Charles de Gaulle to André Malraux, 1958

WAR CLOUDS

Germany took Paris on June 14, 1940, and the president of the Republic and
the prime minister retreated southward toward Africa while Marshal Pétain, 84,
hero of the Verdun battle of World War I, negotiated an armistice with Germany.
Vichy, a health spa often visited by returning colonials, became the new capital,
where, on July 10, the National Assembly gave Marshal Pétain dictatorial powers, sounding the death knell of the Third Republic. What did all this mean for
France overseas?

In World War I, the Empire was an asset because of the troops and materials
it provided and because it made France a global power. As World War II approached, many French believed that once more the country's salvation would
come from its Empire. This time, however, overseas peoples were wary.
Heightened awareness of their inferior status caused many subject peoples to
resist coming to France's aid. "France has given us nothing, why should we die
for France?" was an oft-asked question, and African soldiers sang with bitter
irony:

> France is our mother.
> It is she who feeds us.

With potatoes
And rotten beans![1]

Colonial soldiers feared being sent to the front as cannon fodder. General Bührer, head of colonial troops, hoped for ten divisions of colonial and North African troops to absorb the Germans' frontal attack on the Siegfried Line. Bührer spoke of the need "to conserve French blood to the maximum" and of the necessity "to win the war without wearing out the French race."[2] He was overruled, however, and overseas troops were assigned to regular units. By March 1940 the number of colonial troops in France totaled 89 thousand, 69,500 of them from Africa—considerably short of the 300 thousand called for in re-armament plans and well under the 556 thousand troops who served in World War I. Eventually their numbers rose to 247 thousand troops (1939–1944), approximately 20 to 25 thousand of whom were killed. Almost all of the troops came from the Maghreb or Africa; a few came from Indochina. Losses were heavy: 38% of the Tirailleurs Sénégalese, 29% of the Malagasy troops, and 23% of those from Indochina.[3]

In a symbolic gesture at being an independent government that could act globally at will, part of the Bank of France's gold was sent for safekeeping to Dakar and part was sent to Martinique, escorted by military ships and planes. Vichy propaganda portrayed Marshal Pétain as a wise old mandarin for the Indochinese and "the man with seven golden stars" for the Arabs. Vichy publicists kept alive the vision of France's Empire; a ten-year economic program, as bold as any of Colbert's dreams, was announced for the colonies and the plan for a trans-Saharan railroad was revived, but neither was anything more than a castle in the sky.

Any prospect of cutting back on forced labor recruiting in Africa was squelched during World War II. The Vichy government was unremitting in its demands for laborers, although Pierre Boisson, former governor in Cameroon and governor-general in Dakar, and Vichy's chief recruitment officer, argued that France's system of obtaining forced labor was fast approaching its limits. Boisson did not want African workers diverted from their traditional agricultural employment. "Africa is peasant," he kept saying, cautioning against the spread of industrialization which might expose peasants to the prolitarianization of the workforce with accompanying unsettling political and economic consequences. The winners were the long-established *colons*, who deftly took advantage of the labor debates to strengthen their interests: protect their plantations, maintain low wages, and ensure minimal political meddling from whatever government was in power. To meet the government's growing concern that the labor pool was nearly exhausted, resourceful planters simply extended the duration of contracts, sometimes doubling the length of time they covered.[4] Thus labor contracts, as the fiction of coerced labor was called, rose in the Ivory Coast from 35 thousand in 1939 to 41 thousand in 1942. The Vichy program continued established French colonial practices from the past. Badly in need of new proposals to justify its tenuous existence, the Vichy government seized on several key concepts long discussed by the colonial figures of the 1930s.

For Vichy, the Empire was global proof that France was more than a defeated nation under Axis tutelage; for de Gaulle, the Empire was the launching pad to restore legitimate government and provide troops and wealth for the war effort. Gaullists, writing later from the victor's seat, claim to have enunciated a new colonial vision by the war's end. However, it was little more than a handful of post–Brazzaville Conference suggestions that went nowhere once France entered its postwar political and constitutional debates. The war left France badly over-extended and deeply divided. Both Vichy and Free French efforts to consolidate power consistently ignored signals from Algeria, West Africa, Madagascar, Syria, Lebanon, and Indochina that all was not well with the old order. Nationalism was on the rise, and independence was an immediate or near-term goal. Unbeknownst to French leaders of all parties, the clock was ticking on imperialism's final decades.

France was not an independent agent during World War II and consequently much of its colonial policy was in response to external events rather than internal initiatives. New Caledonia's August 1940 declaration for Free France was supported by Australia. An American military landing in North Africa in November 1942 precipitated the change from Vichy to Free French control there. In Syria and Lebanon, the Allies were in charge and had marginal use for the small Free French forces. In Indochina, the strong Japanese military presence drove French policy for much of the period from 1940 to 1945.

THE TIDE OF WAR TURNS

For General de Gaulle, the Mediterranean in this war was the equivalent of the Marne in World War I. The Allied troop landing in North Africa on November 8, 1942, was the beginning of the end for Vichy France. After the French fleet had been destroyed by its officers and sailors in Toulon harbor, German forces occupied the rest of France, and Admiral François Darlan was left to run a pseudo-government in North Africa for seven months. Meanwhile, President Franklin Roosevelt met the Sultan of Morocco at Anfa, a suburb of Casablanca, promised American assistance, and suggested a postwar three-country trusteeship until Morocco achieved independence. (After their initial meeting, Roosevelt seated the Sultan to his right at dinner, Churchill to his left, and the French *résident général* farther down the table—the sort of calculated slight that could turn a high-ranking French official apoplectic.) De Gaulle, anxious to limit American influence, came to Algeria from London personally to take command of the French military and political operations.

De Gaulle had few cards to play initially. Only the New Hebrides had come out openly for the Free French by July 1940. In Chad, the governor, Félix Éboué, a colonial administrator from French Guiana, declared Chad in support of de Gaulle, followed by Cameroon, Gabon, the Oubangui-Chari region of Central

Africa, Tahiti, and France's Pacific islands. Brazzaville became the Free French capital. (Dakar was closer to France, but it was in Vichy hands.) More than 6 million people and 2,482,000 square kilometers of territory were now nominally under Free French control. While a British fleet stood ready in Dakar harbor, General de Gaulle met with Governor-General Boisson, hoping to persuade him to side with the Free French. He failed and a two-day naval bombardment and sea battle followed on September 23–25, 1940. Vichy troops rounded up the Free French supporters, condemned 115 to death, and sent others to forced labor and prison. Only after Allied troops successfully arrived in North Africa did French West Africa join the Gaullist forces.[5]

It is striking how fragile the Free French military forces were, though no one knew it at the time, and despite propaganda to the contrary, its hold after the war on its colonies would be tenuous as well. The war left colonies with ruined economies buffeted by inflation, severe rationing, and stagnant trade, and with populations acutely hostile to further forced labor conscription. France never got the message. Martin Thomas, a military historian concluded,

It is significant that in all the major colonial federations in which the Free French fought either militarily or politically to assert their control during the Second World War, the transition to an era of decolonization proved violent. . . . The divided French empire of the Second World War never entirely recovered from the rifts that had opened up between rulers and ruled.[6]

THE BRAZZAVILLE CONFERENCE

It was during the Brazzaville Conference of January 30–February 8, 1944, that France outlined a postwar colonial policy more advanced than anything previously discussed, including transforming the Empire into a federation of associated peoples. However, throughout French history, control had remained centered in the *métropole*, reinforcing a top-down political system, and little changed now. At Brazzaville, where 19 governors and governors-general assembled, a vague proposal to create a federated conference with deliberative powers was floated, but not a colonial parliament. No possibility of independence or autonomy outside the French bloc was permissible, and issues involving Indochina or France's Arab holdings were never a matter of public record, if they were discussed at all. Each colony should have its own *personnalité politique* was how de Gaulle's principal colonial spokesman, René Plevan, left it to his satisfaction, but not to the satisfaction of alarmed *colons* or disappointed Africans who found it too politically limiting.[7]

General de Gaulle went farther than any one else at the conference, not out of idealism, but because he was a realist who knew concessions must be made if France were to continue to hold power in a global alliance of francophone states. At Brazzaville he said the goal of French policies would be eventual self-government within a French system. "I do not speak of a French Federation because one can discuss the term, but of a French system where everyone plays their role."[8] All levels of government employment, except the highest ones, would be open to Africans who should receive benefits comparable to Europeans. Additionally, he said, there was a need for a new statute on the place of women in Africa. Delegates agreed that forced labor and the *indigénat* must end. Although reformist language was introduced on recruitment practices, no changes were adopted for the present because of the war effort.

L'HEXAGON ÉTENDU

The colonial empire enjoyed great support at the end of World War II. "Without the Empire France is nothing but a liberated country, thanks to the Empire, she is a conquering country," declared deputy Gaston Monnerville in May 1944. Another deputy added, "One can certainly live without colonies. Only do you want France . . . to fall to the level of a Portugal." It was from the Empire that the liberation of France was launched, and colonial troops had contributed significantly to the military effort. "The black soldier, starting from Chad, entered Strasbourg after having passed through Paris and demonstrates the spirit of all France," a colonial officer wrote. Voltaire once derided France for colonizing only "acres of snow" in Canada, but in March 1945 a deputy wrote, "The history of the acres of snow becoming one of the globe's richest mining regions should serve as a lesson to us."[9] Who knew what riches lay in the Sahara and elsewhere awaiting discovery. France was at a crossroads, politicians of all schools agreed. With more than 100 million people in France and scattered around the globe it would be a world power; with only 40 million inside the Hexagon, it would be "la fin de la République."

Such sentiments ignored rising voices for greater political participation from overseas possessions. The Vietnamese wanted independence. Algerians asked for universal suffrage, a constitution, independence, and association with an Arab (not a French) federation. In Morocco, heavy-handed French police tactics in arresting Istiqlal (Freedom) party political leaders as German collaborators backfired, and nationalists demonstrated in the streets of several towns. News of the repression of workers in Douala and Conakry spread quickly through francophone Africa, as did accounts of the massacre of several thousand Algerians in Guelma and Sétif, near Constantine. (The reporting that appeared in the French press ignored the political aspect of these uprisings, calling them pro-German demonstrations or "uprisings caused by famine.") In 1946 Malagasy separatists and Cameroonian nationalists launched direct appeals to the new United Nations. France could no longer keep the lid on its colonial conflicts.[10]

THE WINDS OF CHANGE

The reforms that emerged a few years later were packaged as a *Union française*, but they came too late. The postwar world was one in which colonial empires were viewed with widespread suspicion. The United Nations and the Universal Declaration of Human Rights made individual rights and political freedom global principles. Despite General de Gaulle's enormous prestige, he operated in difficult political circumstances, with a war-weary country, the specter of Vichy capitulation, the losses of Syria and Lebanon, unrest in Madagascar and North Africa, and growing guerrilla warfare in Vietnam. It is too easy, in retrospect, to fault French policies of the late 1940s and 1950s. They tried to compromise with the inevitable. No French politician in a seat of power could advocate independence, yet North African, Vietnamese, and African leaders by the 1950s could ask for nothing less. When political forces collided, results were swift and unpredictable, but soon the players rearranged themselves within their political space and the drama moved to its conclusion: the emergence of independent states.

A FRENCH-LED FEDERATION?

The word "federation" had been raised at the Brazzaville Conference as the future shape of France's relations with its overseas empire, but it met with stubborn resistance in postwar constitutional deliberations. One deputy stated, "Federation or not, the word is not important; they must solder" the Empire to France. The former Socialist minister Jules Moch was explicit, "I will not allow French delegates to be placed in the minority by black chiefs. . . . I am hostile to giving the same rights to black chiefs as to French representatives. . . . I do not want Queen Makoko to overthrow the French government." "France must not become the colony of its former colonies," another deputy cautioned.[11]

Two equally compelling reasons explain France's failure to engage in political power sharing with overseas peoples. One was openly expressed; France did not want to lose political control. The other was widespread racism, a centuries-old distrust of foreigners, Jews, Arabs, blacks, and Orientals among large segments of the population. Various plans were floated for discussion, ranging from adding colonial deputies to parliament to giving colonies no more than consultative status. Martinique, Guadeloupe, Réunion, and French Guiana became departments of France on March 19, 1946. Some residents celebrated this as "the most important decision since the decrees abolishing slavery in 1848" for their future status was now clear.[12] Articles 77 and 78 of the 1946 constitution provided for elected territorial assemblies that could raise taxes and vote budgets, although real power remained with the governor. The enabling documents from 1946 until the end of empire were as filled with holes as Swiss cheese. Porous and contradictory, they gave participation to overseas peoples but kept ultimate power with France, tossing off lofty constitutional principles that could be annulled by local decrees, ordinances, and extralegal practices.

As might be expected, the result of the postwar talks, the proposed *Union française*, was a compromise that satisfied no one. Algerian and Malagasy delegates called it "a cage that no one would enter"; Maghrebian journalists, "a

Tower of Babel which collapsed before even the construction was completed." When a French constitutional referendum was held in October 1946, the draft faced massive abstentions (32%) and passed by a narrow margin, with strong overseas opposition.[13] Nevertheless, the union idea persisted and led a half-life until 1954 and the fall of Dien Bien Phu. No one believed in it, but no more viable possibility was offered and France kept the chimera of union alive until, one by one, the states it was supposed to attract declared their independence.

The union had no precedents in international law as a political or legal entity. Its compromises displayed the work of many hands, especially supporters of assimilation and federation. The preamble spoke of a union of nations and peoples "sharing in common their resources and efforts." Article 60 defined membership including metropolitan France and its ex-colonies on one hand, and associated territories on the other, a way of incorporating the League of Nations mandate territories, Cameroon and Togo. Associated states included Indochina and the North African protectorates. A special citizenship status for other French Union members was prescribed, but its content was never clear and it attracted no supporters. The proposed legislative bodies were powerless and the assembly could only consider projects referred to it. A High Council of States had a vague mandate to "assist the government in the conduct of the Union."

Putting the various drafts on union and community of these years side by side demonstrates how sieve-like they were, filled with rhetoric about unity and destiny, but without specifics or timetables for real power sharing, and always leaving an escape route for France. Anger, demonstrations, terrorist acts, mistrust, and rejection were the responses of colonial peoples; the French replied with arrests, censorship, deportations, and rule by decree, which further polarized divisions. Both sides ended in a prickly impasse; the French generally changed local governors and military commanders, waited a few years, then agreed to the country's demands. France never wanted to give its overseas territories independence and did so only when there was no other possibility. President Vincent Auriol stated, "I am for giving them the appearance of power and for refusing them the reality [of it]."[14] But he fooled no one.

French political parties likewise reflected the country's equivocal attitude toward the colonies. Socialists were anticolonial when out of power, but more cautious when in office, never envisioning a France without colonies. In the formative 1945–1947 period, the party was accused of offering "that melange of emancipatory phraseology and an incapacity mentally to accept emancipation."[15] Rhetoric oscillated between greater inclusiveness for colonies and cautioning against "fanaticism," supporting "retrograde nationalism," or "separatism, prone to consort with the Stalinists." The Union démocratique et socialiste de la Résistance (UDSR) was another broad-based party, which counted young François Mitterrand among its leaders. A principal political bridge to the overseas world, it claimed ties to both the Indépendants d'outre-mer, which attracted the poet-politician Léopold Sédar Senghor, and the Rassemblement démocratique africain (RDA) whose leader was Félix Houphouët-Boigny, an

Ivory Coast planter and politician. Mitterrand in 1953 articulated the party's support for a moderate evolution of France's overseas possessions "on condition that they respect the military, diplomatic, and economic unity of the French Union."[16]

While the UDSR had ties with Africans overseas, the radical-right party was the party of the *colons* in Algeria and Morocco. Turning back the clock to prewar days was its program, plus nostalgia for Third Republic colonialism as *une grande oeuvre de la civilisation*. Others hesitantly supported revolution, but the radicals said, "We have taken off the baby's diapers before it knows how to walk."[17] For them, the French union was France's "last chance." The Mouvement républicain populaire (MRP) party remained in power for five and one-half years in two different governments, during which Dien Bien Phu fell. One of the few parties with an overseas constituency, it tried unsuccessfully to reconcile innovators like Robert Schuman with traditionalists like Georges Bidault, but it could not reconcile the two positions. With a vagueness typical of the time, the party platform called for a French union *indivisible mais diverse*. Ironically, it was General de Gaulle's party, the Rassemblement du peuple français, that called for "the transformation of the Empire organized in a federative form."[18]

* * *

The international setting of the 1940s and 1950s was not the same as the prewar world for France's overseas empire, but French politicians did not initially grasp this situation. It was as if the gates of the *chasse gardée* (game park) had been opened in several directions, and the once-private preserve would never be the same. Specifically, the United Nations, the United States, and the international labor movement helped open the French Empire to new ideas and political possibilities. Always suspicious of the intentions of others, French politicians were angry at what was happening but powerless to prevent the unfolding of postwar history.

THE UNITED NATIONS

Nothing was more resented by French politicians than the spotlight the United Nations turned on the dark corners of its colonial empire. Syria and Lebanon escaped from being French protectorates and became founding members of the United Nations. Togo and Cameroon used the new international body as a forum to protest French policies. In October 1951 Asian and Arab states urged the General Assembly to investigate French violations of the Universal Declaration of Human Rights in Morocco, and in 1952 the Tunisian protectorate asked the Security Council to resolve differences between France and Tunisia. France kept fending off inquiries with parliamentary ripostes, but Arab and Asian countries found new ways to introduce them, always with accompanying publicity. In the end, some anodyne resolutions made it through the United Nations, but continual negative publicity left France looking like a reactionary power holding on to its colonies at all costs while the young nations of Asia and the Arab world were champions of a righteous cause.

THE UNITED STATES

Franklin Roosevelt was fascinated by France and North Africa. When the Allied invasion of North Africa was planned, Roosevelt made a recording in schoolboy French which was played over international shortwave radio announcing the event. The Atlantic Charter, jointly promulgated by Roosevelt and Churchill, followed the tradition of Woodrow Wilson's 14 Points, supporting self-government, sovereignty, and equal access to world trade. It gave colonial peoples a blueprint for the future. In Tunisia, the American consul, Hooker Doolittle, developed a personal friendship with many of the young nationalist politicians, and he helped Habib Bourguiba, who would later become Tunisia's president, flee to Egypt and escape the French. In the halcyon days before instant communication with Washington, Doolittle was relatively free to implement the broad policy goals of encouraging Tunisian self-determination, which he did with vigor. At French insistence, Doolittle was recalled, but not before he became a hero to a generation of Tunisian nationalists, and the direction of American policy was set, climaxing in an invitation for Bourguiba to visit the United States in 1946, which was shocking to the French. French anti-Americanism on overseas issues was evident in General Alphonse Juin's 1951 statement, shortly after the United States told him it had rejected his plan to remove the Sultan of Morocco. "It is a secret for no one that there is a vast conspiracy where the religious fanaticism and xenophobia of the Middle East joins with American anti-colonialism working actively to ruin our presence in North Africa. Wait now for a sensational appeal before the United Nations."[19]

THE LABOR MOVEMENT, INTERNATIONAL AND LOCAL

The activities of the International Labor Organization (ILO) challenged France's colonial policies in the 1940s and 1950s, adding further pressures toward decolonization. France's socialist government wanted to appear progressive, but many of its colonial practices would not bear scrutiny. The ILO did a great deal to internationalize social and labor issues through its annual conferences, reports, and periodic study missions, which directed the global spotlight on a colonial power's labor practices. Originally the French resisted such attention, calling it interference in a country's internal affairs, but gradually France itself began to participate in ILO surveys of employment and family conditions, maternity benefits, social insurance, worker safety, pensions and retirement benefits, and the nexus of migratory labor issues.

The growing international influence of French labor unions also affected conditions overseas. The Confédération internationale des syndicats libres (CISL), backed by the powerful AFL-CIO unions and the American government, sought to combat Communist influence in the international trade union movement and support "the rights of people to national independence and governmental autonomy."[20] Tunisian trade unionists joined with the CISL, believing it could exert influence on the French government in support of independence. When French terrorists assassinated the Tunisian labor leader Fahrat Hached of the Union générale des travailleurs tunisiens (UGTT), American and North African trade unionists redoubled their support for political emancipation. Nothing was delicate or diplomatic in the trade unionists' approach. They pushed hard for political independence, better salaries, and improved working conditions. Strikes, demonstrations, and inflammatory leaflets were their weapons. For colonial administrators trying to keep the lid on a volatile political setting, the unions were a constant irritant. Communist unions supported traditional French government colonial policies, believing a French colonial system was preferable to the rise of nationalism, which would open the door to American influence and, in North Africa, Moslem feudalism. "The European proletariat benefited from the colonial regime," Senghor wrote in 1959. "They never really, I want to say effectively, opposed it."[21] It was not until 1949 that the Confédération générale du travail (CGT), the Communist union, launched an appeal for peace in Vietnam and for recalling the French expeditionary corps. In Algeria workers denounced "the metropolitan unions and the worker's aristocracy of the CGT." The third union, the Catholic-backed Confédération internationale des syndicats chrétiens (CFTC), hoped to remain apolitical, but in reality it contained members both who opposed colonialism and who supported it.

Labor unions in such places as French West Africa helped redefine the social landscape in two major strikes of the 1940s. From December 1945 to February 1946, African workers struck in Dakar. Although there were 15 thousand wage workers in the capital, not all went out on strike, nor did all groups, including civil servants, commercial sector employees, and dock workers, strike at the same time. However, African trade unionists, skilled at the interplay of negotiations, quickly picked up the vocabulary of French syndicalism and the categories of labor demands, and they struck for improved wages, family allowances, and regional cost-of-living adjustments. The issue of comparable pay for comparable work done by Africans and Europeans was brought to the table. The French government was trapped by its own egalitarian rhetoric, having called for equal treatment of all people with comparable qualifications. Its strategy was to redefine the strike's parameters. As a quick fix, substantial wage increases were offered in hopes that wider issues would be dropped but, as Frederick Cooper wrote, "the terrain would quickly be seized by African trade unionists demanding full equality of family allowances in private and public alike."[22]

The second significant strike, one with an even wider impact, was the French

West African railways strike of October 1947–March 1948, which affected nearly 20 thousand workers in Senegal, Sudan, Dahomey, Guinea, and the Ivory Coast. In this case, the strikers' goal was to achieve economic parity with French workers in the *métropole*. As before, a key issue was the *cadre unique*, the basic demand for similar benefits for African and French workers, a concession that was agreed to by the state-controlled corporation's management (but not by the union of French workers). With consummate timing, the union called for a strike coinciding with the visit of the president of the French Republic and of the minister of colonial affairs to Senegal. Negotiations over implementation of the accord broke down, and the strike began on October 10, 1947, lasting, with few exceptions, until March 19, 1948. The strike worked hardships on the workers, their families, and communities, as depicted in Ousmanne Sembe's novel *God's Bits of Wood* (1960). All major African politicians distanced themselves publicly from the strikers but expressed personal sympathy with their cause. Eventually, Felix Houphouët-Boigny helped negotiate an early end to Ivory Coast's participation in the strike; then a new governor-general, the socialist politician Paul Bécard, held negotiations that brought the strike to an end. By now the railway workers had a real voice in West African economic and political relations. The strike had many characteristics of similar disputes in more politically experienced societies; the workers won major concessions, but the government held. Neither military repression nor revolution resulted. Both sides went face-to-face, survived, and emerged in a relationship different from what they had known in the past.[23]

No less important were the disturbances reported at camps for recently discharged troops or former prisoners of war. The most serious such incident took place on December 1, 1944, near Dakar where more than one thousand former POWs mutinied to protest their failure to receive substantial back pay sums and premiums due them. The French response was swift and brutal. At Thiaroye barracks, 35 Africans were killed and others wounded. Insurrectionists were paraded through the streets, tried, convicted, and sentenced to prison terms before being pardoned by a general amnesty in June 1947. News of the revolt and its repression spread quickly by letter, official circulars, and bush telegraph (word of mouth) throughout West Africa. Most French administrators, and some Africans working for them, defended the French response as important to maintaining discipline and public order, but others, like the rising politician Lamine Guèyre, a respected Senegalese attorney, and Léopold Sédar Senghor, an ex-POW and writer and politician, defended the aggrieved veterans. Thiaroye's impact was deep; Africans, many of whom had fought as well or better than French soldiers, and who had suffered the brutalities of internment, felt betrayed. The French government offered no positive response; in fact, it asked administrators to monitor the activities of ex-POWs. It was not until a changed postwar political climate and the rise of African political parties that African veterans received greater freedoms and more substantial pensions.[24]

FRENCH INTELLECTUALS AND OVERSEAS ÉVOLUÉS

French intellectuals rarely took public positions on colonial political issues until the fall of Dien Bien Phu and later the Algerian war. Rare exceptions included André Gide's criticism of African working conditions based on a trip through parts of Central Africa and André Malraux's novel *La Condition humaine* and other writings. The word *décolonisation*, translated from English, was not used until 1952, the same year the expression *tiers monde* (Third World) appeared. French intellectuals, mostly of the left, were often members of the French Communist party, which claimed to be the intellectual's party. Writers of all political tendencies weighed in on the colonial issue after Dien Bien Phu. François Mauriac, a well-known writer of the Catholic right, spoke of "the vocation of Christians to confront racism, born of fear and greed" and, as events unfolded in the Maghreb, wrote that "justice in North Africa remains the only policy open to France."[25] A few publications, like *Esprit* and *Témoigne chrétien*, began to write about colonial issues, but their circulation was small and their audience largely Christian intellectuals. At the same time, academics like the sociologist, Paul Mus, an expert on Vietnam, and the historian Charles-André Julien, a specialist on Algeria, took anticolonial positions based on their deep knowledge of their subject matter. In contrast, the novelist Jules Romains was an enthusiast for the French Union.

Colonial issues attracted almost no attention in the popular press, but Raymond Aron, one of the best known journalists of the 1950s, wrote lucidly on the subject, taking the unpopular position that France must abandon Indochina if it wanted to consolidate interests in Africa, and that all colonial empires were in a state of decomposition. He said the problem was what to do next, to have *le courage d'innover* (the courage to innovate). Equally important for a decade or so was the work of the influential journalist Raymond Cartier. An original proponent of African independence, Cartier later took a "France first" line, arguing that France would do better to create an Office de la Loire instead of an Office de la Niger to spearhead a massive development plan. In 1964 Cartier published three articles in the mass-circulation magazine *Paris Match*. Armed with statistics about the waste of French aid, he argued that rural France was an undeveloped country: "8 million French get their water from wells as in the year 1,000." "Better Brittany than Dahomey," he added. In Abidjan he found 10 thousand phone lines built without subscribers, while in France hundreds of thousands of persons were without a telephone. Cartier carefully pointed out he was not opposed to all foreign aid, but he wanted it reduced to 1% of the French national budget. French government ministries responded with a flurry of pamphlets defending their actions while opponents of foreign aid had more than enough anecdotes to share with one another about how their taxes were being wasted by new African leaders, whom they called "black kings."[26]

An emerging generation of indigenous writers offered a more substantial view of the overseas world and its complex cultures. These included Senghor's writings on *négritude*, the publication *Présence africaine*, and the political writings of the Martinique poet and politician Aimé Césaire, whose book *Cahier d'un retour au pays natal* became a rallying point for intellectuals in Africa and the Antilles. The plays and novels of a handful of brilliant Algerian writers and Antillian and African intellectuals, including the Haitian writer Jacques Roumain and the Cameroonian Mongo Beti, demonstrated to French readers the creative contribution of overseas societies until then largely ignored.[27]

ÉVOLUÉS

All over the empire a class of *évolués* emerged, people who had studied or worked in France, yet who felt the pangs of discrimination and racism daily in their own countries. General de Gaulle acknowledged their importance in the larger context of the quest for independence when he wrote, "In addition to bringing our civilization we have instituted, in each of our territories, in place of the anarchic divisions of other times, a centralized system prefiguring a national state, and forming elites penetrated with our principles of human rights and liberty and avid to replace us all along the hierarchies."[28]

THE FOURTH REPUBLIC, 1946–1958

After only two months in power, in January 1946, General de Gaulle, not used to not having his way, resigned as head of a coalition government. A constitution was accepted by referendum that October, bringing the Fourth Republic to life for the next 12 years. By now France had developed a three-phase Pavlovian policy reflex to colonial problems. First, there would be overseas petitions, beginning with a modest request for more autonomy, suffrage, or participation in the councils of government. Next would come a vague French reply about giving the country a voice within the greater French political system. The colony's indigenous leadership would reply with demands for independence, often accompanied by terrorist acts. France would respond with force, and an impasse would follow. Finally, France would grudgingly accept the demands of its colonial people, and independence would come within a few years.

The Fourth Republic's colonial policy was a creature of France's cumbersome political structure. Like the Third Republic, it was a barely working parliamentary system, characterized by frequent governmental changes, numerous political parties, a weak presidency, and an impotent bureaucracy. Postwar recovery was the main task facing the nation, and during the late 1940s and 1950s France concentrated on domestic priorities. Entrenched interest groups stymied most colonial reform legislation, as in 1947 when reform of working conditions was successfully blocked by colonial business interests. Only African strikes in 1953 forced their passage in a revised form. Proposals to create local assemblies, decentralize colonial administration, or modify chiefs' roles took several years to pass the French legislature, and they often were overcome by events. African leaders, believing the French were stalling, increased their demands. It was the Cold War now and French politicians who proposed a solution to the Indochinese problem or who wanted to give greater power to Africans could be accused of sympathizing with Moscow. In 1954 overseas French numbered 1.7 million persons including naturalized citizens, 1.5 million in the Maghreb (1,200,000 in Algeria alone), 80 thousand in Africa, 47 thousand in Madagascar, and 30 thousand in Indochina.[29]

MADAGASCAR

In March 1947 Madagascar was shaken by what the former Minister of Colonies Jacques Soustelle described as *"dangereuses éruptions de séparatisme"* (dangerous eruptions of separatism) but which local people called *fikomiana* or "insurrection." Outwardly, Madagascar looked like a tropical "magic island" where peaceful, happy local peoples worked for benevolent colonial masters. However, after the British occupied the island during World War II, French prestige had plummeted. Malagasy troops and treasure had contributed to the war effort with no visible rewards, and the example of growing Indian and South Asian independence movements was there for all to see. Local politicians, backed by numerous secret societies and by Malagasy living in Paris, began advocating independence from France. On March 21, 1946, a proposal went before the Constituent Assembly, an advisory body, abrogating the annexation of Madagascar by France and declaring the country a free state within the French Union. Shortly thereafter Malagasy politicians demanded a popular referendum offering three choices: autonomy, independence, or departmentalization. Surprised by this audacious move, France responded with a divide-and-conquer strategy. Employing Joseph-Simon Gallieni's *politique des races*, they created five territorial assemblies structured along ethnic lines, trying to play the Merina people, located in the interior, against coastal tribes.[30]

During the night of March 29, 1947, hundreds of insurgents struck in a carefully orchestrated campaign. Reviving the old red-and-white flag of the Merina monarchy, to which they added 18 stars, one for each of the island's major tribes, they attacked towns, armed installations, and administrative centers and massacred 180 French military and colonial officials, opposition politicians, and Malagasy *fonctionnaires* loyal to France. France denounced "that democracy imposed by blood" and counterattacked with North African troops sent to reinforce French garrisons. Meanwhile, the insurgents withdrew to thick forests in the island's interior. By November 1948 the armed rebellion was over. Military and civil courts condemned 183 persons to death (27 were executed) and 5,122 persons were found guilty of participating in the uprising. According to French statistics, 11,162 Malagasy died in the encounters: 4,126 were killed in action, 1,646 were killed by the insurgents, and the others died from other causes, including tropical illnesses.[31] The violent events only confirmed Malagasy determination for independence. The French recognized this. General Pellet declared, "The word independence from now on is written in the spirit and heart of the majority of Malagasys." The opposing viewpoint was voiced by François Mitterrand, at that time minister of France for overseas, on January 4, 1951, in Tananarive, "It is not going to be a question of changing Madagascar's statute." The impasse continued until 1953 when the island's Roman Catholic bishops issued a statement supporting legitimate Malagasy aspirations for independence; by then, the trend was irreversible. Independence came on June 26, 1960.[32]

INDOCHINA

"The flower of the colonial Empire," Vietnam was promised "a proper liberty" and participation in France's federal organisms. The improvised plan General de Gaulle put forth on March 24, 1945, was for an "Indochina Federation" within a "French Union," although because they were of different civilizations, races, and traditions, the tripartite division of Tonkin, Annam, and Cochin China would remain, creating three separate "countries." There was no provision for Vietnam to accept or reject this arrangement. As a fillip, France dangled the promise of equal access to government jobs for Vietnamese, economic autonomy, trade unions, and industrialization. As usual in such arrangements, France would retain control over the country's defense and foreign affairs, the governor-general would be the arbiter of local differences, and the French Constituent Assembly would determine the ultimate conditions of political participation.

However, in August 1945, as part of the postwar settlement, the Allied powers met at Potsdam and partitioned Vietnam, frustrating Vietnamese aspirations for a role in the governing of their country, and irritating the French, who regarded Vietnam as their own protectorate. The Allied plan divided the country at the Sixteenth Parallel, giving control of the north to the Chinese and the south to the British. The arrangement did not last long. In the south, the small British forces soon withdrew, and in 1946 General Philippe Leclerc became military commander when the French returned. In the north, the Chinese recognized Ho Chi Minh as head of the Vietnamese government and would not let the French return until after February 28, 1946, when France and China reached an accord giving China commercial concessions on the Yunnan-Hanoi Railway and special status for Chinese nationals living in Indochina.

The French hold on Indochina was precarious. Admiral Jean Decoux, the governor-general from 1940 to 1945, had walked a fine line between accommodating a vastly superior Japanese force and pleasing his Vichy superiors. Although Vichy France was nominally part of the Axis, Decoux, as much a traditional French naval officer as a Vichy collaborator, played a waiting game at the Empire's edge. Japanese demands were heavy, including transit rights to China through northern Tonkin to attack Chiang Kai-shek's Nationalist forces, bases for 25 thousand troops, and steadily mounting requests for rice, rubber, and other commodities. Later Japanese demands broadened to include stationing forces in Cochin China and Cambodia and launching bases for planned invasions of the Philippines, Singapore, and Malaysia. Decoux, with no cards of his own to play, gradually conceded to their demands, as he would for the next four years. At best he could stall and refer questions to headquarters at Vichy for negotiation there.[33]

While sparring with the Japanese, Decoux decided that Vietnamese nationalists must be put down decisively and not be allowed to threaten French rule or make common cause with the Japanese. To this end, he sent Foreign Legion units to burn suspected rebel villages in Cochin China where more than 2 thousand suspects were arrested. Nationalism was in the air by now, and the countryside was full of political, religious, and social groups supporting independence. Their ideologies ranged from a simple desire to rid the country of foreigners of any kind to syncretic amalgams of thought combining Confucian beliefs, Asian nationalism, and French socialism, as in the teachings of the Cao Dai sect, which Decoux viewed with particular suspicion. Many of the groups were barely organized, and some were unaware of the activities of others; still others, like those led by Ho Chi Minh, were built around closely interacting secret cells. French intelligence sources were active, drawing on a countrywide network of paid and voluntary informants. Crackdowns, raids, and interrogations were frequent, but ideas are notoriously hard to imprison and in the end the admiral had little to show for his efforts to extinguish the spread of nationalism.

Decoux had marginally better success in rallying the resident French community to the Vichy cause, and he made a brave effort to win Vietnamese support as well. He employed the standard panoply of nationalistic parades and pageants, literary prizes, art shows, and youth and sports training camps (many future Viet Minh officers were among the participants). The French colonists formed scouting and youth groups, including Jeannettes, named for Joan of Arc; and a 4,100-kilometer Tour d'Indochine cycling race across all of Indochina each year, from 1942 to 1944, was designed to encourage patriotism, while leaving *pneu crevé* (flat tires) across Tonkin, Annam, Cochin China, Cambodia, and Laos. Decoux increased salaries for both French and Vietnamese government officials, and Vietnamese were promoted to responsible administrative positions, less from a desire to install equal employment policies than because the war had diminished the number of French available for such jobs.

It all rang hollow, however, and when the Japanese sprang a military takeover during the night of March 9, 1945, the curtain rang down on Vichy Vietnam. Not that the end was easy. More than 200 French officers and 4 thousand French and Vietnamese soldiers were killed or massacred resisting the Japanese, who moved brutally and effectively to disarm their former "ally." French women and children were used as shields when Japanese units stormed one French fort, and at another the garrison was machined-gunned to death, while singing the *Marseillaise*. Beheadings, concentration camps, and "monkey cages" for prisoners were all part of the Japanese repertoire.[34]

Parenthetically, President Franklin Roosevelt was strongly opposed to the reassertion of French control in Indochina after the war. His sporadic, unfocused comments never constituted a distinct policy statement, but there was no mistaking his anticolonial attitude. Roosevelt did not want American Lend-Lease equipment used to prop up a colonial regime he despised. He told his son Elliott that Indochina had been "liberated in main part by American arms and American troops, and should never simply be handed back to the French to be milked by their imperialists." Later, when he met with de Gaulle, Roosevelt, with the magnanimous gestures he was given to, offered to send de Gaulle skilled Filipino public administration experts to assist France in establishing "a more progressive policy in Indochina." The offer was met with stony silence.[35]

Reflecting Roosevelt's position, the American field commander General Albert Wheyer, assigned to the China command as American chief of staff, was "profoundly hostile to the Gaullist resistance inside Indochina which he judged both corrupt and ineffective."[36] American policy opposed the reassertion of French rule and backed Chiang Kai-shek. However, according to diplomatic-military historian Martin Thomas, "Despite the high quality of information from its own OSS operatives throughout Indochina, the US government failed to appreciate that, while the Viet Minh loathed the French, it feared Chinese expansionism still more. . . . Backing Chiang Kai-shek to offset French or British regional dominance was a policy doomed to failure."[37]

Meanwhile, always suspicious of American intentions, de Gaulle feared the prospect of American troops landing in Saigon and Hanoi without French forces accompanying them. American policy toward Vietnam was left undefined with Roosevelt's death in April 1945. It is an open question as to what Roosevelt would have done had he lived. Americans were quickly tiring of the war effort. The restoration of a French empire was supported by Roosevelt's close collaborator Winston Churchill, who once declared he "had not become the King's First Minister to preside over the liquidation of the British Empire." Would the stubborn and brilliantly impulsive Roosevelt have stayed with his views, or would he have adroitly compromised, as he did so often? The question is the sort that appears on history examinations, but we will never know the answer.

Doc-Lap

When the French returned to power after World War II they faced a determined, carefully organized independence movement, which they refused to take seriously. Ho Chi Minh, a leading Communist politician and resistance hero, led the League for Vietnamese Independence, the Viet Minh. The Viet Minh goal was straightforward: unconditional *doc-lap* (independence). In his Independence Day speech on September 2, 1945, Ho Chi Minh quoted from both the American Declaration of Independence of 1776 and the French Declaration of the Rights of Man and the Citizen of 1791. He chronicled the shortcomings of 80 years of colonialism, its dividing of the country into three parts, the exploitation of land and plundering of mineral wealth, the opium and alcohol sales designed "to weaken our race," and finally France's sellout to Japan. Ho announced he was canceling all treaty obligations signed by the French and was "determined to oppose every plot of the French colonists." He closed with an appeal to the Allied powers (never answered) to support Vietnamese indepen- dence, referring to the exalted language adopted at the Tehran and San Francisco conferences. A French intelligence analyst reported the Independence Day speech as "a bastard combination of bookish internationalism and chauvinistic patriotism, a melange of intellectual Marxism and primitive social demands, corresponding exactly to the aspirations of a section of the backward masses of these Asiatic deltas."[38]

Ho Chi Minh

Ho Chi Minh (he who enlightens), whose Communist guerrilla troops entered Hanoi on August 19, 1945, was partially a product of French colonialism and a rejection of it. Little is certain about his early life, for he was skilled in throwing others off his biographic trail, as befits a revolutionary who spent his first half-century on the move, fleeing police and dodging pursuers. His reported birth year of 1890 is speculative, as are the numerous aliases he used. He was born in the central Vietnamese province of Nghé An, and his father was a minor figure in the traditional imperial administration who, after being dismissed for anti-French activities, finished life as a practitioner of herbal medicine. After attending a village school, Ho attended for several years the prestigious Quoc- Hoc lycée in Hué, founded by an imperial court official desirous of educating a new local elite with Western ideas but free of French indoctrination. After leaving school, apparently for his anti-French activities, he obtained work in Saigon as a *plongeur* (the word meant "diver" or "dishwasher" in French) and as an apprentice pastry cook. This led to jobs on French ships that took him to Europe, America, and along the West African coast. Eventually he was a night cook's assistant at London's Carlton Hotel, where the famed chef Escoffier promoted him to pastry cook. While in America he apparently lived briefly in Harlem. When he later moved to Moscow he wrote a pamphlet called *La Race Noire* (The black race) which was sharply critical of European and American racial practices.

At World War I's end he returned to Paris and became active in socialist politics, supporting himself through his skills with Chinese ink brushes as a photo retoucher and cartoonist in left-wing newspapers. He became a founding member of the French Communist party on December 20, 1920, and in 1924 he moved to Moscow where he attended the University of the Toilers of the East, wrote anti-French articles, sometimes signing them "Nguyen Who Hates the French." An active practitioner rather than a theoretician, he was sent to Canton in December 1924 to recruit, organize, and train Vietnamese exiles as Communist cadre members. Along the way he acquired fluency in French, Rus- sian, English, and three Chinese dialects. His life at this time was one of intense party activity, hiding from the police, being arrested, and making appearances in Moscow (once via the Gobi desert).

Schooled in the world of Moscow tactics and organization of the 1920s and 1930s, Ho tolerated no opposition. Ruthless in liquidating mandarins, intellectuals, leaders of religious sects, and anti-Communist nationalists who stood in his way, he branded opponents "traitors to Vietnam" or "internal enemies of the regime." A convenient way to remove them was to tip French security agents off about their expected arrival at the border. A master propagandist, Ho had immense skills in shaping his message for whatever audience he was dealing with and persuading them to make common cause with him. Pictures of the time show an ascetic figure with alert eyes dressed in simple peasant attire, wearing the familiar Ho Chi Minh rubber sandals cut from used-vehicle tires, the hallmark of peasant farmers and guerrilla fighters in the region. During the winter of 1944–1945 Ho and his close associates courted the American Office of Strategic Services (OSS) South China delegation. American officers accompanied him on his return to Hanoi, and the American flag was flown over their residence, suggesting a degree of cooperation that was not there, but which apparently led the Emperor Bao Dai and his backers to turn over the reins of government to Ho's forces without a struggle.[39]

Americans in the OSS unit working with the Viet Minh urged support for the Vietnamese to the exclusion of the French and Chinese, but Roosevelt was dead now, and a pragmatic Harry Truman had other concerns. France was closer than Indochina, the possibility of cooperation with Ho was dropped, and the agile Vietnamese leader turned elsewhere, to France in the short term and to the Soviet Union for the duration.[40]

In opposition to the highly disciplined, battle-seasoned Ho Chi Minh, the French backed an ineffectual playboy-prince, Bao Dai, who never succeeded in gaining popular support. Militarily, the French never had enough troops to secure the Vietnamese countryside. When Marshal Leclerc led the return of French forces in 1945 it was with 40 thousand soldiers, a small number of troops considering the vast and difficult terrain. The same techniques used in Algeria were employed: *quadrillage*, dividing the countryside into grids, and *ratissage*, raking over the designated area with troops familiar with the terrain and its inhabitants. As soon as the French troops moved on, however, the Viet Minh returned. For several months in 1947 the French army concentrated on Operation Léa, a futile effort to track down Ho Chi Minh. By 1949 the Communist forces were moving freely about the countryside, and the French Army Chief of Staff, General Georges Revers, recommended withdrawal of French troops to the populous, food-producing delta, the so-called *Vietnam utile* (useful Vietnam).

Viet Minh military control of the north gradually expanded, aided by neighboring China, and by 1950 most of the northern part of North Vietnam was in Communist hands. French and colonial troop losses were high; 125 thousand casualties by 1951. Alarmed by the casualty rates, French politicians withdrew 9 thousand soldiers from Vietnam and ordered that French draftees not be assigned to the "police action" there, which further crippled the military effort. The North Vietnamese forces were led by General Vo Nguyen Giap, arguably one of the 20th century's great military commanders, who gradually moved from guerrilla warfare to large-unit tactics as China made more sophisticated weapons available to Vietnam. France appealed for, and received, American financial and material aid, but it was too late.

Dien Bien Phu, the Final Battle

The momentous confrontation came at an isolated air base in North Vietnam, west of Hanoi in a mountainous region covered by thick jungle growth. From a tactical viewpoint, Dien Bien Phu was the worst possible location for France. Isolated and hard to defend, it was of little strategic worth. France had picked it initially as part of a well-intentioned but ill-conceived "land–air base" strategy that would allow highly mobile units to attack quickly behind enemy lines. French forces were few, however, and the enemy was everywhere. The strategy did not work. Additionally, the French underestimated the extent to which the Viet Minh could rain down a merciless stream of artillery fire on the base from well-camouflaged batteries in the nearby hills. General Giap's strategy was a mixture of classical French siege warfare, modern artillery fire, and human-wave troop attacks. The final battle began on March 13, 1954, and ended on May 7; it was said that the French survived for 54 days on instant coffee and cigarettes. Monsoon rains poured down and supplies were hard to come by, as the advancing Vietnamese forces gradually reduced the French bases' landing zone and accurate Viet Minh antiaircraft fire forced the French to drop supplies from an altitude of 8,500 feet. Even the French general's stars and congratulatory bottle of champagne dropped for his battle field promotion landed in enemy territory. French forces were led by Colonel Christian de Castries, a specialist in cavalry and light-armor operations, a daring and impulsive officer ill prepared for siege warfare in a tropical setting. Isolated in his bunker, de Castries dined each evening off family silver set on a crisp white tablecloth, but meanwhile he had lost the confidence of his senior commanders.[41]

The French garrison at Dien Bien Phu had been strengthened to 16 thousand troops, including *Légionnaires* whose numbers included a sizable contingent of German troops who had joined them at the end of World War II, plus Moroccans, Algerians, and Senegalese. Emperor Bao Dai's Vietnamese soldiers were some of the last reinforcements to parachute into the doomed garrison, knowing full well what fate awaited them at the hands of the Viet Minh. Giap had three times as many soldiers as his opponent, plus more than 200 artillery pieces, and an overwhelming strategic advantage.

The French loss of 10 thousand troops and their defeat at Dien Bien Phu marked the end of an era, comparable to the 1905 Japanese victory over the Russian fleet during the Russo-Japanese war, for it sent a message that European powers could be defeated by Asians. By the war's end the French Union forces had sustained 172 thousand casualties, the Viet Minh possibly three times that amount, and another 250 thousand Vietnamese civilians had been killed.[42] Ironically, the French army learned little from its loss in this war of national liberation; its officers moved on to Algeria, determined to gun down and thereby subdue the nebulous spirit of rising nationalism there.

Playing Out the String

The Geneva Conference on the country's future status opened on May 7, the day Dien Bien Phu fell. Negotiations continued until an agreement was signed on July 21, which divided the country into two halves and precipitated a period of further crisis. The accords included a barely maintained cease-fire supervised by an ineffectual International Armistice Control Commission composed of representatives from India, Poland, and Canada. The seventeenth parallel of latitude was to be the temporary boundary until general elections, but the elections were never held. In a preconference statement, the French and the puppet ruler Bao Dai jointly announced a declaration of independence. The ploy had the opposite result from what France wanted. Northern moderates were squeezed from the government now increasingly in Communist hands. Southerners who wanted independence believed they could never find it without a complete break with France. By October 26, 1955, a Republic of Vietnam was proclaimed in the south, and the ineffectual Bao Dai gave way to the quixotic reign of Ngo Dinh Diem, a southern politician with strong Roman Catholic ties. The Vietnamese piastre moved from the franc to the dollar bloc, and the French Expeditionary Corps marched one last time through Saigon to its ships.

Launching the Democratic Republic of Vietnam, as the northern government called itself, was no less rocky. Northern Vietnam was better at fighting a war than governing in peacetime, and its leaders faced famine, a severely damaged irrigation system, and a destroyed road and railway network. Industrial development advice provided by the Soviets and Chinese was barely helpful, and in 1956 peasants revolted in Nghé An and elsewhere against repressive land and agricultural policies. The revolt was severely put down by the Communists. Purges similar to those conducted in other Communist countries removed any traces of nationalist opposition, the news media became government controlled, and the legislature failed to meet from November 1946 until May 1960, except for a single day in 1953 to pass a land-reform law. Over 600 thousand Roman Catholic refugees—65% of the total Catholic population in the north—fled south. Sometimes bishops and clergy led whole dioceses, carrying signs like the "Virgin Mary has departed from the North."[43]

Suppose for a moment that the Orientalist and colonial administrator of an earlier era P.-L.-F. Philastre were there to witness the French evacuation from Hanoi and Saigon. Head of the Office of Native Justice in the 1860s and the translator of the Gia Long legal code into French, Philastre was one of those remarkable figures who appeared from time to time in colonial administration—

one who provided a window into both cultures, French and indigenous. He was as close as France ever came to producing a scholar-mandarin, and in a lengthy memorandum he drew on long experience in colonial affairs to criticize French policy, particularly when the French were replacing a comprehensive indigenous legal code with one imported from France. Though written in 1873, his remarks could have been penned as the planes and ships were leaving Vietnam a century later after Dien Bien Phu:

It has become fashionable to shout out, in all manner of ways, that the Annamite population happily saw us come to deliver it from the oppression which weighed upon it and which it detested.

To say that the Annamites like all our reforms and are proud to live under our domination.

That has been said, said again, written, printed in all fashions, so well that these mistakes have become articles of faith and are generally believed in very good faith.

We have thus reached the point of talking and acting in an atmosphere of convention where our illusions and our desires are taken for reality.

The extraordinary resistance, sometimes violent, sometimes passive in nature, day by day more hateful, which is opposed to us by all classes of the people, is stronger today than at any time since the conquest. It requires, nevertheless, that we open our eyes.

We have proclaimed unceasingly that we respect the customs and the institutions of the conquered people. It was in proclaiming this respect that we required our enemies to lay down their arms, and we pitilessly violate these customs and institutions. . . .

The Annamites are very much aware of this situation, and I do not fear to affirm it, although with pain, to respect the truth, that far from progressing in the spirit of the population, we are less and less well regarded by the Annamites for whom we are no more than adventurers with an unrestrained greed, incapable of governing a people. *This is their own estimation.*[44] (Italics in original.)

MOROCCO AND TUNISIA

The French presence in Vietnam was now declining; North Africa would come next. In Morocco and Tunisia, the business at hand was to remove the long-existing protectorates. France reasoned that in these countries sovereignty rested in the person of the sovereign, not in a particular institution. Therefore, following a practice instigated by Louis-Hubert Lyautey, an uncooperative sovereign could be deposed for a more pliant one. This led to the exile of Bey Moncef in Tunisia (1943) and Sidi Mohammed ben Yousself in Morocco (1953). Meanwhile, the best France would offer Morocco was the possibility of membership in the French Union "in 20 or 21 years." The issue was forced when the sultan refused to sign several *dahirs* (decrees), as he must do to assure their legitimacy under terms of the protectorate, and pointedly ignored the French in a speech at Tangiers in which he alluded favorably to a Moroccan-Arab alliance. France responded in a heavy-handed manner. The choleric General Alphonse Juin, furious he did not have a ruler who could be *téléguidé*, told the sultan,

"You are not the Sultan of Morocco, you are the Sultan of the Istiqlal" political party and announced his support for a traditional rival to the sultan, the pacha of Marrakesh, el-Hadj Thami el-Glaoui, "the lord of the Atlas." Marshal Juin then presided over a "spontaneous" demonstration of 100 thousand Berbers and French-trained Arab troops in front of the royal palace as part of the build up to removing the sultan who, however, remained unmoved and rallied support from his backers.

By now, growing numbers of nationalists and students supported the monarch, who refused to sign more laws and asked France for a statute giving Morocco full sovereignty. The Quai d'Orsay, responsible for Moroccan affairs, failed to respond for six months while the influential *Paris Match* journalist Raymond Cartier wrote on February 1, 1953, *"Le sultan doit changer, ou il faut changer de sultan"* (The sultan should change, or change the sultan).[45] This was accomplished on August 20 by unilateral action of Foreign Minister Georges Bidault, although other cabinet ministers protested when they learned about it. Moroccan responses hardened. Acts of terrorism multiplied, much of the country refused to back the new *sultan des français*, and a state of civil war existed. France took a hard line; it would rather go to war than restore the sultan, now in exile in Madagascar, François Mitterrand declared, with slight exaggeration.

French efforts to stabilize Morocco failed, and 88 French and 700 Moroccans were killed as strikes and terrorist acts increased. The French settlers, fewer in number than in Algeria, formed a *présence française* as intransigent as the Algerian *colons*. The political climate continued to deteriorate, and neither the French *résident général* nor the puppet sultan had any effective power, so all parties did a volte-face and supported the deposed sultan's return. France offered a vague formula of "interdependence," which Moroccans rejected, and on March 2, 1956, granted independence to Morocco, although it retained control over the country's foreign affairs. This was probably because the Quai d'Orsay, which doggedly had held on to responsibility for Morocco and Tunisia for fifty years, feared an independent Moroccan foreign policy would mean collaboration with Algeria and Tunisia against French interests.[46]

In Tunisia, events followed a similar course. The "nationalist bey," Moncef Bey, was exiled in 1943 and died at the moment he might have been recalled. The Néo-Destour nationalist party, led by Habib Bourguiba, who had obtained a law degree in Paris and returned to Tunis and entered politics, seized the moment to campaign for a constitutional monarchy and universal suffrage. In June 1950 the French foreign minister, Robert Schuman, put wind in the sails of Tunisian nationalists by announcing that the mission of the new French *résident général*, Louis Périllier, was to lead Tunisia toward independence. Georges Bidault, president of the governing council, and member of a different political party, rushed to correct the headstrong Schuman. The resident, soon to be recalled, was given a text to read over Radio Tunis that said France would "progressively guide Tunisia toward internal autonomy," an intentionally vague French formula that satisfied no one, inflamed nationalists, and left French politicians with no clear idea of what would come next. In the absence of a policy, France rounded up the usual suspects. The main nationalist party, the Néo-Destour, had been dissolved, but terrorism and French repression grew and the country was a tinderbox. Bourguiba and other nationalists were arrested and exiled as France reasserted the protectorate's "definitive character."

Tunisians responded to French repression with terrorism, which was met with counterterrorism and 70 thousand French troops. Meanwhile, African and Asian states protested French actions before the United Nations Security Council, and tensions heightened with the execution of three nationalists who had been condemned to death. The Quai d'Orsay, embarrassed by growing international criticism, and not having a workable policy, launched a new reform plan, but only a complete change in the political climate would reduce tensions. This was achieved in July 1954 when Pierre Mendès-France announced that France recognized the internal autonomy, but not the independence, of Tunisia. At the bey's request, people renounced violence, and the Néo-Destour party agreed to participate in the government. A Franco-Tunisian protocol was signed on April 21, 1955. France ceded internal governance to the Tunisians but kept control of foreign affairs, the police, and the judiciary. The waiting period turned out to be shorter, however. Tunisian independence came on March 20, 1956, precipitated by Morocco's independence, which was announced in the La Celle-Saint-Cloud declaration of November 6, 1955.[47]

AFRICA

French policy in Africa was no more enlightened than in the Maghreb. Harsh reprisals were taken against protesters in Douala, Cameroon, and Conakry, Guinea; local chiefs, installed and kept in office by the French, were increasingly criticized by the emerging class of *évolués* who reminded the people that the chiefs' main responsibility was collecting taxes and finding bodies to send to war or to work on road gangs. Africans followed events in Cameroon and Togo where local peoples sent their grievances to the United Nations, mindful of their mandate status. The RDA political party gained widespread support in French West Africa. Originally an offshoot of the French Communist party, under the leadership of the moderate Ivory Coast politician Félix Houphouët-Boigny, it gradually moved toward independent political status and a leadership role among West Africa's 26 parties. Houphouët-Boigny, a Roman Catholic chief from the important Baoulé ethnic group, was a physician before he entered politics. He became a cabinet minister in the Mollet government, and in 1956 he was one of the principal drafters of the *loi-cadre*, which created modified executive and legislative governmental organizations in overseas territories, but which was superseded by formation of the Fifth Republic in 1958.[48]

Houphouët-Boigny, who had come from a slave-owning African family, became a leader in the effort to abolish forced labor. He was a leader in the Société agricole africaine (SAA), founded in 1944 with a membership that soon reached

5 thousand Ivory Coast coffee and cocoa planters. At the heart of the SAA's success were good labor contracts which offered one-third of the value of coffee and two-thirds of the value of cocoa harvested, free transportation, food rations, and a minimum salary guarantee of 200 francs a month. This system of tenant farming, widely used by the British in the neighboring Gold Coast, was successfully replicated in the Ivory Coast. The SAA attracted increasing numbers of African members, and soon it became a major political force in the country.

Africans were freed of forced work requirements by a law passed on April 11, 1946, popularly known as the "loi Houphouët-Boigny." The Ivory Coast *colons* made a last-ditch effort to argue that work was a "social duty" that should be required of all eligible African males, but by now the tide against it had turned irrevocably. A requirement for labor for government projects remained, however—the so-called *deuxième position* which had been sanctioned since 1926 as a supplemental levy to traditional military recruitment. The colonial administration's wild card, it allowed local officials to order workers summarily for municipal projects, such as the building of roads, railways, or airports. It, too, was abolished by decree in 1950. Public scrutiny, a changed political climate in the post-1945 period, and the adroitness of a new wave of African politicians had brought one of colonialism's most reprehensible institutions to an end.[49]

THE *LOI-CADRE* OF JUNE 1956

The *loi-cadre* of June 1956, the work of Gaston Defferre and Félix Houphouët-Boigny, decentralized colonial administration, while opening avenues for significant African political participation through territorial councils and assemblies with both elected French and appointed African membership. Suffrage was extended to all French citizens, eliminating the existing two-tier European-African electoral system, but ultimate power remained in the hands of a governor, the *chef du territoire*. That such comprehensive legislation saw the light of day is remarkable in Fourth Republic France, whose political arteries were clogged with draft bills. It took four years for a colonial labor code to move from a proposed bill to law, and long delays were experienced on other reform legislation as well. Experienced administrators like Robert Delavignette had prepared long lists of what needed to be done, but the French political system's sclerotic state prevented their realization. It is difficult to ascertain why the law passed when it did, as such reforms had been proposed before. Some have attributed it to "the spirit of Bandung," the 1956 conference of non-Western peoples, but the French parliament had been impervious to external influences before. Senghor feared the "Balkanization" of Africa could result from the new proposed political structures, but African politicians from places like Upper Volta and Mali criticized "the pretensions of Senegalese and Dahomians to dominate the ex–French West Africa."[50]

If the *loi-cadre*'s bold reforms would have been unthinkable in the 1940s, by

1956 some African leaders called them too little, too late. Some, like Sekou Touré, believed they were calculated to frustrate African independence; still others, like Gabriel d'Arboussier of the RDA, believed they were "an irreversible step in the march toward independence."[51] African political leaders were wary of France's heavy hand in the overall administration. France should send more teachers and health workers, Africans argued, but give Africans control over the police and communications media, including the government radio stations and the weekly newspapers now appearing in most countries. On balance, the *loi-cadre* was more a road map pointing to the direction African politics would take than a codification of political institutions and policies, as might have been France's intention. Africans wanted independence, their own political institutions, and a regional federation, the parameters of which were never set, and they used the language of the *loi-cadre* debates to shape their demands. The *loi-cadre*, which only came into effect in February 1957, was superseded by the Fifth Republic and a new proposal for federation a year later.

THE SHORT INCONCLUSIVE LIFE OF THE COMMUNITY (1958–1960)

État fédéral composé d'états autonomes, décentralisation, nouveau fédéralisme, assimilation, une union librement consentie, état associé, union—the list of possible political structures toyed with by France goes on. This time it was *communauté*, but it would have a no longer shelf life than its predecessors, even if its author was General de Gaulle. The idea, billed as a "new dawn" for French Africa, was put forward at Fort Lamy on August 21, 1958, but it lasted only 18 months. Insubstantial as it might have been, it laid the foundations for future French-African relations; the secretary of state for the community became the secretary of state for cooperation. As anticipated in the 1958 constitution, member states were given autonomy over internal affairs. The community would be governed by a president, an executive committee, and a senate. De Gaulle backed the proposal with his prestige, and he visited several francophone capitals where he presented the idea to huge crowds. It would be voted on by referendum; countries accepting it would reap the benefits of French economic, military, and cultural assistance, those rejecting it would consign themselves to outer darkness. The vote was 7,471,000 *oui* and 1,121,000 *non*. All countries joined except Guinea, whose leader, Sekou Touré, told the general, "*Nous préférons la pauvreté dans la liberté à la richesse dans l'esclavage*" (We prefer to be poor and free [rather than] rich and slaves). "Adieu la Guinée," said the general in departing Conakry airport. The French response was immediate. Phones were ripped out, plumbing fixtures were removed, and files were carted off as part of a departing administrator's luggage or destroyed. Teachers on their way from France to begin the school year were ordered back. Guinea started its independent political life at point zero.[52]

General de Gaulle was elected president of the republic and of the community on December 21, 1958, and on Bastille Day 1959 in Paris gave leaders of each new member state the recently designed community flag, but by now they wanted more—independence. First came Mali, then the Malagasy Republic. By August 1960 all formerly French African states were independent, except Mauritania, whose date was set for November 28, 1960. As a desert wind might blow away a poorly grounded tent, the community collapsed quickly with few traces.[53]

THE COLONIAL VISION OF GENERAL DE GAULLE

It is a supreme irony that the most powerful, charismatic French political figure of the twentieth century, General Charles de Gaulle, presided over the demise of the French Overseas Empire. A successful World War I tank commander and an aide-de-camp to General Pétain, de Gaulle had an acute sense of French history and military strategy. A prisoner of war from 1916 to 1918, he fought in the Russo-Polish war of 1920–1921, served with the general staff in Syria, and held several important troop commands in France before leaving for London with the French defeat in World War II. Relations were never easy between Whitehall, Winston Churchill's headquarters, and the nearby Carlton Gardens, temporary home of the Free French. Nevertheless, Churchill made it clear that, egos aside, de Gaulle's authority was "the only Free French Authority recognized by His Majesty's government."[54] Relations were sorely tested, however, in the Anglo-French dispute over Syria and Lebanon which strengthened the British presence there, crippled the French, and led to the independence of the two countries in 1945. (De Gaulle had a long memory and when Britain's application for the Common Market came up many years later he vetoed it.)

The key to understanding the colonial vision of General de Gaulle is to realize that he was one of the few French officers of the interwar period who never held a command in the Maghreb, Africa, or Indochina; therefore, he did not demonstrate the prevalent narrow views common to most officers of his generation. Although he held a high doctrine of the place of France and its achievements, and saw the Empire as an asset, he was not encumbered by a life-or-death view of the need for France to hold on to each possession as if it were a minor child, and his writings are free of the cant and superior-inferior race rhetoric evident in so many military memoirs. At the advice of Marshal Pétain, de Gaulle spent from 1929 to 1931 in trouble-wracked Syria and Lebanon where he saw firsthand the difficulties of resolving colonial problems. He wrote to an officer friend, "The Levant is a crossroads where everything passes, religions, armies, empires, merchandise, without anything changing. We have been here ten years. My impression is that we have not penetrated here and that the people and we are also strangers (and reciprocally) and it will always be like that." In July 1930 he told Lebanese students, "It is a country you must build . . . aided by the wisdom and strength of France it falls to you to build a state."[55]

During the 1944 Brazzaville Conference, he declared, "France is animated by an ardent will to renew practically" its relations with overseas peoples, contributing materially to their advancement allowing them to "to advance little by little to the level where they will be capable of participating in the management of their own affairs."[56] An advanced political position for the mid-1940s, this viewpoint proved inadequate by the late 1950s. What the general later called *l'idée simple, l'idée conductrice* of his overseas policy from 1944 on became the concept of "federation," with France having the preponderant place, but each member state being part of a "regime of dominions" having a distinct "political personality," whatever that meant.[57]

In late 1944 de Gaulle established France's first postwar government in Paris. Communists (183 seats) represented the largest single parliamentary bloc, due to their presence in the Resistance. Moderate Catholics held 164 seats; socialists, 100 plus. As in Britain at this time, many industries came under state control, including airlines, electricity and coal, and the automobile industry. But while progress was made in postwar construction, de Gaulle grew quickly impatient with the frustrations of coalition government and resigned in January 1946. The Fourth Republic came into being in October 1946, but by then de Gaulle had retreated to the countryside to write his memoirs, only to be called out of retirement in 1958 at the invitation of President René Coty and the National Assembly as chief minister with emergency dictatorial powers for six months. Its failure to solve the Algerian problem resulted in the demise of the Fourth Republic, and in September 1958 the Fifth Republic, with de Gaulle at its head, was ushered in by a four to one popular vote. De Gaulle demanded a new constitution, power to dissolve an unruly National Assembly and call for new elections when desired, and permission to govern by decree in times of national emergency. A later generation of developmental dictators in Africa, when challenged to become more democratic, pointed to the precedents for their actions in French history of this period.

Algeria was the central problem de Gaulle faced. France had been there since the 1830s, and Algerian-French relations showed sharp strains long before they were evident elsewhere. When André Philip counseled him in 1944 to support autonomy for Algeria, de Gaulle replied sharply, "Autonomy, Philip? You know well that all that will end in independence."[58] Several other times from 1944 to 1958 he stated that Algeria would be an independent nation, hopefully aligned with France. Given the political minefield he faced in 1958, de Gaulle could not overtly declare his intentions; later he wrote, "Without ever changing course, I had to maneuver toward the day when, decidedly, good sense would piece the fog. *Larvatus prodeo* [I advance masked]."[59] More a poker player than a theoretician, de Gaulle was prepared to let Algeria move toward independence without ever showing his hand which, as the hour approached, contained few face cards.

"*Les colonies, c'est fini! Il faut faire autre chose*,"[60] he told André Malraux shortly after returning to power as president in 1958. The next step in the federation concept was the idea of the community, but by 1958 time was running out and de Gaulle knew it. He abolished the cabinet office of the minister of France d'outre-mer and on December 1, 1958, told an associate, "The Community, its rubbish! Those people there . . . have but one idea: it's to get out." As African states left the community in quick succession, de Gaulle played his last card: in the future, the magic word would be "cooperation," the economic, political, military, and cultural tie that binds. (Between 1958 and 1965 in 46 television appearances he used the words *coopération* and *coopérer* 63 times, *Empire* and *décolonisation* eight times.) He steered France through the transition "without any joy, but with the certainty of having served France well."[61]

"We have a certain responsibility before history," de Gaulle said, in opening community membership not only to former colonies, but to francophone states like Togo, Cameroon, Zaire, Burundi, and Rwanda. Noting that France had "resources that are not immense," he proclaimed on January 31, 1964, "Yes! In the future cooperation will be France's great ambition."[62] The 7 billion francs he set aside in each annual budget was 2% of France's revenues for a year, and proportionally was much higher than other countries allocated for foreign aid. The money went for education, infrastructure, public health projects, to support the military in states favorable to France, and to bankroll increasingly authoritarian leaders in several countries, of which the megalomaniac Emperor Bokassa of the Central African Republic, one of the world's poorest countries, was the most flagrant example. While some African leaders accused France of using economic assistance as *une aide à la recolonisation*, French power in Africa gradually filtered away in the century's final decades. In 1998 France completed its military withdrawal from the Central African Republic, which served for 80 years as a regional staging base to meet French military needs and to prop up governments favorable to France.

What is most striking, in looking back on de Gaulle's achievement, is that it allowed France to cut away cleanly from potentially permanent entanglements. Except for a few die-hards, France did not speak of the loss of colonies the way it did of war losses to Germany in three successive wars. The trauma of Algeria was short-lived (though not for Algerians), and Dien Bien Phu became a decreasingly bitter nightmare. France could move on to a new, more mature relationship with its former possessions.

De Gaulle's summa on the demise of France's overseas empire, tinged with both nostalgia for past *gloire* and present melancholy, concluded that

in bringing them our civilization, we had established in each of these territories a centralized system prefiguring the nation-State in place of their former anarchic divisions, and trained native elites imbued with our principles of liberty and human rights and eager to replace us from top to bottom of the hierarchy.

"For a man of my age and upbringing, it was bitterly cruel to become through my own choice the overseer of such a transformation," he wrote in his memoirs.

Not so long ago our country had put forth an immense and glorious effort in order to conquer, administer, and develop her overseas dependencies. The colonial epic had been an attempt to compensate for the loss of her distant possessions in the seventeenth and eighteenth centuries and then for her European defeats in 1815 and 1870.

Recalling the work of French proconsuls from Bugeaud in Algeria to Lyautey in Morocco, and of several generations of African and Asian troops, he concluded that France

took pride in the human achievement represented by the basis of modern development laid down in these rough lands as a result of the activities of countless soldiers, administrators, settlers, teachers, missionaries and engineers. What an agonizing ordeal it was to be then for me to hand over our power, furl our flags and close a great chapter of History![63]

ALGERIA

Almost all the Empire was gone now; but there remained Algeria, the Petri dish in which everything was tried and nothing came out right for France, and from which eruptions continued through the century's end. Why was Algeria such a problem for France? From the 1830s on the French and Algerians were on a collision course: Algerians were fiercely independent in temperament, had their own history, religion, and culture, and regarded the French as intruders. When the French came, it was to take the best land as their own and to occupy the country militarily. French *colons* and *pied noirs*, named for the black boots worn by the original occupying soldiers, despised the Algerians, treated them as children, and ruthlessly denied them any possibilities of political participation in their own country. The rupture was deep, compounded by generations of animosity on each side; no quick fix would solve it, such as was repeatedly tried in the war years, from 1954 to 1962. France had several hundred thousand troops in Algeria at one time, but it was never called a real war; the press wrote of *la pacification* (pacification) *or les événements* (happenings) *d'Algérie*. For die-hard French patriots, it was a cause of last resort.

Gradually the thin red line had been pulled back from Indochina, Africa, and North Africa; if Algeria was lost, the Empire was lost. A French writer sympathetic to Algerian aspirations read the handwriting on the wall as early as 1951, "We should prepare ourselves for the coming evacuation of one-million racial brothers in conditions of which the transport planes emptying Hanoi at this very moment gives us a foretaste."[64] There was no Algerian Ho Chi Minh or Vo Nguyen Giap, the FLN (Front de libération nationale) was not as well organized as the Viet Minh, and the number of Algerians was much smaller than the number of Vietnamese. Terrorism and guerrilla raids would be the norm in warfare, instead of direct, large-unit confrontations. Paratroopers and Legionaries, 45 to 50 thousand of them, aided by helicopters, formed the principal

French strike force; meanwhile, the estimated 40 thousand active Algerian opponents also faced a vast army of French conscripts and Africans, who were usually assigned to patrols, roadblocks, and small outposts, endlessly moving about, looking for suspects or responding to terrorist attacks.[65]

A significant ingredient in the Algerian mosaic was the country's economic importance. The land, especially near the coast, was rich, and there were vast oil and mineral deposits and a cheap workforce. Trade, modest but important, accounted for 6.7% of France's 1954 imports (half of it Algerian wines) and 11.3% of its exports. Capital investments were not extensive, owing to chronically unsettled political conditions. The country's budget was always supported by generous grants from France and never even approached economic self-sufficiency.

LA FRANCE ET L'ALGÉRIE DÉCHIRÉE

The war between France and Algeria left both French and Algerians deeply unsettled, and their long, troubled relationship *déchirée* (ripped apart) as well. Most French political parties were torn between classic patriotism and a desire to see a quick solution to the growing, costly war. No one wanted to be responsible for hauling down the *tricolore* but compromises proved illusory. Plagued with internal difficulties and weighed down like Gulliver with parliamentary procedural nets, French politicians of the 1950s had nothing constructive to offer toward resolving the Franco-Algerian crisis. As early as 1954, Algerian bishops, aware of the difficulties of political cohabitation, and responding to a famine, urged the French government to examine the deeper problems of unrest plaguing the country. When the archbishop of Algiers spoke in 1956 of "the necessity to give satisfaction to the Algerian peoples' will for autodetermination" *pieds-noirs* labeled him *Mohammed Duval*. A sharp debate ensued for several years. Thirty-five military clergy visited the cardinal military vicar and asked him to use his influence to curb the army's use of torture against Algerians and to cease other nonmilitary activities. Epitaphs about traitors and *les curés FLN* (FLN priests) were hurled frequently about those who spoke up for the Algerians. Pope John XIII deplored "the fratricidal battles between the sons of France" and "the immoral character of the unjust violence of the OAS," the tattered army of last-ditch French military defenders of the old order.[66]

French intellectuals agonized over the war in Parisian cafés, although few had any direct knowledge of the country or its people. Their perspective had little to do with Algeria as a country or civilization, but much to do about France, its values and its future. Like the Dreyfus affair and the occupation, it was a galvanic event. For the left, led by Jean-Paul Sartre, it was a clear occasion to speak against French militarism, the fascist peril, torture, and other illegal practices. Aware of the decadence that had eaten at French society since the 1920s and 1930s, some argued that ending the festering wound of French-Algerian conflict would help France recover. For the right, it was once more an opportunity to extol *la grandeur de la France*, threatened by communism and Islam's growing encroachment, and a chance to defend the French army's honor, tarnished by the slings and arrows of the *professeurs de trahison* (professors of treason) and *les écrivans fellagas* (writer-partisans). It was *une bataille de l'écrit* (a written battle) fought, not with bullets, but through manifestos, pamphlets, books, and articles in the popular and academic press. What remains striking is how little of the ink war influenced the French public. In 1956 a public opinion poll showed that 45% of the population was willing to accept negotiations for Algeria's independence.[67]

ALBERT CAMUS

Albert Camus (1913–1960), who was raised in Algeria, expressed the French-Algerian dilemma. He called for "a civil truce" during the height of the Algerian crisis. During his 1957 Nobel Prize acceptance speech, he said, "I have always condemned terrorism, and I must condemn a terrorism that works blindly in the streets of Algiers and one day might strike at my mother and my family."[68] His father, a French vineyard foreman, died in World War I when Albert was eight months old; his illiterate Spanish mother spent her life as a charwoman for the poor Algerian French who competed with Arabs for undesirable jobs. Articulate against fascism and totalitarianism, Camus could never support the National Liberation Front; their terrorism was aimed at people like his family and neighborhoods like that in which he lived. Arabs appear only as backdrop figures in his work, and his contacts in Algiers and later in Paris were largely with French leftist intellectuals. Attitudes toward Algeria in his works reflect the dilemmas of an introspective French intellectual in an alien culture. In one of his novels, the Nobel Prize winner had a French farmer in Algeria say,

We're born for each other, since they're as stupid and brutal as we are, but we do share the same blood as human beings. We'll kill each other a little while longer, cut off each other's balls and torture a bit more, and then we'll start to live together as men, which is what the country wants. Would you care for an anisette?

An Algerian writer concluded, "A foreigner and a solitary man, Albert Camus was personally the victim of the social contradictions into which he was born. And perhaps that is why Algerian Arabs today pay him homage, for they too have experienced the heartbreak that comes from living upside down."[69]

On October 3, 1958, General de Gaulle, given to dramatic gestures, announced a sweeping five-year plan in the important provincial city of Constantine. Two-thirds of the country's youth would be sent to schools, 400 thousand new jobs would be created, and a sweeping agricultural reform program would be undertaken. More than 320 thousand new buildings would provide housing for a million persons. (The Moslem population rose 2.5% a year from 1950 to 1954, adding over 223 thousand persons for whom finding food, land, and jobs was a chronic problem.) Chemical and petroleum plants would be built, electric power lines would cover the land, and the textile and agricultural industries would be expanded. But, like the plans of Colbert or Richelieu, these proposals never attracted enough private investment to make them viable. As late as 1961 only a few projects for light industry had been funded, as had 16.2% of the other industrial and 29.4% of the chemical industry expansion plans, despite government guarantees. Neither land reform nor educational programs ever got off the ground, but there was some success with public housing, which had visible results and provided needed employment. A plan for a "thousand new villages" to be constructed in land under French military control was little more than a smoke screen for the French army's *politique de regroupement forcé* (policy of forced regroupment) in which nearly 2 million rural Algerians were removed to over 2 thousand centers under French authority.

DE GAULLE AND THE MILITARY: THE ENDGAME

The French career military's attitude was predictable. Many were recent veterans of the devastating defeat in Indochina, and the 1956 unsuccessful Suez caper rubbed salt in their wounds. France's honor was at stake; it could be saved only by purging the country from decadence and putrefaction (words widely used in 1870). The army were *Centurions* trying to prevent *un Dien Bien Phu diplomatique* in Algeria. Military theorists believed insurgent troops lived like "fish in water" among sympathetic or poorly informed rural populations. Move the rural peoples into zones controlled by the French military, and conduct a successful psychological warfare campaign among them, and the rebel bands would soon be like fish out of water, French strategists argued, in language adopted almost verbatim by later American advisors in Vietnam with similar results. Structures like the 19th century *bureaux arabes* were reestablished in key urban centers, where French commanders exercised complete political and economic control over fiefdoms, with power to recruit troops, arm local militias, and build schools. But French soldiers, increasingly frustrated by their policies' failure, moved beyond permissible conduct, resorting to the widespread use of torture and summary executions of suspected Algerian militants.

On May 13, 1958, French settlers and the military staged a coup d'état, set up a Committee of Public Safety, and urged the intervention of General de Gaulle as the only person who could solve the Algerian problem. The French parliament voted de Gaulle into office on May 27, ending the Fourth Republic and giving him virtual dictatorial powers. Although a patriot, de Gaulle was also a realist who knew French Algeria could never be restored to what it once was. He had to steer between the Scylla of the enraged army and settlers and the Charybdis of enflamed nationalists. Within a year, the army's threat had been reduced when 1,500 officers in Algeria were retired or given postings elsewhere. At a press conference in September 1959, de Gaulle laid out three possible choices for Algeria: the old tie with France (the settlers' option), independence (the nationalists' preference), or some sort of autonomy linking Algeria to France (de Gaulle's preferred choice). Once more, the *colons* balked and seized the center of Algiers in January 1960. The war-weary French people backed their president by a 75% vote in a January 8, 1960, referendum. Angry *colons* and the French army staged a four-day putsch on April 22, 1960. Four former generals took Algiers, supported by a few military units, but the popular uprising the coup leaders counted on never materialized. Key units remained on the sideline, cautious conscripts stayed out of the fray, and the putsch failed.

Was the army to be a law unto itself, or the nonpolitical, loyal servant of the nation? On the answer to that question France's future hung. An army publication laid out the military position, "Yes, the French Army simply fears to be frustrated of its victory. And that victory is [for it] the last chance." General de Gaulle told the troops shortly after becoming president, "As for you, listen to me well! You are not the army for the army. You are the army of France. You do not exist for her [the army], for her and her service. Instead, that which I am . . . should be obeyed by the army so that France lives."[70] De Gaulle made a *tournée des popotes* (round of the mess halls) in March 1960 hoping to quiet military opposition and promote his plan that an *Algérie algérienne* would be the best possible French solution. Eventually he carried the day. Most officers by now supported him, but a bitter strain of violent opposition remained, led by General Raoul Salan and some other officers. After the failed coup attempt, three regiments were dissolved and 530 officers were struck from the lists.

It was then that the Organisation de l'armée secrète (OAS), with Salan as its leader, was formed. Only a handful of active officers supported it, but the OAS spread its brand of terrorism from Algeria to France, claiming 62 deaths and 385 persons wounded in France and 1,622 killed and 5,048 wounded in Algeria. Possibly the OAS counted a thousand members at the peak period of its influence, but its terrorist campaign produced results opposite from what its leaders expected. French citizens of all political persuasions were horrified by its brutality; even those who had been uncertain now concluded that support of *Algérie française* was a dead end and that General de Gaulle's proposed solution was the only possible course of action. Increasingly regarded as a criminal organization, the OAS disintegrated. Salan was arrested and sentenced by a military tribunal, but he was not condemned to death. (The only superior officer given a death sentence was Lieutenant Colonel Jean Marie Bastien-Thiry who was found responsible for two assassination attempts on General de Gaulle's life.) Realizing there was no turning back, de Gaulle entered into serious negotiations with the Algerians, which led to a cease-fire in March 1962 and the formation of a provisional Algerian government. General de Gaulle, who had been returned to power to save French Algeria, four years later liquidated the French Overseas Empire.

THE AFTERMATH: THE NUMBERS

By the late 1990s the number of resident French in Algeria had been reduced to 140 thousand, down from 1,200,000 in 1958. Meanwhile, Algerians offered "the ethnic minority of European origin" (the French) citizenship or status as foreigners, but French passports no longer gave their holders any special status in Algeria. Ironically, the number of North Africans resident in France at the century's end approached 1.5 million, and less than half of them were living there legally. Many had responded to French factories' demands for unskilled labor, but others were attracted by the hope of greater freedom and a better life.

What was surprising was how smoothly France absorbed the shock of the massive, sudden evacuations of the *pieds noirs*; 500 thousand persons in June 1962 alone. The metropolitan government had made no preparation for such an exodus, and many of the returning French received a chilly welcome from bureaucrats who saw them as right-wing intransigents who had brought the problem on themselves. However, once France was freed from the economic burdens of supporting a massive military presence in Algeria, more funds could be redirected to economic projects at home.

There was no backlash from returning veterans, most of whom kept their memories of the recent war to themselves. Likewise, the Algerian war's end, and the end of the Empire rarely registered with the general public, which for five centuries had shown only marginal interest in overseas affairs.[71]

THE BATTLE OF ALGIERS

No examination of the Algerian war and its aftermath is complete without discussing the 1966 film *The Battle of Algiers* (*La Bataille d'Algers*), a fictional documentary based on actual events. The film, which chronicles the conflict between Algerians and French from 1952 to 1957, employs declarations of the FLN and French authorities interspersed with scenes of life in the casbah and in the European town.[72] The Italian director Gillo Pontecorvo, a former Communist who had lived in France, used a newsreel style to show an unemployed street vandal, Ali-la-Pointe, now a revolutionary leader, pitted against Colonel Mathieu, hero of the Resistance and veteran of overseas insurrections in Madagascar and Indochina. Different sequences show the FLN's exertion of gradual control over the town through issuing decrees against the use of alcohol, prostitution, and drugs, conducting clandestine marriage ceremonies, and numerous terrorist acts. The French send in more troops, increase the number of street barriers, and conduct sweeping operations to round up suspects. Since the FLN, like many other similar organizations, was organized so that any one member knew only two others for sure—the person below them and the person above them—the French would pick up as many males as they could and try to unravel the FLN's leadership pyramid, with some success. Colonel Mathieu describes it as a tapeworm-like organizational model, with an infinitesimal number of links that could be cut off before leading to the head. "Basically they are a good people, we've gotten along for 130 years," he observes, echoing a widely held French sentiment. An idealistic Algerian political leader, who later was captured and died in a suspect "suicide" in his cell, observes, "It is difficult to start a revolution, even more difficult to sustain it, and still more difficult to win, and then the real difficulties begin." Reason is lost on all sides; political rhetoric soon disintegrates into violence: Algerians yell "May God be with you" as they set out to bomb ice-cream parlors; and the French call their intensified torture campaign Operation Champagne. Near the film's end Mathieu's paratroopers blow up Ali-la-Pointe's hiding place and declare a victory, having killed or captured most of the resident FLN leadership.

The film gained global popularity as a major work about achieving independence. In the 1990s, however, Algeria's authoritarian government restricted showings of it at home. They feared viewers would equate the actions of the repressive French regime with their own, and they hoped that Islamic fundamentalists would not adopt the organizational techniques used by the Algerians to overthrow the French.

ALGERIA, A MODERN CASE STUDY IN REPRESSION

Following the French departure, a succession of Algerian military or military-backed regimes adopted tactics similar to those employed by France. The result was a society that continued to be repressive. Independent Algeria faced daunting problems. The post-1962 Algerian civil conflict left more than 60 thousand persons dead and caused damage of more than $2 billion to Algeria's infrastructure. It is not that well-intentioned reforms were not tried. From 1989 to 1991, President Chadli Bendjedid, responding to angrily expressed popular demands, launched a series of short-lived initiatives, including multiple political parties, a relatively free press, and an improved human rights climate, ending the National Liberation Front's 30-year stranglehold on the country's political life. A military-backed hard-line government was forced on the country in 1991, after elections were vacated when it appeared Islamic fundamentalists would win. The new government faced a growing tide of Islamic extremism, a distrustful population, and no possibility of gaining popular support. The government resorted to the same methods the French had used: censorship, deporting political opponents, arrests, torture, and terrorism. The Algerian army's language in support of its positions differed little from French military communiqués of previous decades. According to Mona Yacoubian, an analyst of contemporary Algeria,

Lacking indigenous institutions to ground their authority, Algeria's new leaders simply grafted their war-time, clan-based network onto the remnants of the French colonial system. In the summer of 1962, clan infighting triggered a blood-bath as internal rivals battled for primacy. To this day, Algeria's leadership is driven by narrow, clan-based interests, and ultimately by the desire to stay in power. . . . Ruling generals often portray themselves as the embodiment of the national interest, savior of a secular Algeria otherwise doomed to become a backward Islamic republic controlled by a group of religious fanatics.[73]

Islamic opponents of the present regime trace their precedents to the colonial era. One of the most outspoken Islamic leaders was Emir Abd al Kader, who fought the French for nearly two decades while laying plans for an Islamic state. His movement gained strength in the 1930s with the formation of the Association of Algerian Ulama. The *ulamas'* (theologians) battle cry was, "Islam is my religion; Arabic is my language; Algeria is my country."[74] Then, as now, Islam was as much a nationalistic as a religious attraction to those holding deep-seated social grievances—the economically marginal, the politically disenfranchised, and the intellectually cut off from the modern world. The difference was that Algeria's francophone elite of the 1960s had virtually disappeared, emigrated to France, taken jobs elsewhere in the Arab world, been murdered in the recent political upheavals, or, like intellectuals in the Soviet Union during repressive times, withdrawn into their own private worlds. As in the past, demographics and urban overpopulation contributed to a festering political climate. More than 70% of Algerians were under 30 years of age. The term *hittistes* "those who prop up the walls" described the unemployed young males who waited about in cities—55% of the country's population was urban—easy prey for political extremists. Only a handful of French remained in Algeria; many of them were workers in the lucrative oil and gas industry. Algerian terrorists constantly targeted the French for assassinations, including beheading seven monks in the spring of 1996. French policy was to extend generous economic aid with one hand and tighten visa requirements and increase surveillance of Algerians in the *métropole* with the other—a policy that produced few positive results. The shadows of over a century of bitter conflict were long indeed.

LES DAMNÉS DE LA TERRE (THE WRETCHED OF THE EARTH)

All over the former colonial world, the relationship with France produced different responses, from the angst of Frantz Fanon to the Rabelaisian humor of Patrick Chamoiseau. Several authors treated the colonial interaction between France and its subject peoples, including Octave Mannoni, head of the French information services in Madagascar, who likened it to the Prospero-Caliban encounter in Shakespeare's *The Tempest*, and Tunisian Jewish intellectual, Albert Memmi, whose studies of the disruptive bond included *The Statue of Salt* (1953) and *Dominated Man, Notes Toward a Portrait* (1957). A generation later, a skilled West Indian novelist, Patrick Chamoiseau, provided another indigenous interpretation of the colonial encounter through the devastating use of humor.

Frantz Fanon, a Martinique-born psychiatrist, political activist, FLN member, and analyst of Algerian society, viewed the country as a patient and found it dysfunctional, caused in large part by its traumatic relationship with France. A prodigious writer, before he died of cancer at age 36, he had published *Black Skins, White Masks* (1952), *Toward the African Revolution* (1964), and *A Dying Colonialism* (1959). His book, *The Wretched of the Earth*, published in 1962 as the Algerian crisis came to a head, became immensely popular with Third World intellectuals as an exposé of the colonial experience. Fanon believed that colonial domination devalued the conquered peoples' history, myths, and culture and replaced them with the conquering peoples' civilization. The country's intellectuals had traded their own cultural masques for those of the colonizing people and had assumed the colonizers' culture with exquisite sensitivity, welcoming French language, food, clothing, and abstract thought as part of the transformation. Because the relationship was a dysfunctional one for both parties, personal and collective mental illness was its result, as reflected in the upheaval of political institutions. Fanon recommended cathartic violence as a response to colonial control. The "cleansing force of violence" frees the colonized from their inferiority complexes and despair and restores self-respect. Decolonization would be possible only through violent means, he believed, after which human society could be reconstructed along different lines (never detailed by the author). What happens if the successor government is equally authoritarian toward the people or is a developmental dictatorship? Fanon died before the prospect became real, as it did in Algeria and parts of Africa and Asia, and the question remains unanswered.[75]

No less popular was a similar volume, *Prospero and Caliban, a Psychology of Colonization* (1950), by Octave Mannoni, an ex-administrator, which portrays the colonial experience as a "dependency complex" like the interaction in Shakespeare's *The Tempest* of Prospero, the sure, confident possessor of magical powers, which included science, technology, and civilization; and Caliban, the half-formed, impressionistic, aboriginal and emotional creature whose self-realization can come only through his lesser role in a symbiotic relationship with Prospero. Even after achieving liberty, Caliban was left in a disoriented state.[76] Mannoni wrote the book after the 1947 Madagascar uprisings, with an ambiguous viewpoint toward them, and drew heavily on the impressionistic and anecdotal use of anthropological details about various Malagasy societies to create his dependency complex. Like a French essayist of earlier times, Mannoni soared beyond his original purpose to write a psychological-cultural treatise of colonialism and racism in general. If Fanon recommended violence, Mannoni, a mid-level administrator in the French government, dodged the issue, showing sympathy for the oppressed, but offering no solutions.

Albert Memmi, in the words of one of his characters, was "a native in a colonial country, a Jew in an anti-Semitic universe, an African in a world where Europe triumphs." Memmi spent part of World War II in a forced labor camp, was later trained in philosophy at the University of Algiers and the Sorbonne, and taught in Tunisia, then in Paris, where he settled. Caught alternately between two worlds, Tunisia and France, he attempted to describe the psychological relationship between colonizer and colonized as one of implacable dependence which molds their respective characters and dictates their conduct. How could the colonizer be both paternalistic toward farm and factory workers and gun them or their compatriots down in a raid? How could the colonized both hate and want to emulate the colonizer? Colonialism created a double illegitimacy, Memmi reasoned, "A foreigner, having come to a land by the accidents of history . . . has succeeded not merely in creating a place for himself but also in taking away that of the inhabitant, granting himself astounding privileges to the detriment of those rightfully entitled to them." Like Fanon, Memmi prescribed revolt and revolution as the cure for colonial oppression:

We have seen that colonization materially kills the colonized. It must be added that it kills him spiritually. Colonization distorts relationships, destroys or petrifies institutions, and corrupts men, both colonizers and colonized. . . . The liquidation of colonization is nothing but a prelude to complete liberation, to self-recovery. In order to free himself from colonization, the colonized must start with his oppression, the deficiencies of his group. In order that his liberation may be complete, he must free himself from those inevitable conditions of his struggle.[77]

More observant of the colonial situation than Fanon and more systematic in his analysis than Mannoni, Memmi, nevertheless, like them, was better at stating the problem than at suggesting a remedy.

Other Maghrebian writers equally described the conflict of cultures and the yearning for independence. Kateb Yacine's *Nedjma* (1956) is an autobiographical novel about a person living in Algeria torn between its idyllic past and ravaged present. Mohammed Dib, in *Dieu en Barbarie* (1970) and *Le Maître de chasse* (1973), extolls the values of traditional rural life against the intrusions of government bureaucracies, French or Algerian. In a series of novels, the prolific Moroccan writer Driss Chraïbi rails against modern civilization, bourgeois pretentiousness, stultifying Islamic traditionalism, and the cultural clash of the French and Arab worlds.[78]

A more recent treatment of the colonial relationship comes from Patrick Chamoiseau, a writer from Martinique, who covered the major themes of that island's colonial history in a Rabelaisian, irreverent, and culturally disjunctive novel, *Texaco*, published in English in 1997. The book's perspective could be applied to other French overseas possessions as well. Periodization of Martinique's history was based on types of construction material: The Age of Straw, 1823?–1920; The Age of Crate Wood, 1903–1945; The Age of Asbestos, 1946–1960; and The Age of Concrete, 1961–1980. *Texaco* was an unofficial shantytown built near a refinery (hence the name) but was symbolic of *La Cité* (in Creole, *l'En ville*), Fustel de Coulanges' symbolic city as the center of a nation's political, economic, cultural, social, and legal life.[79] Martinique's history was like a manioc root, "the one you take for the master stem . . . is but one stem among many others." History was "a bottleneck where all our stories come

together." (The historian was a "word scratcher.") The book's characters demonstrate an attraction-repulsion for the French language which robs them of
native authenticity yet provides a unique power of expression, as in the school-
teacher who was "a Negro blackman transfigured into a mulatto, transcended to
the White through the incredible power of that beautiful language from
France."[80] In this work, which won the Prix Goncourt in 1992, Chamoiseau did
through the novel what Fanon and others did in essays or plays: described the
deeply disruptive encounter between French and traditional cultures, a conflict
which V. S. Naipaul called "the French colonial monkey game" in *The Middle
Passage* (1962). Characteristic of the encounter were the *maroons*, the slaves
who successfully fled the plantation but could never escape from the small island
and its hermetically sealed culture. As *maroons* depended on the plantations'
wider community for food and friendships, so contemporary overseas people
had similarly ambivalent relationships to France, linked to it through history and
language in ways they sought both to use and to subvert.

THE CONFETTI OF EMPIRE

It would be best to end the story of France's overseas empire now and make
only some final observations at century's end. With Algeria gone, not much
remained, mainly what some observers called "the confetti of empire," or *miettes*
(crumbs). The Comores islands off the east African coast became independent
on July 6, 1975; the territories of Afars and Issas became the Republic of Djibouti on June 27, 1977; and the New Hebrides possessions in the South Pacific
became the State of Vanuatu on July 30, 1980.

That left more than 1,705,000 French nationals on 558,170 square kilometers
on small islands scattered about the DOM-TOM (*départements d'outre-mer*:
Guadeloupe, Martinique, and French Guiana in the West Indies and Réunion in
the Indian Ocean; and *territoires d'outre-mer*: Nouvelle-Calédonie, Wallis et
Futuna, Polynésie française in the South Pacific and a string of other possesions,
the *terres australes et antarctictiques françaises* discussed below). The *vieilles
colonies* of the Antilles, Martinique, Guadeloupe, and French Guiana became
departments of France on March 19, 1946, giving them status similar to that of
an American state, using the French national laws and currency. Some politicians of the left, like the respected writer Aimé Césaire, complained about
French treatment of the Antilles department, but most French observers would
agree with the author Jean Jaurès that they represented "a scrap of French history
shining under other skies."[81]

There are other footnotes to Empire, small islands and coastal establishments
whose stories are more properly the domain of local history. The islands of
Saint-Pierre-et-Miquelon off the Newfoundland coast and Mayotte in the Indian
Ocean had status in between a territory and a department. Several desert islands
remained: Clipperton, a disputed claim off the Mexican coast in the Pacific, les
îles Glorieuse and Tromelin in the Indian Ocean, Bassas da India, Juan de Nova,

and Europa in the Mozambique Channel, plus *les terres australes et antarctiques françaises* (TAAF), including the islands of Saint-Paul and Amsterdam and the Kerguelen and Crozet archipelagos in the South Pacific. Ownership of several of these small islands is disputed, and there remain unresolved claims to the French *terre Adéle*, discovered by France in 1840, but not claimed until 1938 nor established as a territory until 1955. This 400 thousand square kilometers of ice and ocean in Antarctica was more vast than Voltaire's Canadian "acres of snow" but no less chimerical. Thus, what remained of the French Overseas Empire was a scattering of islands, each with fishing rights of 200 nautical miles. What began as a North Atlantic fisherman's empire ended five centuries later in the fishing grounds of the South Pacific.[82]

In addition to this scattering of coasts and islands around the globe, some former colonies have kept active ties with France. France maintains military cooperation agreements with 23 African countries, actual defense pacts with eight countries, and 8,400 troops are stationed in six states. On the average, France has sent its troops into African countries once every two years for the past four decades. Many Africans criticize France for backing some of the continent's most corrupt and brutal dictators, but France has wearied of playing the "gendarme game": times have changed, bases have closed, and troops have been withdrawn.[83]

The Empire's demise was not followed by many success stories as independent states emerged from its shadow. Authoritarian regimes kept power through strong-armed tactics in many former colonies, kleptocracies were numerous, and corruption greased the wheels of government from Vietnam to West Africa. Touré's Guinea was synonymous with brutal repression, and Ho Chi Minh's Vietnam was Asia's economic basket case. To be sure, health conditions improved in places, schools were built, and transportation and communication infrastructures were expanded, but a less positive picture emerged in the evolution of political and legal institutions, the advancement of human rights, and the lot of individual citizens. Given such a problematic present, the past looks brighter than it actually was, but then empires often look better from a distance.

L'EMPIRE ENGLOUTIE (THE SUNKEN EMPIRE, AS IN DEBUSSY'S "SUNKEN CATHEDRAL")

As the Empire's power and presence faded, so too did the influence of the French language. At a November 1997 conference held in Hanoi, presided over by President Jacques Chirac, representatives of 46 francophone countries met to discuss the state of the French language overseas. The picture was sobering. Less than 1% of 75 million Vietnamese spoke French. In most of the old Empire French was the language of from 10% to 30% of the population. The world's French-speaking population was estimated at 105 million persons, half the population of the United States and less than the population of Portuguese-speaking Brazil. The francophone world's aggregate gross national product represented

10% of the world's economy and 9% of its population, spread across the globe. In France, restrictions were in place to block the spread of English; French radio and television had quotas of French songs to play and films to show—40% of the songs on popular radio stations—and jurists struggled to prevent the creeping use of phrases like *Votre Honneur* in court instead of *Monsieur le Juge*.

The attendees at the 7th Conference of Chiefs of State and Governments Having French in Common were united in opposing the spread of English as a global language, but outside the doors of the Hanoi conference hall for every Vietnamese student studying French 30 were learning English. Margie Sudre, former secretary of state for francophone affairs in the Foreign Ministry, where administration of the threads of Empire had come to rest, declared, "The English that is spreading around the world is Anglo-American, not the pure English of Shakespeare,"[84] although few English ever spoke like Hamlet or Lear. France spent nearly $1 billion a year supporting the French language and culture globally, plus $100 million a year to finance 1,056 Alliance Française centers in 134 countries. Boutros Boutros-Ghali, an Egyptian diplomat and former secretary general of the United Nations, was named secretary general of a French-sponsored organization to promote francophone interests. (Ghali spoke perfect French; learning French was a hallmark of Egyptian intellectuals and affluent landowners of his generation.) If Sudre was the *assimilationist*—"We don't want the French language to lose its richness and purity"—Ghali was the *associationist*. Defending the value of cultural regionalism, he said, "If everyone wears the same clothes, speaks the same language, has the same customs, we risk having a global fascist-type regime." The lines between the two camps were drawn again, this time not over land but over language.[85]

As I finished this work, the image of Claude Debussy's *cathédrale englouti* (sunken cathedral) came to mind. The sunken cathedral, once a large, harmonious structure, was now only visible in partial images reflected through moving water and sunlight. Not that the French Overseas Empire was ever that vast or harmonious, except for a few brief decades. The reasons for its expansions and contractions have become clear in the telling. Explorers, traders, settlers, missionaries, and soldiers struck out to the Americas, Africa, or Asia, hoping for a groundswell of governmental or public support, which was only hesitantly or temporarily forthcoming in the best of times. France always looked first to itself and then to the Continent. Two sides of the eternal Hexagon faced water, but France never became a world maritime power nor did its population ever pour out of the country in the numbers the British did; just the opposite, most stayed at home. And when they did go abroad, the Gallic penchant to control everything from the center made local adaptation, so necessary in colonies, impossible to achieve. Hoped-for troops never came, moneys required to launch an enterprise were not raised, needed political and diplomatic backing shifted or was withdrawn, disease ravaged colonizer and colonized. No wonder the edifice finally sank.

Consider France's claimed achievements: the sweeping charters granted, impressive expanses of the earth once claimed, engrossing explorers' accounts, colonial expositions, virgin lands brought under cultivation, industries launched, numbers of indigenous peoples converted, and local peoples taught to read and write French. Many then studied in the *métropole*, learned the intricacies of the French legal system, and became skilled players at parliamentary politics. Others benefited from advancements in science and technology; still others were successful in business and academic careers. Despite those who were left behind, what remained at century's end was *la francophonie*, even if its visibility was much refracted by the adaptations of overseas societies in long-departed outposts of Empire.

NOTES

1. Quoted in Myron J. Echenberg, *Colonial Conscripts: The Tirailleurs Sénégalais in French West Africa, 1857–1960* (Portsmouth, N.H.: Heinemann, 1991), p. 164. The song was recorded and translated by Nancy E. Lawler, "Soldiers of Misfortune: The *Tirailleurs Sénégalais* of the Côte d'Ivoire in World War I," 3 vols., Ph.D. diss., Northwestern University, 1988, vol. 2, p. 439; published by Ohio University Press, 1992.

2. Charles-Robert Ageron, "De l'empire à la dislocation de l'Union française (1939–1956)," in *Histoire de la France coloniale, 1914–1990*, eds. Jacques Thobie, Gilbert Meynier, Catherine Coquery-Vidrovitch, and Charles-Robert Ageron (Paris: Armand Colin, 1991), p. 314.

3. Ibid., pp. 312–314.

4. Frederick Cooper, *Decolonization and African Society, the Labor Question in French and British Africa* (Cambridge: Cambridge University Press, 1996), pp. 148–150.

5. Ageron, "De l'empire à la dislocation," pp. 334–335.

6. Martin Thomas, *The French Empire at War, 1940–1945* (New York: Manchester University Press, 1998), p. 263.

7. Brian Weinstein, *Éboué* (New York: Oxford University Press, 1972), pp. 299–303.

8. Ageron, "De l'empire à la dislocation," pp. 349–352.

9. Ibid., pp. 355–357, 431.

10. Martin-René Atangana, *Capitalisme et nationalisme au Cameroun au lendemain de la seconde guerre mondiale, 1946–1956* (Paris: Publications de la Sorbonne, 1998), pp. 87–100, 257–274.

11. Ageron, "De l'empire à la dislocation," p. 366.

12. Ibid., p. 368.

13. Ibid., pp. 369–370, 403.

14. Ibid., pp. 366–368, 436.

15. Ibid., p. 430.

16. Ibid., p. 433.

17. Ibid., pp. 403, 434–436.

18. Ibid., p. 435.

19. Ibid., p. 397.

20. Ibid., p. 398.

21. Ibid., p. 440.

22. Cooper, *Decolonization and African Society*, pp. 222–234.

23. Ibid., pp. 241–248.

24. Echenberg, *Colonial Conscripts*, pp. 99–104.

25. Ageron, "De l'empire à la dislocation," p. 438.

26. Ibid., pp. 475–484.

27. Ibid., pp. 437–440.

28. Charles de Gaulle, *Mémoires d'espoir*, vol. 1, *Le renouveau, 1958–1962* (Paris: Plon, Livre de poche, 1970), pp. 50–51.

29. D. Bruce Marshall, *The French Colonial Myth and Constitution-Making in the Fourth Republic* (New Haven, Conn.: Yale University Press, 1973).

30. Ageron, "De l'empire à la dislocation," pp. 373–377.

31. Ibid., pp. 375–376.

32. Ibid., pp. 376–377.

33. Amiral Jean Decoux, A *la barre de l'Indochine: Histoire de mon governeur général (1940–1945)* (Paris: Libraire Plon), 1954.

34. Thomas, *French Empire at War*, pp. 191–216.

35. Bernard B. Fall, *The Two Vietnams: A Political and Military Analysis* (New York: Frederick A. Praeger, 1963), pp. 53–54.

36. Thomas, *French Empire at War*, p. 209.

37. Ibid., p. 209.

38. "Le Viet Minh," Report of June 25, 1946, p. 37, in AOM, INF, c. 138–39 d. 1247, Archives d'Outre-Mer, Aix-en-Provence, Indochine nouveau fonds, in David G. Marr, *Vietnam, 1945: The Quest for Power* (Berkeley: University of California Press, 1997), p. 539.

39. Ibid., pp. 439–449.

40. Fall, *The Two Vietnams*, p. 101.

41. Marr, *Vietnam, 1945*, pp. 284–290, 489–501, 525–535.

42. Bernard B. Fall, "Dien Bien Phu: A Battle to Remember," in *Viet Nam: History, Documents, and Opinions on a Major World Crisis*, ed. Marvin E. Gettleman (Greenwich, Conn.: Fawcett Crest Books, 1965), pp. 105–114.

43. Fall, *The Two Vietnams*, pp. 153–154; Douglas Porch, *The French Foreign Legion, a Complete History of the Legendary Fighting Force* (San Francisco: HarperCollins, 1991), pp. 505–555; Philippe Devillers, *Histoire du Viet-Nam* (Paris: Emm. Grevin et Fils, 1952); Paul Mus, *Viet-Nam: Sociologie d'une guerre* (Paris: Éditions du Seuil, 1952); Decoux, *A la barre de l'Indochine*; Jean Chesneaux, *Contribution à l'histoire de la nation vietnamienne* (Paris: Éditions Sociales, 1955); Edward Rice-Maximin, *Accommodation and Resistance: The French Left, Indochina and the Cold War, 1944–1954* (Westport, Conn.: Greenwood Press, 1986).

44. Quoted in Milton E. Osborne, *The French Presence in Cochinchina and Cambodia: Rule and Response (1859–1905)* (Ithaca, N.Y.: Cornell University Press, 1969), pp. 45–46.

45. Ageron, "De l'empire à la dislocation," p. 384.

46. Ibid., pp. 382–386, 405–408.

47. Ibid., pp. 386–389, 403–404; Charles F. Gallagher, *Tunesia*, in *African One-Party States*, ed. Gwendolen M. Carter (Ithaca, N.Y.: Cornell University Press, 1962); Jean Planchais, *L'Empire embrasé, 1946/1962* (Paris: Denoël, 1990), pp. 119–165.

48. Pierre Messmer, *Les Blancs s'en vont; Récits de décolonisation* (Paris: Albin Michel, 1998), pp. 73–112.

49. Cooper, *Decolonization and African Society*, pp. 191–200.

50. Ageron, "De l'empire à la dislocation," p. 494.

51. Ibid., p. 496.

52. L. Gray Cowan, *Guinea*, in *African One-Party States*, ed. Gwendolen M. Carter (Ithaca, N.Y.: Cornell University Press, 1962); Ageron, "De l'empire à la dislocation," pp. 498–499.

53. Ageron, "De l'empire à la dislocation," pp. 498–505.

54. Thomas, *French Empire at War*, p. 94.

55. Ageron, "De l'empire à la dislocation," pp. 533–534.

56. Ibid., p. 353.

57. Ibid., p. 532.

58. Ibid., p. 536.

59. Ibid., p. 539.

60. Ibid., p. 537.

61. Ibid., p. 545.

62. Ibid., p. 543.

63. Charles de Gaulle, *Memoirs of Hope: Renewal and Endeavor*, trans. Terence Kilmartin (New York: Simon and Schuster, 1971), pp. 37–38.

64. Ageron, "De l'empire à la dislocation," pp. 549–550.

65. Porch, *French Foreign Legion*, pp. 565–616.

66. Ageron, "De l'empire à la dislocation," pp. 526–532, 539–542.

67. Ageron, "De l'empire à la dislocation," p. 522; Pierre Lelulliette, *St. Michael and the Dragon*, trans. John Edmonds (Boston: Houghton Mifflin, 1964); Alister Horne, *A Savage War of Peace, 1954–1962* (New York: Viking Press, 1977); Alf Andrew Heggoy, *Insurgency and Counterinsurgency in Algeria* (Bloomington: Indiana University Press, 1972); David L. Schalk, *War and the Ivory Tower: Algeria and Vietnam* (New York: Oxford University Press, 1991); Messmer, *Les Blancs s'en vont*, pp. 159–180.

68. Olivier Todd, *Albert Camus: A Life* (New York: Alfred A. Knopf, 1997), p. 378.

69. Ibid., p. 420.

70. Ageron, "De l'empire à la dislocation," p. 532.

71. Martin Stone, *The Agony of Algeria* (New York: Columbia University Press, 1997).

72. Film, *The Battle of Algiers,* directed by Gillo Pontecorvo, Igore Film, Rome, 1966.

73. Mona Yacoubian, *Algeria's Struggle for Democracy*, Occasional Paper Series, no. 3 (New York: Council on Foreign Relations, 1997), p. 16.

74. Stone, *Agony of Algeria*, p. 148.

75. Frantz Fanon, *The Wretched of the Earth*, trans. Constance Farrington (New York: Grove Press, n.d.); Irene L. Gendzier, *Frantz Fanon: A Critical Study* (New York: Pantheon Books, 1973), pp. 198–205.

76. Octave Mannoni, *Prospero and Caliban: A Psychology of Colonization* (Ann Arbor, Mich.: Ann Arbor Paperbacks, 1990).

77. Albert Memmi, *The Colonizer and the Colonized* (New York: Orion Press, 1965), pp. ix, 151–152.

78. Jean Déjeux, *La Littérature maghrébine d'expression française* (Paris: P.U.F., Que sais-je?, 1992).

79. Patrick Chamoiseau, *Texaco*, trans. Rose-Myriam Réjouis and Val Vinokurou (New York: Alfred A. Knopf, 1997).

80. Shirley Crew, "In the Creole Quarter," *Times Literary Supplement*, March 21, 1997, p. 14.

81. Ageron, "De l'empire à la dislocation," pp. 554–559.

82. Denise Bouche, *Histoire de la colonisation française*, vol. 2 (Paris: Fayard, 1991), pp. 494–496; Messmer, *Les Blancs s'en vont*, pp. 181–203.

83. "France, a New Foreign Policy?," *The Economist* (London), September 6, 1997, p. 54.

84. Craig R. Whitney, "French Speakers Meet Where Few Will Hear, Hanoi Prefers Vietnamese (or English)," *New York Times*, November 15, 1997, A4.

85. Ibid.

Chronology

1608	Samuel de Champlain founds Québec.
1609	Champlain sides with Hurons against Iroquois.
1611	French East India Company is founded.
1611	Jesuit missionaries go to Canada.
1620	Massachusetts colony is settled by the English.
1624–1642	Era of Richelieu.
1625	French tobacco plantation is established on Saint-Christophe's in West Indies.
1626	Richelieu creates several companies, most of which soon fail.
1627	Company of 100 Associates, also called Company of New France, is created and lasts until 1663.
1630s	French buccaneers arrive on Tortuga island off the northern coast of Saint-Domingue.
1633	Unsuccessful French attempt is made at colonizing Guiana on northern rim of South America.
1635	Martinique and Guadeloupe are claimed for France.
1635	Champlain dies.
1639	British are at Madras and establish a presence in India.
1640	Sugar production begins in Barbados.
1644	Coffee is introduced into Europe.
1650	Sugar production begins in French Caribbean islands.
1661–1683	Era of Colbert.
1663	Canada is under direct administration of the French crown.
1664	Colbert creates West India Company, which lasts until 1674; East India counterpart company is formed to trade in Asia, India, and Madagascar.
1672	Jacques Marquette and Louis Joliet explore the Mississippi.
1672	Comte de Frontenac governs in New France (1672–1682, 1696–1698).
1674	Sugar production expands in West Indies.
1676	French *comptoir* (trading post) is established at Pondicherry on Indian coast.
1683	French navy grows under Jean-Baptiste Colbert.
1685	Code Noir is issued to govern slave life in the Antilles.
1698–1702	Le Moyne d'Iberville arrives at the mouth of the Mississippi and establishes a French colony.
1701–1713	War of Spanish Succession.
1723	Coffee is introduced as a crop in Martinique.
1740–1748	War of Austrian Succession.
1742–1754	Joseph-François Dupleix is French governor in India.

1749	Port-au-Prince is established as the capital of Saint-Domingue.
1755	Acadians are deported by English from Nova Scotia.
1756–1763	Seven Years' War.
1757	Robert Clive defeats French-supported forces at Plassey; Indian trade passes into British hands; French India is no more.
1760	Montréal falls to British.
1766–1769	Louis-Antoine de Bougainville circumnavigates the globe.
1776	American Declaration of Independence is written.
1781	French armed forces and Americans defeat British at the Battle of Yorktown on September 5.
1787	American constitution creates federal government with Bill of Rights.
1788	Société des Amis des Noirs is created in France; Estates General meet at Versailles.
1789	Declaration of the Rights of Man and the Citizen is issued in France; debates occur over their applicability to colonies.
1791	Slave uprisings occur in Saint-Domingue.
1794	Convention formally abolishes slavery.
1802	Toussaint Louverture surrenders and is deported to France.
1803	General uprising occurs in Saint-Domingue; French army capitulates and leaves island; Napoléon Bonaparte renounces his dream for an American empire and sells Louisiana to America.
1804–1811	Napoleonic Empire.
1816	Colonial activity expands under Louis XVIII (1815–1824); plans are made to colonize Senegal.
1822	L'Oeuvre pour la Propagation de la Foi is founded at Lyon; Catholic missionary activity increases overseas.
1824–1830	Charles X reigns; French interest in Algeria grows.
1830	French occupy Algeria.
1833	Great Britain abolishes slavery in colonies.
1837	Tafna Convention is held in Algeria with Abd al Kader and General Thomas Bugeaud.
1842	French protectorate is established in Tahiti.
1843	French coastal forts are established in Gabon and Côte d'Ivoire.
1847	Abd al Kader surrenders after several years of warfare.
1848	Second Republic abolishes slavery in all French colonies.
1849	Libreville, Gabon, is founded for freed slaves.
1852–1870	Second Empire; Louis-Napoléon becomes Napoléon III and supports expansionist policies.
1853	French arrive in New Caledonia.

1854	Louis Faidherbe arrives in Senegal.
1859	Saigon is seized by Admiral Rigault de Genouilly.
1863	Treaty gives France protection of Cambodia.
1863–1867	French are present in Mexico.
1867	Monsigneur Lavigerie, Archbishop of Alger, later of Carthage, founds Société des Missions d'Afrique (White Fathers).
1869	Suez Canal is inaugurated.
1870–1871	Franco-Prussian War; France is defeated and Napoléon III is taken prisoner.
1874	Paul Leroy-Beaulieu's *De la colonisation chez les peuples modernes* is published.
1877	Victoria is crowned Empress of India.
1878	Savorgnan de Brazza explores Ogooué River, Congo.
1879–1881	Joseph-Simon Gallieni moves inland and secures French presence in Sudan.
1880–1881, 1883–1885	Jules Ferry is prime minister.
1880	The annexation of Tahiti is proclaimed.
1881	The protectorate of Tunisia is declared.
1881	Undersecretary of State for Colonies is established.
1883	Treaty of protection is imposed on Annam.
1884–1885	Berlin Conference on status of Africa is held.
1885	Ferry government falls over Lang-Son incident.
1885	Treaty of protection proclaimed over Merina kingdom, Madagascar.
1885–1889	Africa is partitioned.
1886	Brazza becomes *commissaire général* for French Congo.
1891	First Pasteur Institute overseas is founded in Saigon.
1893	Dahomey, Côte-d'Ivoire, and Guinea become French colonies.
1894	French occupy Timbuktu.
1894	Ministry of Colonies is created.
1896–1905	Gallieni is *governor général* of Madagascar.
1897–1902	Paul Doumer is *governor général* of Indochina.
1898	French government recalls Jean-Baptiste Marchand from Fashoda, ending conflict with British.
1904	Government of l'Afrique occidentale française (AOF) is organized.
1905	Russo-Japanese War ends.
1905	Decree is made against slavery in AOF and French Congo.

1910	Government of l'Afrique équatoriale française (AEF) is organized.
1912	Treaty of Fez establishes French protectorate over Morocco.
1912–1925	Louis-Hubert Lyautey is *résident général* in Morocco.
1914–1918	World War I.
1916	Statute accords citizenship to inhabitants of four communes of Senegal without bringing them under French civil code.
1917	Russian Revolution.
1918	Wilson's Fourteen Points is promulgated.
1919	Cameroon and Togo, former German possessions, are placed under French control as League of Nations mandate territories.
1920	League of Nations gives French mandate over Syria and Lebanon as part of post–World War I settlement.
1923	Albert Sarraut's *La Mise en valeur des colonies françaises* is published.
1924	Confédération générale des travailleurs tunisiens (CGTT) is founded; labor unions are established in Africa.
1924	Daladier government limits application of *indigénat* code in AOF.
1925	Abd el Krim attacks French in Morocco; Rif war begins and lasts one year.
1927	Nationalist political party (VNQDD) is founded in Vietnam.
1929	*Le Bled*, film by Jean Renoir, is released.
1930	Yen-Bay mutiny in Vietnam occurs.
1931	Colonial Exposition is held in Vincennes.
1931	Association of Reformist Ulamas (religious leaders) is founded in Algeria by Shiek Ben Badis.
1932	First native Vietnamese bishop is consecrated.
1934	"Pacification" of Morocco is complete.
1936–1937	Popular Front is in power and attempts colonial reforms.
1936	Protocols are signed giving eventual independence to French mandate territories Syria and Lebanon.
1937	*Légion d'Honneur*, film by Maurice Gleize, is released.
1939	France enters World War II in September.
1940	General Charles de Gaulle, now in London, is recognized as head of Free French movement by British government on June 28.
1940	Vichy government gives power to Marshal Philippe Pétain, World War I hero, on July 10.
1940	AEF and Cameroon side with Free French; Governor Félix Éboué of Chad backs de Gaulle in August.
1941	Viet Minh is formed in South China.

1941	Japanese troops occupy Indochina.
1943	Casablanca Conference held; Franklin Roosevelt meets with the sultan of Morocco.
1944	Brazzaville Conference (January–February) considers postwar reforms.
1944	French repress indigenous troop uprising at Camp Thiaroye, Senegal.
1945	Germany surrenders on May 8, followed by Japan on August 14; World War II ends.
1945	The Democratic Republic of Vietnam is proclaimed by Ho Chi Minh on September 2; French administration is reinstalled in Saigon.
1945	General strike occurs in September in Douala, Cameroon; uprisings take place in Guelma and Sétif, Algeria.
1946	General de Gaulle is elected president of the provisional government but resigns on January 20, 1946; *Union française* is proclaimed.
1946	Félix Houphouët-Boigny, African leader in French Assembly, passes legislation on April 11 abolishing forced work requirements in overseas territories.
1946	Rassemblement démocratique africain (RDA) political party is founded in Bamako on October 21.
1947	Independence of India is declared on August 15.
1947	*Présence afraiciane* begins publication.
1949	France recognizes independence of Vietnam, Laos, and Cambodia, which are given associated states status.
1950	Moroccans and Tunisians are granted observer status at the United Nations.
1952	New Workers' Code is promulgated in overseas territories.
1953	Franco-Lao Treaty of Amity and Association is promulgated on October 2.
1953	Cambodia proclaims full independence from France on November 9.
1954	French capitulate at Dien Bien Phu on May 7.
1954	Geneva Accords on Indochina are reached on July 20.
1956	Moroccan independence is declared on March 2.
1956	Tunisian independence is declared on March 20.
1957	Independence of Ghana is declared on March 6.
1958	French Assembly votes on June 2 to give full powers to General de Gaulle; the Fifth Republic is formed by constitution of September 28.
1958	Independence of Guinea is declared on October 2.
1959	Etat fédéral du Mali is formed.

1959	French community flag is raised in presence of African chiefs of state on July 14.
1959	De Gaulle announces plan for autodetermination of Algeria on September 16.
1960	Executive Committee of Community meets for last time on March 21.
1960	French generals in Algeria stage unsuccessful putsch on April 21–26.
1960	Independence is given to remaining AOF and AEF states and Madagascar between June and September.
1960	United Nations General Assembly resolution of December 14 favors immediate and unconditional independence for all colonial people.
1961	French Ministry of Cooperation is created in May as future agent for contact with overseas countries.
1962	Frantz Fanon's *The Wretched of the Earth* is published.
1962	Evian Accords on Algerian independence are declared on March 18.
1962	Independence of Algeria is proclaimed on July 3.

MAPS

France in 18th Century North America: Canada, Louisiana, and the English Colonies, 1760

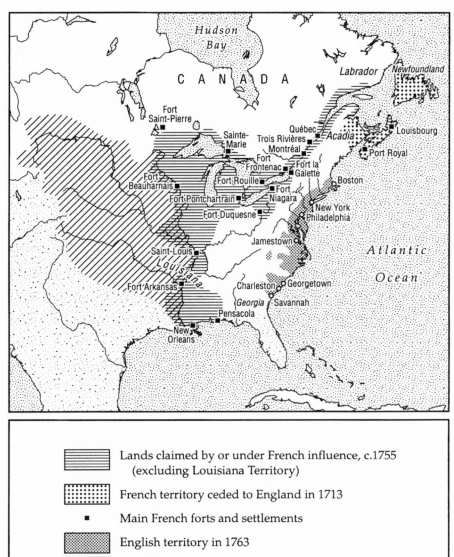

Lands claimed by or under French influence, c.1755 (excluding Louisiana Territory)

French territory ceded to England in 1713

■ Main French forts and settlements

English territory in 1763

Spanish possessions, including Spanish Florida

Louisiana Purchase, 1803

The Remnants of Empire, 1962

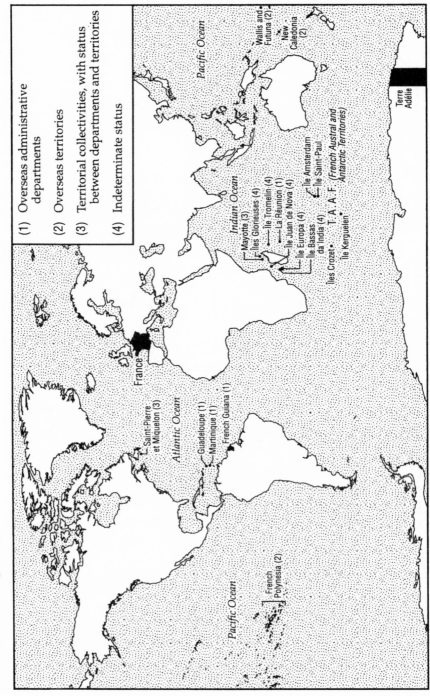

(1) Overseas administrative departments

(2) Overseas territories

(3) Territorial collectivities, with status between departments and territories

(4) Indeterminate status

Pacific Ocean

Walls and Futuna (2)

New Caledonia (2)

Terre Adélie

Indian Ocean

Mayotte (3)

Îles Glorieuses (4)

Île Tromelin (4)

La Réunion (1)

Île Juan de Nova (4)

Île Europa (4)

Île Bassas da India (4)

Île Amsterdam

Île Saint-Paul

Îles Crozet

Île Kerguelen

T. A. A. F. (*French Austral and Antarctic Territories*)

France

Saint-Pierre et Miquelon (3)

Atlantic Ocean

Guadeloupe (1)

Martinique (1)

French Guiana (1)

Pacific Ocean

French Polynesia (2)

French Indochina

French West Africa (AOF) and Togo

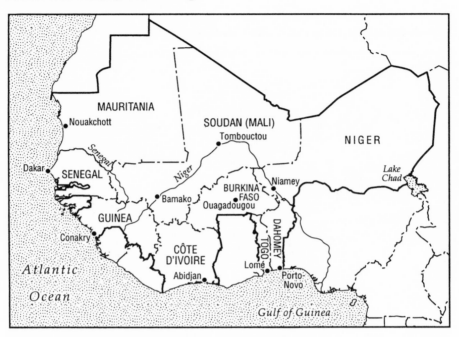

France in the West Indies, 1755

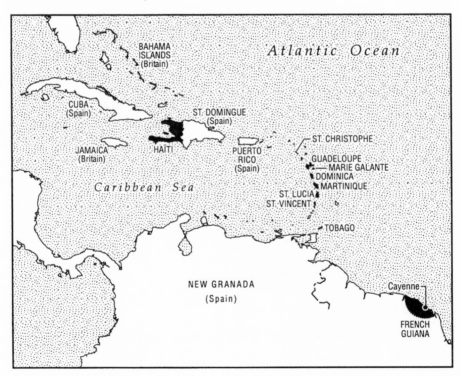

French Equatorial Africa (AEF) with Cameroon

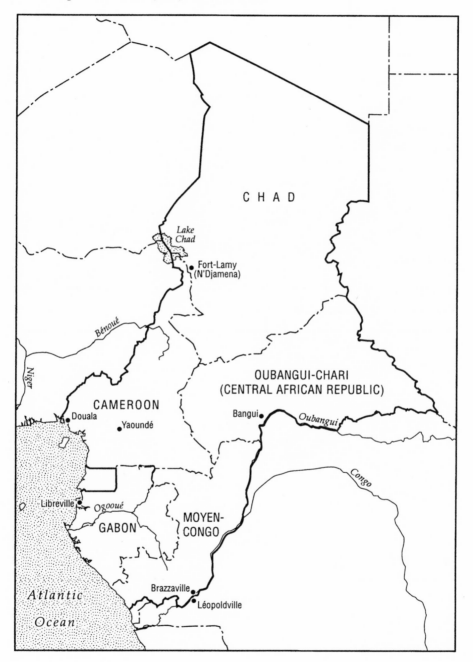

North Africa

France in India, 18th Century

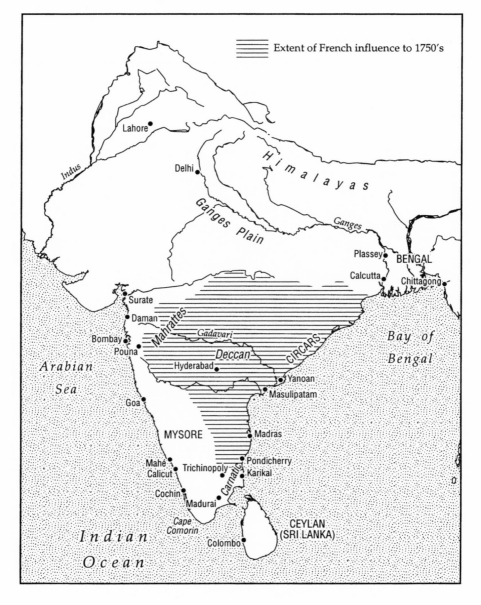

France in the Indian Ocean

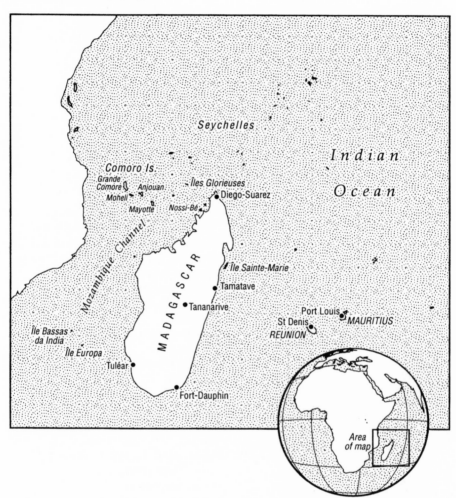

Index

About the Author

FREDERICK QUINN, an American diplomat and historian, is a frequent visitor to the French Empire and has written about the country's overseas presence for nearly three decades. His foreign service assignments in Francophone countries include Morocco, Haiti, Burkina Faso, Vietnam, and Cameroon. The Times Literary Supplement named his book *Democracy at Dawn: Notes from Poland and Points East* one of its international books of the year for 1998.

ISBN 0-275-96799-9

90000>

EAN

9 780275 967994

HARDCOVER BAR CODE